THE JEWELERS' MANUAL

Books by the Same Publishers

Dictionary of Gems and Gemology

Robert M. Shipley

The Diamond Dictionary

*Lawrence L. Copeland, Richard T. Liddicoat, Jr.,
Lester B. Benson, Jr., Jeanne G. M. Martin,
G. Robert Crowningshield*

Handbook of Gem Identification

Richard T. Liddicoat, Jr.

Diamonds... Famous, Notable and Unique

Lawrence L. Copeland

THE JEWELERS' MANUAL

THE
JEWELERS'
MANUAL

by

RICHARD T. LIDDICOAT, JR.

Executive Director

and

LAWRENCE L. COPELAND

Course Editor

of the

GEMOLOGICAL INSTITUTE OF AMERICA

Copyright 1967

by the

GEMOLOGICAL INSTITUTE OF AMERICA

First Edition
1964

Second Edition
1967

Second Edition
Second Printing
1970

Second Edition
Third Printing
1974

All rights reserved. No part of this work may be reproduced without the written permission of the authors and the publishers.

PRINTED IN THE UNITED STATES OF AMERICA
ISBN 0-87311-003-X

Preface

The *Jewelers' Manual* is a successor to the popular *Jewelers' Pocket Reference Book*, edited by Robert M. Shipley and published by the Gemological Institute of America in five editions, from 1947 through 1951. The present work is all new, differing in scope, purpose and format from the original publication; hence, the change of title.

The purpose of the *Manual* is to offer a concise, comprehensive, accurate presentation of information and data pertaining to the major categories of merchandise in the jewelry industry and related trades. It is designed to provide an easy-to-use, authoritative reference for the busy jeweler in his daily activities, and to answer the multitude of questions asked by inquiring customers. It is particularly valuable as a means of orienting the salesperson who is new to the jewelry business.

Liddicoat wrote the diamond, pearl and gem-testing sections, as well as a portion of the glossary, and acted in the capacity of supervising editor. Copeland shared the writing task and was responsible for the overall compilation and editing, including the required literary research, rewriting and coordination of text and illustrative material. Jeanne G. M. Martin prepared the layout and artwork, typed the final manuscript for the printer and assisted with the proofreading; she also took the photographs of diamond imperfections, cutting discrepancies and famous-diamond replicas.

We are indebted to many jewelry suppliers, manufacturers and trade associations for providing artwork and information for some of the tables and text; their contributions are acknowledged throughout the book.

Los Angeles, California   RTL
July, 1967   LLC

TABLE OF CONTENTS

Preface

Diamonds

    Formation & Occurrence 1
    Sources 4
    Mining 4
    World Production of Gem & Industrial Diamonds
        for a Recent Year 5
    Marketing of Rough 16
    Cutting 17
    Grading & Evaluation 29
    Comparison of Three Different Diamond
        Color-Grading Systems 30
    Typical Diamond Inclusions &
        Surface Characteristics 33
    Diamond-Grading & -Merchandising Instruments 39
    Diameters & Corresponding Weights of Round,
        Ideally-Proportioned Brilliant-Cut Diamonds 45
    Sizes & Weights of Some Pear-Shaped, Marquise
        & Emerald-Cut Diamonds 46
    The More Important Famous Diamonds 47
    How to Learn More About Diamonds 55

Colored Stones

    GEM TESTING

        Examination by Unaided Eye or
            Low-Power Magnification 57
        The Refractometer 58
        High Magnification 58
        Inclusions that Characterize Some Natural
            & Artificial Gem Materials 59
        The Polariscope 61
        The Dichroscope 61

THE JEWELERS' MANUAL

The Spectroscope 61
Specific Gravity 62
Fluorescence 62
GIA Thermal Reaction Tester 63
Hardness 63

GEM-TESTING INSTRUMENTS

Gemolite 64
GIA Diamond Grader 64
Gem Detector 65
Duplex II Refractometer 65
Illuminator Polariscope 65
GIA Spectroscope 66
Ultraviolet Lamp 66
GIA Thermal Reaction Tester 66
Optivisor 66
Specific-Gravity Liquids 67
Specific-Gravity Attachments 67
Tweezers 67
Immersion Cell 67
Hardness Points 67
GIA Dichroscope 67
Emerald Filter 67

PROPERTY TABLES

Color 68
Refractive Index 74
Specific Gravity 76
Hardness 78
Pleochroism 79
Birefringence 81
Dispersion 81
Cleavage, Fracture & Relative Toughness 81

CRYSTAL SYSTEMS 83
RECOMMENDED NAMES for the MORE IMPORTANT
 GEMSTONES 85

x

Table of Contents

TRADE NAMES & RECOMMENDED NAMES for
   SYNTHETIC STONES 90
BIRTHSTONES 92
ZODIACAL, or ASTRAL, STONES 94
FOREIGN EQUIVALENTS of some of the
   MORE IMPORTANT GEM NAMES 95
"PRECIOUS" & "SEMIPRECIOUS" STONES 99
SHAPES & STYLES of CUTTING 99
COLORED-STONE SIZES 113
CARE of GEMSTONES 113

Natural, Cultured & Imitation Pearls 115

Pearl Testing 116
Base-Price System 117
Weight Estimations of Round Natural
   & Cultured Pearls 119

Wedding-Anniversary List 121

Traditional Wedding-Anniversary List Recommended
by Social Authorities 121

Precious Metals

Markings & Descriptions 122
Karat Gold 122
Silver 123
Platinum Metals 123
Silver & Karat Gold 124
Karat Gold & Platinum Metals 124
Stainless Steel & Karat Gold 125
Gold-Filled & Rolled-Gold Plate 125
Palladium-Filled & Rolled-Palladium Plate 126
Gold Electroplate 126
Property Table 127
Acid Tests 128
Gold Content of Karat Alloys 128

Basic Kinds of Jewelry Findings 130

xi

THE JEWELERS' MANUAL

Basic Kinds of Mountings & Settings 139

United States & British Ring-Size Equivalents 140

Basic Styles of Jewelry Chains 141

Important Emblems of Fraternal Orders & Civic Groups 145

Hallmarks 149

Silverware

    Care of Silverware 155
    Sterling Flatware 156
    Sterling Holloware 158

Examples of Styles for Jewelry & Silver Engraving 177

Ornaments & Designs 179

Watches & Clocks

    How a Watch Works 181
    Factors Contributing to Quality 183
    Wearing a Watch to Bed 184
    The Meaning of Jewels 184
    Winding a Watch 184
    Self-Winding Watches 185
    "Shockproof" Watches 185
    Antimagnetic Watches 186
    Waterproof Watches 186
    Round Versus Square Watches 187
    Chronographs 187
    Chronometers 187
    Swiss Versus American Watches 187
    The Meaning of Adjusting to Position 187
    Cleaning 188
    The Electric Watch 188
    The Electronic Watch 189
    The Parts of a Watch Mechanism 191

Table of Contents

    Modern Watch Hands & Their Names 193
    Watch Sizes 194
    Basic Shapes & Kinds of Clocks 196

Trade Associations 200

Glossary 214

Weights & Measurements 345

Bibliography

    Gemology 346
    History, Lore & Romance of Gems & Jewelry 347
    Mineralogy, Mineral Collecting & Localities . . . 349
    Gem Cutting 350
    Jewelry Making & Repairing,
        Silversmithing & Enameling 351
    Engraving 352
    Horology 353
    China & Glassware 354
    Dictionaries & Reference Works 355
    Periodicals 355

What is Gemology?

    Definition 357
    How do Gemologists Serve? 357
    Training Required 357
    Opportunities 358

The Gemological Institute of America

    Educational Activities 359
    The GIA Gem-Trade Laboratories 360
    Instruments 360
    Publishing 360
    Staff 360
    Board of Governors 361
    Locations 361

Diamonds

Probably the most remarkable material known to man—certainly the most remarkable gem mineral—is diamond. Nothing in nature compares to diamond in hardness; in its crystal clarity, too, it is unsurpassed. Yet, it is made of *carbon*, the element in *charcoal* and *graphite*, two of the dark, opaque, soft materials so diametrically opposite to diamond in appearance and properties. Graphite is lustrous but is comparable in hardness to talc, number one on the 1-to-ten hardness scale, representing one of the softest materials known. There is probably no greater contrast in nature than that between diamond and graphite, and it is attributable only to the difference in the arrangement and bonding of the carbon atoms.

Formation & Occurrence

Diamond is found in nature either in a rock called *kimberlite* or in secondary deposits, such as river gravels. Kimberlite crystallized from molten rock; it is so called because it was the first primary rock in which diamonds were found, at Kimberley, South Africa, about 1870. The popular name for kimberlite is *blueground*, because of its greenish blue-gray color. In this area and elsewhere, it is found in nearly vertical deposits with a roughly circular outline. They were the necks of ancient (approximately sixty million years), long-extinct volcanoes; such deposits are called *pipes*. *Dikes* (tabular bodies of once-molten rock) of kimberlite are also found in Africa.

Diamond is formed in nature under conditions of extreme heat and pressure. The tiny stones of industrial quality that are made synthetically by the General Electric Company (and since GE's initial success, in 1955, by several other firms, both here and abroad) show clearly that the conditions under which diamond, rather than graphite, crystallized from carbon were indeed extreme. They were conditions that were thought to exist at depths of approximately 200 to 250 miles beneath the surface of the earth. Unless such temperatures and pressures existed in the place of diamond's formation, carbon would have crystallized as graphite, rather than diamond.

THE JEWELERS' MANUAL

Diamonds

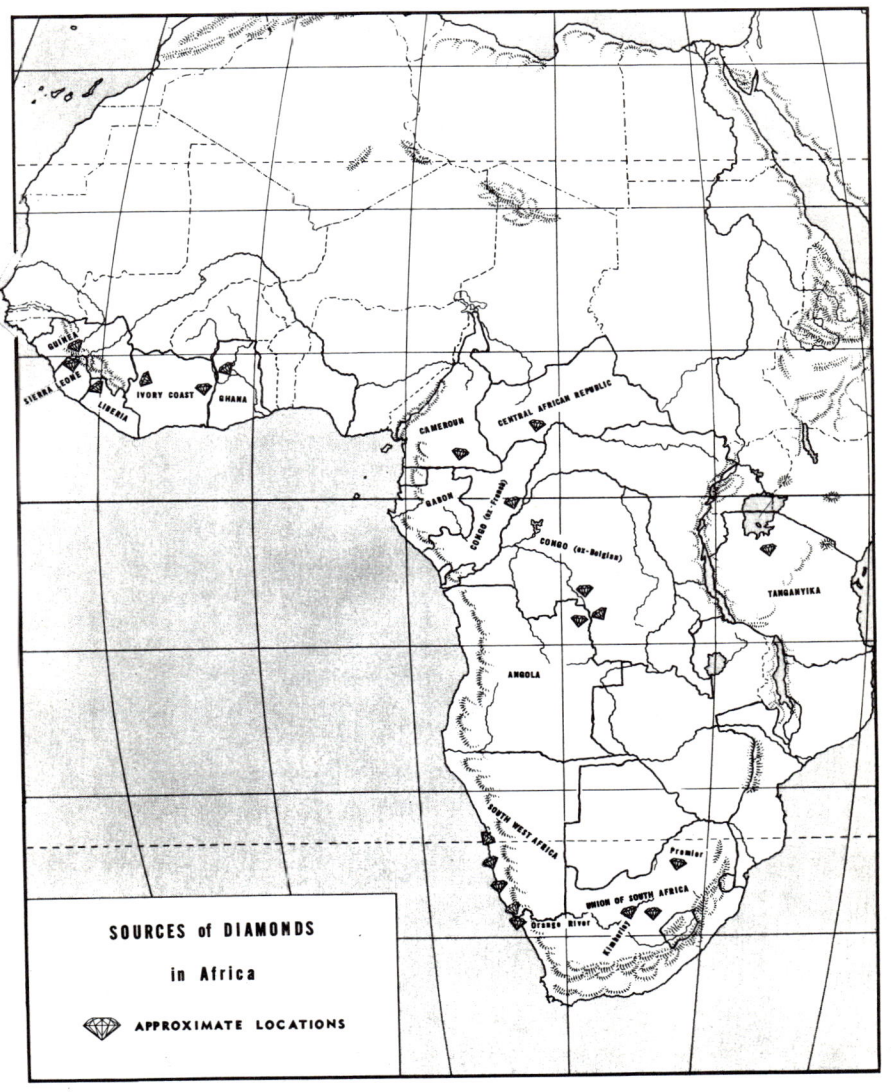

THE JEWELERS' MANUAL

Sources

Although diamonds have been found on all continents but Antarctica, the bulk of the world's production is mined in Africa. Asia and South America are comparatively insignificant producers.

African sources include the Union of South Africa, South-West Africa, Tanganyika, Sierra Leone, Ghana, the Republic of the Congo (formerly the Belgian Congo), Angola and some of the former French African territories. The vast production of the Kasai area of the Congo is almost exclusively of industrial quality. Many of the other major sources, such as Ghana, Angola and the Premier Mine (a pipe deposit), also produce mostly industrials.

The four countries that produce most of the gem-quality diamonds in Africa are South-West Africa, Sierra Leone, and the pipe mines of Tanganyika and South Africa, except the Premier Mine.

Mining

The very low proportion of diamonds to the rock or gravel in which they are found is such that man's ability to extract them profitably is a tribute to his ingenuity. Most kimberlite pipes are either barren of diamonds or, like those in Arkansas, so poor in quantity of diamonds as to be uneconomic to mine. Those that contain diamonds in sufficient number and size to be practical to exploit are worked first from the surface. If they are rich enough in yield to warrant, they are mined by subsurface shaft operations, when it is no longer safe or practical to work them from the surface. The blueground is drilled, blasted and crushed, much as if the product sought were an ordinary base metal, instead of perhaps the most precious commodity known to man.

A shaft is sunk in nondiamond-bearing ground away from the pipe and tunnels are cut across the pipe and around it; they are sloped toward the shaft, so that the mine cars are moved easily when loaded. The ore is guided through conical ore passes to lower levels, where chutes are operated as necessary to fill the cars; these, in turn, are pulled to the shaft by electric locomotive. Near the shaft a screen and crusher operate, which reduce the size of those chunks over six inches in diameter. The smaller material, plus the blueground that has passed through this coarse crusher, is dumped into storage bins at the foot of the shaft; it is then hauled to the surface in ore skips for the extraction process.

At the surface, the blueground is put through two stages of crushing, and an opportunity is afforded before each crushing to detect any large diamonds and remove them from the danger of being broken. It then goes through a *heavy-media* separation plant.

Diamonds

World Production of Gem & Industrial Diamonds for a Recent Year

AFRICA

Country	Carats
Republic of the Congo (ex-Belgian)	12,500,000
Union of South Africa	5,160,000
Republic of the Congo (ex-French)	5,000,000
South-West Africa	2,300,000
Ghana	2,000,000
Angola	1,450,000
Sierra Leone	1,300,000
Liberia	800,000
Tanzania	710,000
Central African Republic	442,000
Guinea	300,000
Ivory Coast	116,000

OTHER SOURCES

USSR	3,500,000
Brazil	600,000
Venezuela	100,000
British Guiana	100,000
India & other countries	50,000
TOTAL	36,428,000

Heavy-media equipment consists of a large cone in which a slurry of ferro-silicon and water is maintained to an effective specific gravity of approximately 2.85 to 3.0, depending on the density of the blueground. Diamonds and other heavy minerals sink to the bottom, whereas the great bulk of the material having specific gravities below this level floats on across the cone and is spilled out at the other side. Material that has passed through the heavy-media separator and that is still large enough to contain tiny diamonds is sent to another crusher, and it is once again passed over a heavy-media cone; if it is the size of sand grains, it is separated by a *jig*.

The concentrates from the heavy-media cone and from the jigs are passed over a series of *grease tables*. Here, a stream of water carrying the heavy pebbles over the grease washes materials other than diamonds on over the tables, whereas diamonds, to which water does not adhere, stick to the grease. The other materials have a wet surface and do not adhere. Concentrates from surface mining have to be treated with sodium-oleate solution and caustic soda to remove a wettable film from the diamonds, so they will adhere to the grease. Periodically, the grease is scraped from the tables and boiling releases the diamonds. At each of the stages where barren, fine-size material is separated from the potentially diamond-bearing material, the worthless particles are discarded. In some plants, the concentrates are given an *electrostatic-separation* treatment, by which fine-size diamonds are separated from other tiny materials.

In the Premier Mine, the largest pipe operation and one of the richer ones, the yield is one part diamond for every fourteen million times its weight in rock; at the Williamson Mine it is one part in every fifty million. One carat of diamond is recovered from over three tons of blueground at Premier and about eleven tons at Williamson. The approximately one hundred thirty-five thousand carats recovered monthly at the Premier Mine is made possible by an output of about sixteen thousand tons of blueground mined and treated daily. Many workmen have never seen a diamond in the mine.

After the diamonds have been removed from the grease, they are hand sorted to remove metal, garnet and other minerals occasionally found with them. They are then sorted according to size and classified for either gem or industrial use.

The tendency in this country is to assume that monopoly means artificially high prices. An examination of the facts in relation to other extractive industries reveals some interesting comparisons. First, the yield in diamonds varies widely from deposit to deposit. Of course, average-quality differences among deposits are also large; therefore, weight yield is not always the key factor in value yield from a mine or a wet digging. The Williamson Mine was shown to yield about nine carats from each one hundred tons. The Jagersfontein Mine is not much higher, and even more tonnage must be moved for one carat in South-West Africa. On the other hand, some areas in Ghana produce more than one carat for each ton of ore mined, on the average.

Because the Premier output is largely industrial and that of Consolidated Diamond Mines of South-West Africa's is primarily large gem quality, the latter is much more profitable. If no monopoly existed, low-cost producers could "freeze out" high-cost operators; however, they could not come close to meeting world demand. Thus, if the monopoly were to end and prices drop, demand would surely force prices high enough to bring in the higher cost producers, just as they have been brought in by the monopoly. The jeweler and the public would both be happy to see lower prices, but they would not welcome wild price gyrations.

To assess the monopoly's price structure, suppose we compare it to a gold mine. Even the largest and most efficient gold mine in the United

Diamonds

Drilling blast holes in kimberlite in a pipe mine

Photos courtesy N.W. Ayer & Son, Inc., New York City

THE JEWELERS' MANUAL

Conveyor belt carrying kimberlite to shaft for transportation to surface

Diamonds

Prospecting trench in a South-West African alluvial deposit

THE JEWELERS' MANUAL

Recovering diamond-bearing gravel with a large vacuuming machine in a South-West African alluvial deposit

Diamonds

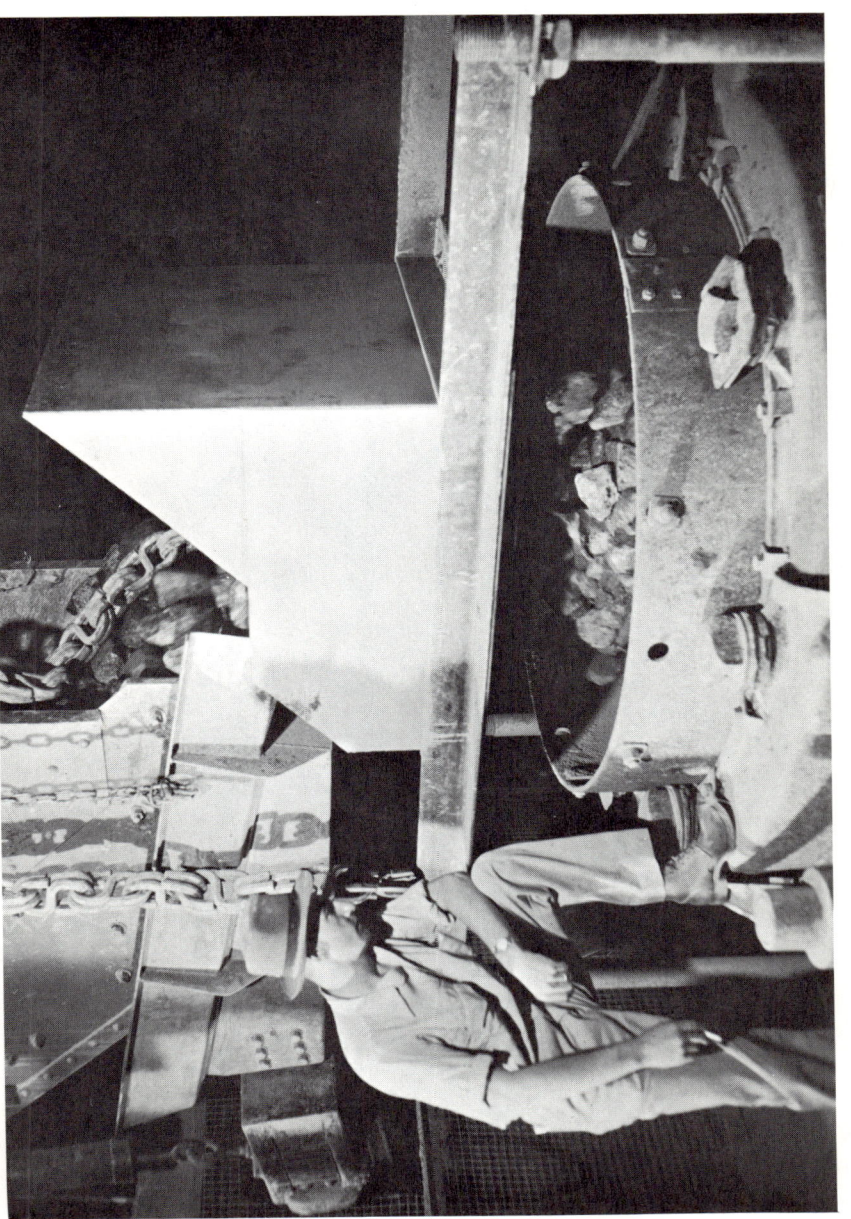

Crushing kimberlite

THE JEWELERS' MANUAL

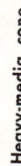

Heavy-media cone

Diamonds

Grease table

THE JEWELERS' MANUAL

Scraping diamonds from the grease table

Diamonds

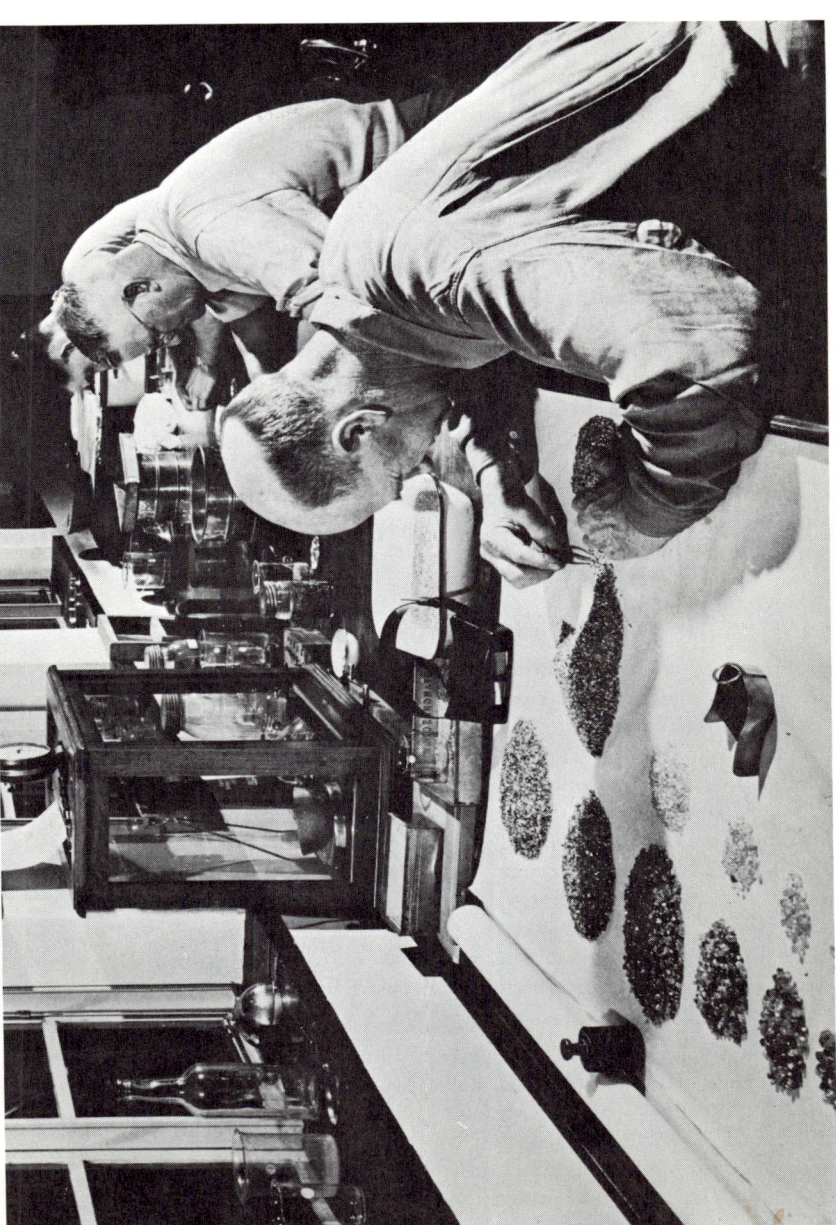

Sorting and classifying diamonds at the mine

THE JEWELERS' MANUAL

States needs ore that averages about twenty-eight hundred carats in each one hundred loads to operate; this is more than one hundred times the yield of the rich Premier Mine. A comparison of the gross income realized from each ton of ore treated shows that diamonds are sold by De Beers at a substantially lower average return than the gold produced by North American underground operations. On this basis, the monopoly is certainly in a defensible position with respect to price.

Unless important new diamond deposits are discovered in the near future, the present rate of exploitation will shortly cause production to fall off rapidly. With the exception of the Premier Mine, most of the South African pipe mines are now being worked at great depths, so not too many years should see them reach a point below which further exploitation will not be feasible. Reserves of alluvial (stream-gravel) deposits are also being depleted fairly rapidly, and undoubtedly will be worked out in the not-to-distant future. Stability in diamond prices, then, is possible only if new deposits are found and exploited in the next few years. It is too early to tell whether the recently discovered deposits in Siberia and off the coast of South-West Africa will extend the period of relatively adequate supply for any appreciable length of time.

Marketing of Rough

Diamond production in the key producing countries of the Union of South Africa, South-West Africa and Tanganyika is controlled directly by De Beers Consolidated Mines, Ltd., for the most part. Production from the Congo, Angola and the newly developed deposits off the coast of South-West Africa is subject to purchase agreement by the Diamond Corporation, Ltd. (a De Beers affiliate), through a subsidiary, the Diamond Purchasing & Trading Co., Ltd. The only significant production on the African continent that is not directly or fully contracted for by a member of the De Beers group is that from Sierra Leone and Ghana. Consolidated African Selection Trust, Ltd., a company that operates in these countries, sells fifty percent through the Corporation and fifty percent independently. Also, native miners sell their production to licensed buyers, some of whom are independent.

The Diamond Producers' Association, Ltd., comprised of De Beers and its subsidiaries, plus the South African Government, sets the price that will be paid for the goods of its members and for that purchased from other companies. The rough is purchased by the Diamond Purchasing & Trading Co., Ltd., and gem rough is sold through the Diamond Trading Co., at *sights*. Industrial material is purchased by Industrial Distributors (1946), Ltd., and sold by Industrial Distributors (Sales), Ltd.

Diamonds

At a sight, the Diamond Trading Co., Ltd., offers its goods to diamond-cutting firms and, to a lesser extent, to brokers. Complete sights are offered on a take-it-or-leave-it basis, although the purchaser has the opportunity to indicate what kind and quantity he wants. Sights are priced as closely as possible to an equal basis for all buyers; the result is a highly competitive market. In other words, since prices start at the same level for rough of comparable size and quality, there is little opportunity for a cutter to gain a competitive edge of any magnitude. Lower cutting costs abroad are offset in the United States by a 10% import duty on sizes over one-half carat and 8% on sizes of one-half carat and under. This means that American cutters cannot compete on small sizes where cutting cost represents a higher proportion of value, but on large sizes the tariff makes it possible for them to compete effectively.

There are large apparent differences in prices at which retailers are offered merchandise. Yet, if weight retention from the rough is determined accurately, it can be shown that prices are actually very close together; in other words, the high prices charged by a cutter who cuts to approximately ideal proportions stand up well against the prices of one who cuts to spread proportions, if weight retention is taken into consideration.

Cutting

The diamond cutter is among the most skilled of artisans. Through long experience, he does most of the angle setting and indexing by eye alone.

The first step in diamond cutting is careful examination of the stone under magnification by the *planner*, who usually is a member of the firm or a key employee. Sometimes, he has one or more flat surfaces polished on the edge of a crystal, to give him more assurance in locating the exact position of an inclusion. Most diamonds are marked with India ink, to indicate the plane or planes along which sawing or cleaving should be undertaken. If inclusions are large and will reduce materially the clarity grade of any stone cut from the rough, its separation usually is planned so that either the saw blade or a cleavage goes through the unsightly inclusions, thus removing them from the final product.

Since all cutters pay approximately the same price for their rough, the difference between making a profit or failing to do so is in effective positioning of the cut stones in the rough to get maximum value yield. This encompasses a wide variety of considerations: which shape or shapes, how placed, of what grade, and of what size.

A factor to consider is cutting to salable shapes and sizes. If with no greater weight loss a cutter is able to get two .50-carat stones in round brilliants, instead of a slightly greater weight yield in odd sizes, it may be advantageous. In other words, assuming that he can saw the rough through the center and produce two .50's or saw off center and produce perhaps a .41 and a .65, he may prefer the two 50-point stones. Usually, off-center sawing of an octahedron yields a slightly greater weight; therefore, this is preferred, unless there is some offsetting advantage.

All of these decisions are made by the planner when he studies a piece of rough. If he is dealing only with octahedra, inclusions and distortions of shape are the factors that he considers, together with the weight of the finished stones. It becomes much more difficult to plan stones from odd shapes, such as the larger sizes of irregular rough with few or no crystal faces. The larger the misshapen mass, the more difficult it is to visualize clearly the possibilities to ensure minimum weight loss and produce attractive and salable merchandise. Thus, planning is a very important factor in cutting.

Diamond has four directions parallel to faces of the octahedron in which it can be split to yield flat, clean surfaces; when this method of separation is utilized, the process is called *cleaving*.

The diamond to be cleaved is first grooved with the corner of another diamond crystal; this abrades a tiny trench along the trace of the cleavage plane on the surface. A successive series of grooves are then made, starting with a relatively wide aperture and using increasingly sharper crystals, thus making the trough narrower at the bottom.

After the stone has been mounted in a special dop with the cleavage direction perpendicular to the upright holder, a rather coarse, steel blade is inserted in the cut. The cement in which the stone is held is relatively soft, so that the diamond gives slightly under the blow of a mallet striking the blade. The blade acts not as a knife but as a wedge, much in the manner in which a wedge is used to split wood; in other words, the force of the blow is delivered to the sides of the groove and forces the diamond apart, as opposed to the cutting action of a sharp knife. In this way, if the blow is not perfectly delivered, there is less chance of damage to the diamond than if a knife action were attempted, because any misdirection of a sharp blade could cause shattering.

Although there is always a certain amount of potential danger connected with cleaving, it is not ordinarily a very dangerous procedure. Diamonds sometimes break on the saw, too, but breakage is rare in either separation process.

Sawing is much to be preferred as a means of separating a diamond crystal, if the shape of the rough makes it possible, because usually the weight retention from the shapes produced by this method is greater than from cleaving the usual crystal forms. In addition, one person can operate an entire bank of saws, whereas cleavage requires considerable work on each stone by a highly skilled man.

The stone to be sawed is mounted in a holder called a *dop*. The dop contains an adhesive with a low melting point, usually a combination of wax and shellac but sometimes a low-melting-point metal, and the stone is placed in the head of the dop at an angle that permits it to be mounted against the saw correctly for it to cut in a proper plane.

Sawing is performed in a direction that is softest for diamond. A mixture of diamond powder and olive oil is used to charge the saw blade. which is made of soft phosphor-bronze. Usually, the blade that is used to start the cut is heavier than the one used for later cutting; a thinner blade is then used to reduce weight loss to a minimum.

The length of time required to saw a diamond depends on the thickness of the blade, how much weight is placed on the saw, and whether an electrical charge is placed across the diamond-blade contact. A one-carat diamond usually can be sawed in approximately two hours, if a heavy blade is used and a heavy weight holds the stone against the blade. If a thinner blade (.003 inch) is used, to avoid unnecessary weight loss, and little weight is on the blade (as a safety precaution), six to eight hours may be required.

After the blade has been charged with a combination of diamond powder and olive oil several times early in the cutting process, the material coming off the stone serves to recharge the blade. The diamond dust is able to cut through the stone, because the softest direction of diamond is utilized for sawing and the dust consists of cleavage fragments that expose the mineral's hardest direction. As a result, the soft metal holding the sharp fragments of diamond bring them repeatedly against the saw cut and provides the abrasive action that ultimately saws the stone in half.

After an octahedron has been sawed, the resulting four-sided shape must be *rounded up*, if a round brilliant is to be cut. This is accomplished by mounting the stone in the head of a lathe that spins at a high rate of speed. Against it another diamond is held firmly, to act as a cutter to chip off tiny pieces from the spinning stone. If this is done very carefully and not too rapidly, the girdle of a well-turned diamond assumes almost a waxy luster; it seems very nearly polished, it is so smooth.

This operation, which is the only one that can be strictly referred to as cutting, is performed by a workman called the *cutter*, or *bruter*. The head of a dop is mounted in a long holder that is secured under one armpit. The holder is grasped by both hands and rested against a support beside the lathe, so that the diamond can be held steadily as it is forced against the rapidly revolving stone in the lathe. Unless it is held very securely, a "chattering" effect can result and shatter the diamond being rounded up.

This is the only operation in diamond cutting in which the material cut away from the stone is saved. In the sawing and polishing operations, some of the material remains as dust to help cut other stones; in rounding up, however, a pan is kept under the lathe to catch as many of the tiny diamond fragments as possible.

The placing, grinding and polishing of the facets on a diamond are often referred to collectively as *polishing*, but this is often called *diamond cutting*, as if it were the complete operation.

Faceting is usually accomplished in two steps, because the major facets are placed by a man called the *blocker*, or *lapper*, and the remaining facets are placed by a less-experienced workman known as a *brillianteerer*. Usually, the blocker polishes the table, the eight bezel facets, the eight pavilion-main facets, the table and the culet; this establishes the proportions of the stone. The brillianteerer then adds the forty remaining facets, including the eight star facets, the sixteen upper-girdle facets, and the sixteen lower-girdle facets.

Polishing is usually done on a lap that is also known as a *scaife;* it is a relatively porous, cast-iron wheel that is charged frequently with diamond dust by the polisher. Usually, a slightly coarser grain size of diamond powder is used for the initial grinding and a finer grain size for polishing. The wheel must be balanced very carefully, since it operates at 3000 rpm. An experienced cutter uses the same wheel for a number of months, because he does not like to break in a new one. Occasionally, they are resurfaced on a lathe and scored to form grooves in which diamond dust and olive oil will accumulate to charge the wheel.

The diamond is mounted either in a dop with a metallic bonding agent or in a so-called mechanical dop, which consists of metal "fingers" in which the stone is gripped firmly. During grinding and polishing, the diamond is attached to a *tang*, a contrivance that permits the stone to rest on the spinning lap, with the facet being polished making the third of three legs; the other two are the wooden supports of the tang, which rest on the cutting bench beside the lap. If a large facet is being polished, it requires a considerable length of time; therefore, it is common practice to put a weight on the tang and let it run, while facets on other stones are being polished simultaneously. Care must be taken, of course, to avoid polishing a facet too deeply, because this means that either the symmetry of the stone is ruined or that it must be reblocked and recut to a smaller size. Usually, when cutters are working on small stones, they use only one tang at a time and lift it frequently to examine the facet under a loupe, to be certain that it is being polished correctly.

Usually, the dop is attached to the tang by a thick copper wire; it is the bending of this wire that sets the angle of the facet to the girdle plane. The cutter must have an exceedingly keen eye to set this angle evenly all the way around the stone and to index its turning properly, so that the eightfold symmetry is maintained and adjoining facets meet at a point or a straight line, as they should. When setting and indexing are done correctly, a symmetrical pattern of reflections is presented to the eye, which contributes importantly to maximum beauty.

Unless a diamond is polished very carefully, wheel marks, or minute grooves, are left on the surface; this causes a diffraction effect and a distinct loss of brilliancy. If facets are polished too rapidly, the heat generated by friction can cause burn marks to appear, which cloud the surface and also reduce brilliancy.

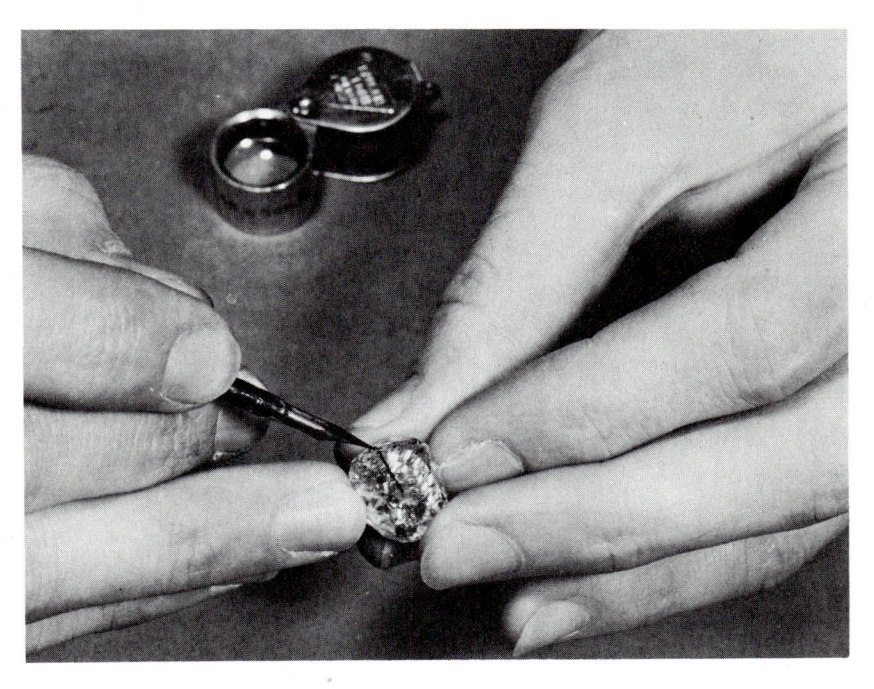

Marking a diamond crystal with India ink, to indicate the correct sawing direction

THE JEWELERS' MANUAL

Grooving a diamond preparatory to cleaving

Diamonds

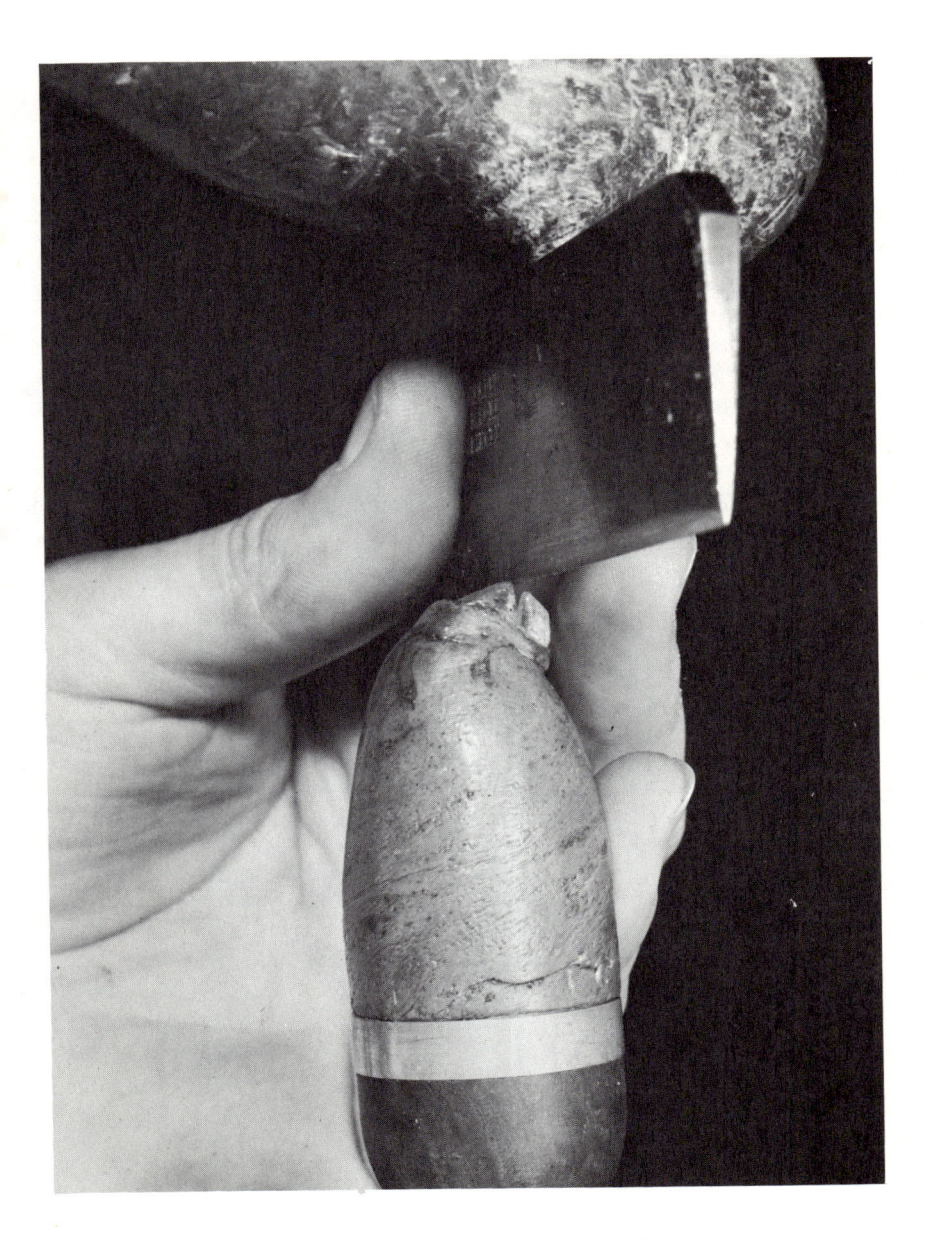

A cleaved diamond, showing cleaver's knife and mallet in position

THE JEWELERS' MANUAL

Sawing

Diamonds

Bottom: holder with one part of sawed diamond; other part shown at left

Rounding up

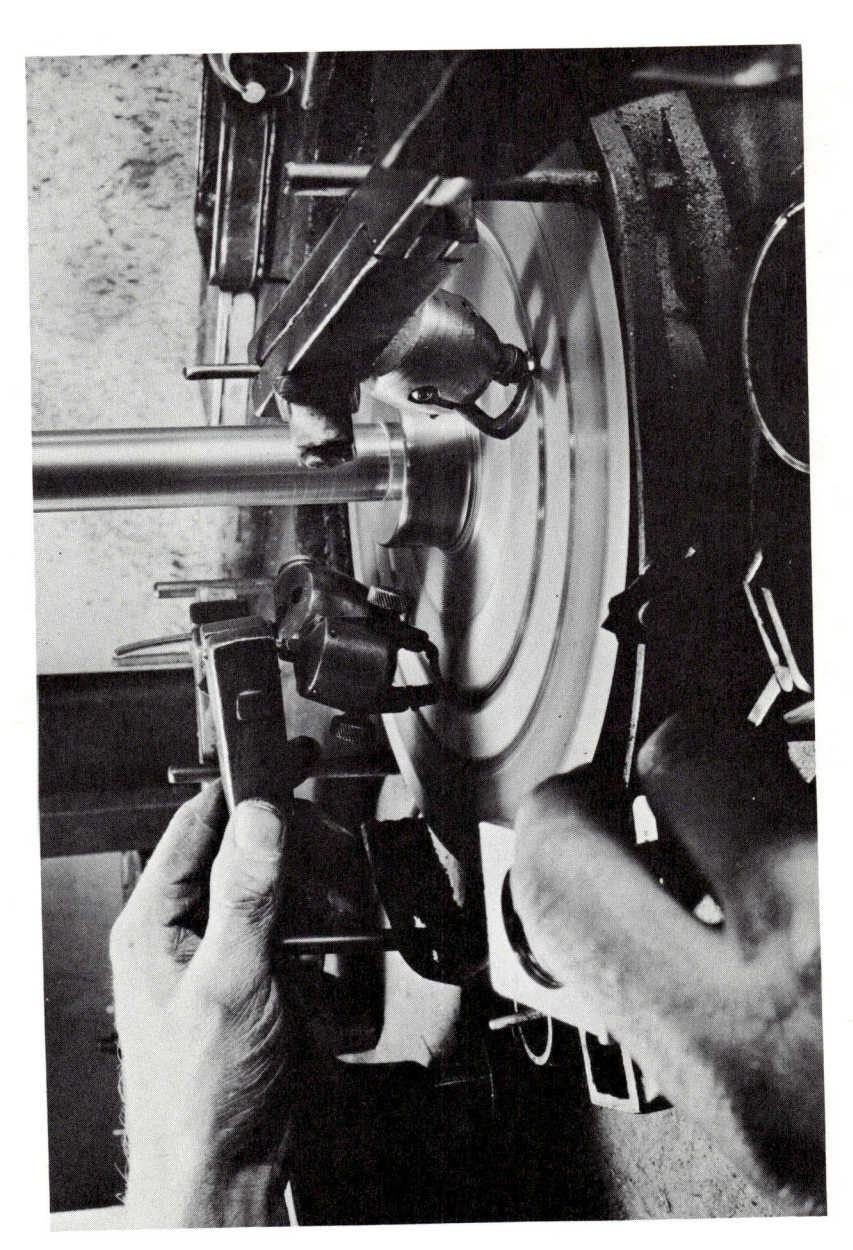

Diamonds

Polishing

THE JEWELERS' MANUAL

Finished diamonds

Diamonds

Grading & Evaluation

The value of a diamond is based largely on rarity and desirability. On this basis, *color, clarity* and *cutting quality*, together with *carat weight*, comprise the so-called *Four C's* that measure a diamond's value. These factors can be judged much more accurately and readily in loose stones than in those that have been mounted.

Many terms have been used to describe degrees of freedom from color in a diamond. The most valuable diamond is one that is completely devoid of color and highly transparent. The only exception to this is a stone with a decided tint of color other than yellow or brown. Diamonds with enough body color to be an asset are called *fancies;* those in greatest demand have a strong tint of pink, blue, green or violet. Such stones may command a considerably higher price than colorless ones; otherwise, colorless is considered the finest. Most diamonds have a tint of greenish yellow or brown; when either tint is obvious to the unaided eye, they are less attractive to most persons.

In the diamond industry, a number of different color grades are recognized, the number depending on the sales methods of the supplier. A few importers use as many as nine or ten grades and many use only four or five, combining several grades into broader ones. Over a period of time, and in the absence of precise standards, grading terminology has become almost meaningless.

One system long in use that is being slowly replaced is that in which the finest is called a *river,* followed by *top Wesselton, Wesselton, top crystal, crystal, top cape, cape, light yellow* and *yellow.* A river should be entirely devoid of body color and highly transparent. A top Wesselton should have a minimum of color and be slightly less transparent. Each successive grade in this system shows slightly more yellow than the preceding one. In a stone of approximately one carat, the tint usually is visible face up to the unaided eye in a crystal or top cape.

Another system is that in which *blue-white* is considered the finest, followed by *fine white, white* and sometimes by *commercial white*, before the cape and yellow grades. The term blue-white has been particularly abused, since the majority of stones represented and sold under this label are *not* colorless but slightly *yellow*. The degree to which they are tinted depends on the knowledge or ethics of the retailer. Some misrepresent through ignorance; others do so intentionally. A consumer who visits an established store need not be concerned about another material being substituted for the diamond he buys, but trading with such a store is *not* a guarantee against misrepresentation of *quality*. Knowledge about dia-

Comparison of Three Different Diamond Color-Grading Systems

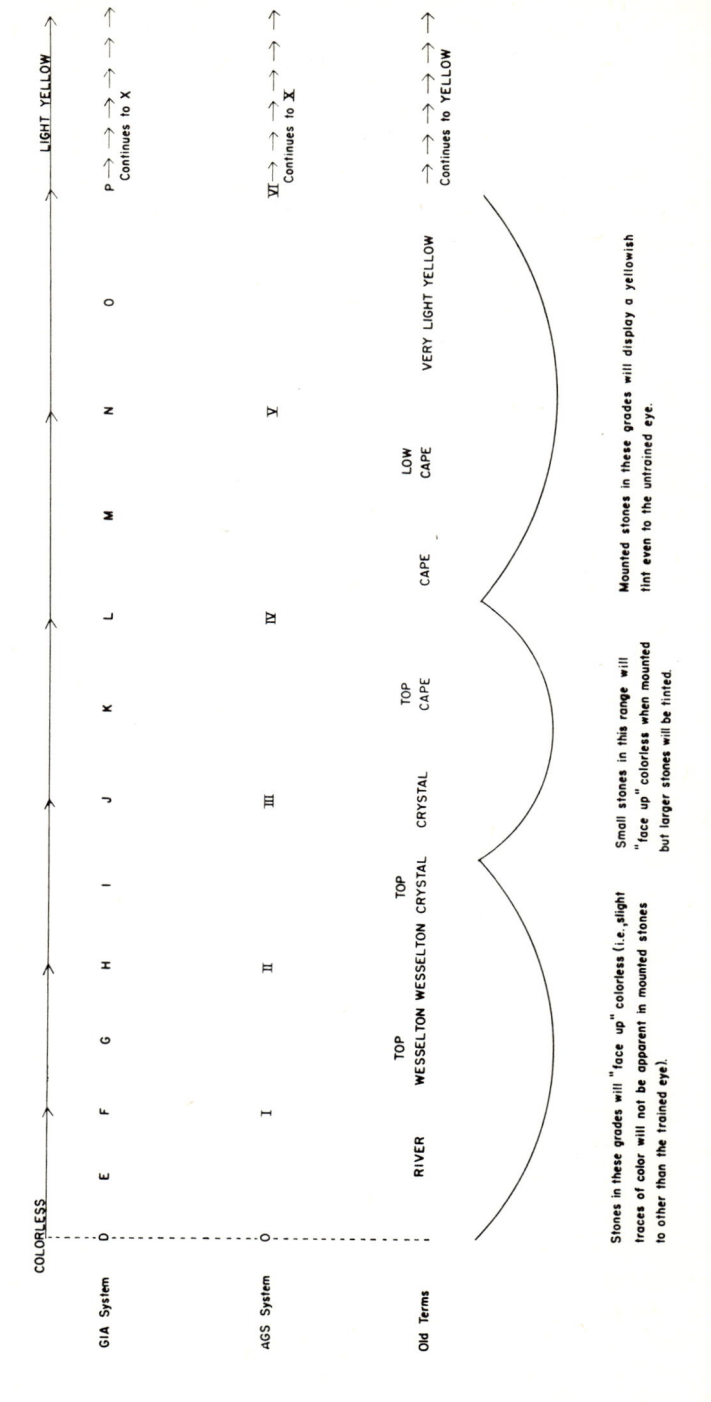

	COLORLESS →						→					→				→ LIGHT YELLOW →
GIA System	D	E	F	G	H	I	J	K	L	M	N	O	P → → → → → → Continues to X
AGS System	0	I			II		III		IV		V		VI → → → → → → Continues to X
Old Terms	RIVER		TOP WESSELTON	WESSELTON	TOP CRYSTAL	CRYSTAL		TOP CAPE	CAPE		LOW CAPE		VERY LIGHT YELLOW	→ → → → → → Continues to YELLOW

Stones in these grades will "face up" colorless (i.e., slight traces of color will not be apparent in mounted stones to other than the trained eye).

Small stones in this range will "face up" colorless when mounted but larger stones will be tinted.

Mounted stones in these grades will display a yellowish tint even to the untrained eye.

30

Diamonds

monds is certainly as essential as good ethics on the part of the proprietor.

There are two grading systems based on absolutes. One is a *numerical* system, using an *electronic colorimeter*, an instrument developed for the American Gem Society. The other is a *letter* system, developed by the Gemological Institute of America, which utilizes *color-comparison stones* under controlled lighting conditions, to ensure that grading results are always identical.

On the basis of rarity and desirability, in view of the popularity of diamonds with an absence of body color, there is a strong price differential between limpid, colorless stones and those that are noticeably yellow. From the finest colorless stone to one that is sufficiently yellow to be unattractive, but not enough to be appealing, the drop in price exceeds 50%. However, the percentage of price drop depends on other factors as well, such as clarity grade and size of the stone. The price drops at the rate of 5% to 15% a color grade from the value of a flawless, colorless, well-cut stone of the same weight, depending on the number of grades used and other factors that control value. If a stone is flawless and the cutter uses nine grades, the drop from the finest color to the next grade is likely to be 6% to 8%. There is little change in the drop from grade to grade, until a point is reached at which color becomes obvious to the unaided eye. In the first grade with obvious color, the price drop is abrupt. Stated another way, the difference in price between a grade in which color in a given stone size is not obvious to the unaided eye to the first lower grade in which it becomes apparent, even to a layman, is much greater than between other adjacent pairs of grades.

Color usually is graded either in north daylight in a room as free from color reflections as possible, or in an instrument called the *Diamondlite*, which furnishes a light that is corrected to the equivalent of north daylight but with the ultraviolet removed. This device has the advantage of providing a diffused, low-intensity light that reduces greatly a diamond's surface reflection and makes it easier to study the stone's interior and judge its color. In addition, the unit has a separate source of ultraviolet light that is not turned on during grading, except to determine whether a stone is fluorescent. Flourescent diamonds usually glow blue under ultraviolet radiation. Daylight contains sufficient ultraviolet so that it makes a stone of this kind appear much better than in artificial light; it is often referred to as a *false-colored diamond*. There are two principal kinds that are likely to have this appearance. One is the so-called *Jager* (Yah"-ger), a stone that is either colorless or nearly so under artificial light but that fluoresces blue in daylight. The other, known as a *Premier*, is definitely yellow in artificial light but, because of strong blue fluorescence, appears blue in daylight. It is sometimes called "coal-oil blue," because the fluorescence is so strong that it resembles kerosene, or coal oil, when viewed in ultraviolet-rich light.

Fluorescence lowers value, if it reduces transparency so much that the gem is cloudy in daylight or if the fluorescent color is unattractive; the latter condition is rare, however. It increases value slightly, if it makes a colorless stone blue or if it changes a stone from yellow in artificial light to a fine color in daylight. In each case, the increase in value is minor.

The *clarity* of a diamond (i.e., the degree to which it is free from inclusions or surface blemishes) is rated on a scale ranging from *flawless* (or *perfect*) to *imperfect*. On this scale, there are approximately as many divisions as in color grading. Some importers use three to five clarity grades; others use ten or eleven. The Federal Trade Commission defines the term *perfect* as follows:

"It is an unfair trade practice to use the word *perfect*, or any other word, expression or representation of similar import, as descriptive of any diamond that discloses flaws, cracks, carbon spots, clouds or other blemishes or imperfections of any sort when examined in normal daylight, or its equivalent, by a trained eye under a ten-power, corrected diamond eye loupe or other equal magnifier."

The American Gem Society defines the term *flawless* as follows:

"The term *flawless* shall be used to describe a diamond that is free from all internal and external flaws, inclusions or blemishes under skilled observation in normal, natural or artificial light with a ten-power loupe corrected for chromatic and spherical aberration; binocular magnification under dark-field illumination is preferred. No other use of the term *flawless*, as applied to diamonds, shall be permitted.

"(Note: In the interest of clarifying trade practice, an *extra facet* shall be considered a blemish only when it can be seen directly through, or is located on, the crown. A *natural* shall be considered a blemish only when it extends beyond the maximum width of the girdle, breaks the symmetry of the shape or can be seen on, or directly through, the crown. *Growth lines* will be classified as flaws when they exhibit color or break the surface of the stone.)"

The clarity grades used by the Gemological Institute of America are as follows: *flawless*, VVS_1, VVS_2, VS_1, VS_2, SI_1, SI_2, I_1 and I_2. Although it is not an invariable rule, a diamond that is flawless to the unaided eye falls into one of the first seven grades. Some of the *internal* discrepancies that may occur in diamond include tiny diamond crystals

Diamonds

Typical Diamond Inclusions & Surface Characteristics
Photos GIA

Scratches

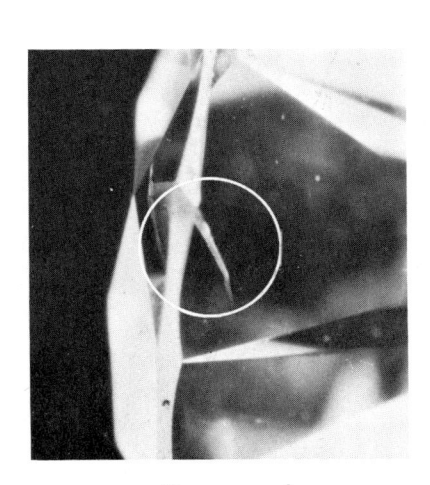

Cleavage crack

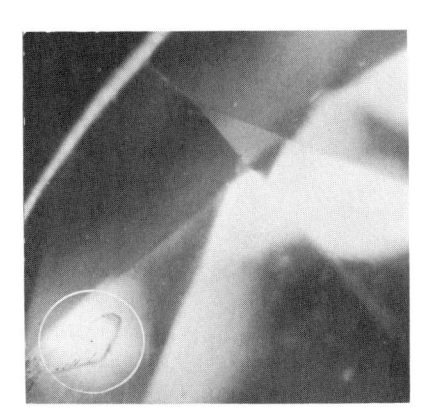

Knot

THE JEWELERS' MANUAL

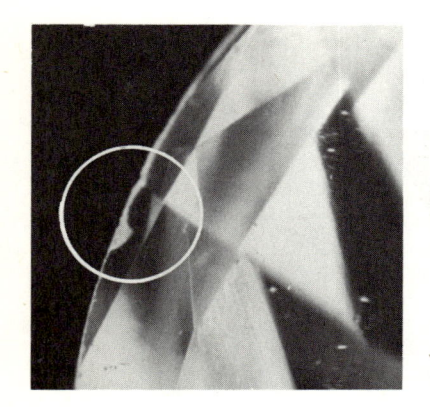

Nicks

Cavity

Natural

Diamonds

Cloud

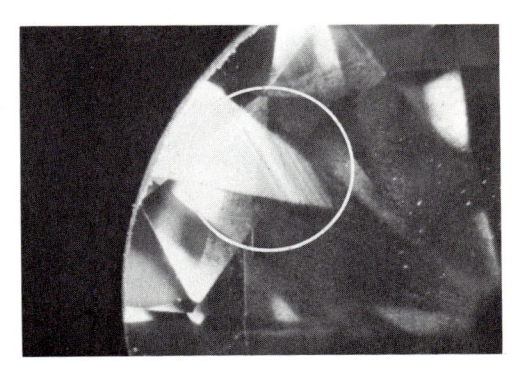

Polishing marks

oriented differently from the surrounding crystal, crystals of other minerals, tiny cleavages (separations parallel to the grain), cloudy inclusions consisting of tiny gas-filled spaces, twinning lines (or planes), which mark a change of direction of crystal growth, etc. *External* blemishes include tiny cavities, nicks, scratches, abrasions, polishing-wheel marks, extra facets and naturals (small portions of the original outer surface of the diamond that were not polished away).

Unfortunately, very few diamonds meet the exacting standards for flawless or perfect. Many stones that are free from internal imperfections or that reveal only very minute inclusions under 10x are sold as "perfect"

THE JEWELERS' MANUAL

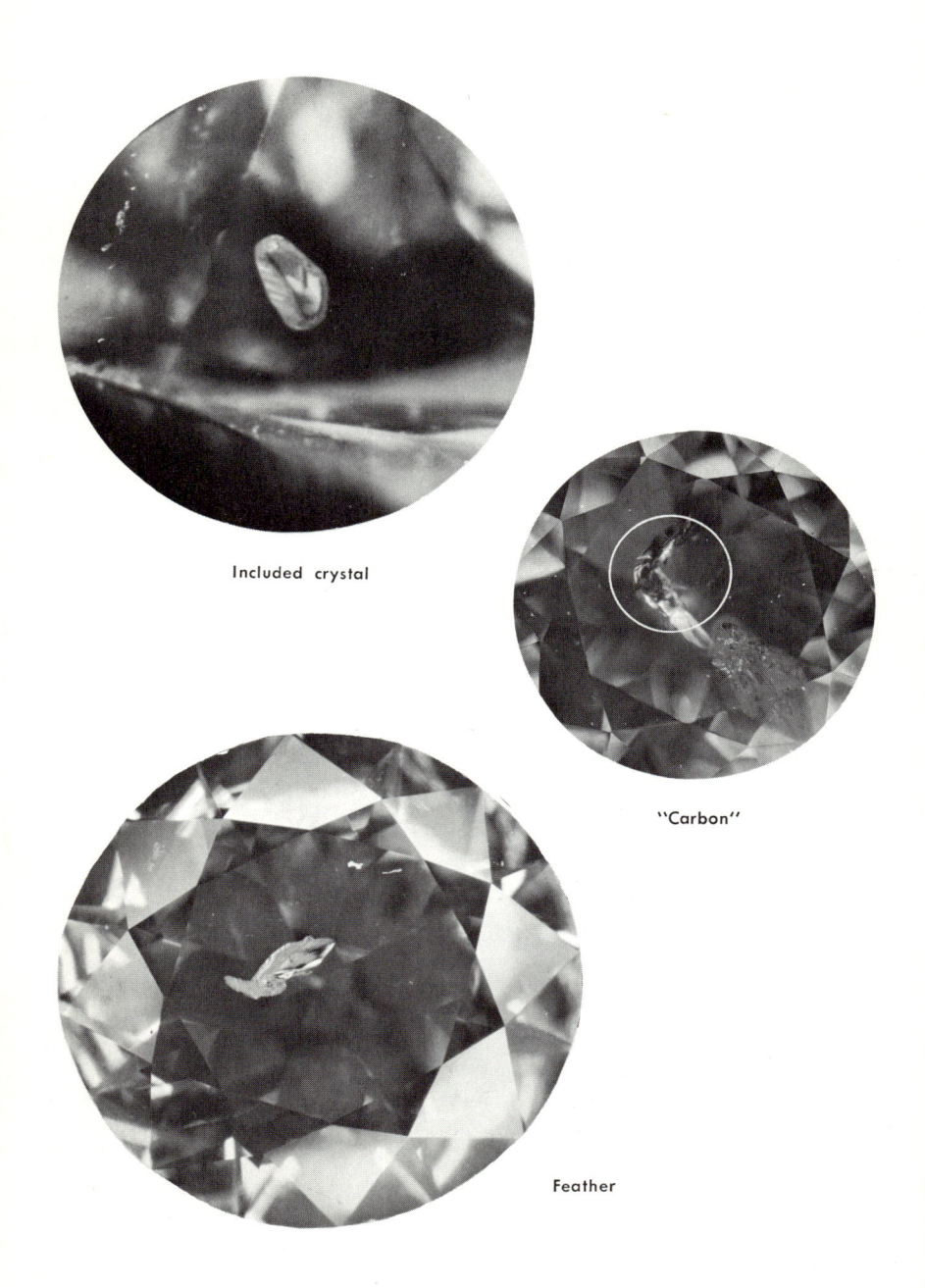

Included crystal

"Carbon"

Feather

Diamonds

—despite the presence of many *surface* blemishes. One frequently-encountered blemish of this kind is the so-called bearded girdle. This is a condition that remains after a diamond has been turned on a lathe too rapidly, with the result that many "chatter" marks (tiny hairline fractures) extend into the gem from the girdle. Such stones are often guaranteed to be "perfect," but they fail by a significant margin to qualify according to the FTC or AGS definition of the finest clarity grade.

Diamonds are purchased and esteemed because of their beauty, which, in turn, depends on their brilliancy, fire and limpidity. A stone may be perfect according to the FTC definition and absolutely devoid of body color, yet be lacking seriously in brilliancy and fire, unless its *proportions* are good and its *angles* in relation to the plane of the girdle are reasonably close to ideal figures. If the pavilion angle of a stone is too flat, the result is a "dead" appearance in the center (i.e., a lack of brilliancy) and it is known to diamond men as a *fisheye*. If the pavilion angle is too steep, the result is a black center when the stone is viewed from above; it is sometimes called a *lumpy stone*. The ideal angle for the pavilion of a brilliant-cut diamond is $40\frac{3}{4}$ to $41°$. A departure of even one degree is detectable in appearance, and a departure of more than two degrees is obvious.

The angle and thickness of the crown determine the degree to which *dispersion*, or *fire*, is displayed; i.e., the degree to which white light is separated into the flashing, brilliant colors of the spectrum. The crown angle (the angle of the bezel facets, which extend from table to girdle) should be approximately 34 to $34\frac{1}{2}°$ and the table less than 60% of the girdle diameter, for an optimum degree of fire to be in evidence. Failure to adhere to this angle closely is immediately apparent in appearance. The spread table and thin crown seen frequently today reduce materially the fire that should be displayed in a well-cut diamond, even though the effect of crown angle on brilliancy is much less. The reason for using angles and proportions that reduce fire and brilliancy is an effort to achieve maximum weight retention from the rough, to permit lower prices. All too few jewelers are sufficiently familiar with the appearance of a well-cut diamond to recognize what is wrong with one that is poorly cut, so they buy unattractive stones on price alone; such stones do not sell themselves because of their inherent appeal.

Poor angles and proportions are not the only common cutting faults employed to retain extra weight; others are very poor symmetry, in the form of off-center tables and culets; tilted tables; and squared or oval girdle outlines. The girdle is often wavy in places, which is caused by failing to remove enough of the diamond in the rounding-up or blocking

THE JEWELERS' MANUAL

processes to produce a truly circular girdle all in one plane. Huge, unattractive naturals, representing the "skin" of the original rough crystal, often remain as flats that extend well down from the girdle onto the pavilion. Sometimes, naturals are seen even on the crown.

Faults in cutting are frequently much more obvious to the eye than the difference caused by several color or clarity grades. When beauty is the goal, poor cutting is perhaps the worst place to attempt to save money. The majority of the diamonds on the market today depart materially from even the modern modifications of ideal figures.

Finish is also important. A stone should be so well polished that brilliancy is not reduced by the diffraction effect that occurs when the surface is "washboarded" with wheel marks that are visible under a loupe. Extra facets and a rough girdle are also characteristic of a poor finish. Facets should meet at proper points, and opposite facets on the crown and pavilion should be mirror images of one another. There should be a tiny culet, the girdle surface should be so smooth that it has almost a waxy luster (if not polished), and the table (on a round brilliant) should be octagonal.

The cutting factor is certainly not the least—perhaps it is the most—important of the Four C's.

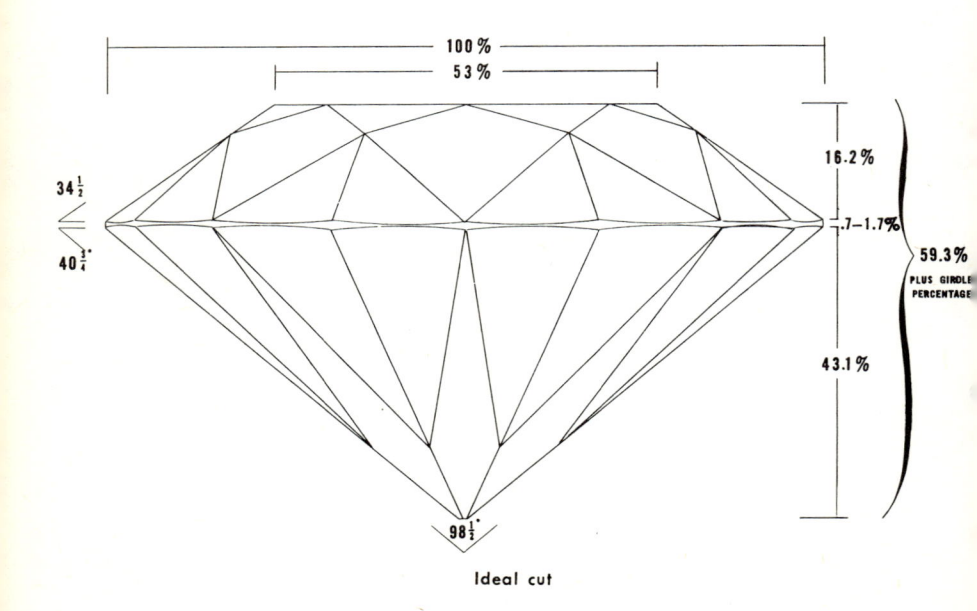

Ideal cut

Diamonds

Diamond-Grading & -Merchandising Instruments

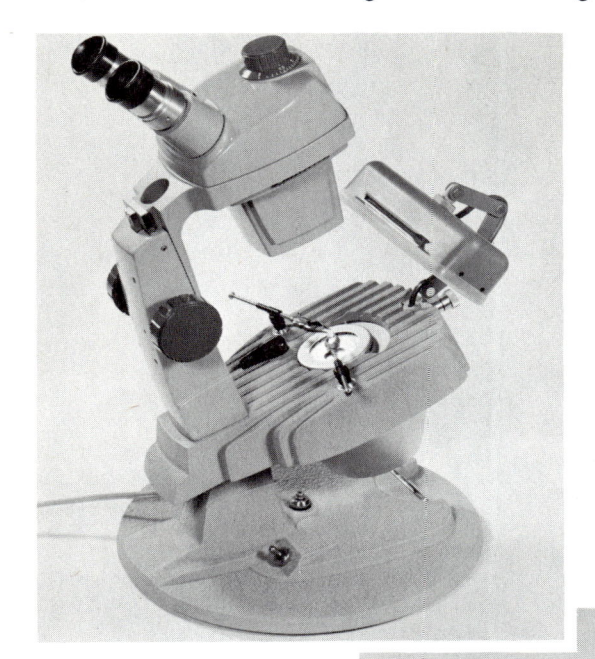

Gemolite

GIA Diamond Grader

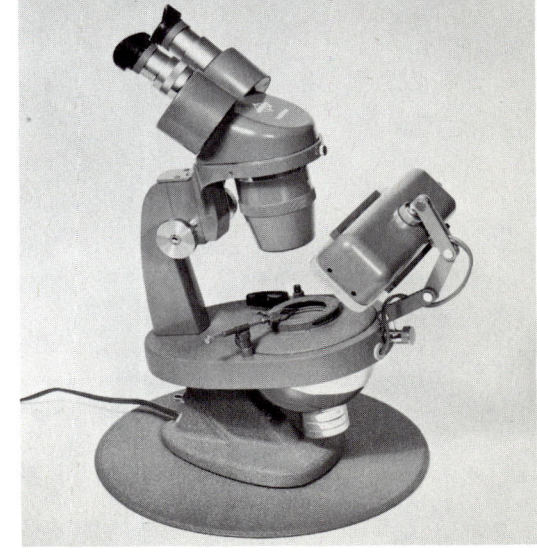

THE JEWELERS' MANUAL

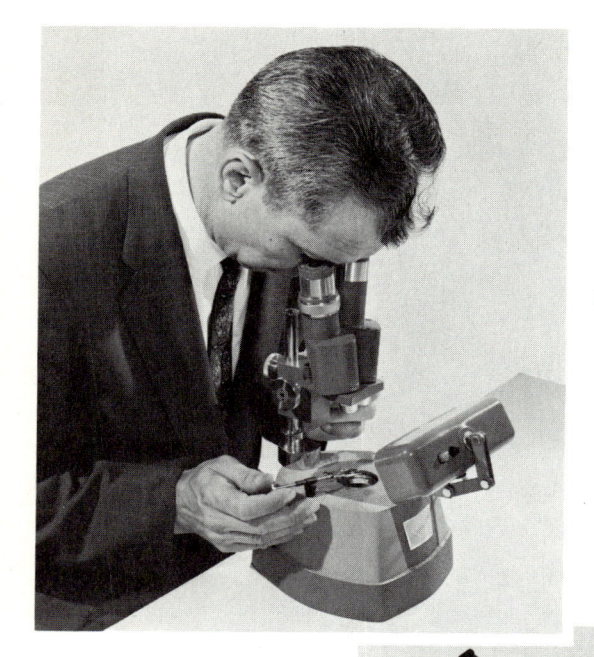

Gem Detector

GIA Color Grader on Gemolite

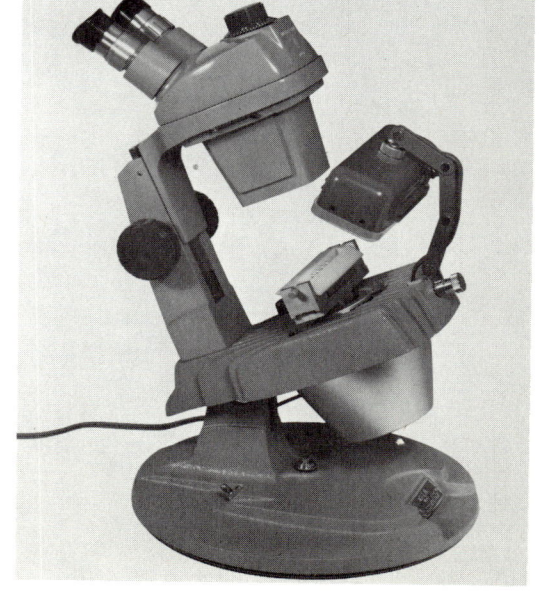

Diamonds

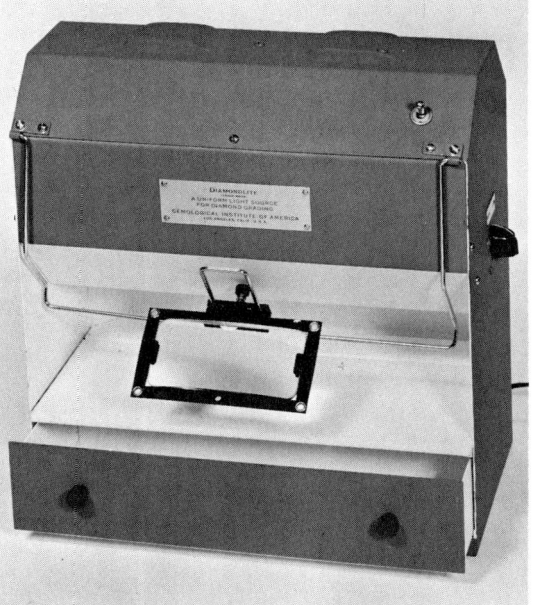

Diamondlite

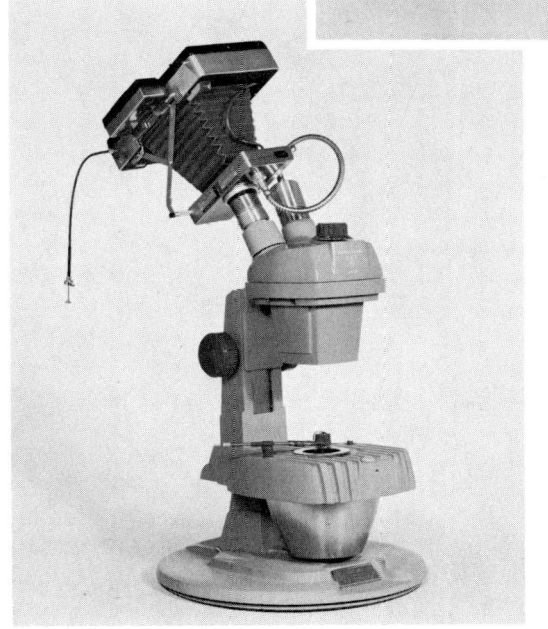

Photoscope on Gemolite

THE JEWELERS' MANUAL

Diamond Balance

ProportionScope

Diamonds

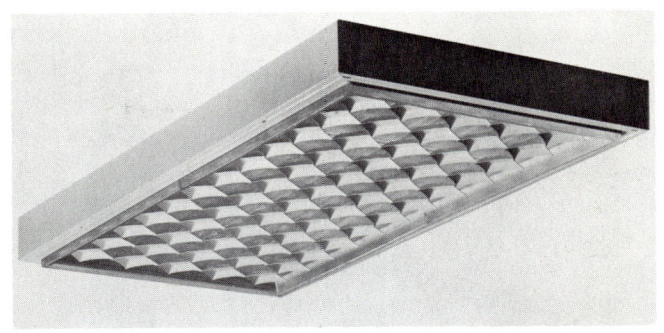

Diamondlux

Hand loupe

Eye loupe

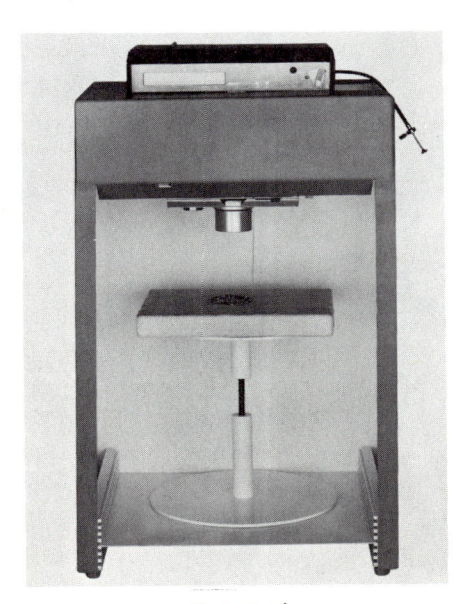

Photostand

THE JEWELERS' MANUAL

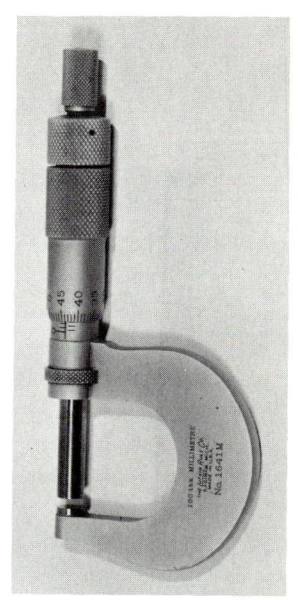

Leveridge gauge

Micrometer

Moe gauge

44

Diamonds

Diameters & Corresponding Weights of Round, Ideally Proportioned, Brilliant-Cut Diamonds

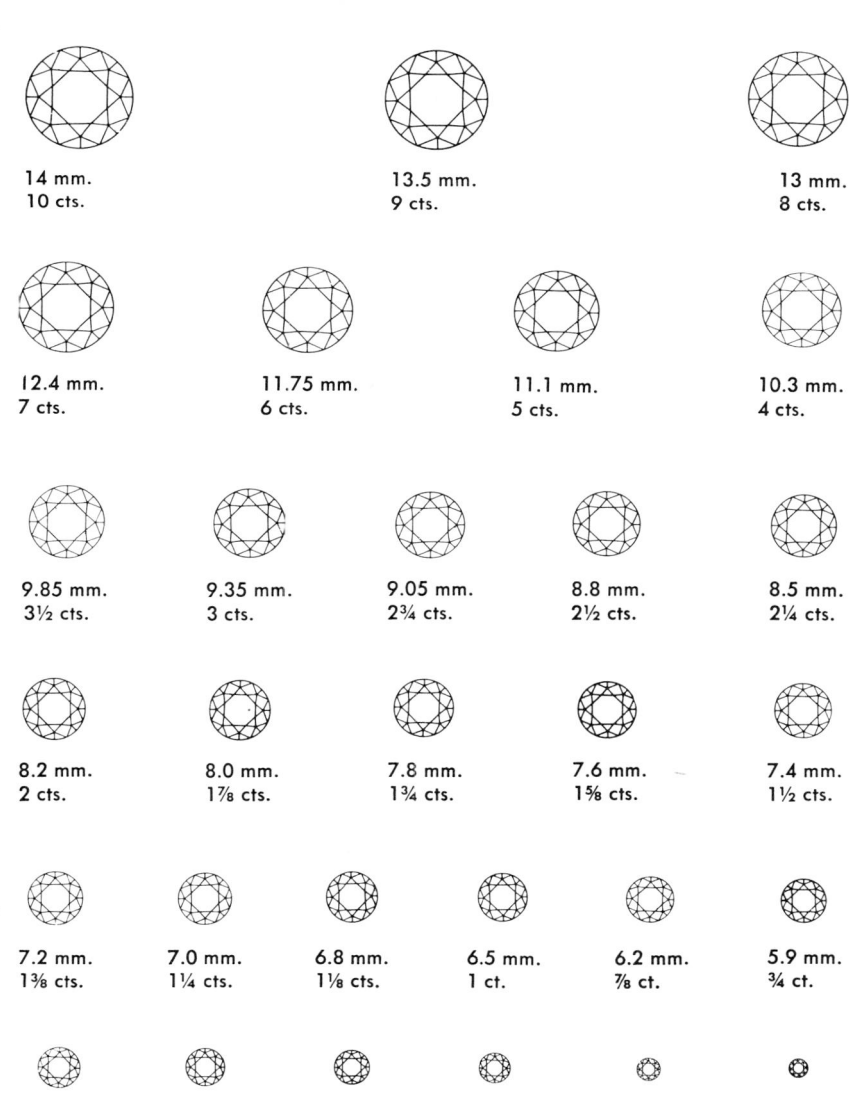

14 mm. 10 cts.	13.5 mm. 9 cts.	13 mm. 8 cts.

12.4 mm. 7 cts.	11.75 mm. 6 cts.	11.1 mm. 5 cts.	10.3 mm. 4 cts.

9.85 mm. 3½ cts.	9.35 mm. 3 cts.	9.05 mm. 2¾ cts.	8.8 mm. 2½ cts.	8.5 mm. 2¼ cts.

8.2 mm. 2 cts.	8.0 mm. 1⅞ cts.	7.8 mm. 1¾ cts.	7.6 mm. 1⅝ cts.	7.4 mm. 1½ cts.

7.2 mm. 1⅜ cts.	7.0 mm. 1¼ cts.	6.8 mm. 1⅛ cts.	6.5 mm. 1 ct.	6.2 mm. ⅞ ct.	5.9 mm. ¾ ct.

5.55 mm. ⅝ ct.	5.15 mm. ½ ct.	4.68 mm. ⅜ ct.	4.1 mm. ¼ ct.	3.25 mm. ⅛ ct.	2.58 mm. 1/16 ct.

THE JEWELERS' MANUAL

Sizes & Weights of Some Pear-Shaped, Marquise & Emerald-Cut Diamonds

ct. weight	Emerald	Marquise	Pear
½	▭	◇	◊
¾	▭	◇	◊
1	▭	◇	◊
1¼	▭	◇	◊
1½	▭	◇	◊
2	▭	◇	◊
2½	▭	◇	◊
3	▭	◇	◊
4	▭	◇	◊
5	▭	◇	◊

Diamonds

The More Important Famous Diamonds
(Described in Glossary)

Name	Date Found	Weight in Rough	Weight After Cutting
Braganza (Not illustrated)	Unknown	Unknown	1680 cts.
Cullinan	1905	3,106.00 Cts.	530.20 cts., plus 8 major gems & 96 smaller stones
Dresden Green	Unknown	Unknown	41.00 cts.
Empress Eugenie	Unknown	Unknown	51.00 cts.
English Dresden	1857	119.50 cts.	76.50 cts.
Excelsior (Not illustrated)	1893	995.20 cts.	70.00 cts., plus 21 smaller stones
Florentine	Unknown	Unknown	137.27 cts.
Great Mogul	Unknown	787.50 cts.	280.00 cts.
Hope	Unknown	Unknown	44.50 cts.
Jonker (Not illustrated)	1934	726.00 cts.	125.65 cts., plus 11 smaller stones
Jubilee	1895	650.80 cts.	245.35 cts.
Kohinoor	Unknown	Unknown	186.00 cts. (original), 108.93 cts. (recut)
Matan	1787	367.00 cts.	Uncut
Nassak (Not illustrated)	Unknown	Unknown	90.00 cts. (original) 80.59 cts. (1st recutting) 43.38 cts. (2nd recutting)
Nizam	Unknown	340.00 cts.? 440.00 cts.?	277.00 cts.
Orloff	Unknown	Unknown	199.60 cts.
Pasha of Egypt	Unknown	Unknown	40.00 cts.
Pigott	Unknown	Unknown	49.00 cts.?
Polar Star	Unknown	Unknown	40.00 cts.
Presidente Vargas	1938	726.60 cts.	48.26 cts., plus 22 smaller stones
Regent	1701	410.00 cts.	140.00 cts.
Sancy	Unknown	Unknown	55.00 cts.
Shah	Unknown	Unknown	88.70 cts.
Star of Este	Unknown	Unknown	26.16 cts.
Star of South Africa	1869	83.50 cts.	47.75 cts.
Star of the South	1853	261.88 cts.	128.50 cts.
Stewart	1872	296.00 cts.	123.00 cts.
Tiffany	1878	287.42 cts.	128.51 cts.
Victoria (Not illustrated)	Unknown	469.00 cts.	184.50 cts.

THE JEWELERS' MANUAL

Florentine

Tiffany

The Presidente Vargas

Cullinan I

Diamonds

English Dresden

Hope

Polar Star

Jubilee

THE JEWELERS' MANUAL

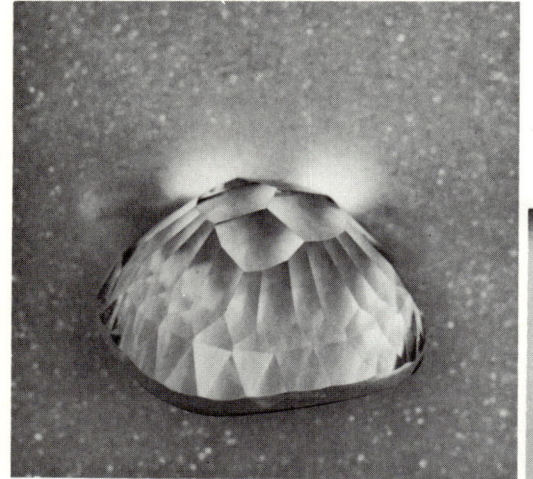

Kohinoor Diamond before re-cutting

Kohinoor Diamond after recutting

Regent

Nizam

Diamonds

Piggot

Star of the South

Star of South Africa

THE JEWELERS' MANUAL

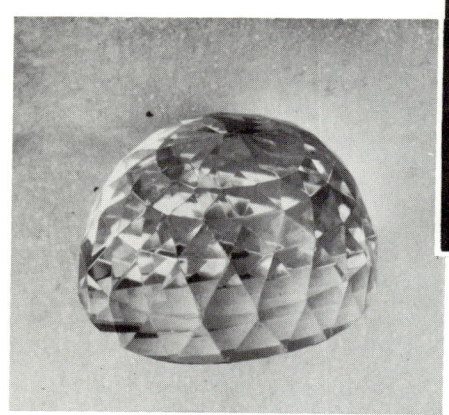

Pasha of Egypt

Great Mogul

Stewart

Diamonds

Sancy

Dresden Green

Orloff

THE JEWELERS' MANUAL

Star of Este

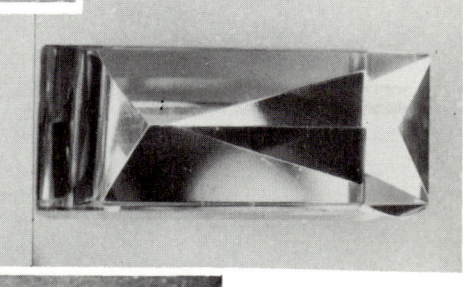

Empress Eugenie

Shah

Matan

Diamonds

How to Learn More About Diamonds

A limited knowledge of diamonds may be acquired by reading many of the books on this subject that have been published in the past fifty years. For example, the reader can gain from the *GIA Diamond Dictionary* and a number of other books some information on diamond properties, mining, cutting and notable stones. A practical knowledge of grading and appraising, however, *cannot* be gained in this manner, since there are no published textbooks that deal with these vital aspects of the diamond industry. Prices change rapidly and diamonds are needed to teach diamond grading and appraising; therefore, books would have to be too general to serve a useful purpose.

Thorough diamond training for jewelers and for those preparing to enter this profession is available *only* in the *Diamond Course* of the Gemological Institute of America. This course is offered entirely by correspondence or, alternatively, partly by correspondence and partly in residence; the latter is presented in the form of one-week classes in cities throughout the country. Whether studying at home or in a class, the student grades and appraises many diamonds according to the unique GIA system. Many of the stones used for grading and appraising practice were donated by De Beers Consolidated Mines, Ltd. An adequate supply of diamonds has made possible a wholly practical training by correspondence. In one-week classes, in addition to working with thousands of dollars worth of diamonds, each student is given the use of a *Gemolite* and has access to Leveridge gauges, *Diamondlites*, color-comparison stones and other equipment and materials. The use of such equipment speeds the mastering of the GIA grading-and-appraising system.

The *Diamond Course* is divided into forty-four general subjects, or assignments, including a number of diamond-grading projects and a written examination. Successful completion of the course leads to the *GIA Diamond Certificate*.

The first ten assignments discuss, among other subjects, the mining and processing of diamonds and their key properties and methods of synthesis, as well as related subjects that have a direct bearing on the distribution and pricing of both rough and cut stones.

The next eight assignments discuss the importance to the jeweler of the nature of the American diamond market, as it is affected by the price of rough goods established by the Diamond Corporation, Ltd., the country in which the rough is cut, and the mode of operation of the American distributor. The grading of rough, price controls, and cutting and proportions are all given careful consideration.

THE JEWELERS' MANUAL

The following fourteen assignments provide a complete system of grading and appraising. Step-by-step instructions for color, clarity, proportion and finish grading, together with comprehensive wholesale price charts, are followed by intensive practice in grading and appraising, using GIA diamonds. In addition to round brilliants, the pricing of fancy shapes is given close attention. The student grades and appraises stones until his instructor is convinced that the system is understood thoroughly.

The remaining assignments are concerned with establishing an appraisal service, detecting substitutes and treated diamonds, handling jewelers' insurance and legal problems, layout and lighting for display and sales areas, and other subjects of vital importance to the diamond retailer.

Gem Testing

Most gemstones and many substitutes are *crystalline solids* with characteristic chemical compositions and crystal structures; as such, they have physical and optical properties that are relatively constant. Even opal and jet, which are noncrystalline (*amorphous*), have nearly constant properties. The other nonmineral gem materials, pearl and coral, are actually mostly crystalline; their property values, too, are almost invariable.

By using destructive tests, it is not too difficult to determine the structure and composition of a gemstone; however, even these tests will not distinguish synthetic from natural stones. Since there are not many gem materials, compared to the number of crystalline solids known to man, separating them can be accomplished usually by the measurement of comparatively few properties. The properties chosen must be diagnostic but measurable, without in any manner harming the stone or the mounting in which it is set. The mineralogist and the chemist usually have no need to avoid destruction of the material they are testing; therefore, destructive tests are perfectly satisfactory. To the gemologist, however, the tremendous value of gemstones, or the fact that they are cherished by their owners, limits the tests to those that are not harmful; this is one reason why he never uses the hardness test on a transparent stone.

These constant properties, for the most part, are measurable by relatively simple instruments that can be used by any well-trained person. In the following paragraphs, these properties and instruments will be discussed briefly.

Examination by Unaided Eye or Low-Power Magnification

One key test that is applied by an expert gemtester is a very careful examination of the stone by the unaided eye or with a low-power loupe. At this time, he notes color, luster, quality of polish, the girdle surface, heft, amount of dispersion (fire), whether doubling of the back-facet junctions is obvious, and whether dichroism is evident. He also studies any cleavages or fractures that may be present and notes the kind of luster on these surfaces. These characteristics, together with distribution of color and degree of transparency, are helpful to an experienced gemologist. On this basis, he can eliminate many of the possibilities the stone might have seemed to be at first glance.

The Refractometer

Perhaps the most important property in gem identification is *refractive index*. This is a measure of a gem's ability to bend a light ray as it enters or leaves. It is measured by the simple, nondestructive means provided by a *refractometer* (re'-frak-tom"-eh-ter). If a stone has a well-polished convex or flat surface, this instrument can be used to obtain a very accurate R.I., ranging from a minimum of 1.30 to a maximum of 1.81. The upper limit is the refractive index of a contact liquid, which is needed to form an optical contact between the gemstone and the hemicylinder of the instrument. Although it is possible to obtain a refractometer with a diamond hemicylinder, it is exceedingly expensive and seldom used. This is not too important in gemtesting, since, of the major gemstones, only zircon and some garnets have indices above the normal refractometer's scale, but within the added range made possible by a diamond hemicylinder; these stones can be separated readily by other means.

Since many gemstones are doubly refractive, two readings are possible at one time, and these readings may vary widely as the stone is rotated on the hemicylinder. However, both the R.I. range and the *birefringence* may be obtained, so that, in effect, two properties are being determined at one time. In each case, the number of possibilities among the gem materials at any one point on the scale is very limited; for this reason, refractive index is an important test.

High Magnification

Probably the next most important test to a practicing gemologist is *high magnification;* often, it is the only practical means of separating synthetic from natural stones. For example, the refractive index and other properties of ruby and synthetic ruby are identical. However, magnification reveals the curved growth lines and spherical gas bubbles that typify the synthetic and the angular inclusions and hexagonal color banding of the natural.

Other gemstones also have characteristic inclusions or other features that are diagnostic to the trained observer. The unusual surface appearance of a diamond's lathe-turned girdle, together with characteristic growth markings or shiny, unpolished remnants of the original crystal surface, may be detected readily under magnification.

Gem Testing

Inclusions That Characterize
Some Natural & Artificial Gem Materials

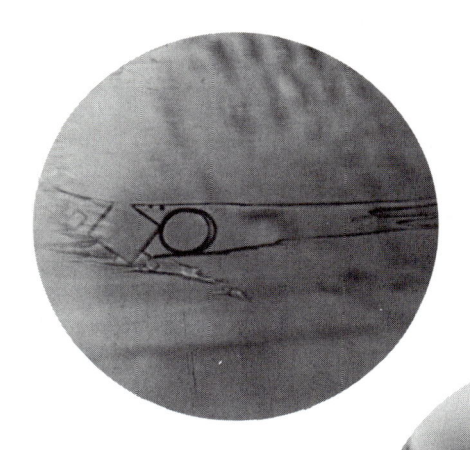

Three-phase inclusion in emerald

Liquid- and air-filled fissure in sapphire

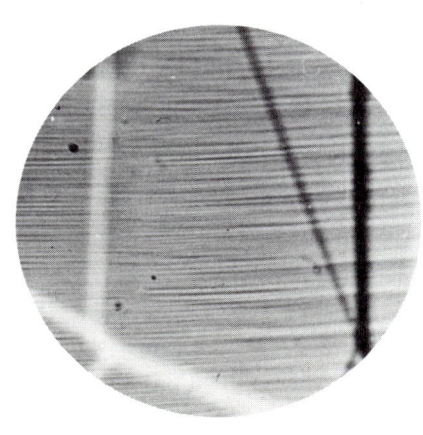

Gas bubbles and curved striae in synthetic ruby

THE JEWELERS' MANUAL

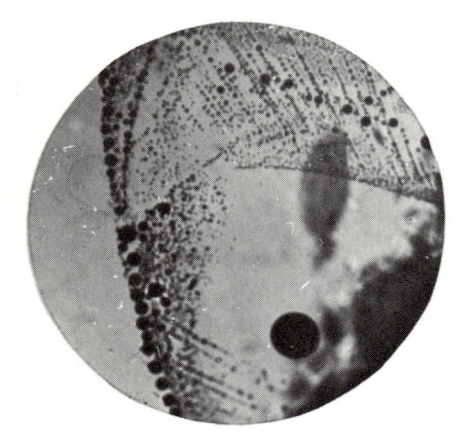

A concentration of gas bubbles in glass

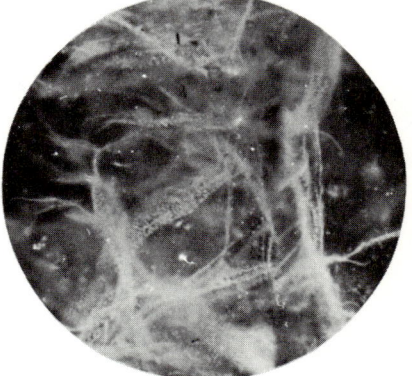

Wisplike liquid feathers in synthetic emerald

Gas bubbles and natural inclusions in garnet-and-glass doublet

Gem Testing

The Polariscope

Another valuable test is to determine whether a gem is *singly* or *doubly refractive*. A doubly-refractive material polarizes light transmitted through it into two beams that vibrate at right angles to one another. This property is detected readily with a *polariscope* (po-lare"-ih-scope), an instrument consisting essentially of two Polaroid plates that are set with the planes of vibration at right angles to one another. When a transparent gem is rotated between crossed Polaroid plates (i.e., in the dark position), a doubly-refractive material becomes alternately light and dark, whereas a singly-refractive material remains dark in all positions. Although there are factors that tend to complicate this testing method somewhat, it is relatively simple to use, after a certain amount of instruction and practice.

The Dichroscope

Singly- and doubly-refractive materials may also be separated with a *dichroscope* (die"-kro-scope). This small instrument incorporates a piece of highly birefringent, transparent, colorless calcite that separates the two beams into which a gem has polarized light and permits the gem-tester to examine the color of the transmission in those two vibration directions. Many gemstones, such as ruby and sapphire, have very strong *pleochroism* (ple"-oh-kro'-izm), which is a difference in the color of light transmitted in different vibration directions through the same stone; it is detected with this instrument. Singly-refractive colored stones show no difference in color transmission in the two windows of the dichroscope.

The Spectroscope

Some gemstones have the ability to absorb certain portions of the spectrum of light transmitted through, or reflected from, them. Characteristic absorption is analyzed by an instrument called a *spectroscope*. Although it has always been a useful tool to gemologists, the importance of the spectroscope has grown in the past few years with the discovery in the laboratories of the Gemological Institute of America of its value in distinguishing between irradiated and naturally-colored diamonds and between dyed and naturally-colored jadeite. It is also very useful in distinguishing jadeite from substitutes; natural from synthetic blue, green and yellow sapphire; garnet from ruby or synthetic ruby; pyrope from spinel; and in many other separations.

The key to successful use of the gemologist's prism spectroscope is excellent lighting. The two general methods of illumination are (1) to pass light through the specimen or (2) reflect it from the gem's surface.

In general, a powerful light source is necessary for maximum efficiency. The GIA Spectroscope Unit employs a small Beck prism-type instrument with a wavelength scale and a powerful lamp that can be changed readily to a cool source of transmitted light (by passing it through a prism) or a directly-reflected beam.

Specific Gravity

Another property of value in gem testing is *specific gravity*. This is the ratio of the weight of a gem compared to the weight of an equal volume of water; i.e., a measure of how many times heavier a gemstone is than an equal volume of water. Of course, this test is limited by the fact that it is applicable only to loose stones; mounted gems cannot be tested by this means.

Specific gravity is determined by two principal methods. In the *hydrostatic method*, the gem is first weighed in air and again in water; the density is then obtained by dividing the loss of weight in water into the the weight in air.

The second method utilizes *heavy liquids*; i.e., those with densities considerably greater than that of water. The principal ones are *bromoform*, either in pure form, at 2.89, or diluted with *xylene* (zy″-lene) to lower figures; *methylene iodide*, with an S.G. at room temperature of 3.32; and, occasionally, *Clerici's solution*, a water solution of a combination of thallium malonate and thallium formate. The problem with the latter is that it is highly toxic and dangerous to use. In a saturated solution at room temperature, it has an S.G. of approximately 4.25; it may be diluted with water to any desired density between 1 and 4.25.

Fluorescence

Also useful to the gemologist is *fluorescence*; i.e., the reaction of a gemstone to *ultraviolet light*. Some gems fluoresce and others do not. Some varieties of the same species fluoresce but others fail to react; in fact, a variety from one source may fluoresce and the same variety from another mine will not.

Although fluorescence is usually more of an indication than a positive test, there are times when it is very helpful in an identification; e.g., synthetic yellow sapphire does not fluoresce, whereas natural yellow sapphire from Ceylon reacts in an orangy color. In general, synthetic ruby fluoresces more strongly than natural material of comparable color, and it tends to phosphoresce after exposure to X-rays. Synthetic emerald fluoresces deep red but the natural usually does not, although occasional fine stones do react slightly.

Gem Testing

Thermal Reaction Tester

An instrument that is rarely needed but that is sometimes very helpful is an electrically-heated needle, called a *hot point*. If the point is brought near an oiled turquois or one that has been impregnated with paraffin, moisture may be seen under magnification. Plastic imitations or plastic-impregnated turquois can be detected by odor when the point is touched against the stone.

Hardness

Historically, *hardness* was the jeweler's standard test; however, it is not only dangerous but is very likely to be misleading, so it is avoided by the gemologist. A file drawn across a knife-edge girdle of a diamond can appear to have "bitten" into the stone, whereas it has actually fractured its edge. Just as a glazier scratches glass to weaken it before being broken, a scratch on a gemstone can weaken it so much that breakage results, either at the time or later. Even if breakage does not occur, a scratch usually defaces a stone noticeably. Thus, hardness is a test that should *never* be used on a *transparent* stone and used only with *caution* on the back of an *opaque* one, but only then when all else has failed.

Armed with this battery of tests, the competent gemologist is able to identify gemstones.

THE JEWELERS' MANUAL

Gem-Testing Instruments

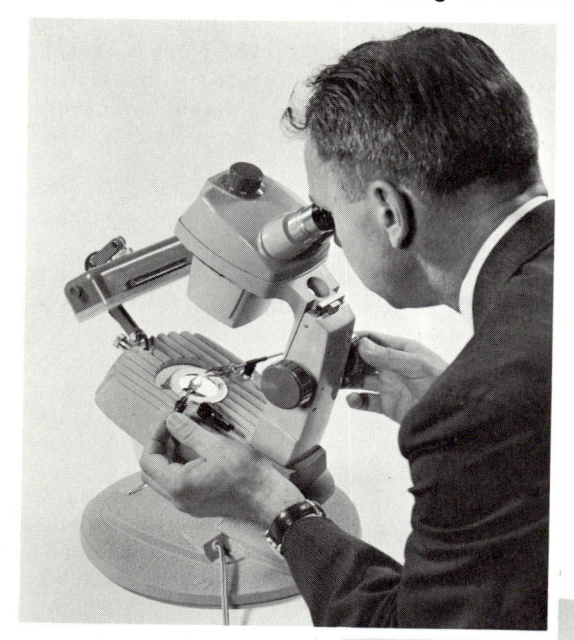

Gemolite

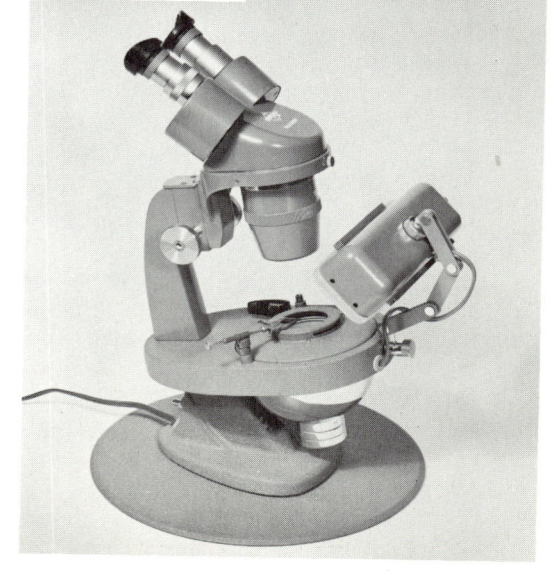

GIA Diamond Grader

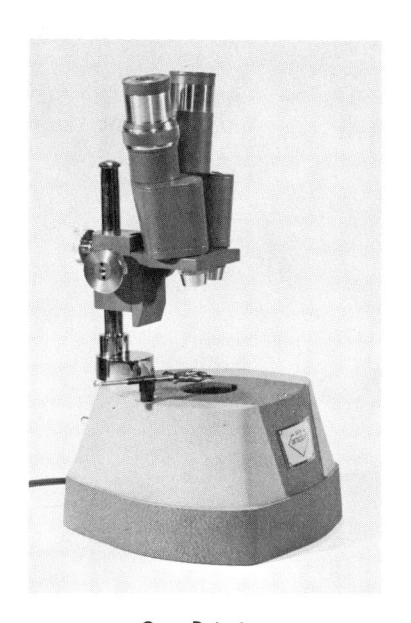

Gem-Testing Instruments

Gem Detector

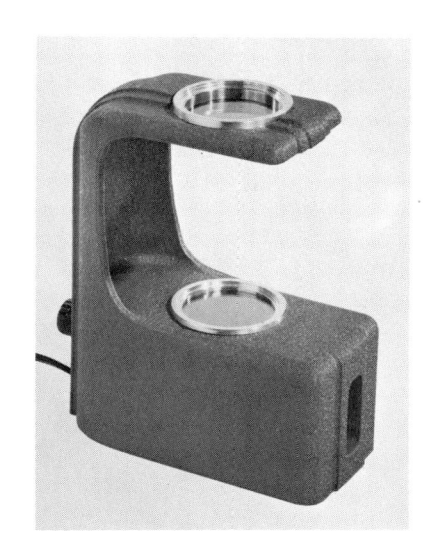

Illuminator Polariscope

Duplex II Refractometer

THE JEWELERS' MANUAL

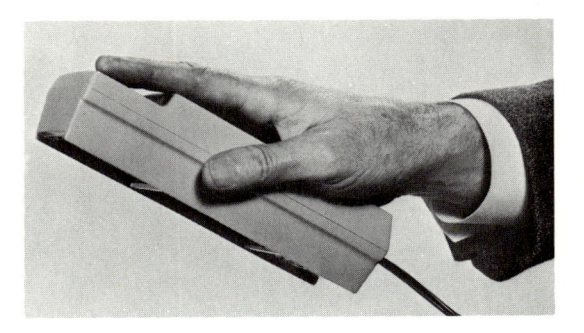

Ultraviolet lamp

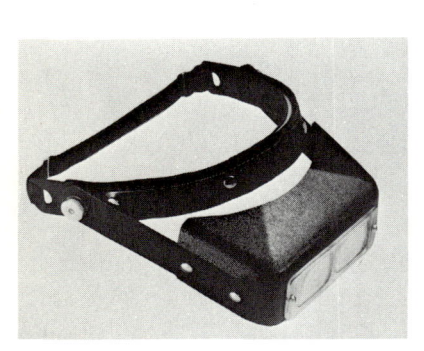

Optivisor

GIA Thermal Reaction Tester

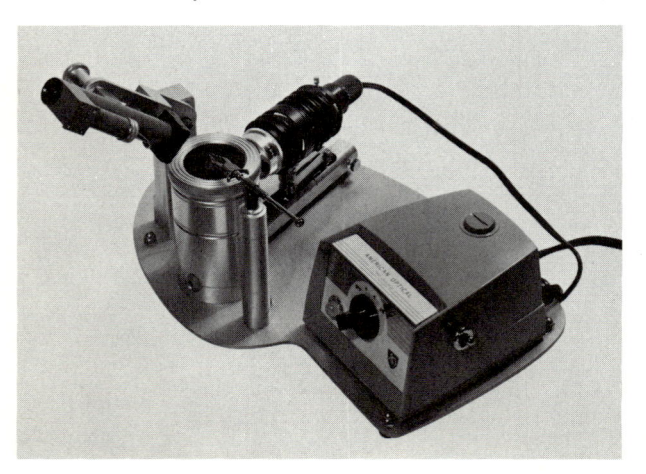

GIA Spectroscope Unit

Gem-Testing Instruments

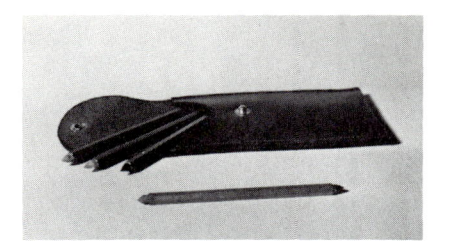

Hardness points

Immersion cell

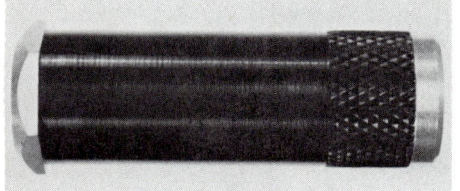

GIA Dichroscope

Emerald filter

Tweezers

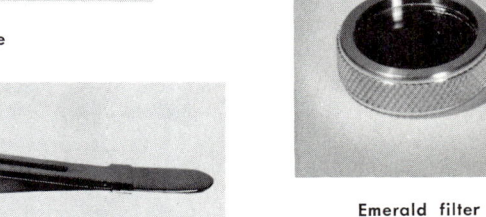

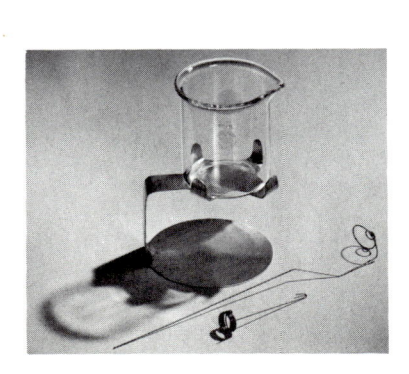

Specific-gravity attachments

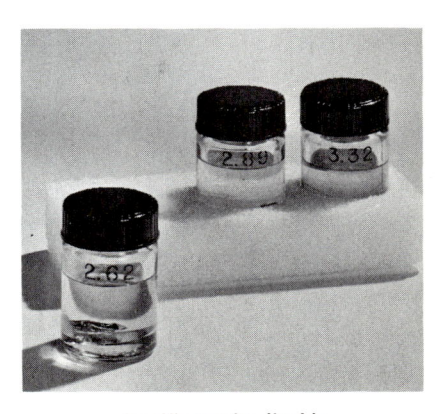

Specific-gravity liquids

THE JEWELERS' MANUAL

Color

Purple and Violet Gemstones and Their Substitutes

Transparent

Almandite garnet
Beryl (morganite)
Chrysoberyl (alexandrite)
Corundum (sapphire)
Diamond
Glass
Plastics
Pyrope garnet
Quartz (amethyst)

Rhodolite garnet
Spinel
Spodumene (kunzite)
Synthetic corundum
Synthetic spinel
Topaz
Tourmaline
Zircon
Doublets

Gems infrequently encountered in the jewelry trade:

Andalusite
Apatite
Axinite
Fluorite

Iolite
Scapolite
Taaffeite

Nontransparent

Almandite garnet
Corundum (star sapphire)
Jadeite

Quartz (chalcedonic)
Stichtite
Thomsonite

Blue Gemstones and Their Substitutes

Transparent

Beryl (aquamarine)
Corundum (sapphire)
Diamond
Glass
Iolite
Plastics
Quartz (dyed)
Chalcedony (dyed and natural)
Opal
Spinel

Synthetic corundum
Synthetic rutile
Synthetic spinel
Topaz
Tourmaline
Zircon
Doublets
Triplets
Foilbacks

Gems infrequently encountered in the jewelry trade:

Apatite
Benitoite
Euclase
Fluorite

Kornerupine
Kyanite
Lazulite
Sillimanite

Nontransparent

Azurite
Chalcedonic quartz
  (chrysocolla quartz and
  dyed chalcedony)
Corundum (star sapphire)
Glass
Jadeite
Labradorite feldspar
Lazurite (lapis-lazuli)

Opal (black opal)
Plastics
Quartz (cat's-eye quartz)
Sintered synthetic spinel
Synthetic corundum
Turquois
Doublets
Foilbacks

Color

Gems infrequently encountered in the jewelry trade:
- Diopside
- Dumortierite
- Lazulite
- Odontolite
- Smithsonite
- Sodalite

Green Gemstones and Their Substitutes

Transparent

- Andradite garnet (demantoid)
- Beryl (emerald)
- Chrysoberyl (including cat's-eye and alexandrite)
- Corundum (green sapphire)
- Diamond
- Glass
- Peridot
- Plastics
- Chalcedonic quartz (chrysoprase)
- Quartz
- Spinel
- Synthetic corundum
- Synthetic emerald
- Synthetic rutile
- Synthetic spinel
- Topaz
- Tourmaline
- Zircon
- Doublets
- Triplets

Gems infrequently encountered in the jewelry trade:
- Andalusite
- Apatite
- Brazilianite
- Datolite
- Diopside
- Dioptase
- Ekanite
- Enstatite
- Epidote
- Euclase
- Fluorite
- Gahnite
- Gahnospinel
- Jadeite
- Kornerupine
- Kyanite
- Moldavite
- Obsidian
- Sphalerite
- Sphene
- Spodumene
- Willemite

Nontransparent

- Agalmatolite
- Beryl
- Calcite (dyed onyx marble)
- Chalcedonic quartz (chrysoprase or bloodstone and dyed chalcedony)
- Chlorastrolite
- Chrysoberyl (cat's-eye)
- Corundum
- Glass
- Grossularite garnet
- Idocrase
- Jadeite jade
- Labradorite feldspar
- Malachite
- Microcline feldspar (amazonite)
- Nephrite jade
- Opal (black opal)
- Prehnite
- Pseudophite
- Quartz (aventurine)
- Saussurite
- Serpentine
- Sillimanite
- Smithsonite
- Steatite
- Synthetic emerald
- Tourmaline
- Turquois
- Variscite
- Verdite

Yellow Gemstones and Their Substitutes

Transparent

Amber	Spessartite garnet
Beryl	Spodumene
Chrysoberyl	Synthetic corundum
Corundum	Synthetic rutile
Diamond	Synthetic spinel
Glass	Topaz
Grossularite garnet (hessonite)	Tourmaline
Opal	Zircon
Peridot	Doublets
Plastics	Triplets
Quartz (citrine)	Foil backs

Gems infrequently encountered in the jewelry trade:

Apatite	Labradorite feldspar
Axinite	Orthoclase feldspar
Beryllonite	Phenakite
Brazilianite	Scapolite
Cassiterite	Smithsonite
Copal	Sphene
Danburite	Spinel
Fluorite	Stibiotantalite

Nontransparent

Amber	Jadeite jade
Chalcedonic quartz	Plastics
Chrysoberyl (cat's-eye)	Smithsonite

Brown and Orange Gemstones and Their Substitutes

Transparent

Amber and pressed amber	Quartz
Beryl	Chalcedony
Chrysoberyl	Sinhalite
Copal (and other natural resins)	Spinel
Corundum	Synthetic corundum
Diamond	Synthetic rutile
Doublets	Synthetic spinel
Glass	Topaz
Grossularite garnet (hessonite)	Tourmaline
Opal (fire opal)	Triplets
Plastics	Zircon

Gems infrequently encountered in the jewelry trade:

Anatase	Obsidian
Andalusite	Peridot
Axinite	Scheelite
Cassiterite	Spessartite garnet
Copal	Sphalerite
Enstatite	Sphene
Idocrase	Staurolite
Kornerupine	Willemite

Color

Nontransparent

Amber	Plastics
Chalcedonic quartz	Quartz tiger's-eye
Chrysoberyl (cat's-eye)	Smithsonite
Jadeite jade	Sunstone
Opal	Synthetic corundum

Red and Pink Gemstones and Their Substitutes
Transparent

Almandite garnet	Rhodolite garnet
Beryl (morganite)	Spinel
Chrysoberyl (alexandrite)	Spodumene (kunzite)
Corundum (ruby and pink sapphire)	Synthetic corundum
	Synthetic rutile
Diamond	Synthetic spinel
Glass	Topaz
Opal (fire opal)	Tourmaline (rubellite and Bordeaux tourmaline)
Plastics	
Pyrope garnet	Zircon
Quartz (rose quartz)	Doublets
Chalcedony (carnelian and sard)	Triplets
	Foilbacks

Gems infrequently encountered in the jewelry trade:

Amber	Phenakite
Andalusite	Pollucite
Apatite	Rhodochrosite
Apophyllite	Rutile
Cassiterite	Scapolite
Danburite	Spessartite
Epidote	Sphalerite
Fluorite	Zincite
Painite	

Nontransparent

Almandite garnet (star garnet)	Plastics
	Quartz (cat's-eye quartz)
Chalcedonic quartz (sard, sardonyx, and carnelian)	Rhodochrosite
	Rhodonite
Conch pearl	Scapolite
Coral	Stichtite
Corundum (star ruby)	Synthetic corundum
Glass	Thomsonite
Grossularite	Zoisite (thulite)
Jadeite	Foilbacks

Colorless Gemstones and Their Substitutes
Transparent

Beryl
Corundum (white sapphire)
Diamond
Glass
Opal
Orthoclase feldspar (moonstone)
Plastics
Quartz (rock crystal)

Spinel
Strontium titanate
Synthetic corundum
Synthetic rutile
Synthetic spinel
Topaz
Tourmaline
Zircon (jargoon)

Gems and their substitutes infrequently encountered in the jewelry trade:

Amblygonite
Apatite
Augelite
Benitoite
Beryllonite
Brazilianite
Danburite
Euclase
Fluorite
Hambergite
Jadeite

Labradorite
Leucite
Petalite
Phenakite
Pollucite
Rhodizite
Scapolite
Scheelite
Spodumene
Doublets

White Gemstones and Their Substitutes
Nontransparent

Alabaster
Chalcedonic quartz
 (chalcedony moonstone)
Coral
Corundum
Glass
Jadeite jade
Nephrite jade

Onyx marble
Opal
Opal doublets
Orthoclase feldspar (moonstone)
Plastics
Synthetic corundum
Synthetic spinel

Black Gemstones and Their Substitutes
Nontransparent

Andradite garnet (melanite)
Black coral
Chalcedonic quartz
 (black onyx)
Corundum (star sapphire)
Diamond
Glass
Hematite
Hemetine

Jadeite jade
Jet
Nephrite jade
Obsidian
Opal
Opal doublets
Plastics
Psilomelane
Tourmaline

Color

Gray Gemstones and Their Substitutes
Nontransparent

Chalcedonic quartz (agate)
Corundum (star sapphire)
Hematite
Hemetine
Jadeite jade
Labradorite feldspar
Nephrite jade
Sintered synthetic corundum

Refractive Index

Refractive Index

Rutile & Syn	2.616	2.903
Anatase	2.493	2.554
Diamond	2.417	
Strontium titanate	2.409	
Stibiotantalite	2.37	2.45
Sphalerite	2.37	
Zincite	2.013	2.029
Cassiterite	1.997	2.093
Zircon (high)	1.925	1.984
Scheelite	1.918	1.934
Sphene	1.900(±.018)	2.034(±.020)
Zircon (medium)	1.875(±.045)	1.905(±.075)
Andradite garnet	1.875(±.020)	
Zircon (low)	1.810(±.020)	1.815(±.020)
Spessartite garnet	1.81(±.010)	
Almandite garnet	1.80(±.030)	
Gahnite	1.80	
Painite	1.787	1.816
Corundum	1.762(−.003,+.007)	1.770(−.003,+.008)
Synthetic corundum	1.762	1.770
Rhodolite garnet	1.76(±.010)	
Benitoite	1.757	1.804
Gahnospinel	1.76(±.02)	
Pyrope garnet	1.746(−.026,+.010)	
Chrysoberyl	1.746(±.004)	1.755(±.005)
Staurolite	1.736	1.746
Grossularite garnet	1.735(±.015)	
Azurite	1.73(±.010)	1.84(±.010)
Rhodonite	1.73	1.74
Epidote	1.729(−.015,+.006)	1.768(−.035,+.012)
Synthetic spinel	1.73(±.01)	
Spinel	1.718(−.006,+.044)	
Taafeite	1.719	1.723
Kyanite	1.716(±.004)	1.731(±.004)
Idocrase	1.713(±.012)	1.718(±.014)
Zoisite	1.700	1.706
Willemite	1.69	1.72
Rhodizite	1.69	
Dumortierite	1.678	1.689
Axinite	1.678	1.688
Diopside	1.675(−.010,+.027)	1.701(−.007,+.029)
Sinhalite	1.668(±.003)	1.707(±.003)
Kornerupine	1.667(±.002)	1.680(±.003)
Malachite	1.66	1.91
Spodumene	1.660(±.005)	1.676(±.005)
Sillimanite	1.659	1.68
Jet	1.66(±.020)	
Enstatite	1.658(±.005)	1.668(±.005)
Dioptase	1.655(±.011)	1.708(±.012)
Jadeite	1.654	1.667
Euclase	1.654(±.004)	1.673(±.004)
Phenakite	1.654(−.003,+.017)	1.670(−.004,+.026)
Peridot	1.654(±.020)	1.690(±.020)
Apatite	1.642(.−012,+.003)	1.646(−.014,+.005)

THE JEWELERS' MANUAL

Refractive Index

Andalusite	1.634(±.006)	1.643(±.004)
Danburite	1.630(±.003)	1.636(±.003)
Datolite	1.626	1.670
Tourmaline	1.624(±.005)	1.644(±.006)
Smithsonite	1.621	1.849
Topaz	1.619(±.010)	1.627(±.010)
Prehnite	1.615	1.646
Turquois	1.61	1.65
Lazulite	1.612	1.643
Amblygonite	1.612	1.636
Bakelite	1.61(±.06)	
Nephrite	1.606	1.632
Brazilianite	1.602	1.621
Odontolite	1.60(±.03)	1.61(±.03)
Ekanite	1.597	
Rhodochrosite	1.597	1.817
Verdite	1.580	
Beryl	1.577(±.016)	1.583(±.017)
Synthetic emerald (Linde)	1.575	1.581
Augelite	1.574	1.588
Pseudophite	1.57	1.58
Synthetic emerald (Chatham)	1.561	1.565
Variscite	1.56	1.59
Coral (black)	1.56	1.57
Labradorite feldspar	1.559	1.568
Hambergite	1.555	1.625
Beryllonite	1.552	1.562
Agalmatolite	1.55	1.66
Scapolite	1.55	1.572
Quartz	1.544(±.00)	1.553(±.00)
Iolite	1.542(—.010,+.002)	1.551(—.011,+.045)
Steatite	1.54	1.590
Amber	1.540	
Chalcedony quartz	1.535	1.539
Apophyllite	1.535	1.537
Albite-oligoclase	1.532(±.007)	1.542(±.005)
Pollucite	1.525	
Microcline	1.522	1.530
Orthoclase	1.518	1.526
Thomsonite	1.515	1.540
Stichtite	1.516	1.542
Leucite	1.508	
Petalite	1.502	1.518
Lazurite (lapis-lazuli)	1.500	
Obsidian	1.500	
Lucite	1.495(±.005)	
Serpentine	1.56(—.07)	1.570(—.07)
Calcite	1.486	1.658
Coral	1.486	1.658
Sodalite	1.483(±.003)	
Moldavite	1.48	
Opal	1.45(—.080,+.020)	
Fluorite	1.434	
Glass (normal)	1.48 - 1.70	
(extreme)	1.44 - 1.77	

75

THE JEWELERS' MANUAL

Specific Gravity

Stibiotantalite	7.50(±.30)	Ekanite . . .	3.28
Cassiterite . .	6.95(±.08)	Enstatite . .	3.25(±.02)
Scheelite . .	6.12	Sillimanite . .	3.25(±.02)
Zincite . . .	5.70	Chlorastrolite .	3.30
Hematite . .	5.20(±.08)	Fluorite . . .	3.18(±.01)
Strontium		Apatite . . .	3.19(±.02)
titanate . .	5.13(±.02)	Spodumene . .	3.19(±.03)
Pyrite . . .	5.00(±.10)	Andalusite . .	3.17(±.04)
Marcasite . .	4.85(±.05)	Euclase . . .	3.10(±.01)
Zircon		Odontolite . .	3.10
(high) . .	4.70(±.03)	Lazulite . . .	3.09(±.05)
(medium) .	4.32(±.25)	Tourmaline .	3.06(—.05,+.15)
Gahnite . .	4.55	Amblygonite .	3.02
Smithsonite .	4.30(±.10)	Danburite . .	3.00(±.01)
Rutile & Syn. .	4.26(±.02)	Psilomelane .	3.0
Spessartite . .	4.15(±.03)	Nephrite . .	2.95(±.05)
Almandite . .	4.05(±.12)	Phenakite . .	2.95(±.01)
Sphalerite . .	4.05(±.02)	Datolite . . .	2.95
Painite . . .	4.01	Brazilianite . .	2.94
Gahnospinel .	4.01(±.40)	Pollucite . .	2.92
Zircon (low) .	4.00(±.07)	Verdite . . .	2.90
Corundum		Prehnite . .	2.88(±.06)
& Syn. . .	4.00(±.03)	Beryllonite . .	2.85(±.02)
Malachite . .	3.95(—.70,+.15)	Conch Pearl .	2.85
Anatase . . .	3.90	Agamatolite .	2.80
Andradite . .	3.84(±.03)	Turquois . .	2.76(—45,+.08)
Rhodolite . .	3.84(±.10)	Steatite . . .	2.75
Azurite . . .	3.80(—.50,+.07)	Lapis-lazuli .	2.75(±.25)
Pyrope . . .	3.78(—.16,+.09)	Beryl	2.72(—.05,+.12)
Chrysoberyl .	3.73(±.02)	Pearl	2.70(—.02,+.15)
Staurolite . .	3.71(±.06)	Labradorite .	2.70(±.05)
Rhodochrosite	3.70	Augelite . .	2.70
Syn. spinel . .	3.65(—.12,+.02)	Pseudophite .	2.70
Benitoite . .	3.64(±.03)	Calcite . . .	2.70
Kyanite . . .	3.62(±.06)	Scapolite . .	2.68(±.06)
Grossularite .	3.61(±.14)	Quartz . . .	2.66(±.01)
Spinel . . .	3.60(—.03,+.30)	Syn. emerald	
Taaffeite . .	3.61	(Linde) . .	2.68(±.03)
Topaz . . .	3.53(±.04)	(Chatham) .	2.66(±.01)
Diamond . .	3.52(±.01)	Oligoclase . .	2.65(±.02)
Sphene . . .	3.52(±.02)	Coral . . .	2.65(±.05)
Sinhalite . .	3.48	Iolite	2.63(±.05)
Rhodonite . .	3.50(±.20)	Chalcedony .	2.60(±.05)
Idocrase . .	3.40(±.10)	Serpentine . .	2.57(±.06)
Epidote . . .	3.40(±.08)	Orthoclase . .	2.56(±.01)
Rhodizite . .	3.40	Microcline . .	2.56(±.01)
Peridot . . .	3.34(—.03,+.14)	Variscite . .	2.50(±.08)
Jadeite . . .	3.34(±.04)	Leucite . . .	2.50
Zoisite . . .	3.30(±.10)	Obsidian . .	2.45(±.10)
Dioptase . .	3.30(±.05)	Moldavite . .	2.40(±.04)
Kornerupine .	3.30(±.05)	Petalite . . .	2.40
Saussurite . .	3.30	Apophyllite .	2.40(±.10)
Dumortierite .	3.30	Alabaster . .	2.30
Diopside . .	3.29(±.03)	Thomsonite .	2.35(±.05)
Axinite . . .	3.29(—.02)	Hambergite .	2.35

Specific Gravity

Specific Gravity

Glass	2.3 to 4.5
Sodalite . . .	2.24 (±.05)
Chrysocolla .	2.20 (±.10)
Stichtite . .	2.18 (±.02)
Opal	2.15 (−.17, +.07)
Coral (black) .	1.37
Jet	1.32 (±.02)
Plastics . . .	1.30 (±.25)
Amber . . .	1.08 (±.02)

THE JEWELERS' MANUAL

Hardness

Diamond	10	Petalite	6
Silicon carbide	9¼	Hematite	5½-6½
Corundum & Syn.	9	Rhodonite	5½-6½
Chrysoberyl	8½	Beryllonite	5½-6
Spinel & Syn.	8	Anatase	5½-6
Painite	8	Brazilianite	5½
Topaz	8	Enstatite	5½
Taaffeite	8	Willemite	5½
Rhodizite	8	Moldavite	5½
Beryl & syn. emerald	7½-8	Thomsonite	5½
Phenakite	7½-8	Opal	5-6½
Zircon	7½	Diopside	5-6
Almandite garnet	7½	Glass	5-6
Hambergite	7½	Strontium titanate	5-6
Euclase	7½	Lazulite	5-6
Gahnite	7½	Lapis-lazuli	5-6
Gahnospinel	7½	Turquois	5-6
Rhodolite garnet	7-7½	Sodalite	5-6
Pyrope garnet	7-7½	Chlorastrolite	5-6
Spessartite garnet	7-7½	Sphene	5-5½
Tourmaline	7-7½	Obsidian	5-5½
Andalusite	7-7½	Datolite	5-5½
Iolite	7-7½	Bowenite (serpentine)	5-5½
Staurolite	7-7½	Apatite	5
Grossularite garnet	7	Scheelite	5
Quartz	7	Dioptase	5
Danburite	7	Smithsonite	5
Dumortierite	7	Odontolite	5
Chalcedony	6½-7	Stibiotantalite	5
Peridot	6½-7	Apophyllite	4½-5
Jadeite	6½-7	Zincite	4½
Andradite garnet	6½-7	Kyanite	4-7
Axinite	6½-7	Variscite	4-5
Saussurite	6½-7	Augelite	4
Idocrase	6½	Fluorite	4
Scapolite	6½	Rhodochrosite	3½-4½
Kornerupine	6½	Malachite	3½-4
Pollucite	6½	Azurite	3½-4
Spodumene	6-7	Sphalerite	3½-4
Sinhalite	6-7	Coral	3½
Epidote	6-7	Conch pearl	3½
Sillimanite	6-7	Calcite	3
Cassiterite	6-7	Verdite	3
Zoisite	6-7	Black coral	3
Rutile & Syn.	6-6½	Hemetine	2½-6
Microcline	6-6½	Pearl	2½-4½
Orthoclase	6-6½	Jet	2½-4
Nephrite	6-6½	Pseudophite	2½
Pyrite	6-6½	Agalmatolite	2½
Benitoite	6-6½	Serpentine	2-4
Marcasite	6-6½	Amber	2-2½
Prehnite	6-6½	Copal	2
Labradorite	6	Alabaster	2
Amblygonite	6	Stichtite	1½-2
Leucite	6	Steatite (soapstone)	1-1½

Pleochroism

The symbols S, D, W, and VW signify strong, distinct, weak, and very weak pleochroism. Only two colors are given for biaxial gemstones when little color difference is detectable between two of the three directions. Colors may vary from those described, depending on hue and depth of color.

Purple or violet gemstones

Corundum (sapphire) (S) ....Violet and orange
Tourmaline (S) ....Purple and light purple
Andalusite (S) ....Brownish green and dark red to purple
Spodumene (kunzite) (S) ....Violet to purple and colorless to pink
Beryl (D-S) ....Violet and colorless
Chrysoberyl (alexandrite) (S)....Dark red-purple, orange and dark green
(trichroic)
Topaz (D-S) ....Light to very light purple

Blue gemstones

Beryl (W-D) ....Light blue and darker blue
Corundum (S) ....Dark violetish blue and light greenish blue
Topaz (W-D) ....Colorless and light blue
Tourmaline (S) ....Dark blue and light blue
Zircon (S) ....Medium blue and colorless to gray
Apatite (S) ....Blue and yellow
Benitoite (S) ....Colorless and dark blue
Iolite (S) ....Colorless to yellow, blue and dark blue-violet
(trichroic)

Green gemstones

Beryl (emerald) (S) ....Green and blue-green
Corundum (sapphire) (S) ....Green and yellow-green
Tourmaline (S) ....Blue-green to dark brownish green and yellow-green
Zircon (W) ....Brownish green and green
Topaz (D) ....Blue-green and light green
Sphene (D) ....Brownish green and blue-green
Andalusite (S) ....Brownish green and dark red
Chrysoberyl (alexandrite) (S) ....Dark red, orange and green
(trichroic)
Peridot (W) ....Yellow-green and green

Yellow gemstones

Beryl (W) ....Light greenish yellow and light blue-green
Chrysoberyl (D) ....Colorless, very light yellow and greenish yellow
(trichroic)
Corundum (W) ....Yellow and light yellow
Danburite (W) ....Very light yellow and light yellow
Phenakite (D) ....Colorless and orange-yellow
Quartz (citrine) (VW) ....Light yellow and very light yellow
Spodumene (D) ....Light yellow and very light yellow
Topaz (D) ....Brownish yellow, yellow and orange-yellow
(trichroic)
Tourmaline (D) ....Light yellow and dark yellow
Zircon (W) ....Yellow-brown and yellow

THE JEWELERS' MANUAL

Brown and orange gemstones

Axinite (S)	Violet, yellow-brown and green (trichroic)
Corundum (S)	Yellow-brown to orange and colorless
Quartz (W)	Brown and reddish brown
Topaz (D)	Yellow-brown and brown
Tourmaline (S)	Yellowish brown—dark greenish brown
Zircon (W-D)	Brownish yellow and purplish brown

Pink and red gemstones

Andalusite (S)	Dark red and brownish green
Beryl (morganite) (D)	Light red and red-violet
Chrysoberyl (alexandrite) (S)	Dark red, orange, and green (trichroic)
Corundum (ruby) (S)	Violetish red and orangy red
Synthetic corundum (S)	Violetish red and orangy red
Spodumene (kunzite) (S)	Light red to purple and colorless
Topaz (D to S)	Light red and yellow
Tourmaline (S)	Dark red and light red
Zircon (D)	Reddish purple and reddish brown

Birefringence

Birefringence

This table includes only those doubly-refractive materials that normally possess sufficient transparency to make the visual detection of birefringence practical.

(Note: although seldom cut as a gemstone, calcite is listed here because of its application in the dichroscope and its value as an aid to the proper understanding of the optical property of double refraction.)

Synthetic rutile	.287	Corundum	.008
Calcite	.172	Synthetic corundum	.008
Zircon (high)	.059	Topaz	.008
Peridot	.038	Feldspars	.008 to .010
Tourmaline	.020	Beryl	.005 to .009
Spodumene	.015	Synthetic emerald	.003 to .005
Quartz	.009	Zircon (low)	.003 to .015
Chrysoberyl	.009		

Dispersion

Silica glass	.010	Spinel	.020
Orthoclase feldspar	.012	Synthetic spinel	.020
Quartz	.013	Almandite garnet	.024
Beryl	.014	Rhodolite garnet	.026
Synthetic emerald	.014	Pyrope garnet	.027
Topaz	.014	Spessartite garnet	.027
Chrysoberyl	.015	Grossularite garnet	.028
Crown glass	.016	Zircon	.038
Tourmaline	.017	Diamond	.044
Spodumene	.017	Andradite garnet	.057
Corundum	.018	Strontium titanate	.190
Synthetic corundum	.018	Synthetic rutile	.330
Peridot	.020		

Cleavage, Fracture & Relative Toughness

The following classification of gems, listed in order of decreasing toughness, is divided into two groups, as shown below in the left-hand column: (1) faceted transparent stones and (2) cabochon-cut translucent to opaque stones (usually crystalline aggregates).

It is impossible to make a direct comparison between these two basic classifications, since too many unrelated factors are involved. For example, nephrite jade, if fashioned with a thin girdle similar to that on most diamonds, would withstand little abuse without chipping; on the other hand, a nephrite cabochon with a thick girdle would be exceptionally resistant to breakage.

THE JEWELERS' MANUAL

Among both of these groups are extreme variations in each species, since the number and nature of flaws, perfection of structure, and purity of composition all have a marked effect on comparative durability. Some diamonds with no visible flaws have been known to shatter under temperature changes alone, without pressure being applied. This is in marked contrast to the usual good durability of most diamonds. Thus, when considering the relative durability of any species, including diamond, it must be remembered that some specimens of that species may be broken more easily than others.

Order of Decreasing Toughness	Cleavage	Fracture	Luster of Fracture
Group #1			
Corundum (synthetic & natural)	None	Conchoidal	Vitreous to subadamantine
Diamond	Easy	Conchoidal	Adamantine
Spinel (synthetic & natural)	None	Conchoidal	Vitreous
Chrysoberyl	None	Conchoidal	Vitreous to subadamantine
Quartz	None	Conchoidal	Vitreous
Garnet	None	Conchoidal	Vitreous to subadamantine
Tourmaline	None	Conchoidal	Vitreous
Synthetic emerald	None	Conchoidal	Vitreous
Beryl	None	Conchoidal	Vitreous
Topaz	Easy	Conchoidal	Vitreous
Peridot	None	Conchoidal	Vitreous to subvitreous
Zircon (heat treated)	None	Conchoidal	Subadamantine
Spodumene	Easy	Splintery	Vitreous
Feldspar	Easy	Splintery	Vitreous to pearly
Synthetic rutile	None	Conchoidal	Vitreous
Glass	None	Conchoidal	Vitreous
Strontium titanate	None	Conchoidal	Vitreous
Group #2			
Nephrite	None	Granular	Dull
Jadeite	None	Granular	Dull
Plastics	None	Conchoidal	Vitreous, resinous or dull
Chalcedony	None	Conchoidal	Waxy to dull
Hematite	None	Splintery	Metallic to dull
Lapis-lazuli	None	Granular	Dull
Coral	None	Uneven	Dull to waxy
Pearl	None	Uneven	Pearly to dull
Shell	None	Splintery	Dull
Turquois	None	Conchoidal, granular	Waxy to dull
Amber	None	Conchoidal	Resinous
Opal	None	Conchoidal	Subvitreous

Crystal Systems

Almost all minerals and most of the other solid materials with which we are familiar possess a geometrically-ordered arrangement of their constituent atoms. This pattern by which the various atoms that make up a material are repeated in space is called *crystal structure*. Scientists today usually refer to substances that have a definite internal structure as *crystals*, whether or not they are bounded by plane surfaces. However, the classic definition of a crystal is a solid body that has a regular arrangement of constituent atoms and that is bounded by plane surfaces.

There are two hundred thirty possible three-dimensional patterns that are capable of unlimited repetition in the same order in space. These two hundred thirty patterns can be grouped into thirty-two *crystal classes* and further into six *crystal systems*. Every crystalline substance can be classified under one of these six systems.

Crystallographers distinguish between the various systems by the use of imaginary *crystal axes, planes of symmetry, centers of symmetry,* and *axes of symmetry*. The reference axes are arranged in a manner that gives the greatest possible symmetry for that shape; i.e., that yields the simplest possible mathematical relationship between the various faces of the crystal. For example, the *dodecahedron* (doe′-dek-ah-he″-dron), a twelve-sided form in the most symmetrical crystal system (*cubic*), could also be described as a crystal in the *hexagonal* (hex-ag″-oh-nal) system, but it has more elements of symmetry than is possible in the hexagonal system.

These are the axial relationships that are characteristic of the six crystal systems (see accompanying illustrations):

1. **Cubic (or isometric) System.** Three axes, all of which are equal in length and mutually perpendicular. Examples: diamond, spinel, garnet.

2. **Hexagonal (hex-ag″-oh-nal) System.** Three axes of equal length at sixty degrees to one another, and a fourth that is perpendicular to the plane of the first three and unequal in length to them. (Some crystallographers describe the lower symmetry, or *trigonal* (trig″-oh-nal), class of this system as a seventh crystal system, the *rhombohedral* (rom-bo-he″-dral). Examples: ruby, sapphire, emerald, aquamarine.

3. **Tetragonal (teh-trag″-oh-nal) System.** Three mutually perpendicular axes, two equal in length and one either longer or shorter than the other two. Example: zircon.

4. **Orthorhombic (or′-tho-rom″-bik) System.** Three mutually perpendicular axes, all unequal in length. Examples: topaz, chrysoberyl.

5. **Monoclinic (mon′-oh-klin″-ik) System.** Three axes of unequal length, one of which is perpendicular to the other two but the other two are not perpendicular to each other. Examples: jadeite, nephrite.

6. **Triclinic (tri-klin″-ik) System.** Three axes at oblique angles to one another and unequal in length. Examples: labradorite, microcline feldspar.

THE JEWELERS' MANUAL

Models of the Six Crystal Systems

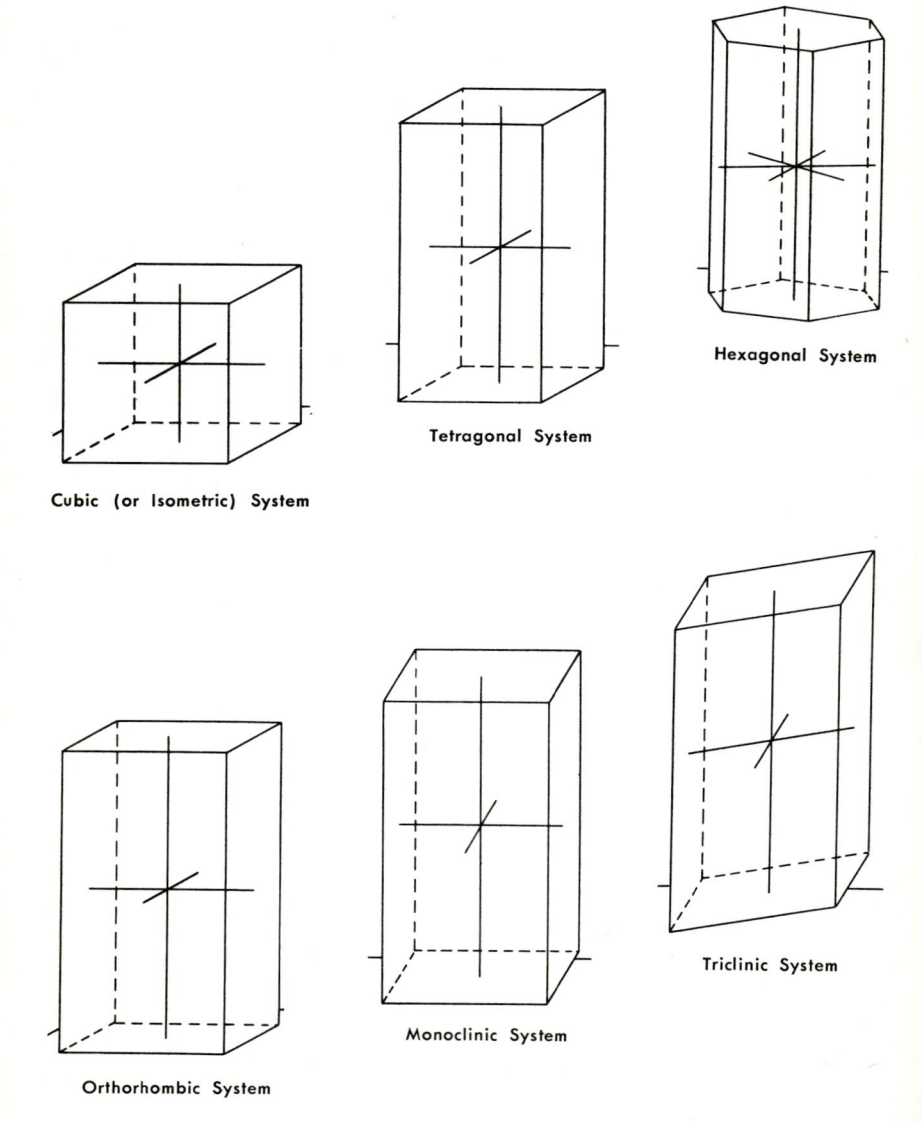

Cubic (or Isometric) System

Tetragonal System

Hexagonal System

Orthorhombic System

Monoclinic System

Triclinic System

Recommended Names for the More Important Gemstones

Recommended Names for the More Important Gemstones

Prepared by the Educational Advisory Board of the Gemological Institute of America

Species	Description	Recommended Names
Diamond	Transparent. Colorless and all colors, usually in very light tones. Also black	Diamond
Corundum	Transparent red (excluding pink or other light tones of red)	Ruby
	Transparent blue	Sapphire
	Transparent. Other colors	Pink sapphire, yellow sapphire, purple sapphire, green sapphire, etc.
	Transparent colorless to pale bluish white	White or colorless sapphire
	Asteria. Six-rayed star in semitransparent to semitranslucent gray and all above colors, except red; also black and brown	Star sapphire
	Red asteria	Star ruby
Chrysoberyl	Transparent greenish yellow, green, yellowish green, greenish brown to brown	Chrysoberyl
	Transparent to translucent. Any of the above colors exhibiting chatoyancy (a distinct, movable band of light)	Chrysoberyl cat's-eye
	Transparent green in daylight; red to purple in most artificial light	Alexandrite
	Transparent to translucent, as above, but chatoyant	Alexandrite cat's-eye
Spinel	Transparent red, pink, blue, yellow to orange-red, green, purple, violet, red-brown; also opaque, very dark green to black	Spinel, red spinel, etc.
Topaz	Transparent yellow, light blue, very light red to red, orange, colorless, brown or green	Topaz, yellow topaz, blue topaz, pink topaz, etc.
Beryl	Transparent intense green to bluish green	Emerald
	Transparent light green	Beryl
	Transparent yellow	Golden beryl
	Transparent light blue to greenish blue	Aquamarine

THE JEWELERS' MANUAL

Species	Description	Recommended Names
	Transparent light red (rose or pink) or light purple	Morganite
	Transparent. Other colors	Beryl
Zircon	Transparent colorless, yellow, blue, green, orange to orange-brown, violet, etc.	Zircon, blue zircon, green zircon, etc.
Tourmaline	Transparent. All colors and colorless	Tourmaline, green tourmaline, red tourmaline, colorless tourmaline, etc.
	Transparent to translucent chatoyant band of light	Tourmaline cat's-eye
Garnet group	All colors in which the mineral occurs	Garnet
Almandite	Transparent red to purple	Almandine or almandite garnet
Pyrope	Transparent red to reddish brown	Pyrope garnet or pyrope
Rhodolite	Transparent light to medium red-purple to violet	Rhodolite garnet or rhodolite
Grossularite	Transparent yellow to orange-brown	Hessonite garnet or hessonite
	Transparent yellow-brown to reddish brown	Hessonite or cinnamon stone
	Translucent to semitranslucent yellowish green	Grossularite or green garnet
Andradite	Transparent green	Demantoid garnet or demantoid
Peridot	Transparent light to dark yellowish green, brown, light yellow-green to yellow	Peridot
Quartz	Transparent violet to purple	Amethyst
(Crystalline)	Transparent to translucent light red (pink) or light purplish red (rose)	Rose quartz
	Asteria. Six-rayed star in pale tones of same color	Star rose quartz or star quartz
	Transparent yellow, orange, yellow-brown or red-brown	Citrine or topaz quartz
	Transparent grayish brown to almost black	Cairngorm or smoky quartz
	Translulent grayish green, light gray, greenish yellow, brownish, brownish red or bluish exhibiting chatoyancy (a distinct, movable band of light)	Quartz cat's-eye

Recommended Names for the More Important Gemstones

Species	Description	Recommended Names
(Cryptocrystalline, or chalcedony, quartz)	Translucent yellowish to brown with silky sheen as stone is moved. Also dyed brownish red and gray	Tiger's-eye
	Translucent bluish with silky-gray sheen	Hawk's-eye
	Translucent grayish, yellowish, brownish or brownish red glittering with red spangles. Green with silver spangles	Aventurine or aventurine quartz
	Semitransparent to translucent white to bluish Sometimes dyed blue, green, yellow, brown, etc. Dyed chalcedony long known in trade as "onyx," with color prefix	Chalcedony, white chalcedony, etc.
	Opaque black (usually dyed)	Black chalcedony
	Translucent red to brownish red to orange-brown	Carnelian
	Translucent red-brown or yellowish brown to brown	Sard
	Translucent to opaque. Flat parallel layers of gray or black or any color but red, orange or brown, alternating with white	Onyx
	Translucent to opaque. Flat parallel layers of carnelian or sard, alternating with white or black chalcedony	Sardonyx
	Semitranslucent dark green with red spots	Bloodstone or heliotrope
	Semitransparent to translucent light yellowish green (apple green)	Chrysoprase
	Translucent. Curved bands alternating in various colors	Agate or banded agate
	Translucent white with green, black, brown or reddish moss-like inclusions	Moss agate
	Opaque red or yellow-brown; sometimes green or white	Jasper
Spodumene	Transparent light yellow to greenish yellow or bright yellowish green to green	Spodumene
	Transparent rose-pink or violet	Kunzite

THE JEWELERS' MANUAL

Species	Description	Recommended Names
Jadeite	Semitransparent to opaque green, white or white with green inclusions; also brown, orange, reddish pink, violet, bluish or dark green to almost black	Jadeite
Nephrite	Semitransparent to opaque green; also gray, brown, reddish, bluish, light bluish violet, yellow, black or white	Nephrite
Opal	Transparent to semitransparent white to colorless with play of color	Opal or white opal
	Transparent to translucent black or very dark gray, blue or green with play of color	Black opal
	Transparent orange-yellow to red (may show play of color)	Fire opal
Feldspar group	Transparent colorless to light yellow	Orthoclase
Orthoclase	Colorless to milky with billowy bluish light	Moonstone or adularia
Microcline	Semitranslucent bluish green to yellowish green	Amazonite or amazonstone
Albite	White to nearly colorless with moving light	Moonstone
Oligoclase	White to nearly colorless with moving light	Moonstone
Labradorite	Semitranslucent grayish with overall flashes of bluish, greenish, yellowish, reddish orange or bronze; also transparent yellow	Labradorite
Lapis-lazuli	Opaque, intense greenish blue to violetish blue, usually with pyrite inclusions	Lapis-lazuli
	Light blue with veins of white matrix and often tinged or spotted with green	Lapis-lazuli
	Light blue to blue with large proportion of matrix	Lapis matrix
Turquois	Opaque light blue to light blue-green, sometimes with veins of brown limonite	Turquois or turquoise
	Same colors with larger amounts of limonite or other matrix	Turquois matrix
Pearl	Translucent white, creamy, pinkish, light yellow, green, blue, violet, gray, etc.	Pearl

Recommended Names for the More Important Gemstones

Species	Description	Recommended Names
	Semitranslucent mother-of-pearl bead covered with layers of pearl nacre of above colors	Cultured pearl
	Semitranslucent purplish red or blue to almost black; also light grayish yellow	Clam pearl
	Semitranslucent dark metallic blue, brown, etc.	Black pearl
	Semitranslucent pink or white without nacre	Conch pearl
Amber	Transparent to opaque pale yellow to reddish brown to dark brown. May be tinged with green or blue; also whitish or cloudy	Amber
	Translucent pale yellow to dark brown, reconstructed by softening small pieces and bonding by pressure	Pressed amber
Coral	Semitranslucent to opaque white to dark red, cream, brown, blue and black	Coral
Jet	Opaque black	Jet

THE JEWELERS' MANUAL

Trade Names & Recommended Names for Synthetic Stones

Stone	Trade Names	Recommended Names
Synthetic corundum		
Red		Synthetic ruby
Red (asteriated)		Synthetic star ruby
Dark red	"Synthetic garnet"	Synthetic Siamese ruby
Pink	"Rose kunzite," "kunzite," "rose sapphire," "rose topaz," "synthetic rose topaz"	Synthetic pink sapphire
Blue (asteriated)	"Hope sapphire"	Synthetic star sapphire
Light blue	"Synthetic aquamarine," "synthetic zircon"	Synthetic sapphire or synthetic Ceylon sapphire
Purple or violet	"Synthetic amethyst," "Ultralite," "Violete"	Synthetic amethystine sapphire
Yellow	"Synthetic topaz"	Synthetic golden sapphire
Alexandritelike	"Synthetic alexandrite"	Synthetic alexandritelike sapphire
Orange	"Padparadsha"	Synthetic padparadsha sapphire or synthetic hyacinth sapphire
Dark green	"Synthetic tourmaline"	Synthetic green sapphire
Green	"Synthetic emerald," "scientific emerald"	Synthetic green sapphire
Yellowish green	"Synthetic chrysolite," Amaryl	Synthetic green sapphire or synthetic chrysolite sapphire
White (asteriated)		Synthetic star sapphire
Black (asteriated)		Synthetic star sapphire
Colorless	"White sapphire," "white zircon," "Diamondite," "Mr. Diamond," "Zircolite," "Brillite," "Emperor-lite," Ledo Frozen Fire, "Strongite," "Vega Gem," "Vespa Gem," "Walderite," Thrilliant	Synthetic colorless sapphire
Synthetic spinel		
Red & Pink	"Rozircon," "rose kunzite," "rose topaz," "Berylite"	Synthetic red or pink spinel
Red-violet	"Synthetic almandine," "synthetic almandite"	Synthetic almandine spinel
Dark blue	"Synthetic zircon," "synthetic sapphire"	Synthetic sapphire spinel or synthetic blue spinel
Light blue	"Synthetic aquamarine," "synthetic zircon"	Synthetic aquamarine spinel or synthetic blue spinel

Trade Names & Recommended Names for Synthetic Stones

Stone	Trade Names	Recommended Names
Violet		Synthetic amethystine spinel
Light green	"Perigem," Erinide, "synthetic chrysolite"	Synthetic chrysolite spinel
Green	"Dirigem," "synthetic emerald," "scientific emerald," "synthetic peridot"	Synthetic green spinel
Dark green	"Synthetic tourmaline"	Synthetic green spinel
Alexandritelike	"Synthetic alexandrite"	Synthetic alexandritelike spinel
Yellow		Synthetic yellow spinel
Colorless	Alumag	Synthetic colorless spinel
Synthetic emerald		
Green	"Cultured emerald"	Synthetic emerald
Green	"Linde Synthetic Emerald"	Synthetic emerald overgrowth on beryl
Green	"Created emerald"	Synthetic emerald
Synthetic rutile		
Light yellow, blue, bluish green, orange, orangey brown	"Diamonite," "Diamothyst," "Rainbow Magic Diamond," "Rainbow Diamond," "Java Gem," "Kenya Gem," "Johannes Gem," "Kimberlite Gem," "Rainbow Gem," Miridis, Rutania, Star*Tania, "Tiru Gem," "Titangem," Titania, Titania Brilliant, "Titania Midnight Stone," Titanium Rutile, "Titanstone," "Lusterite," "Kenya Stone," "Capri Gem," "Capra Gem," "Kima Gem," Sapphirized Titania, Astryl, "Ultimate"	Synthetic rutile
Strontium titanate		
Colorless	"Fabulite," "Starilian," "Zenithite"	Synthetic strontium titanate

Note: Technically, any trade or trademarked name that ends in *ite* suggests that the product is a mineral, and is therefore misleading as the name for a synthetic. A name containing the word *gem* or *stone* is also misleading, because either implies that the synthetic or imitation is a gem.

THE JEWELERS' MANUAL

Birthstones

In 1952, the Jewelry Industry Council sponsored the following birthstone list, which was subsequently accepted and approved by the American National Retail Jewelers' Association, National Jewelers' Association (now the Retail Jewelers' Association), American Stone Importers' Association, and the American Gem Society. It will be noted that the major changes consisted of adding alexandrite as a choice for June and replacing lapis-lazuli with zircon for December.

UNITED STATES

Month	Natural Stone	Synthetic Stone
January	Garnet	Synthetic corundum
February	Amethyst	Synthetic corundum
March	Aquamarine or bloodstone	Synthetic spinel
April	Diamond	Synthetic spinel
May	Emerald	Synthetic spinel or emerald
June	Pearl, moonstone or alexandrite	Cultured pearl or synthetic corundum
July	Ruby	Synthetic ruby
August	Peridot or sardonyx	Synthetic spinel
September	Sapphire	Synthetic sapphire
October	Opal or pink tourmaline	Synthetic corundum
November	Topaz or citrine	Synthetic corundum
December	Turquois or zircon	Synthetic spinel

GREAT BRITAIN

Month	Stone
January	Garnet
February	Amethyst
March	Aquamarine or bloodstone
April	Diamond or rock crystal
May	Emerald or chrysoprase
June	Pearl or moonstone
July	Ruby or carnelian
August	Peridot or sardonyx
September	Sapphire or lapis-lazuli
October	Opal
November	Topaz
December	Turquois

Birthstones

UNION OF SOUTH AFRICA

Month	Stone
January	Garnet or tourmaline
February	Amethyst
March	Aquamarine
April	Diamond or colorless sapphire
May	Emerald
June	Pearl
July	Ruby
August	Peridot or green tourmaline
September	Blue sapphire
October	Opal
November	Topaz
December	Turquois

AUSTRALIA

Month	Stone
January	Garnet
February	Amethyst
March	Aquamarine or bloodstone
April	Diamond or zircon
May	Emerald or green tourmaline
June	Pearl or moonstone
July	Ruby or carnelian
August	Peridot or sardonyx
September	Sapphire or lapis-lazuli
October	Opal
November	Topaz
December	Turquois

CANADA

Month	Stone
January	Garnet
February	Amethyst
March	Aquamarine
April	Diamond
May	Emerald
June	Cameo or pearl
July	Ruby
August	Peridot or sardonyx
September	Sapphire
October	Opal or tiger's-eye
November	Topaz
December	Onyx or zircon

THE JEWELERS' MANUAL

Birthstones for the Hours

1 AM	Smoky quartz	1 PM	Zircon
2 AM	Hematite	2 PM	Emerald
3 AM	Malachite	3 PM	Beryl
4 AM	Lapis-lazuli	4 PM	Topaz
5 AM	Turquois	5 PM	Ruby
6 AM	Tourmaline	6 PM	Opal
7 AM	Chrysolite	7 PM	Sardonyx
8 AM	Amethyst	8 PM	Chalcedony
9 AM	Kunzite	9 PM	Jade
10 AM	Sapphire	10 PM	Jasper
11 AM	Garnet	11 PM	Lodestone
12 AM	Diamond	12 PM	Onyx

Birthstones for the Week Days

Sunday	Topaz
Monday	Pearl or rock crystal
Tuesday	Ruby or emerald
Wednesday	Amethyst or lodestone
Thursday	Sapphire or carnelian
Friday	Emerald or cat's-eye
Saturday	Turquois or diamond

Phenomenal Birthstones for the Week Days

Sunday	Sunstone
Monday	Moonstone
Tuesday	Star sapphire
Wednesday	Star ruby
Thursday	Cat's-eye
Friday	Alexandrite
Saturday	Labradorite

Zodiacal, or Astral, Stones

(Gems believed to be peculiarly and mystically related to the zodiacal signs)

Aquarius (January 20 to February 18)	Garnet
Pisces (February 19 to March 20)	Amethyst
Aries (March 21 to April 19)	Bloodstone
Taurus (April 20 to May 20)	Sapphire
Gemini (May 21 to June 21)	Agate
Cancer (June 22 to July 22)	Emerald
Leo (July 23 to August 23)	Onyx
Virgo (August 23 to September 22)	Carnelian
Libra (September 23 to October 23)	Chrysolite
Scorpio (October 24 to November 21)	Beryl
Sagittarius (November 22 to December 21)	Topaz
Capricorn (December 22 to January 19)	Ruby

Foreign Equivalents of Some of the More Important English Gem Names

ENGLISH	FRENCH	GERMAN
Diamond	Diamant	Diamant
Corundum	Corindon	Korund
Ruby	Rubis	Rubin
Sapphire	Saphir	Saphir
Chrysoberyl	Chrysobéryl	Chrysoberyll
Alexandrite	Alexandrite	Alexandrit
Cat's-eye	Oeil de chat	Katzenauge
Beryl	Béryl	Beryll
Emerald	Emeraude	Smaragd
Aquamarine	Aiguemarine	Aquamarin
Spinel	Spinelle	Spinell
Topaz	Topaze	Topas
Zircon	Zircon	Zirkon
Tourmaline	Tourmaline	Turmalin
Garnet	Grenat	Granat
Almandite	Almandin	Almandin
Pyrope	Pyrope	Pyrop
Grossularite	Grossulaire	Grossularit
Hessonite	Essonite	Hessonit
Spessartite	Spessartine	Spessartin
Andradite		Andradit
Demantoid	Démantoide	Demantoid
Quartz	Quartz	Quarz
Rock crystal	Cristal de roche	Bergkristall
Amethyst	Améthyste	Amethyst
Citrine	Quartz jaune	Citrin
Smoky quartz	Quartz-enfumée	Rauchquarz
Rose quartz	Quartz-rosé	Rosenquarz
Aventurine	Aventurine	Avanturinquarz
Tiger's-eye	Oeil de tigre	Tigerauge
Quartz cat's-eye	Quartz oeil de chat	Quarzkatzenauge
Chalcedony	Calcédoine	Calcedon
Chrysoprase	Chrysoprase	Chrysopras
Carnelian	Cornaline	Karneol
Sard	Sardoine	Sard
Heliotrope	Heliotrope	Heliotrop
Agate	Agate	Achat
Onyx	Onyx	Onyx
Jasper	Jaspe	Jaspis
Peridot	Péridot	Peridot
Jadeite	Jadéite	Jadeit
Nephrite	Néphrite	Nephrit
Spodumene	Spodumène	Spodemen
Kunzite	Kunzite	Kunzit
Feldspar	Feldspath	Feldspat
Amazonite	Amazonite	Amazonit
Moonstone	Pierre de lune	Mondstein
Labradorite	Labradorite	Labradorit
Sunstone	Pierre de soliel	Sonnenstein
Turquois	Turquoise	Türkis
Lapis-lazuli	Lapis-lazuli	Lapis-lazuli
Opal	Opale	Opal
Hematite	Hématite	Hämatit
Pearl	Perle	Perle
Coral	Corail	Koralle
Amber	Ambre	Bernstein
Jet	Jais	Gagat

Foreign Equivalents of Some of the More Important English Gem Names

ENGLISH	ITALIAN	SPANISH
Diamond	Diamante	Diamante
Corundum	Corindone	Corindón
Ruby	Rubino	Rubí
Sapphire	Zaffiro	Zafiro
Chrysoberyl	Crisoberillo	Crisoberilo
Alexandrite	Alessandrite	Alexandrita
Cat's-eye	Occhio di gatto	Ojo de gato
Beryl	Berillo	Berilo
Emerald	Smeraldo	Esmeralda
Aquamarine	Acquamarina	Aguamarina
Spinel	Spinello	Espinela
Topaz	Topazio	Topacio
Zircon	Zircone	Circón
Tourmaline	Tourmalina	Turmalina
Garnet	Granato	Granate
Almandite	Almandino	Almandina
Pyrope	Piropo	Piropo
Grossularite	Grossularia	Grosularia
Hessonite	Essonite	Essonita
Spessartite	Spessartina	Spessartita
Andradite	Andradite	Andradita
Demantoid	Demantoide	Demantoide
Quartz	Quarzo	Cuarzo
Rock crystal	Cristallo di rocca	Cristal de roca
Amethyst	Ametista	Amatista
Citrine	Quarzo citrino	Citrine
Smoky quartz	Quarzo affumicato	Cuarzo ahumado
Rose quartz	Quarzo rosa	Cuarzo rosa
Aventurine	Quarzo avventurina	Aventurina
Tiger's-eye	Occhio di tigre	Ojo de tigre
Quartz cat's-eye	Quarzo occhio di gatto	Cuarzo ojo de gato
Chalcedony	Calcedonio	Calcedonia
Chrysoprase	Crisoprasio	Crisoprasa
Carnelian	Corniola	Cornalina
Sard	Sarda	Sarda
Heliotrope	Eliotropio	Heliotropo
Agate	Ágata	Ágata
Onyx	Onici	Onix
Jasper	Diaspro	Jaspe
Peridot	Peridoto	Peridoto
Jadeite	Giadeite	Jade
Nephrite	Nefrite	Nefrita
Spodumene	Spodumeno	Espodumena
Kunzite	Kunzite	Kunzita
Feldspar	Feldspati	Feldespato
Amazonite	Amazzonite	Amazonita
Moonstone	Pietra di luna	Piedra de luna
Labradorite	Labradorite	Labradorita
Sunstone	Pietra di sole	Piedra del sol
Turquois	Turchese	Turquesa
Lapis-lazuli	Lapis-lazzuli	Lapis-lazuli
Opal	Opale	Ópalo
Hematite	Ematite	Hematita
Pearl	Perle	Perla
Coral	Corallo	Coral
Amber	Ambra	Ámbar
Jet	Gagate	Azabache

Foreign Equivalents
of Some of the More Important English Gem Names

ENGLISH	PORTUGUESE	DUTCH
Diamond	Diamante	Diamant
Corundum	Coríndon	Korund
Ruby	Rubí	Robijn
Sapphire	Safíra	Saffier
Chrysoberyl	Crisoberilo	Chrysoberyl
Alexandrite	Alexandrita	Alexandriet
Cat's-eye	Ôlho de gato	Chrysoberylkatoog
Beryl	Berilo	Beryl
Emerald	Esmeralda	Smaragd
Aquamarine	Águamarinha	Aquamarijn
Spinel	Espinélio	Spinel
Topaz	Topázio	Topaas
Zircon	Zircônio	Zirkoon
Tourmaline	Turmalina	Toermalijn
Garnet	Granada	Granaat
Almandite	Almandita	Almandien
Pyrope	Pirôpo	Pyroop
Grossularite	Grosularita	Grossulaar
Hessonite	Essonita	Hessoniet
Spessartite	Spessartita	Spessartien
Andradite	Andradite	Andradiet
Demantoid	Demantoide	Demantoïd
Quartz	Quartzo	Kwarts
Rock crystal	Cristal de rocha	Bergkristal
Amethyst	Ametista	Ametist
Citrine	Citrino	Citrien
Smoky quartz	Quartzo enfumaçado	Rookkwarts
Rose quartz	Quartzo rosa	Rosenkwarts
Aventurine	Aventurina	Aventurijnkwartz
Tiger's-eye	Ôlho de tigre	Tijgeroog
Quartz cat's-eye	Quartzo ôlho de gato	Kwartskatoog
Chalcedony	Calcedônia	Chalcedoon
Chrysoprase	Crisópraso	Chrysopraas
Carnelian	Carneol	Karneool
Sard	Sardonica	Sarder
Heliotrope	Heliotrópe	Heliotroop
Agate	Ágata	Agaat
Onyx	Ónix	Onyx
Jasper	Jaspe	Jaspis
Peridot	Peridoto	Peridot
Jadeite	Jadeita	Jadeiet
Nephrite	Nefrita	Nefriet
Spodumene	Trifana	Spodumeen
Kunzite	Kunzita	Kunziet
Feldspar	Feldspato	Veldspaat
Amazonite	Amazonita	Amazoniet
Moonstone	Pedra da lua	Maansteen
Labradorite	Labradorita	Labradoriet
Sunstone	Pedra do sol	Zonnesteen
Turquois	Turquesa	Turkoois
Lapis-lazuli	Lápis-lazúli	Lapis-lazuli
Opal	Ópalo	Opaal
Hematite	Hematita	Hematiet
Pearl	Pérola	Parel
Coral	Coral	Koraal
Amber	Âmbar	Barnsteen
Jet	Azeviche	Git

Foreign Equivalents of Some of the More Important English Gem Names

ENGLISH	SWEDISH	FINNISH
Diamond	Diamant	Timantti
Corundum	Korund	Korundi
Ruby	Rubin	Rubiini
Sapphire	Safir	Safiiri
Chrysoberyl	Krysoberyll	Krysoberylli
Alexandrite	Alexandrit	Aleksandriitti
Cat's-eye	Krysoberyllkattoga	Kissansilmä
Beryl	Beryll	Berylli
Emerald	Smaragd	Smaragdi
Aquamarine	Akvamarin	Akvamariini
Spinel	Spinell	Spinelli
Topaz	Topas	Topaasi
Zircon	Zirkon	Zirkoni
Tourmaline	Turmalin	Turmaliini
Garnet	Granat	Granaatti
Almandite	Almandin	Almandiini
Pyrope	Pyrop	Pyrooppi
Grossularite	Grossular	Grossulaari
Hessonite	Essonit	Hessoniitti
Spessartite	Spessartit	Spessartiitti
Andradite	Andradit	Andradiitti
Demantoid	Demantoid	Demantoidi
Quartz	Kvarts	Kvartsi
Rock crystal	Bergkristal	Vuorikristalli
Amethyst	Ametist	Ametisti
Citrine	Citrin	Sitriini
Smoky quartz	Rökkvartsen	Savukvartsi
Rose quartz	Rosakvarts	Ruusukvartsi
Aventurine	Aventurinkvarts	Avanturiinikvartsi
Tiger's-eye	Tigeröga	Tiikerinsilmä
Quartz cat's-eye	Kvartskattöga	Kvartsikissansilmä
Chalcedony	Kalsedon	Kalsedoni
Chrysoprase	Krysopras	Krysoprsaasi
Carnelian	Karneol	Karneoli
Sard	Sard	Sard
Heliotrope	Heliotrop	Heliotrooppi
Agate	Agat	Akatti
Onyx	Onyx	Oniksi
Jasper	Jaspis	Jaspis
Peridot	Peridot	Peridootti
Jadeite	Jade	Jadeiitti
Nephrite	Nefrit	Nefriitti
Spodumene	Spodumen	Spodumeni
Kunzite	Kunzit	Kuntsiitti
Feldspar	Fältspat	Maasälpä
Amazonite	Amasonsten	Amatsoniitti
Moonstone	Månsten	Kuukivi
Labradorite	Labradorit	Labradori
Sunstone	Solsten	Aurinkokivi
Turquois	Turkos	Turkoosi
Lapis-lazuli	Lapis-lazuli	Lasuurikivi
Opal	Opal	Opaali
Hematite	Hämatit	Hematiiti
Pearl	Pärla	Helmi
Coral	Korall	Koralli
Amber	Bärnsten	Meripihka
Jet	Jet	Gagaatti

"Precious" & "Semiprecious" Stones

For many years, authorities have differed markedly in their classification of gemstones as "precious" and "semiprecious." Because of the diversity of opinion, the European International Federation of Jewelry Associations resolved that the term *gemstone* be used as a replacement. The Gemological Institute of America also recommends the elimination of these two confusing and misleading terms and the use of the word *gemstone* for all stones having the necessary beauty, durability and rarity to be desirable for jewelry purposes.

Undoubtedly, the term "semiprecious" indicates to most laymen a comparatively undesirable gem; it is still popularly applied to all gems except those that, as a class, are more expensive (i.e., ruby, diamond, sapphire, emerald and pearl). However, alexandrite and cat's-eye, so-called semiprecious stones, are, as a class, more expensive than many sapphires (especially fancy colors), which are so-called precious stones; and many individual specimens of jade, opal and many other colored stones are more expensive than poor specimens of the so-called precious types.

By calling stones "semiprecious," their value is lessened in the eyes of the general public, and the desirability and sale of many gems of great merit are thus decreased substantially.

Shapes & Styles of Cutting

Many shapes and styles of cutting are diagrammed on the following pages. In the interest of uniformity, top and bottom views perpendicular to the girdle outline are used, with rare exceptions. The principal types are the *brilliant cut* and the *step cut*. In the former, most of the facets are triangular and the others are more or less kite shaped; the most important is the *standard, round, 58-facet brilliant* (see plate). The crown consists of 33 facets; one table, eight star facets, eight bezel facets, and 16 upper-girdle facets. The pavilion consists of 25 facets: one culet, eight pavilion facets, and 16 lower-girdle facets. The culet is sometimes omitted, in which case the pavilion consists of 24 facets. Modifications include the *marquise, pear shape, heart shape, briolette* and many others.

The step-cut style is distinguished by the fact that one or more of the edges of *all* the inclined facets are parallel to the girdle edge. The facets are usually arranged in rows, or tiers, that resemble a flight of stairs; hence, the name. The most important of this style is the *emerald cut*. It usually is rectangular but is sometimes square, in which case it is known as the *square emerald cut*. It has rows of elongated, rectangular facets on the crown and pavilion, parallel to the girdle, and with corner facets.

THE JEWELERS' MANUAL

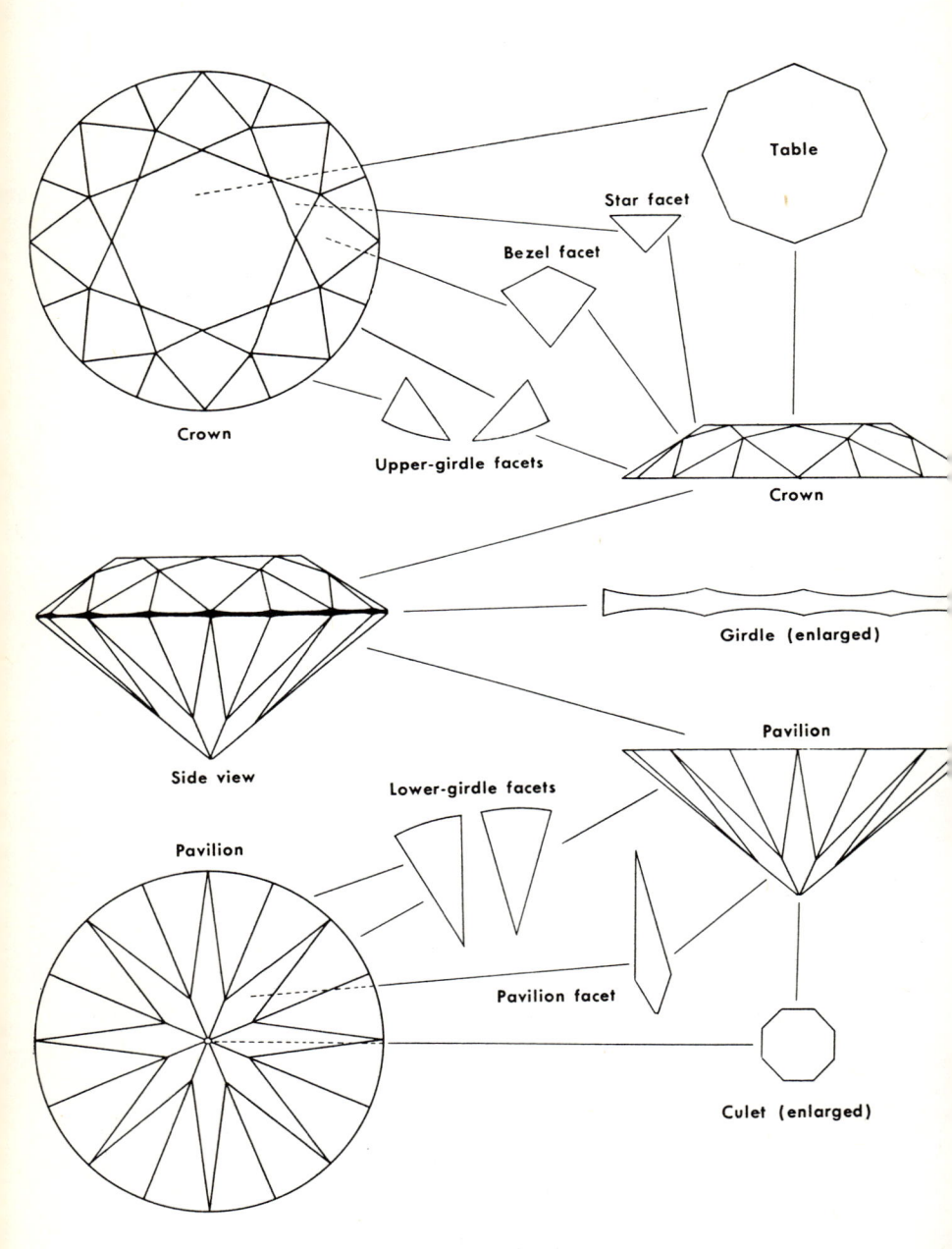

BRILLIANT CUT (ROUND)

Shapes & Styles of Cutting

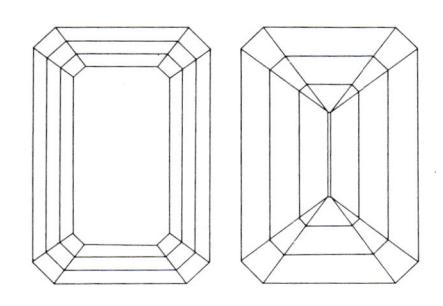

Emerald cut

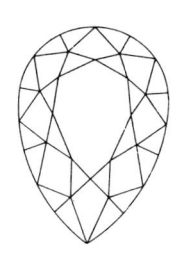

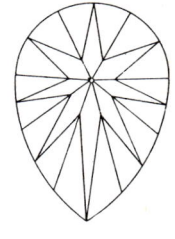

Pear-shaped cut

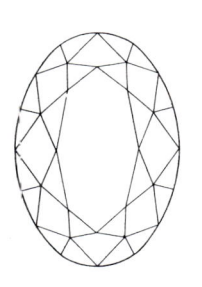

Oval cut

Marquise cut

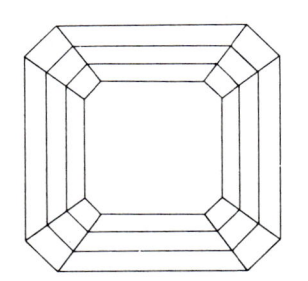

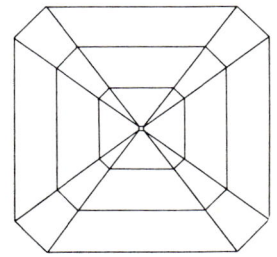

Square emerald cut

THE JEWELERS' MANUAL

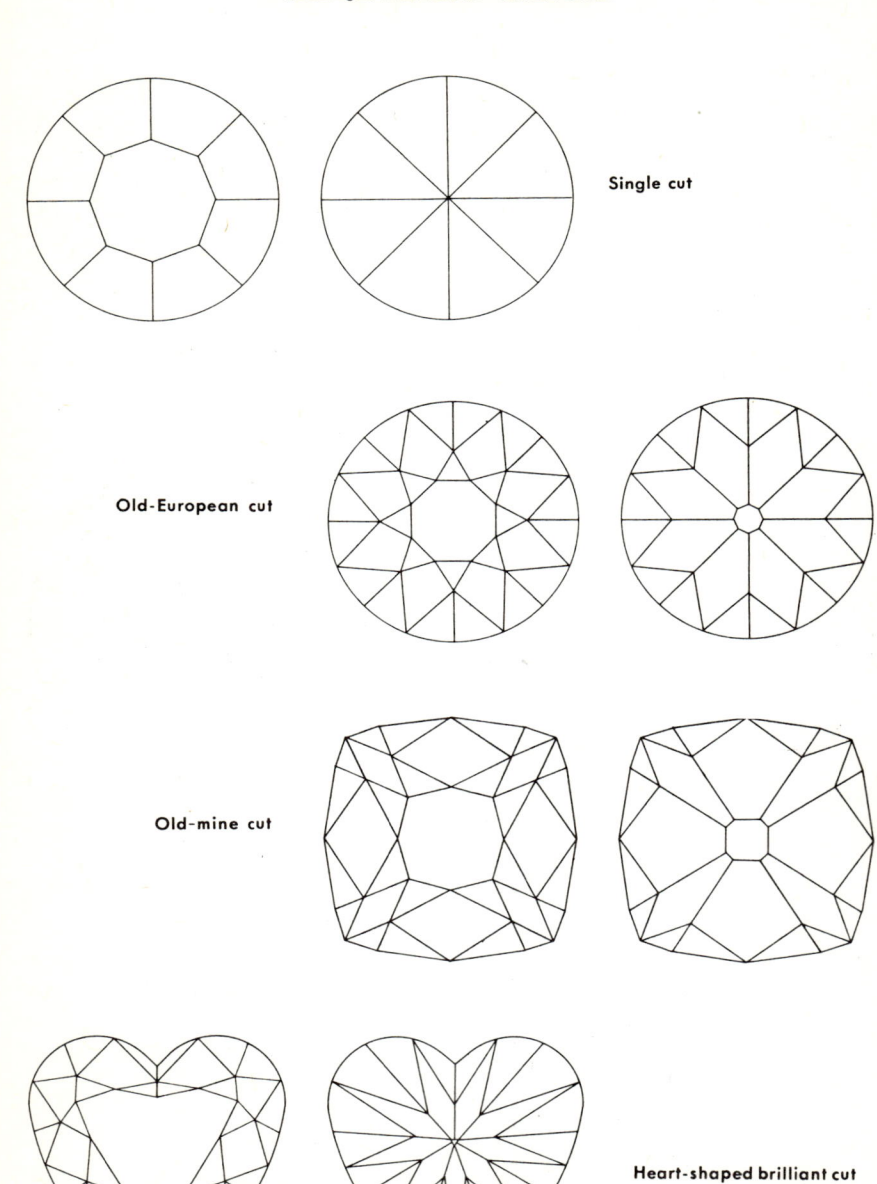

Single cut

Old-European cut

Old-mine cut

Heart-shaped brilliant cut

Shapes & Styles of Cutting

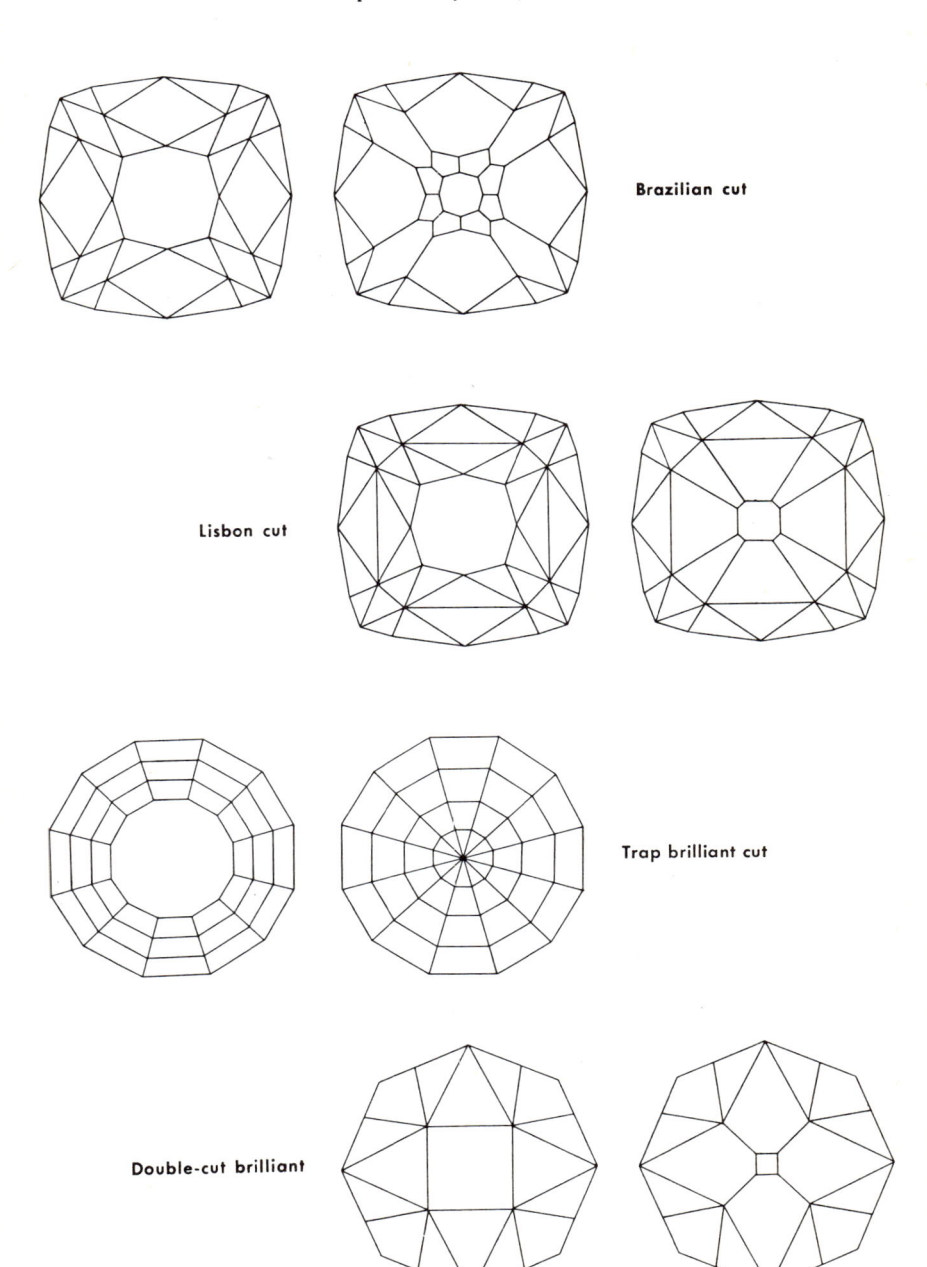

Brazilian cut

Lisbon cut

Trap brilliant cut

Double-cut brilliant

THE JEWELERS' MANUAL

English square-cut brilliant

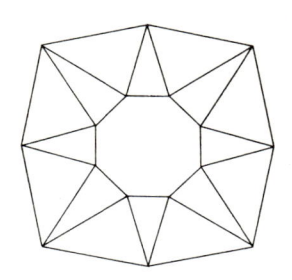

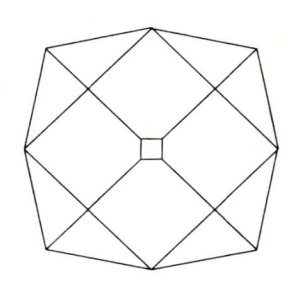

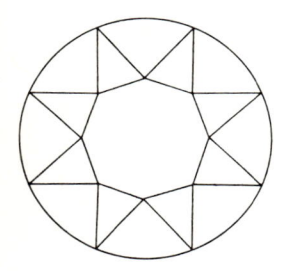

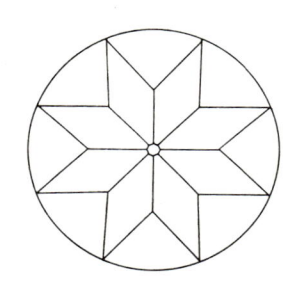

Swiss cut

Split-brilliant cut

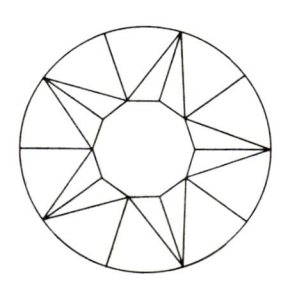

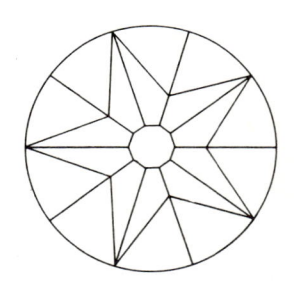

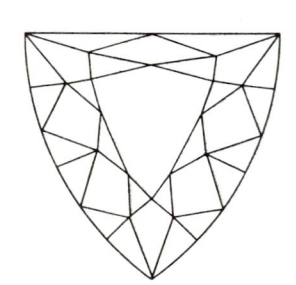

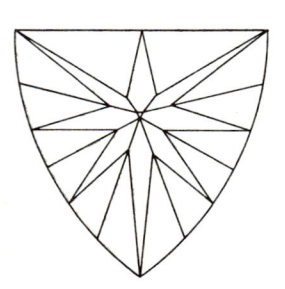

Seminavette

Shapes & Styles of Cutting

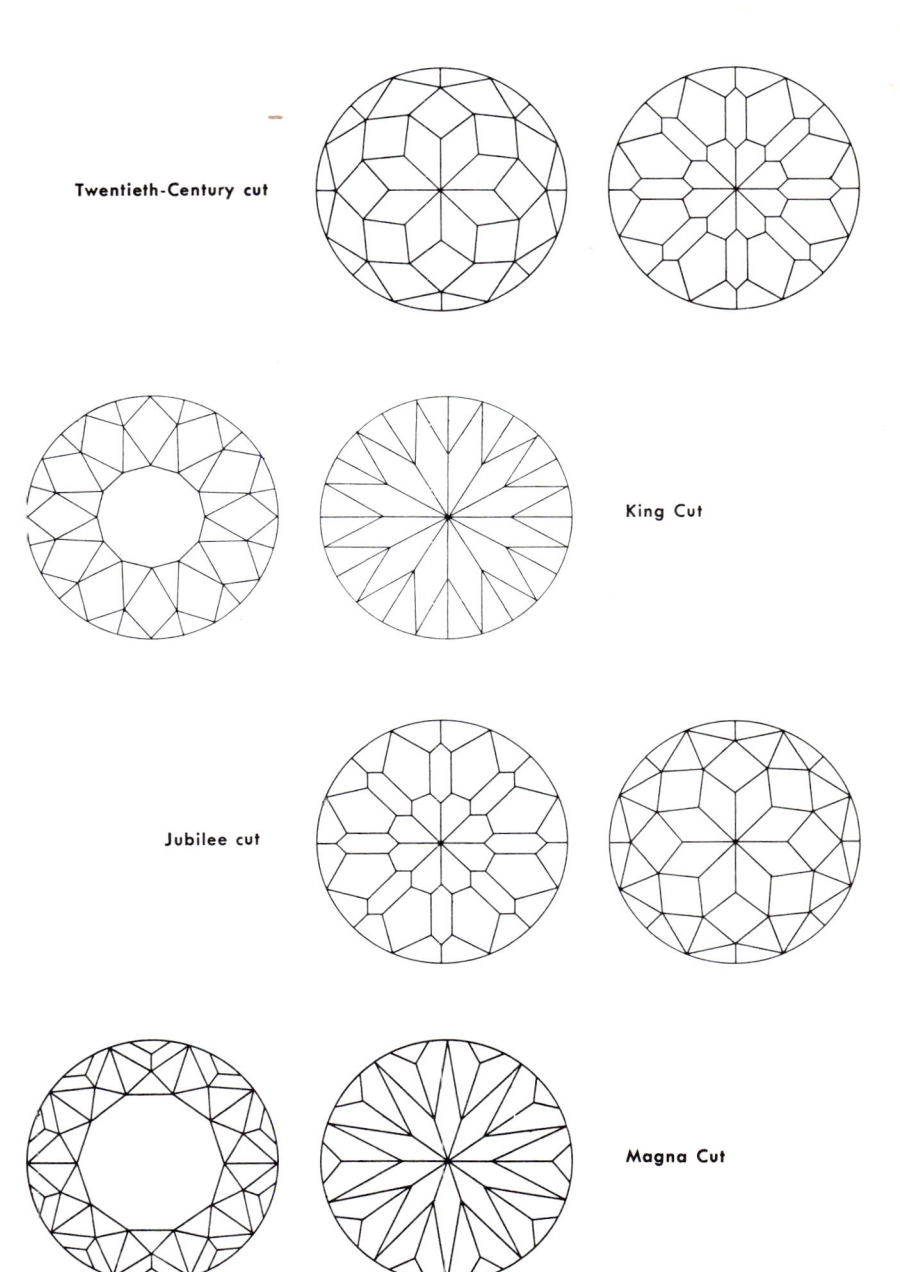

Twentieth-Century cut

King Cut

Jubilee cut

Magna Cut

105

THE JEWELERS' MANUAL

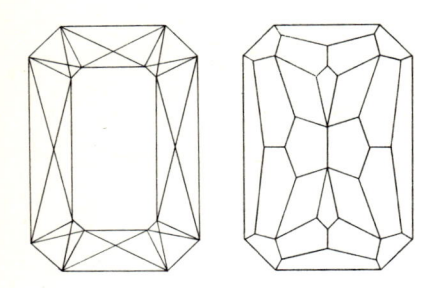

Scissors cut

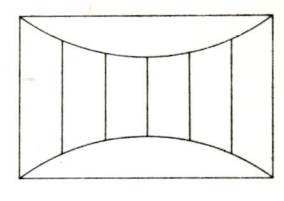

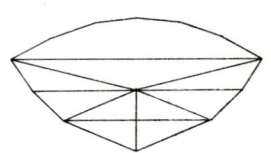

Bent-top cut

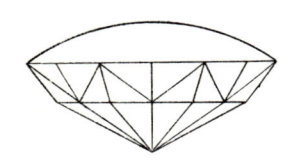

Buff-top cut

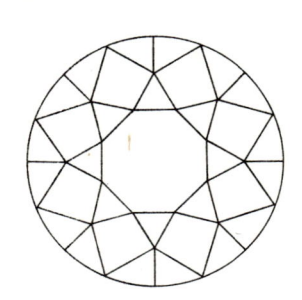

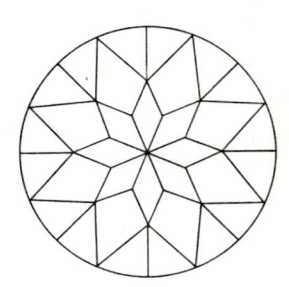

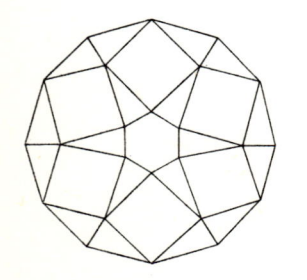

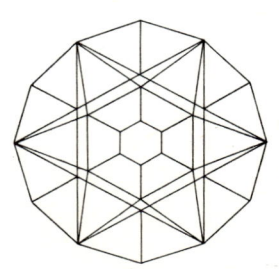

Zircon cut

Cairo cut

Shapes & Styles of Cutting

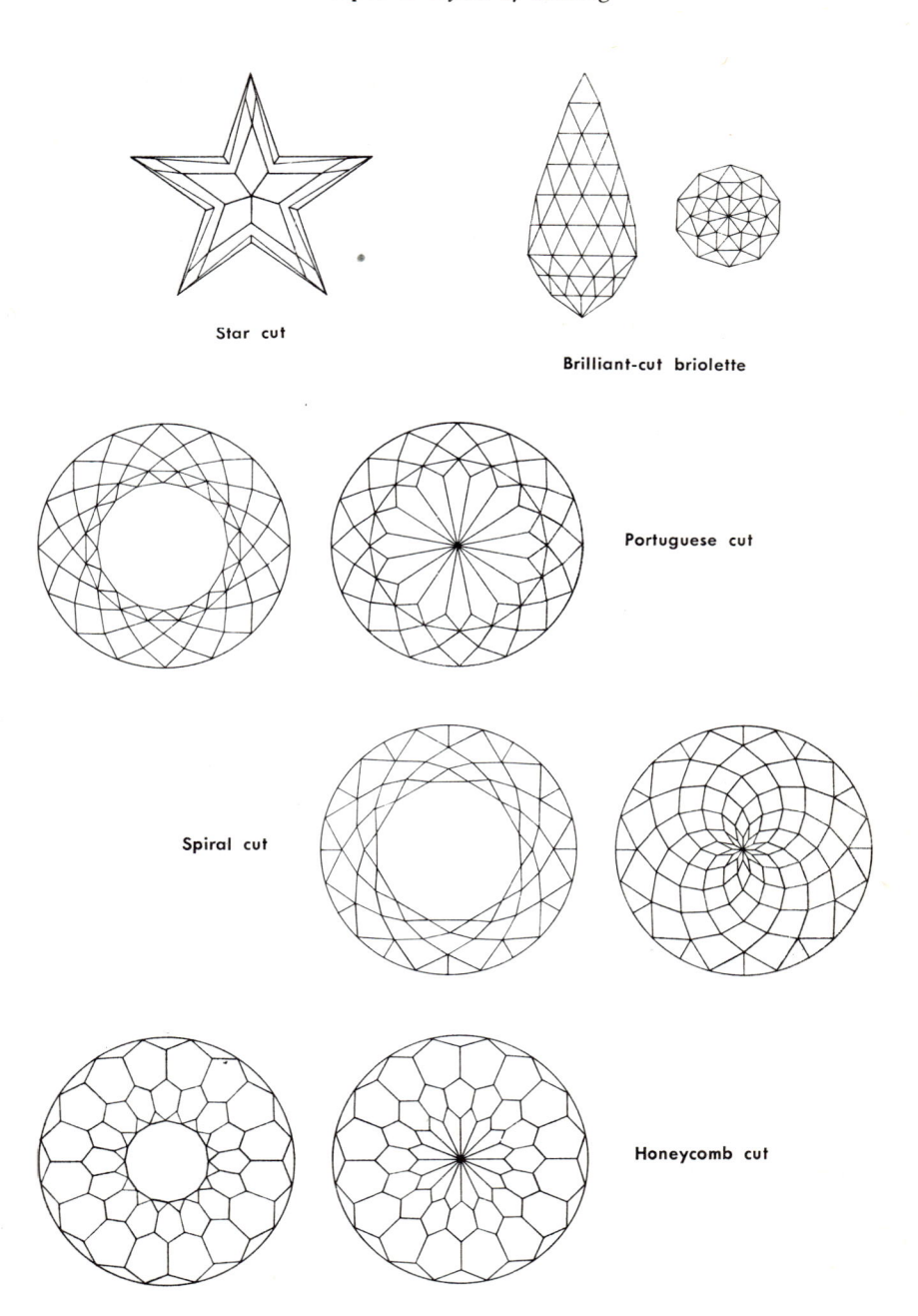

Star cut

Brilliant-cut briolette

Portuguese cut

Spiral cut

Honeycomb cut

THE JEWELERS' MANUAL

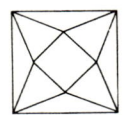

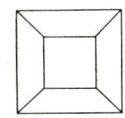

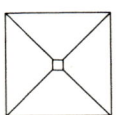

French cut

Table cut

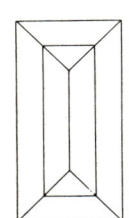

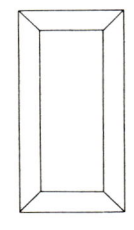

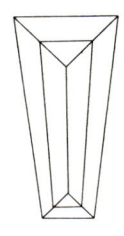

Baguette

Tapered baguette

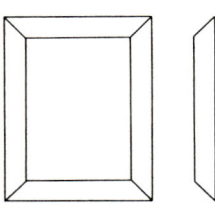

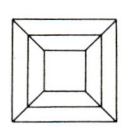

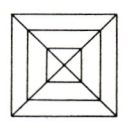

Bevel cut

Square cut

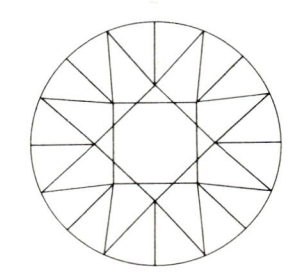

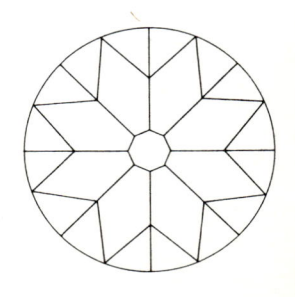

English round-cut brilliant

Shapes & Styles of Cutting

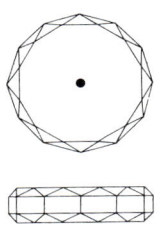

Rondelle

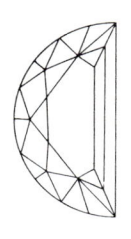

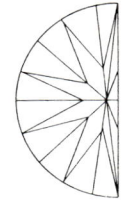

Half-moon cut

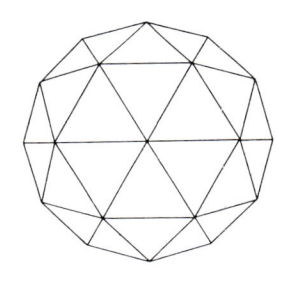

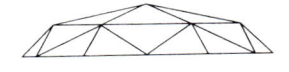

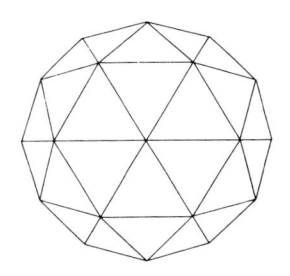

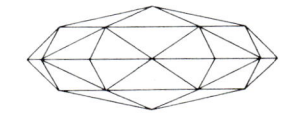

Full-Dutch (or full-Holland) rose cut

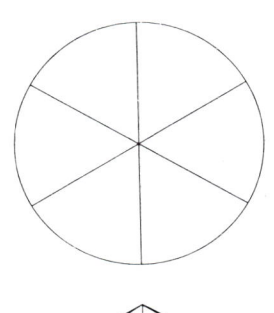

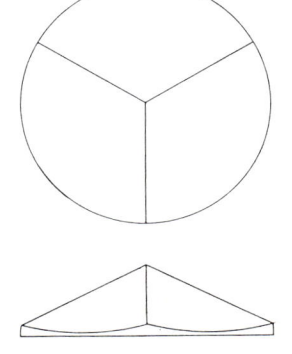

Double-rose cut

Six-facet rose cut

Three-facet rose cut

THE JEWELERS' MANUAL

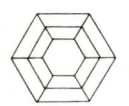

Hexagon cut

Pentagon cut

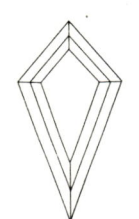

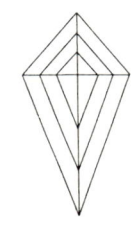

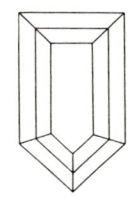

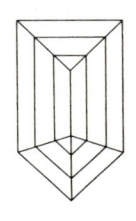

Kite cut

Bullet cut

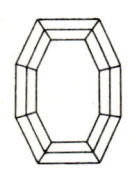

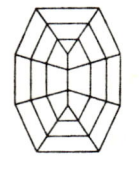

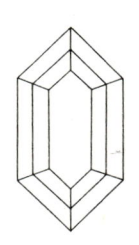

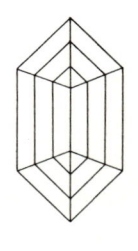

Long octagon cut

Long hexagon cut

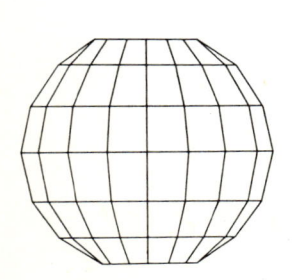

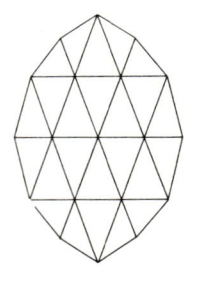

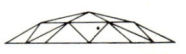

Step-cut bead

Boat-shape rose cut

Pear-shaped rose cut

Shapes & Styles of Cutting

Tapered pentacut

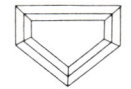

Epaulet (or epaulette) cut

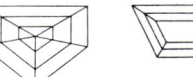

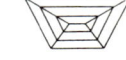

Trapeze cut

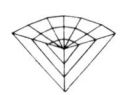

Fan-shape cut

Triangle cut

Calf's-head cut

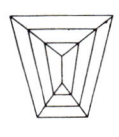

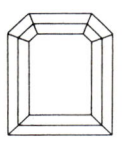

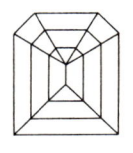

Shield cut

Keystone cut

Window cut

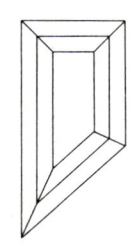

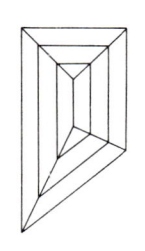

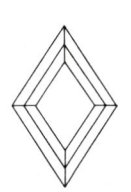

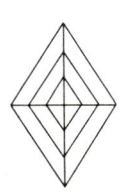

Whistle cut

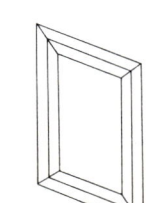

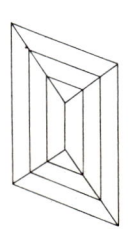

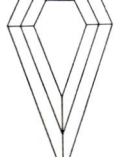

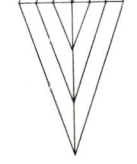

Lozenge cut

Cut-corner triangle cut

Rhomboid cut

THE JEWELERS' MANUAL

Cross-Sectional Views of Basic Cabochon Styles

Single cabochon

Lentil cabochon

Hollow cabochon

Reverse cabochon

Double cabochon

Cross-Sectional Views of Carved & Engraved Gems

Cameo

Intaglio (in-tal"-yo)

Cuvette (koo-vet")

Chevee (sheh-vey")

Care of Gemstones

Usually, corresponding facets are placed on the girdle. The number of rows, or steps, may vary; the usual number is 58, including the eight on the girdle. In addition to the emerald cut and the square emerald cut, modifications include *baguette, keystone, table cut* and many others.

Combinations of the brilliant- and step-cut styles are called *mixed cuts*. By combining the outline name with the above terms, the style of the cut can be classified; e.g., a *square step cut* or a *rectangular mixed cut*.

Colored-Stone Sizes

Stone Size	Millimeter Size	Stone Size	Millimeter Size
No. 1	1 mm.	No. 23	5 mm.
No. 3	1¼ mm.	No. 24	5¼ mm.
No. 4	1½ mm.	No. 26	5½ mm.
No. 5	1¾ mm.	No. 27	5¾ mm.
No. 6	2 mm.	Nos. 28-29	6 mm.
No. 8	2¼ mm.	No. 30	6½ mm.
No. 9	2½ mm.	No. 32	6¾ mm.
No. 10	2¾ mm.	Nos. 33-34	7 mm.
No. 11	3 mm.	Nos. 35-36	7½ mm.
No. 12	3⅛ mm.	No. 38	8 mm.
No. 13	3¼ mm.	No. 40	8½ mm.
No. 15	3½ mm.	No. 42	9 mm.
No. 16	3¾ mm.	No. 44	10 mm.
No. 17	4 mm.	No. 46	10½ mm.
No. 18	4⅛ mm.	No. 47	11 mm.
No. 19	4¼ mm.	No. 48	11½ mm.
No. 21	4½ mm.	No. 50	12 mm.
No. 22	4¾ mm.		

Care of Gemstones

Even in a jewel case, the harder and tougher stones should be separated from the more easily damaged ones. Moreover, damage can occur to gems in jewelers' stocks, because of a lack of knowledge of stones and pearls.

Grease has an extraordinary affinity for diamond. At the mines, diamonds are separated from other minerals by passing the disintegrated blueground (diamond-bearing rock) over grease tables, to which diamonds alone adhere. Likewise, grease from soap and water or from the atmosphere quickly coats the pavilion, or back, of a diamond. If the pavilion is covered with a film of grease or other foreign matter, much of the stone's brilliancy is lost; this is true of all transparent gems.

Diamonds and other faceted gems should be cleaned every week or two with a small brush (such as a toothbrush) in warm water with a detergent added (and ammonia, if available). Then they should be dried with a soft, clean cloth or tissue.

Turquois is a lovely but delicate gem. It may become discolored from perspiration, acids, cosmetics, perfume or soap. This is more true of paraffin-treated material than of the fine qualities; however, all must be given special care. If it is subjected to localized heat, such as that from a match flame, it will break into pieces (decrepitate). The only cleaning recommended for turquois is gentle wiping with a damp chamois. A turquois ring or bracelet should never be worn while washing the hands.

Heat, excessive perspiration, face powder, hair sprays, direct contact with skin oils or perfume, or constant contact with hard, rough-textured fabrics may damage the delicate surface of pearls.

Wearing pearls so that they come in contact with other jewelry will cause them to become scratched and worn.

Pearls should be strung with knots between them; otherwise, the friction caused by the pearls coming in contact with one another will cause wear around the drill holes. Also, if the string is broken, the knots will prevent the loss of more than one pearl.

Care must be exercised in repairing pearl jewelry, because heat may split the pearls and turn them brown. Acids will attack them violently.

Although many pearls retain their beauty in full measure for centuries, they are subject to a gradual loss of water from the organic conchiolin binding agent. The greater the amount of conchiolin, the more the pearls will show evidence of deterioration. It may take generations for yellowing, surface cracking or other signs to become evident, however.

If properly cared for, Oriental pearls will last for many lifetimes. Constant contact with acid skin secretions is perhaps the more damaging situation.

Natural, Cultured & Imitation Pearls

Defined very loosely, a *pearl* is any calcareous concretion that is produced by a shellfish and that is unattached to its shell. There are many kinds of invertebrates in which such concretions form, but only a few have the necessary combination of *orient* and *luster* to qualify as gem pearls.

Orient is the multihued diffraction effect that is produced by millions of tiny overlapping plates of *nacre* (nay″-ker). Pearl nacre consists of a multitude of layers of calcium carbonate in the form of *aragonite* (ah-rag″-o-nite), the crystals of which are held together by cartilagelike *conchiolin* (kahn-ky″-o-lin). Lustrous, iridescent nacre must be present for a pearl to be considered a gem. A glance at the interior of a shell of any shellfish species is enough to show its potential as gem-pearl producer. The absence of nacreous layers renders the concretions found in edible oysters valueless. Sometimes, laymen have the attractively-shaped concretions found in cherrystone clams set in jewelry, but they have only a curiosity value.

Pearls start to form only if an object works itself though the *mantle tissue*, which separates the body mass from the shell. If some shell-building outer *epithelial* (ep-ih-thee″-le-al) cells come though the mantle with the foreign matter, the animal secretes nacre to surround the intruder. One started, the process continues.

The important hosts for salt-water pearls are all of the oyster genus *Pinctada*, a type regarded in America as nonedible. There are three main species of *Pinctadas*: *Margaritifera, Maxima* and *Martensii*. At full growth, *Maxima* is fully twelve inches in diameter, in contrast to about seven inches for *Margaritifera* and four inches for *Martensii*. *Margaritifera* is the most important producer of natural pearls; varieties of this species are found in the Persian Gulf, the Indian Ocean, the South Seas and off Australia. *Martenseii* is the host mollusc for most Japanese cultured pearls. Other natural-pearl hosts are the *abalone* and the *Unio* family of fresh-water clams. Many rivers in the United States have produced lovely fresh-water pearls.

Most *cultured* pearls are produced by inserting a large bead of *mother-of-pearl*, plus a square of mantle tissue, into a channel, cut usually in the foot muscle of a Japanese oyster. In a three-and-one-half-year period, the mollusc usually adds about one-half millimeter of nacre. Thus, a 6.6-millimeter bead, to which a one-half-millimeter layer has been added, increases in diameter by one millimeter, to 7.6 millimeters.

In the fresh-water clams of Japan's Lake Biwa, *baroque* pearls are cultured by inserting only mantle tissue into a row of incisions. A second and even a third crop is possible in this type, becoming more spherical with each crop.

Margaritifera and *Maxima* species are used in normal salt-water cultured-pearl farming off Burma and northern Australia. Because of the warmer water and the use of larger species, larger pearls are produced.

Blister pearls are protrusions attached to the shell. These are cut off and the shell side is either ground smooth or, if hollow, filled with mother-of-pearl. *Cultured blisters* are made by attaching a foreign object to the shell, so that an evenly-rounded protrusion will be covered with nacre; this is later filled with a mother-of-pearl core that has been cut to fit. The result is called a *mabe* (mah"-be), or *Japan pearl*.

Imitation pearls are made by coating glass or other kinds of beads with many layers of *essence d'orient*. This material is made by extracting lustrous guanine crystals from fish scales and suspending them in a transparent substance that hardens after application.

Pearl Testing

Pearl testing differs from most gem-testing problems, because shell with approximately the same composition as a pearl is coated with a thin layer of nacre by another mollusc. This means that when the pearl is undrilled, there is no essential outward difference between the cultured and the natural; however, each pearl-bearing mollusc species stamps an individuality on the pearl it produces. Since cultured pearls are produced primarily in Japan, they have the characteristics of those produced by the Japanese oyster, *Pinctada Martensii*. For practical purposes, it may be assumed that no Japanese *natural* pearls are marketed at the present time. If a pearl dealer sees obvious characteristics of the Japanese product in a pearl, its value is sure to be less—regardless.

There are several features that serve as indications of the Japanese salt-water cultured pearl. When the mollusc is brought to the surface for the operation of inserting the bead and piece of mantle tissue into the incision, the oyster is sickened and produces first a relatively thick layer of conchiolin. When the initial shock is past, nacre is produced. The conchiolin sometimes causes welts on the surface, and probably contributes to the greenish cast that is expected in undyed cultured pearls. Today, however, almost all cultured pearls are tinted, so a *rosé* color does not necessarily suggest the natural.

In a strand with a thin coating of nacre, *candling* usually discloses a number of mother-of-pearl beads that show characteristic agatelike banding when light is transmitted through them. Since a natural pearl has concentric layers, the striped effect is a safe means of detection, if all beads in a strand show it. Of course, it is possible to have mixed strands or an unusually thick layer of nacre or conchiolin, which would make it impossible to detect the bonding by the candling method. For this means of detection, a slightly darkened room and a bright light are needed. Even in an all-cultured strand with a thin coating of nacre, many of the beads are likely to show no stripes. Only thin-coated pearls give obvious results. The light source should be used with an opaque shield that has an opening that can be reduced or enlarged, or a series of openings of various sizes, so the pearl can be placed over a hole of appropriate size.

For undrilled pearls and for inexpensive cultured strands with a very thin nacreous coating, the only safe method of identification is *X-radiography*. A check test is provided by *X-ray fluorescence*. The pearls are first examined in a dark room through the lead-glass shield of an X-ray unit, to determine whether fluorescence is visible. In general, cultured pearls fluoresce when exposed to strong X-ray beams, as do fresh-water natural pearls, whereas natural salt-water pearls fail to react. This is not a certain test but is a good indication, particularly of a mixed natural-and-cultured strand.

In the X-radiographic method, a film is exposed to record the degree to which the X-ray beam passes through an object in the path of the beam. For satisfactory results, the pearls must be immersed in a liquid that has approximately the same density to X-rays as the pearls. The conchiolin is so transparent to X-rays that it shows on the film as a dark ring surrounding the mother-of-pearl bead but inside the usually thin layer of nacre.

Some testers continue to use *endoscopes* for drilled pearls. This instrument provides a positive test for natural pearls but is negative for cultureds and useless for undrilled pearls. Thus, X-ray is more practical, particularly since a strand must be unstrung to apply a drill-hole-test technique, such as that required with the endoscope.

Base-Price System for Pearls

Pearl appraising is even more complicated than diamond evaluation. Most retailers handle too few strands of natural pearls to justify obtaining

THE JEWELERS' MANUAL

Natural & Cultured Pearls

Cross section of a natural salt-water pearl

Cross section of a drilled cultured pearl

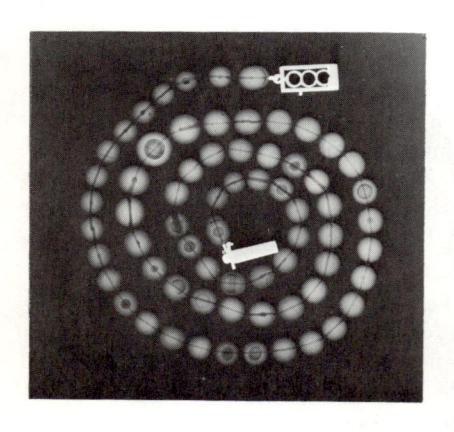

Radiograph of a natural-pearl strand

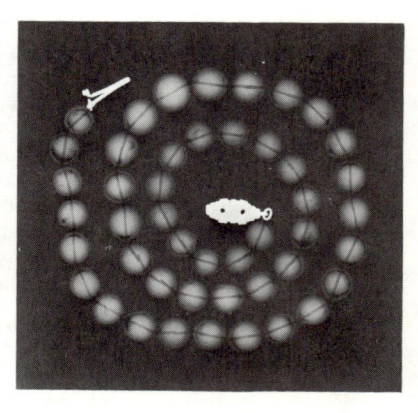

Radiograph of a cultured-pearl strand

Natural, Cultured & Imitation Pearls

Weight Estimations of Round Natural & Cultured Pearls

Diameter in Millimeters	Pearl Grains	Diameter in Millimeters	Pearl Grains	Diameter in Millimeters	Pearl Grains
1.0	.02	5.7	5.25	10.4	32.00
1.1	.03	5.8	5.50	10.5	33.00
1.2	.04	5.9	5.75	10.6	34.00
1.3	.05	6.0	6.00	10.7	35.00
1.4	.06	6.1	6.50	10.8	36.00
1.5	.08	6.2	6.75	10.9	37.00
1.6	.11	6.3	7.00	11.0	38.00
1.7	.14	6.4	7.50	11.1	39.00
1.8	.18	6.5	7.75	11.2	40.00
1.9	.21	6.6	8.00	11.3	41.00
2.0	.25	6.7	8.50	11.4	42.00
2.1	.28	6.8	9.00	11.5	43.00
2.2	.32	6.9	9.25	11.6	44.00
2.3	.36	7.0	9.75	11.7	45.00
2.4	.42	7.1	10.00	11.8	46.00
2.5	.50	7.2	10.50	11.9	47.00
2.6	.53	7.3	11.00	12.0	48.00
2.7	.59	7.4	11.50	12.1	49.00
2.8	.65	7.5	12.00	12.2	50.00
2.9	.70	7.6	12.50	12.3	51.00
3.0	.75	7.7	13.00	12.4	52.00
3.1	.82	7.8	13.50	12.5	53.00
3.2	.90	7.9	14.00	12.6	54.00
3.3	1.00	8.0	14.50	12.7	55.00
3.4	1.10	8.1	15.00	12.8	56.00
3.5	1.25	8.2	15.50	12.9	59.00
3.6	1.30	8.3	16.00	13.0	61.00
3.7	1.40	8.4	16.50	13.1	63.00
3.8	1.50	8.5	17.00	13.2	65.00
3.9	1.60	8.6	17.50	13.3	67.00
4.0	1.75	8.7	18.00	13.4	69.00
4.1	1.90	8.8	18.50	13.5	71.00
4.2	2.00	8.9	19.00	13.6	73.00
4.3	2.25	9.0	19.50	13.7	75.00
4.4	2.40	9.1	20.00	13.8	77.00
4.5	2.50	9.2	20.50	13.9	79.00
4.6	2.75	9.3	21.00	14.0	81.00
4.7	2.90	9.4	22.00	14.1	83.00
4.8	3.00	9.5	23.00	14.2	85.00
4.9	3.25	9.6	24.00	14.3	87.00
5.0	3.50	9.7	25.00	14.4	89.00
5.1	3.75	9.8	26.00	14.5	91.00
5.2	4.00	9.9	27.00	14.6	93.00
5.3	4.25	10.0	28.00	14.7	95.00
5.4	4.50	10.1	29.00	14.8	97.00
5.5	4.75	10.2	30.00	14.9	99.00
5.6	5.00	10.3	31.00	15.0	101.00

One metric carat equals four pearl grains; one metric gram equals twenty pearl grains, or five carats; one momme (used for weighing cultured pearls) equals seventy-five pearl grains, or 18.75 metric carats.

the lengthy training and experience that is necessary to appraise accurately. The rarity of pearls increases even more rapidly with increasing size than diamonds. In addition, a pair of matched pearls is worth much more in the pearl trade than the two pearls before matching.

To take into account such complicated relationships, pearl importers use a system based on what they call the *once* of a pearl or a group of pearls, which considers size and a base rate covering quality and matching. Since this system is very rarely used by the retailer, it will be discussed briefly by citing two examples of its use.

The price of a single pearl is computed by squaring its weight in grains and multiplying the result by the base rate. The quality of a single pearl and the quality, plus matching, of two or more, determines the base rate. For example, if a pearl weighs 8.65 grains and the base rate is $6, 8.65 x 8.65 x $6 = $448.92. As another example, two matched pearls of nearly equal size weigh 17.30 grains. Advancing the base rate to $12, because of excellent matching, their value would be computed as follows: 17.30 x 17.30 = 299.29; 299.29 ÷ 2 = approximately 150; 150 x $12 = $1800. (Note: When a pair of matched pearls is being priced, the base rate is increased to compensate for rarity; in this case, the base rate actually would have been doubled, had the pearls been perfectly matched. When the price of two pearls of unequal size is being calculated, the once figure is obtained by adding the squares of the two weights.)

To compute the price of a necklace, pairs or groups of pearls of equal or nearly equal size at an equal distance on each side of the center pearl are worked out by this method and then added together until all are accounted for.

This complicated system is employed more frequently in the original pricing of a newly made-up strand than in appraising pearls on the resale market. Dealers who handle quantities of pearl jewelry often estimate value without detailed determinations.

Wedding-Anniversary List

Wedding-Anniversary List

In 1948, the following list was sponsored by the Jewelry Industry Council and approved by the National Wholesale Jewelers' Association, American National Retail Jewelers' Association and National Jewelers' Association (the latter two organizations merged in 1957 to form the Retail Jewelers of America, Inc.).

1. Clocks
2. China
3. Crystal and glass
4. Electrical appliances
5. Silverware
6. Wood
7. Desk sets, pen-and-pencil sets
8. Linen and laces
9. Leather
10. Diamond jewelry
11. Silver, gold, gold-filled and gold-plated fashion jewelry and accessories
12. Pearls or colored stones
13. Textiles and furs
14. Gold jewelry
15. Watches
16. Silver holloware (sterling or plate)
17. Furniture
18. Porcelain
19. Bronze
20. Platinum
25. Sterling-silver jubilee
30. Diamond
35. Jade
40. Ruby
45. Sapphire
50. Golden jubilee
55. Emerald
60. Diamond jubilee

Traditional Wedding-Anniversary List Recommended by Social Authorities

1. Paper
2. Cotton
3. Leather
4. Fruit and flowers, or silk
5. Wood
6. Sugar and candy, or iron
7. Wool or copper
8. Bronze or pottery
9. Willow or pottery
10. Tin or aluminum
11. Steel
12. Silk or linen
13. Lace
14. Ivory
15. Crystal
20. China
25. Sterling-silver jubilee
30. Pearl
35. Coral
40. Ruby
45. Sapphire
50. Golden jubilee
55. Emerald
60 & 75. Diamond jubilee

Markings & Descriptions of Precious Metals

The following is a brief summary of the main provisions of the Federal Trade Commission's Trade Practice Rules, the U.S. Commercial Standards, and the Federal Stamping Law. It is, of necessity, condensed and does not cover every specific problem; it is not intended as the final word concerning markings and descriptions. For those who need to consult the complete, official texts of these publications, they are available from the Jewelers' Vigilance Committee, 15 W. 44th St., New York 36, N. Y.

Karat Gold

Karat-gold articles should be marked and described to show the fineness of the gold alloy of which they are made; for example, 10-*Kt. Gold.* or 14-*Karat Gold,* or the shorter forms 10 *K.* or 14 *Kt.*

The Federal Stamping Law provides for a tolerance of one-half karat (.0208) in the fineness of karat-gold articles containing no solder and for each individual part of a soldered article. In addition, soldered articles must assay in their entirety within one karat of their marked quality.

Watchcases and flatware have a fineness tolerance of only .003 where no solder is used or for an individual part. However, as with other karat-gold articles, a full karat is allowed on the overall assay of the article as a whole where solder is included.

The Federal Trade Commission has ruled that the terms *Gold* and *Solid Gold* mean *fine gold;* i.e., gold of 24-karat quality. If a karat-gold article is solid, in the sense that it does not have a hollow center, this fact may be indicated in a mark or description; for example, *Solid* 14-*Kt. Gold.* Such a mark as "10-Kt. Solid Gold" is incorrect. The word *solid* should always preface the term 10-*Kt. Gold.*

If the quality of an alloy is less than 10 karat, or if the article is weighted, it *cannot* be represented as karat gold, marked in any manner with the karat mark, or described as "gold" or "karat gold."

The Federal Trade Commission has likewise condemned the use of such coined words and terms as "Dirigold," "Duragold," "Mirigold,"

Markings & Descriptions of Precious Metals

"Gold Ray," "Gold Craft," "Goldine," "Gold Tone" or similar language that may be misleading.

Silver

Articles made of an alloy of silver (i.e., containing not less than 925/1000 parts of fine silver) may be marked and described as *Sterling* or *Sterling Silver*; if desired, *Silver* or *Solid Silver* can be used.

Articles made of coin silver (i.e., an alloy containing not less than 900/1000 of fine silver) may be marked and described as *Coin* or *Coin Silver*.

A tolerance of .004 is allowed for articles where no solder is used and for individual parts of soldered articles. In addition, soldered articles as a whole must assay within .010 of the quality indicated by the mark.

The terms *Sterling* and *Coin* should never be abbreviated.

If the quality of the alloy is less than 900/1000 fine, the article *cannot* be represented as silver.

The Federal Stamping Law prohibits the use of either the word *Sterling* or *Coin*, alone or with other words or marks, on *plated* articles; for example, "Sterling Plate" or "Coin Plate."

If an article is weighted and the term *Sterling* or *Coin* is applied to it, the mark must also show that it is weighted or otherwise reinforced. To be so marked, the weight or reinforcement must *not* be metal.

Platinum Metals

Articles made of platinum alloys and one or more of the related platinum metals (iridium, palladium, ruthenium, rhodium and osmium), consisting of not less than 985 parts per thousand of such metals where solder is not used and at least 950 parts per thousand where solder is used, should be marked and described as follows:

If the alloy is predominantly pure platinum, with no more than 50 parts per thousand being of the related metals, the correct mark or description is simply *Platinum*.

If the platinum content of the alloy is at least 750 parts per thousand, the word *Platinum* may be used, if immediately preceding such term there appears the name or abbreviation of the other most dominant related metal, which must be more than 50 parts per thousand of the entire article; for example, *Iridium Platinum* or *Ruth. Plat.*

Should the platinum content of the alloy be 500 parts per thousand or more, but less than 750, the proportion, in thousands, of each of the platinum-group metals contained in the article must be indicated, provided such proportion is more than 50 parts per thousand; for example, .600 *Plat.*, .350 *Pall.* or .500 *Plat.*, .200 *Pall.*, .150 *Ruth.*, .100 *Rhod.*

If the platinum content of the alloy is less than 500 parts per thousand, the word *Platinum* cannot be used.

The term "Platinum Plate" is never correct, either in marks or advertising, and the use of such expressions as "Platinum Top" and "Platinum Clad" have also been held to be unlawful.

Articles made of palladium, containing at least 950 parts per thousand of such metal, should be marked and described as *Palladium.*

The recognized abbreviations for the various metals of the platinum group are *Plat., Irid., Pall., Ruth., Rhod.* and *Osmi.*

Silver & Karat Gold

Articles made of sterling or coin silver and karat gold should be marked and described to show affirmatively the presence of both metals and the fineness of the karat gold; for example, *Sterling & 12 Kt.* or *Coin & 10 K.*

In order to use the combination mark, the karat gold must be at least 5% by weight of all metals in the article.

The mark may also, if desired, include a fraction that shows the proportionate weight of the karat gold; for example, *Sterling & 1/5 12 Kt.* or *Coin & 1/10 10 K.* Such a mark is particularly desirable when the article consists of sterling or coin silver combined with white karat gold.

The karat mark and its prefix, if used, should always follow the *Sterling* or *Coin* mark. An exception to this is when the karat-gold content is one-half or more of the weight of the article, in which case the karat mark may precede the silver mark; for example, 10 *K. & Coin Silver* or 5/8 12 *K. & Sterling.*

Combination articles of the type described in this section should never be marked or described as "Gold Top," "10-Kt. Front" or "Part Gold."

Articles made of mechanically plated material with a silver base should not be represented as combinations of silver and karat gold (see section entitled *Gold Filled & Rolled-Gold Plate*).

Karat Gold & Platinum Metals

Articles made of karat gold and platinum may be marked with the karat mark and the platinum mark, provided the fineness of the karat gold is correctly stated, the proportion of the platinum is not less than 5% of the weight of all metal in the article, and the platinum mark follows the karat mark; for example, 18 K. & *Platinum* or 14 *k.-Plat.*

If desired, the quality mark may also include a fraction showing the proportional weight of the platinum; for example, 18 K. & 1/8 *Platinum* or 14 K.-1/10 *Plat.*

Articles made of karat gold and palladium should be similarly marked and described; for example, 14 *Kt. & Palladium* or 10 *K.-Pall.* If the palladium content is one-half or more of the weight of the article, the mark may be *Palladium & 12 Kt.*

Stainless Steel & Karat Gold

Articles made of stainless steel and karat gold may be marked and described to show the presence of both metals; for example, *Stainless Steel & 12 Kt.* The karat mark should always follow the stainless-steel mark. A fractional prefix may be added, to indicate the proportion of the weight of the karat gold, if desired; for example, *Stainless Steel & 1/5 12 Kt.* An exception is when the gold content is one-half or more of the weight of all metal in the article. In this case, the karat mark may precede the stainless-steel mark; for example, 10 *K. & Stainless Steel.*

If white karat gold is combined with stainless steel, the use of the prefix fraction showing the proportion of the weight of the karat gold to the weight of the entire article is highly desirable.

Abbreviations such as "SS" or "ss" should never be used for stainless steel. Also, the term *Stainless Steel* should always be in the same size type as the karat designation and the word *Gold*.

The general opinion in the trade is that no reference should be made to karat gold, if it is less than 1/10 by weight of all metal in the article.

Articles made of mechanically plated material with a steel base should not be presented as combinations of stainless steel and karat gold (see following section).

Gold-Filled & Rolled-Gold Plate

Gold filled and rolled-gold plate are materials made with a metal base upon one or more sides or surfaces of which there is affixed continuously by soldering, brazing, welding, or other mechanical means a sheet or sheets or covering of karat gold that is at least 10 Kt. fine. The covering of gold is rolled, drawn or pressed to an indicated ratio before uniting with the base metal, and this ratio is maintained during further rolling, drawing or pressing.

THE JEWELERS' MANUAL

The term *Gold Filled* is used properly only when 1/20 or more of the total weight of all metal is karat gold of the quality stated. The term *Rolled-Gold Plate* may be used to describe materials in which proportion of the karat gold is less than 1/20.

Articles, other than watchcases, made of gold-filled or rolled-gold-plate material should be marked and described as plated, and should show the proportion of the weight of the karat-gold covering to the weight of all metal in the article and the fineness of the gold in the plating; for example, 1/10 12 *K. Gold Filled* or 1/30 *K. Rolled-Gold Plate.*

Watchcases made of gold filled or rolled-gold plate should be marked and described to show that the case is plated and to indicate the fineness of the karat gold in the plating. If the thickness of the plate is *not less* than 3/1000 of an inch (.003), the term *Gold Filled* may be used; for example, 14 *K. Gold Filled.* If the thickness of the plate is less than .003 of an inch, but less than .0015, the correct designation or description is *Rolled-Gold Plate.*

No quality mark indicating the presence of karat gold can be applied to a watchcase in which the thickness of the plate is *less* than .0015 of an inch.

No article having an alloyed-gold covering of less than 10-karat fineness can be marked or described as *Gold Filled* or *Rolled-Gold Plate.*

Palladium-Filled & Rolled-Palladium Plate

Articles made of palladium-filled and rolled-palladium plate should be marked and described in the same manner as gold filled and rolled-gold-plate articles, the word *Palladium* or the abbreviation *Pall.* being substituted in the mark or description for the word *Gold* and the karat mark being omitted; for example, 1/20 *Palladium Filled* and 1/40 *Rolled-Palladium Plate.*

Gold Electroplate

Articles plated electrolytically with gold or an alloy of gold are frequently referred to as *Gold Plated.* However, the better practice is to describe them affirmatively as *Gold Electroplate* or *Gold Electroplated,* since the term *Gold Plate* is an all-inclusive one embracing both rolled-gold plate and gold electroplate.

The FTC has ruled that the karat mark *cannot* be used to refer to an electroplated item. It has ruled further that an article must be covered with a "substantial amount of gold" to be properly called *Plate* or *Plated.* If the covering is not of a substantial character, the Commission prohibits the use of these terms and, if the word *Gold* is used, requires that it be

Properties of Precious Metals

Metal	Chemical Symbol	Specific Gravity	Mohs' Hardness	Brinell Hardness	Melting Point °C	Melting Point °F	Solubility	Source and Occurrence
Gold	Au	19.3	2½-3	25	1063°	1945°	Insoluble in single acids; soluble in aqua regia*.	Chiefly as native metal in placer and vein deposits; rarely as telluride. USSR, USA, Canada, South Africa.
Silver	Ag	10.5	2½-3	30	961°	1761°	Soluble in nitric acid.	Native silver, chloride, sulphide. USA, Mexico, Canada.
Platinum	Pt	21.5	4-4½	42	1773.5°	3224°	Soluble in hot aqua regia.	Native metal in placer deposits; by-product of nickel industry. Canada, USSR, Colombia.
Palladium	Pd	12.0	4-4½	46	1554°	2831°	Soluble in hot nitric acid.	Occurs with platinum.
Iridium	Ir	22.4	6½	172	2454°	4449°	Insoluble in aqua regia.	Occurs with platinum, usually in minor amounts. Also as osmiridium.
Rhodium	Rh	12.4	5	135	1966°	3551°	Insoluble in aqua regia.	Occurs with platinum, usually in minor amounts.
Osmium	Os	22.5	7	350	2700°	4892°	Virtually insoluble in aqua regia.	Occurs with platinum, usually in minor amounts. Also as osmiridium.
Ruthenium	Ru	12.2	6½	220	2450°	4442°	Virtually insoluble in aqua regia.	Occurs with platinum, usually in minor amounts.

* Aqua regia is a mixture of hydrochloric and nitric acids.

Gold Content of Karat Alloys

Karat	Gold Percentage	Karat	Gold Percentage
24	100.00%	12	50.00%
23½	97.92%	11½	47.92%
23	95.83%	11	45.83%
22½	93.75%	10½	43.75%
22	91.67%	10	41.67%
21½	89.58%	9½	39.58%
21	87.50%	9	37.50%
20½	85.42%	8½	35.42%
20	83.33%	8	33.33%
19½	81.25%	7½	31.25%
19	79.17%	7	29.17%
18½	77.08%	6½	27.08%
18	75.00%	6	25.00%
17½	72.92%	5½	22.92%
17	70.83%	5	20.83%
16½	68.75%	4½	18.75%
16	66.67%	4	16.67%
15½	64.58%	3½	14.58%
15	62.50%	3	12.50%
14½	60.42%	2½	10.42%
14	58.33%	2	8.33%
13½	56.25%	1½	6.25%
13	54.17%	1	4.17%
12½	52.08%	½	2.08%

properly qualified; for example, *Gold Flash*, *Gold Finish* or *Gold Color*. (By "substantial" is meant .00001 of an inch in thickness, to less a tolerance of .000003.)

Acid Tests for Precious Metals

Gold: For the acid test to determine the gold content of an article, the following equipment is required: a touchstone slab; karat needles; and a bottle each of nitric acid, aqua regia, diluted nitric acid, and diluted aqua regia.

First, file a deep notch in the article and apply a drop of nitric acid. Little or no reaction indicates more than 10-karat gold; a slight reaction, 10 karat; a pinkish-cream color, gold plate on silver; a bright-green reaction, plated gold. Green gold reacts more slowly than yellow because of the silver content. Because of the presence of nickel or palladium, white gold reacts slowly.

Markings & Descriptions of Precious Metals

To determine the karat, rub the touchstone with a cleanly filed portion of the article, making a clear mark on the stone. Beside the mark, make an equally heavy one with a karat needle of whatever karat and color you estimate the gold content of the unknown to be. Using nitric acid for 10 karat or less and aqua regia for higher karats, apply acids to both marks at the same time. A too-quick reaction of the karat needle indicates too low a needle; a too-slow reaction, that the needle is too high. The correct karat is found when the reactions of the two marks are identical.

Platinum: To test for platinum metals, the procedure is similar to that for gold, except that needles of platinum, iridio-platinum, palladium-platinum and palladium are used. Aqua regia is used to determine the reactions. Platinum and iridio-platinum react very slowly; lower-grade alloys that contain palladium, gold and base metals react rapidly.

Silver: The test for silver is similar to that for gold. When nitric acid is applied to the article, sterling turns a cloudy-cream color; plated silver green; and coin silver, blackish. Silver of 750 fineness and lower shows a green reaction, which deepens as the fineness is reduced. Comparative tests with silver of known fineness is a good check.

THE JEWELERS' MANUAL

Basic Kinds of Jewelry Findings

Illustrations courtesy A.E. Waller Co., Providence, R.I.; W.R. Cobb Co., Cranston, R.I.; Grieger's, Inc., Pasadena, Calif.

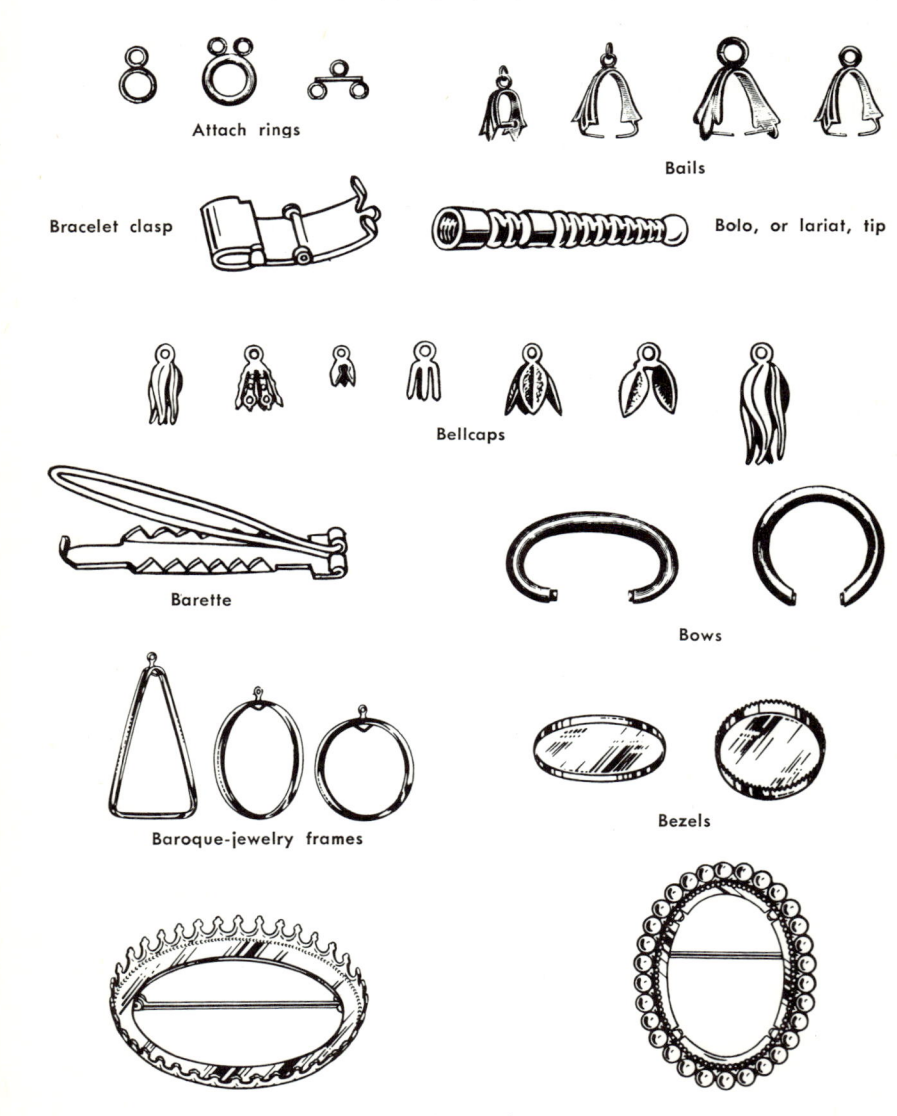

Attach rings

Bails

Bracelet clasp

Bolo, or lariat, tip

Bellcaps

Barette

Bows

Baroque-jewelry frames

Bezels

Brooch mountings

130

Basic Kinds of Jewelry Findings

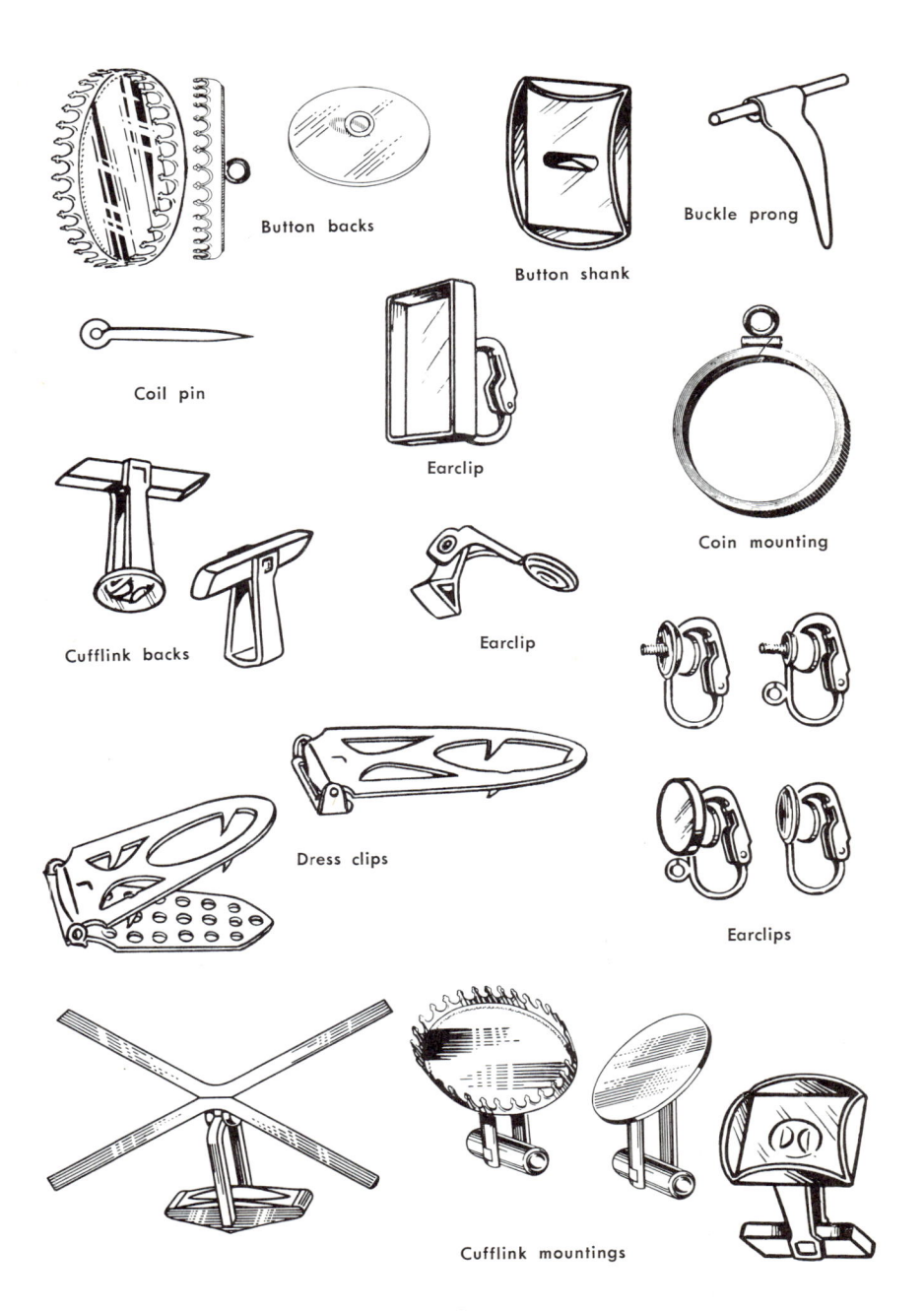

Button backs

Button shank

Buckle prong

Coil pin

Earclip

Coin mounting

Cufflink backs

Earclip

Earclips

Dress clips

Cufflink mountings

THE JEWELERS' MANUAL

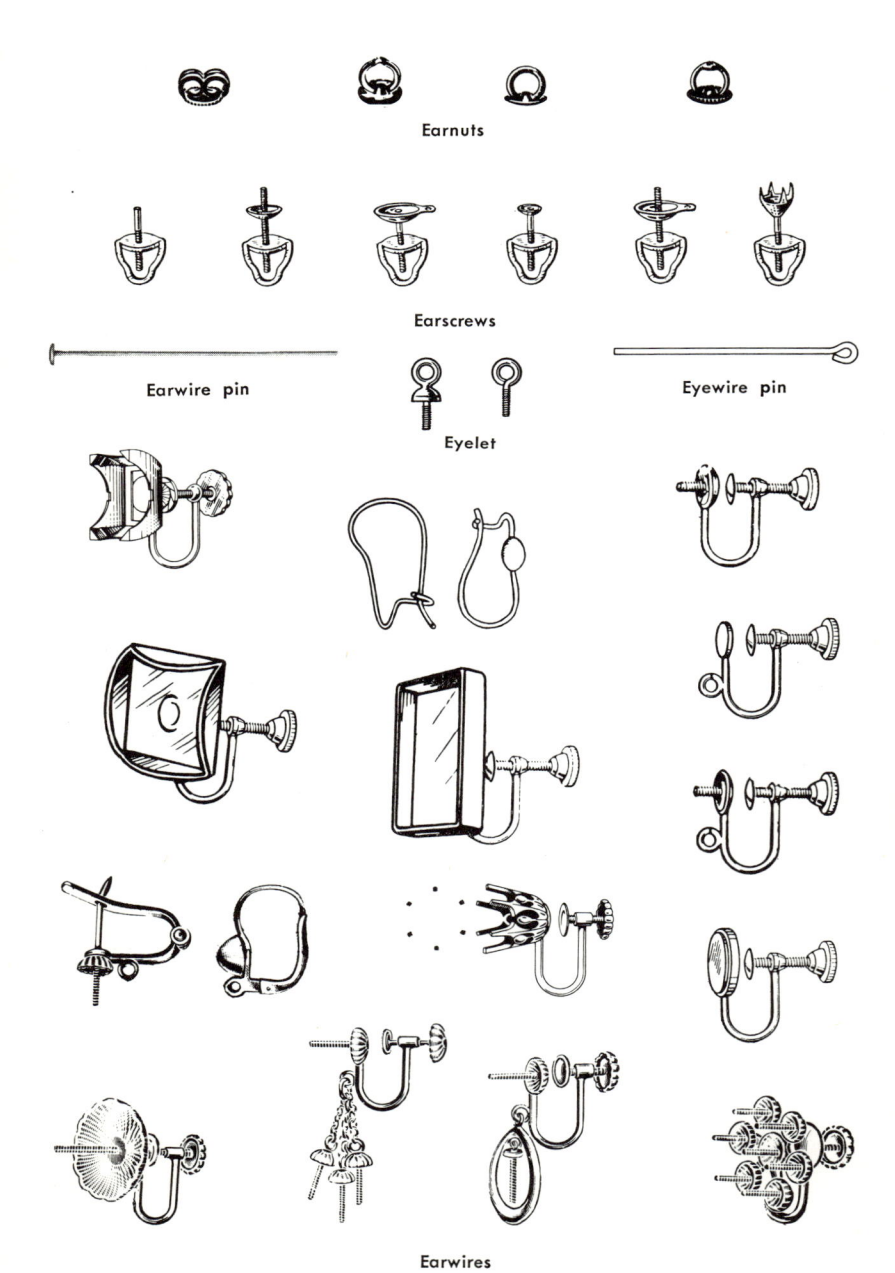

Earnuts

Earscrews

Earwire pin

Eyelet

Eyewire pin

Earwires

132

Basic Kinds of Jewelry Mountings

Hoop earring

Joint

Joint & pinstem

Hairclip

Gallery wire

Jump rings

Guard chain

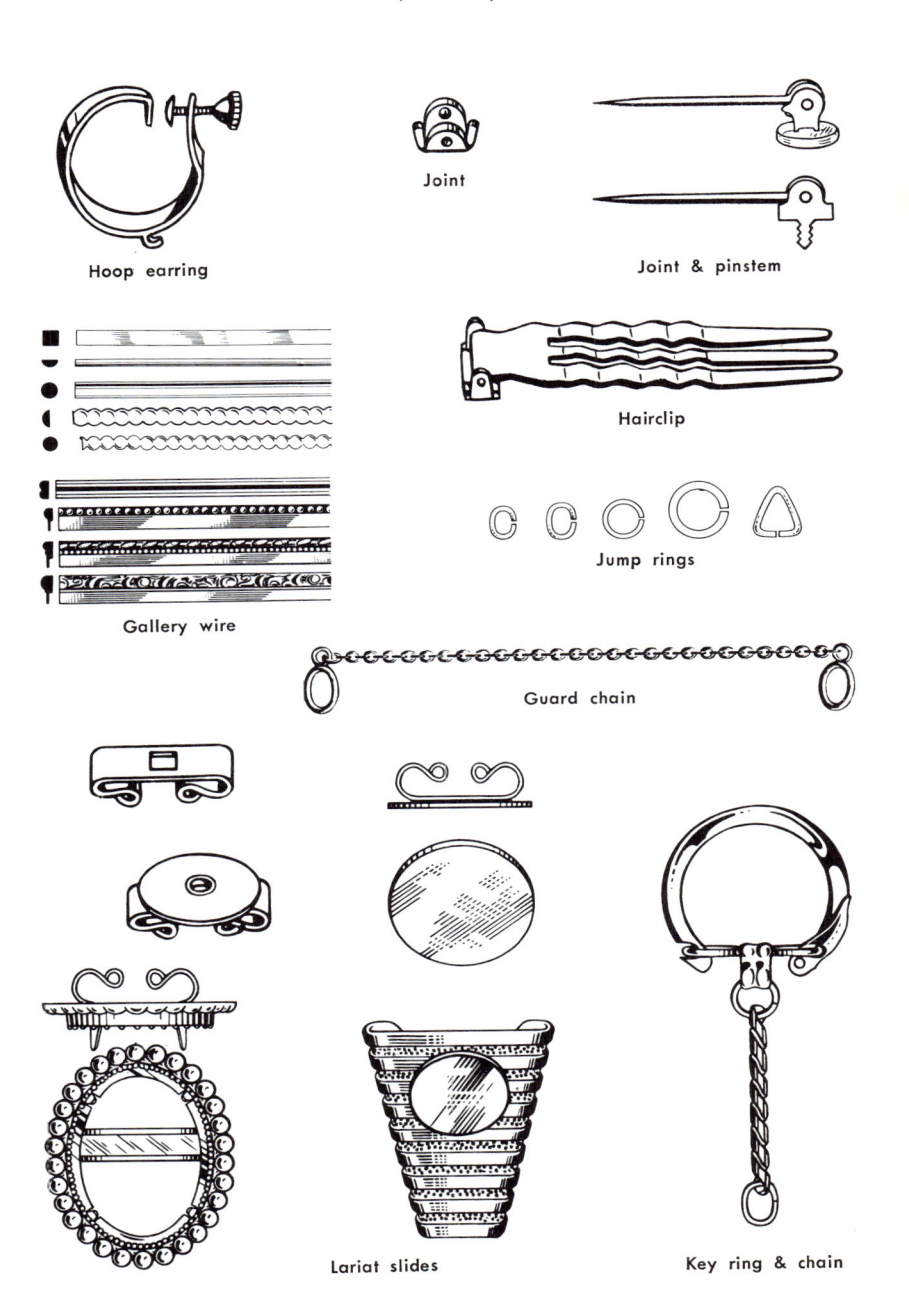

Lariat slides

Key ring & chain

THE JEWELERS' MANUAL

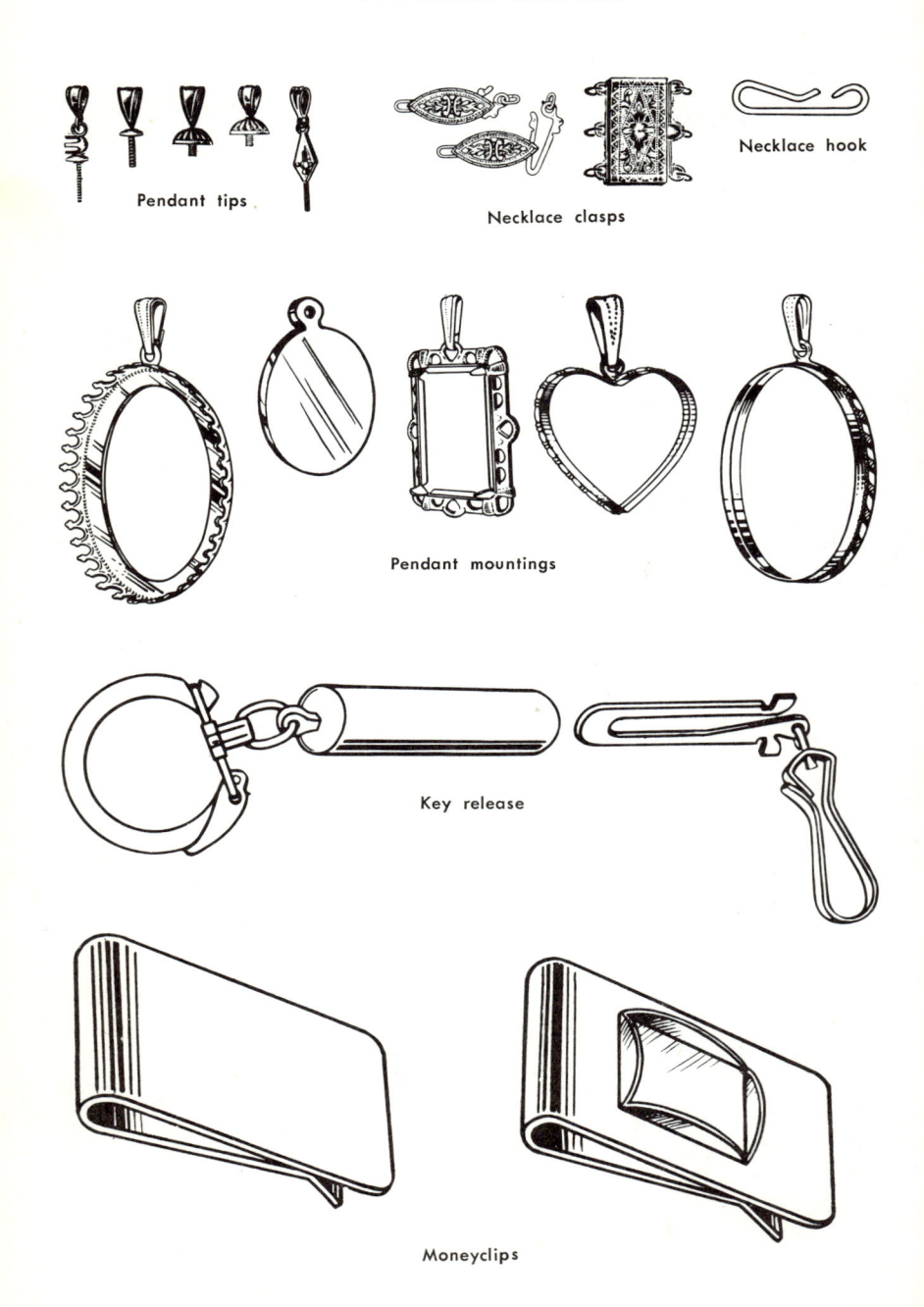

Pendant tips

Necklace clasps

Necklace hook

Pendant mountings

Key release

Moneyclips

Basic Kinds of Jewelery Mountings

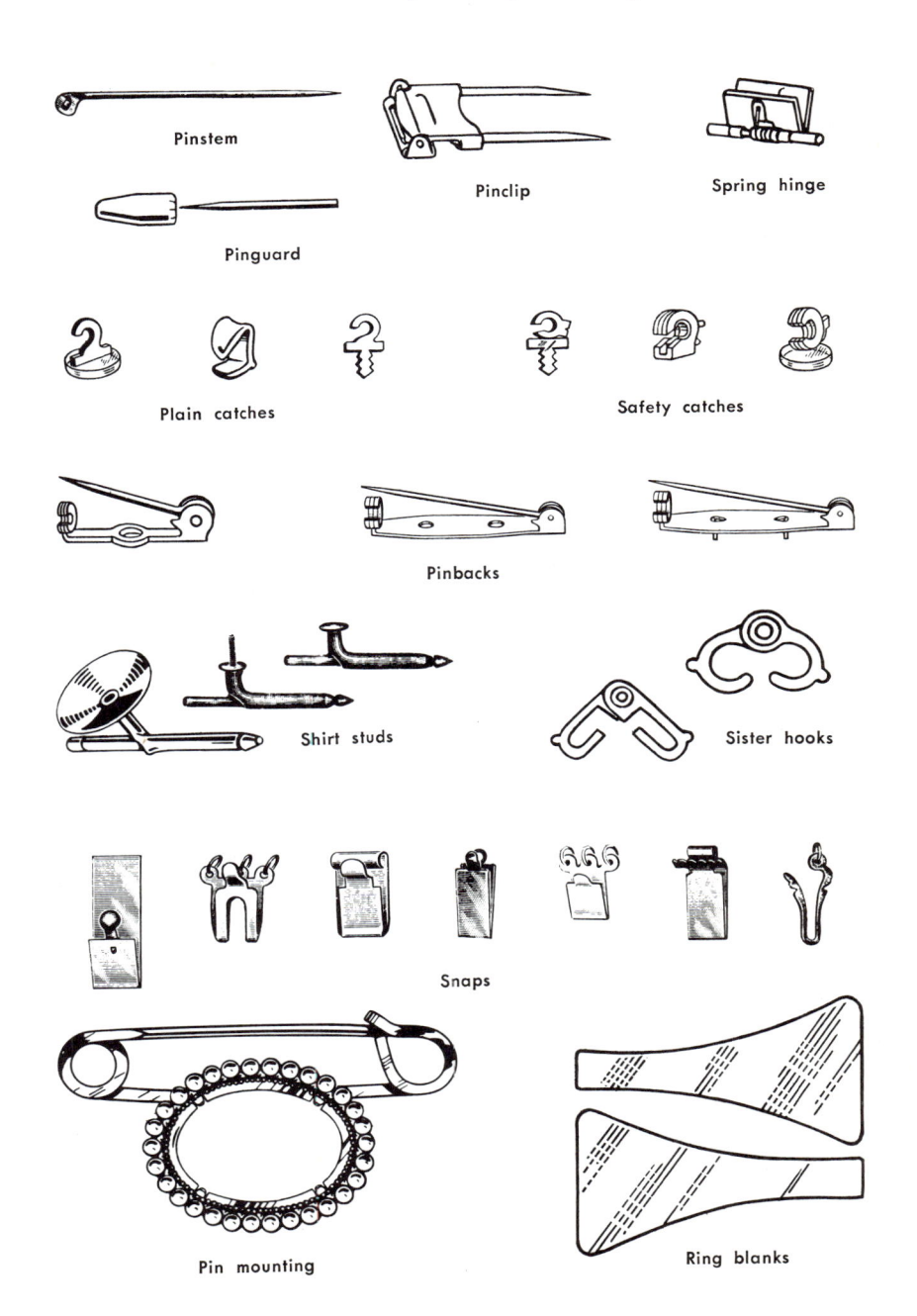

Pinstem

Pinclip

Spring hinge

Pinguard

Plain catches

Safety catches

Pinbacks

Shirt studs

Sister hooks

Snaps

Pin mounting

Ring blanks

135

THE JEWELERS' MANUAL

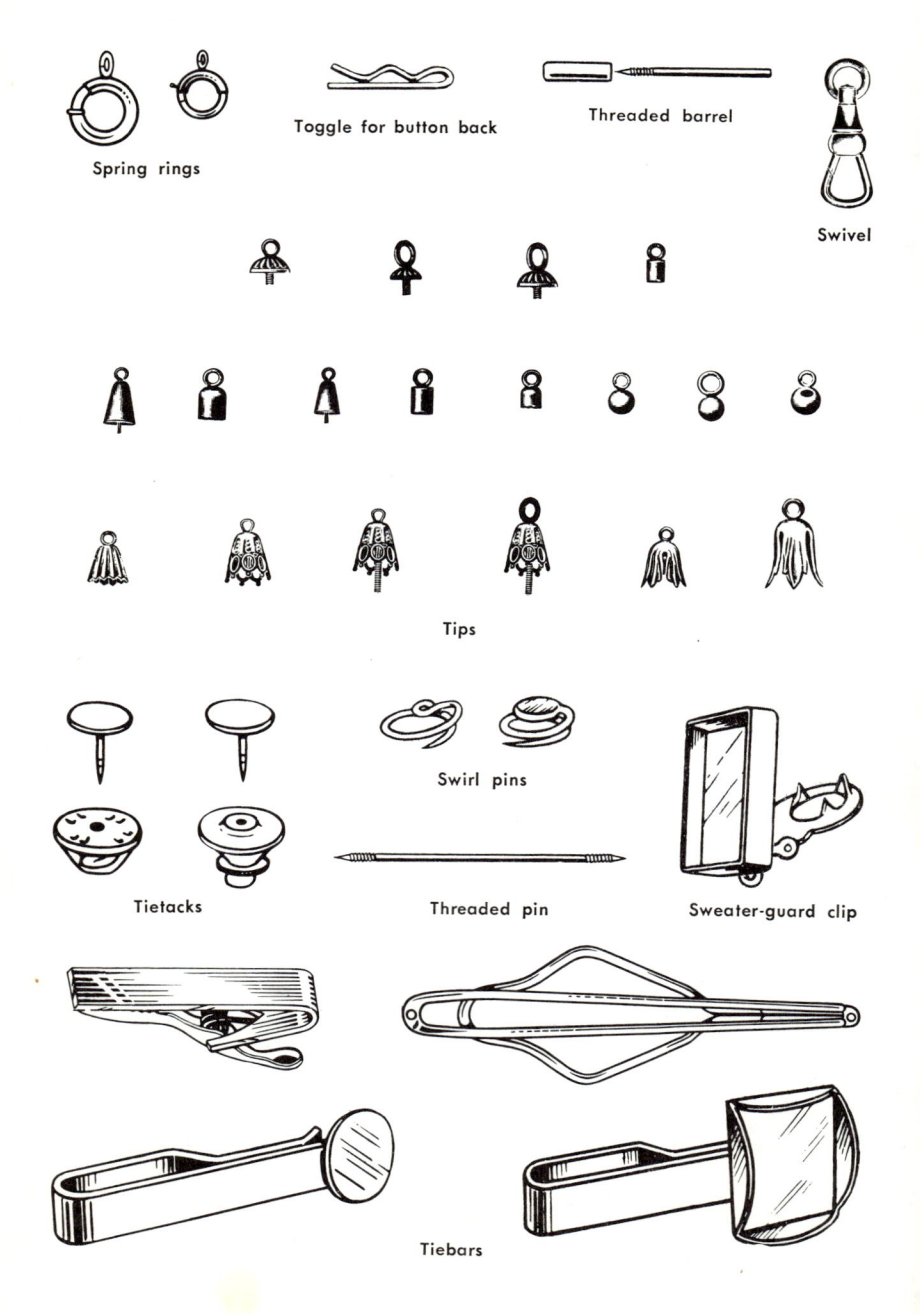

Spring rings

Toggle for button back

Threaded barrel

Swivel

Tips

Tietacks

Swirl pins

Threaded pin

Sweater-guard clip

Tiebars

136

Basic Kinds of Mountings & Settings

Basic Kinds of Mountings & Settings

Illustrations courtesy Karlan & Bleicher, Inc., New York City; Jewelers' Circular-Keystone, Philadelphia, Pa.

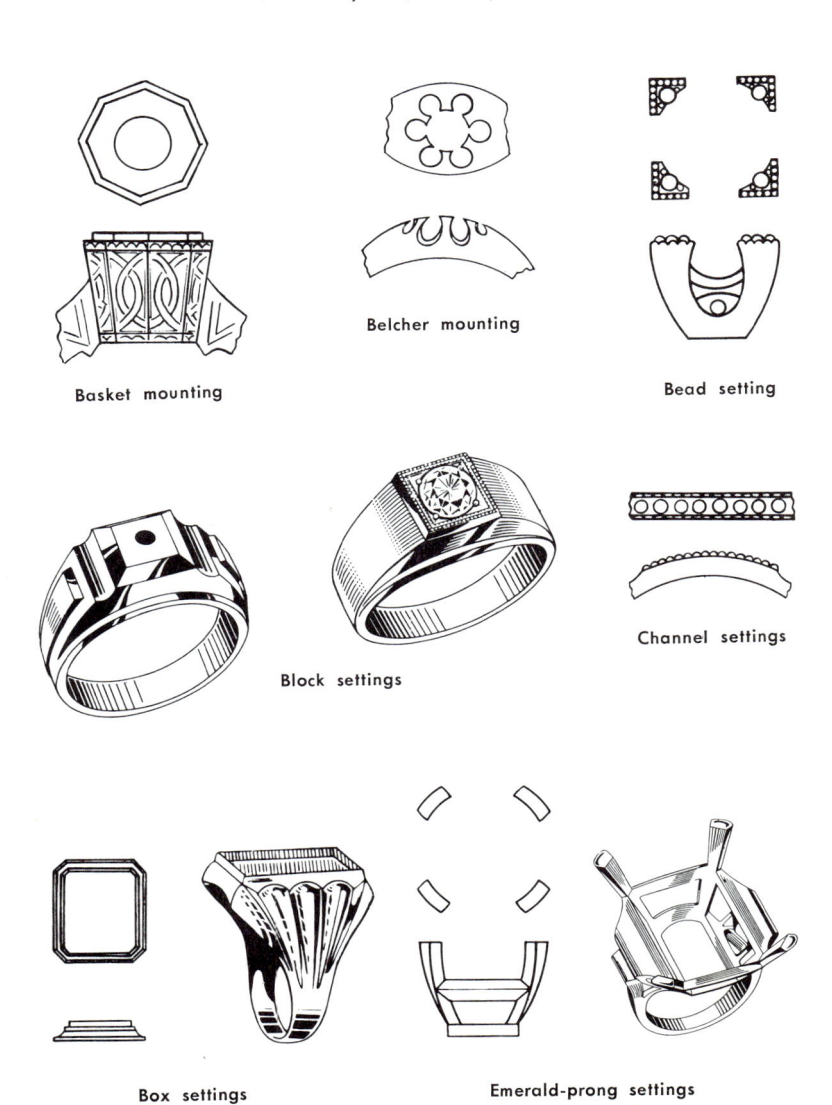

Basket mounting

Belcher mounting

Bead setting

Block settings

Channel settings

Box settings

Emerald-prong settings

137

THE JEWELERS' MANUAL

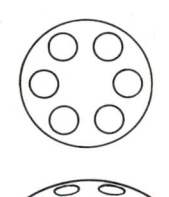

Cluster settings

Four-piece mounting

Two-piece wedding rings

Gypsy mountings

Fishtail settings

Basic Kinds of Mountings & Settings

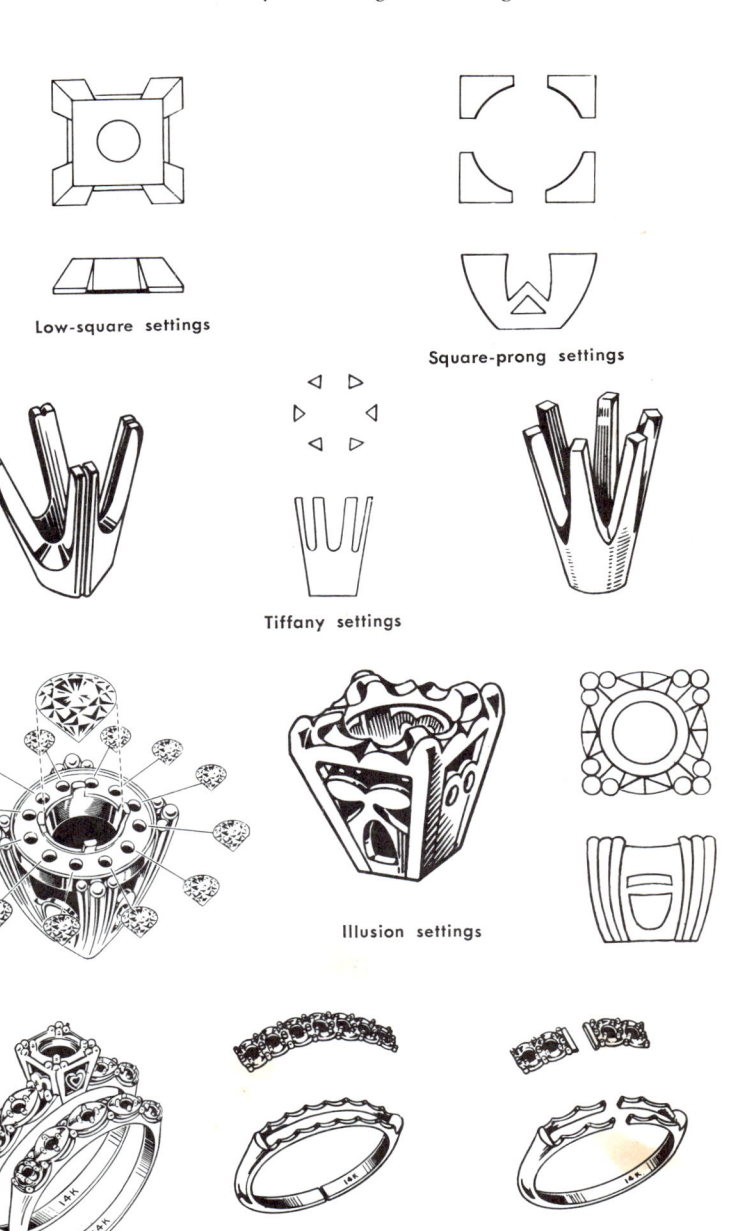

Low-square settings

Square-prong settings

Tiffany settings

Illusion settings

Needlepoint settings

139

United States & British Ring-Size Equivalents

United States	Average Diameter in Inches	British Equivalent	United States	Average Diameter in Inches	British Equivalent
000	.39		6¾		N ½
00	.422		7	.683	O
0	.454		7¼		O ½
½		A	7½	.699	P
¾		A ½	7¾		P ½
1	.487	B	8	.716	Q
1¼		B ½	8¼		Q ½
1½	.503	C	8½	.732	
1¾		C ½	8⅝		R
2	.520	D	8⅞		R ½
2¼		D ½	9	.748	
2½	.536	E	9⅛		S
2¾		E ½	9⅜		S ½
3	.553	F	9½	.764	
3⅛		F ½	9⅝		T
3⅜		G	10	.781	T ½
3½	.569		10¼		U
3⅝		G ½	10½	.797	U ½
3¾		H	10⅝		V
4	.585	H ½	11	.814	V ½
4¼		I	11⅛		W
4½	.601	I ½	11⅜		W ½
4⅝		J	11½	.830	
5	.618	J ½	11⅝		X
5⅛		K	11⅞		X ½
5⅜		K ½	12	.846	Y
5½	.634	L	12¼		Y ½
5⅞		L ½	12½	.862	Z
6	.650	M	12¾		Z ½
6¼		M ½	13	.879	
6½	.666	N			

Basic Styles of Jewelry Chains

Chains courtesy Armbrust Chain Co., Providence, R.I.

Lace

Buckle

Bracelet

Ring

Belt

THE JEWELERS' MANUAL

Disc

Double-link curb

Double-oval link

Double cable

Double ring

Triple cable

Cable

Basic Styles of Jewelry Chains

French rope

Soldered curb

Round filed

Bevel filed

Flat filed

Double curb

Flat curb

Swedged cable

Swedged curb

THE JEWELERS' MANUAL

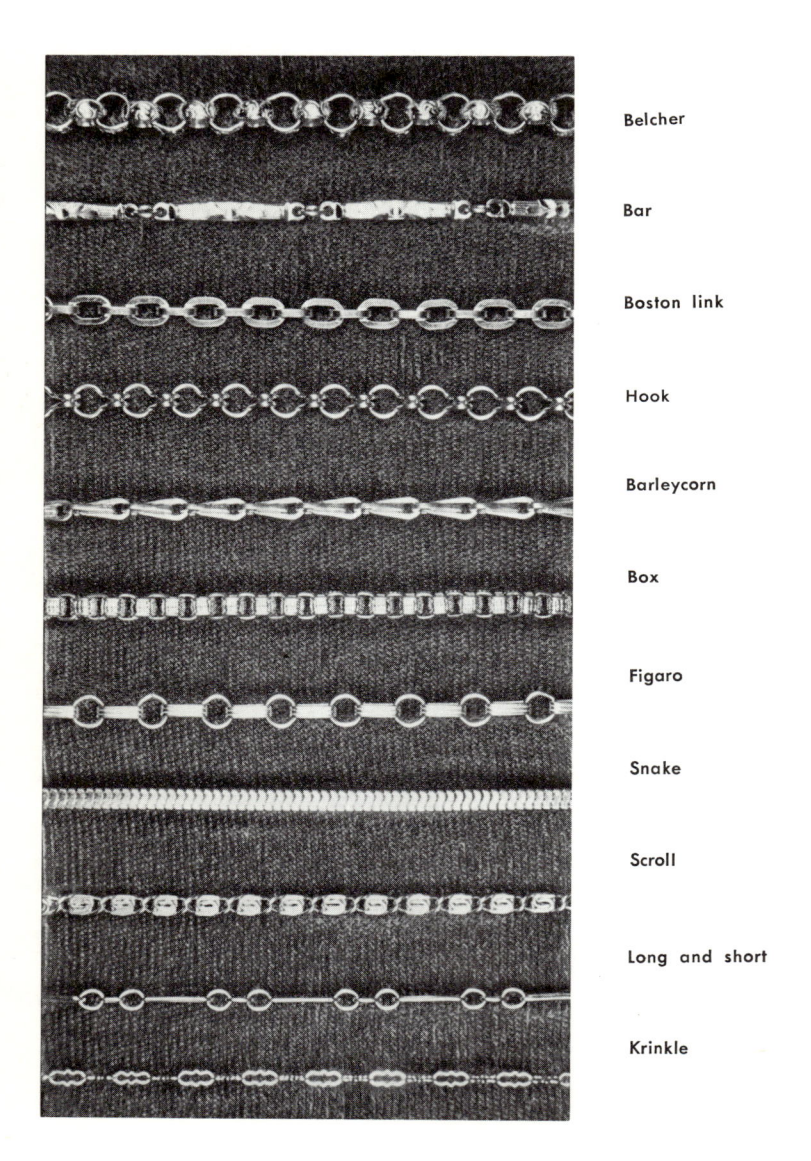

Belcher

Bar

Boston link

Hook

Barleycorn

Box

Figaro

Snake

Scroll

Long and short

Krinkle

Important Emblems of Fraternal Orders & Civic Groups

Important Emblems of Fraternal Orders & Civic Groups

Illustrations courtesy Rabin-Tobar, Inc., New York City

Masonic, Blue Lodge	Masonic, Tubal Cane	Masonic, Trowel
Masonic, Slipper	Masonic, Master Square	Masonic, Past Master
Masonic, District Deputy	Masonic, Knight Templar	Masonic, 32nd Degree
Masonic, 33rd Degree	Mystic Shrine	Mystic Shrine

145

THE JEWELERS' MANUAL

Mystic Shrine	Mystic Shrine, Fez	Knights of Columbus, 3rd Degree
Knights of Columbus, 4th Degree	Knights of Pythias	Knights of Pythias
D.O.K.K.	Benevolent & Protective Order of Elks	B.P.O.E., Past Exalted Ruler
Caduceus	Lions International	 Rotary International

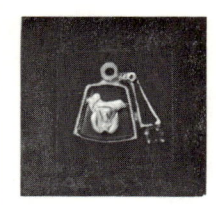

Important Emblems of Fraternal Orders & Civic Groups

Kiwanis International

Fraternal Order of Eagles

Improved Order of Redmen

Independent Order of Odd Fellows

Loyal Order of Moose

Modern Woodmen of America

Woodmen of the World

Eastern Star

Eastern Star, Past Matron

THE JEWELERS' MANUAL

Eastern Star, Past Patron

Order of Amaranth

Daughters of Rebekah

Order of Amaranth, Past Patron

White Shrine of Jerusalem

White Shrine of Jerusalem

Hallmarks

A hallmark is a stamp applied by an authorized organization to articles of precious metals, after test by assay, to denote fineness of quality. Although both gold and silver are stamped and many countries use a hallmarking system, only articles made of silver in England and Scotland are discussed here.

The four marks stamped on British sterling are listed and described below:

The Hallmark
(also called the *assay-office mark* or the *town mark*)

There are four official assay offices in England and two in Scotland, each of which has its characteristic mark. In the early days, these offices were referred to as "halls"; hence the term hallmark. Note that, of the four marks that appear on British silver, the assay-office mark is the hallmark, *not* the other three. These are the six offices and their marks (see illustrations):

1. **London.** A leopard's head. If the head is crowned, it was marked before 1820; if uncrowned, after 1820.
2. **Birmingham.** An anchor.
3. **Sheffield.** A crown.
4. **Chester.** Three sheaves and a sword.
5. **Edinburgh.** A castle.
6. **Glasgow.** Tree, bird, bell, fish and ring. This mark is also the city's coat-of-arms.

England also had, at various times, nineteen other assay offices, the names and marks of which are given in the books on hallmarking mentioned in a subsequent paragraph.

In addition, each office has a second mark that is used on goods not made in England; it identifies the office that does the stamping and indicates that the goods are imported. All precious-metal articles imported into Great Britain must go directly to one of the assay offices

THE JEWELERS' MANUAL

and be marked before they can be sold in that country. Following are the hallmarks used on importations (see illustrations):

1. **London.** Sign of constellation Leo.
2. **Birmingham.** A triangle.
3. **Sheffield.** Sign of constellation Libra.
4. **Chester.** An acorn and two leaves.
5. **Edinburgh.** St. Andrew's Cross.
6. **Glasgow.** Two letters "F" on their sides.

Quality Mark

(also called *standard mark*)

This is equivalent to the sterling stamp used in the United States. The quality marks used for sterling-silver articles made in England are as follows (see illustrations):

1. **London.** Lion passant (a full side view of a lion with its head facing straight ahead and its right foreleg raised).
2. **Birmingham.** Lion passant.
3. **Sheffield.** Lion passant guardant (same as lion passant but with its head turned *toward* the observer. As used in heraldry, the word *guardant* merely means acting as a guard or guardian).
4. **Chester.** Lion passant guardant.
5. **Edinburgh.** A thistle.
6. **Glasgow.** Also a thistle but of a different shape than the one used by Edinburgh. There is also a second mark that shows a lion rampant but on a shield of different outline (the word *rampant* means *standing and reared up, with one foreleg raised above the other*).

Each of these quality marks is superimposed on a shield of different shape. Thus, although both London and Birmingham use the lion passant, they can be distinguished by the shape of the shield.

England has a second and higher grade of silver known as *Britannia silver*, but it is not used extensively. It is 958.4 parts per thousand fine silver and the balance, base metal. The quality mark for this alloy is the Lady Britannia, seated, with a shield and spear. Chester and London use a second shield, in addition to the one showing Britannia, that bears a lion's head erased (in the language of heraldry, the word *erased* means *torn from the body with a jagged edge;* hence, the head is shown with an irregular edge at its base).

A different quality mark is used on silver articles imported into Great Britain. For sterling, it is the number .925 on an oval shield; Britannia silver is represented by the number .9584 on an oval shield (see illustrations).

Hallmarks

Hallmarks, Quality Marks & Date Letters

London	Birmingham	Sheffield

Chester	Edinburgh	Glasgow

Hallmarks on British-Made Sterling

London	Birmingham	Sheffield

Chester	Edinburgh	Glasgow

Hallmarks on Sterling Imported Into Britain

THE JEWELERS' MANUAL

London · Birmingham · Sheffield

Chester · Edinburgh · Glasgow

Quality Marks on British-Made Sterling

·925
Quality Mark for Sterling Imported Into Britain

·9584
Quality Mark for Britannia Ware Imported Into Britain

Quality Mark for British-Made Britannia Ware

The Irish Quality Mark

The Irish Hallmark

Examples of Date Letters

London	Birmingham	Sheffield	Chester	Edinburgh	Glasgow
1836	1824	1868	1884	1882	1871
1856	1849	1893	1901	1906	1897
1876	1875	1918	1926	1931	1923

152

Hallmarks

Date Letter

This mark, which consists basically of a letter on a shield, indicates the year in which an article was made. Each assay office has its own code of date letters. The system is based on the idea of using the letters of the alphabet and changing them annually, thus producing definite cycles that can be repeated. For example, when date lettering first began, the authorities decided to use the letter A for the first year, B for the second, C for the third, etc., all in the same type style and on the same shape shield throughout the entire alphabet. This, they reasoned, would permit them to use a wide variety of printing styles and shield outlines and thus provide endless different combinations to avoid duplication among cycles.

However, because each assay office eliminates certain letters of the alphabet, the length of the cycle varies. London, for example, when it first started dating sterling articles in 1478, decided to use only the letters A through U and eliminate J, thus producing a twenty-year cycle. Both Birmingham and Sheffield have twenty-five-year cycles, eliminating either J or I. Chester and Edinburgh always omit the J. (The reason for eliminating the J's and I's is believed to be the fact that, in certain type faces, the two letters look very much alike, particularly after much wear.)

As mentioned above, each office changes its letters annually but at different times, as follows: London, May 29; Birmingham, Sheffield and Chester, July 1; Edinburgh, the second or third week of October; Glasgow, the first Monday in July. The reason for the different dates is that each office began its date-stamping at a different time. A given date letter is therefore in use not only for the rest of the calendar year following the starting date, but for part of the year following. On the other hand, the early part of the calendar year finds goods being marked with the letter belonging to the still-unfinished year of the previous term.

In further reference to the shield, it is interesting to note that its shape, or outline, is not necessarily changed with each new cycle. In practice, it is only Edinburgh that alters the shield shape for each new alphabetical series. The other offices maintain the same shield for two or more consecutive series, but this is done only when the style of the letters in each series is sufficiently different to avoid confusion.

For further information, consult: *Hallmark & Date Letters*, by Arthur Tremayn, NAG press, Ltd, London, 1944; *British & Irish Silver Assay-Office Marks*, by Frederick Bradbury, J. W. Northend, Ltd., Sheffield; and *The Law & Practice of Hallmarking Gold & Silver Wares*, by J. Paul de Castro, Crosby, Lockwood & Son, 1935.

THE JEWELERS' MANUAL

The accompanying examples of British date letters show the type styles and shield outlines that have been used by the various offices. The year shown under each mark is the one in which that particular letter and shield commenced to be used.

Maker's Mark

This stamp corresponds to our American trademark. It must be registered with the assay office and, of course, shows who made the article. But there is one important point to note: a retailer or wholesaler can employ his own mark; a manufacturer may make the article but put on the stamp of the retailer or wholesaler. The mark must also be registered; this means that the retailer or wholesaler must accept the responsibility for the quality of the goods. The point to be emphasized is that the maker's mark does not necessarily indicate who made the article.

The early maker's mark consisted of his initials or a device or the two combined. On Britannia silver, the mark was the first two letters of the maker's surname. The modern system is to use the initials of an individual, the partners of a firm, or a company. The maker's mark usually begins or ends the series of stamps on a piece of British silver, although there is no particular rule or law governing the order in which the four marks should appear.

From time to time, other marks have been authorized in England besides the conventional hallmark, quality mark, date letter and maker's mark. For example, from the year 1784 to 1890, duty marks were used, which consisted of a stamping of the ruling sovereign's head. In 1935, the jubilee mark was authorized; it consisted of the heads of King George V and Queen Mary in profile. A special coronation mark was used in 1953 at the time of the coronation of Queen Elizabeth. Most books on hallmarking discuss and illustrate these marks.

Until 1922, the Dublin, Ireland, Assay Office was part of the British system, but when Eire became a separate country, the Dublin office came under the jurisdiction of that nation. However, their hallmarking follows the British method, with but few differences. The Irish hallmark is a figure of a woman known as Hibernia, who is seated facing sideways with a small harp by her left hand and a spray of palm leaves in her right hand; the quality mark is a crowned harp (see illustrations). Britannia silver is not recognized. Irish goods imported into the United Kingdom must be sent to one of the six assay offices to be stamped, just as goods imported from other countries.

Care of Silverware

One of the most important rules in the care of silver is to use it daily and wash it thoroughly after each meal. Constant use not only retards tarnishing but actually increases beauty. The richness, mellowness and depth of color of fine old museum pieces is the result of generations of daily usage. The fear of scratching newly acquired silver is natural; however, a mulitude of fine scratches imparts a more durable, practical and beautiful finish than can be produced mechanically.

The major enemies of silverware are rubber, salt, eggs (sulphur), gases and smoke. If salad dressing is left on a fork, knife or spoon, discoloration will result. Salty foods may cause tarnish and black spots. Wash the articles in hot, soapy water and dry immediately; then wipe thoroughly with a clean, soft cloth. Be sure that all pieces are completely dry before being stored.

Even with these precautions, silver requires occasional repolishing. Choose a good brand of polish. Rub each piece lengthwise, never crosswise or with a circular motion. After the surface has been given the desired color, wash thoroughly in hot, soapy water and rinse in clean, hot water. If the silver is highly ornamented, remove the polish in the crevices with a small brush. After cleaning and drying, polish it with a soft flannel cloth or chamois.

Silver can be cleaned chemically by boiling the pieces in an aluminum container in a solution of water, soda and salt. This process removes tarnish but also removes patina; therefore, it is wise to follow with a regular silver polish. Of course, there are some pieces that, because of their nature, are not used daily; these should be kept in tarnishproof chests, bags or rolls.

THE JEWELERS' MANUAL

Sterling Flatware

Photo courtesy Reed & Barton, Taunton, Mass.

1. Flat-handled spreader
2. Hollow-handled spreader
3. Bouillion spoon
4. Cream-soup spoon
5. Soup spoon
6. Dessert or cereal spoon
7. Place spoon
8. Teaspoon
9. Salad or pastry fork
10. Place fork
11. Large place fork
12. Large place knife
13. Place knife
14. Individual steak knife
15. Fruit knife
16. Tea fork
17. Tea knife
18. Five-o'clock spoon
19. Iced-beverage spoon
20. Grapefruit, orange or melon spoon
21. Cocktail or oyster fork
22. Ice-cream fork
23. Coffee or cocktail spoon
24. Cake slicer
25. Pastry server
26. Cake server
27. Small salad or serving spoon
28. Tomato or flat server
29. Table or serving spoon
30. Pierced tablespoon
31. Salad-serving set
32. Cheese-serving knife
33. Buffet or cold-meat fork
34. Large buffet or cold-meat fork
35. Large salad or serving spoon
36. Large salad or serving fork
37. Pie- or cake-serving knife
38. Fish-serving fork
39. Fish-serving knife
40. Carver's assistant
41. Poultry shears
42. Cake breaker
43. Salt-serving spoon
44. Spoon pin
45. Individual fish knife
46. Individual fish fork
47. Letter opener
48. Flat-handled butter-serving knife
49. Hollow-handled butter-serving knife
50. Lemon fork
51. Olive or pickle fork
52. Butter fork
53. Bon bon or nut spoon
54. Jelly server
55. Baby fork and baby spoon
56. Child's fork, knife and spoon
57. Infant-feeding spoon
58. Sugar spoon
59. Small sugar spoon
60. Steak-carving fork and knife
61. Roast-carving fork, steel and knife
62. Cream or sauce ladle
63. Gravy ladle
64. Soup ladle
65. Platter or dressing spoon
66. Punch ladle
67. Sugar tongs
68. Ice tongs
69. Wedding-cake knife
70. Bar service: short, flat handled mixing spoon; olive or pickle fork; hollow-handled muddler; bar knife; long, hollow-handled mixing spoon.
71. Bottle opener
72. Candle snuffer

Sterling Flatware

157

THE JEWELERS' MANUAL

Sterling Holloware

Since most of the various pieces of holloware may be used for a variety of purposes, it is a dubious practice to give them individual names. A name does, however, serve to distinguish them one from another in conversation or for convenience in ordering.

Baby cup

Berry bowl

Ash trays

158

Sterling Holloware

Bon bon dish

Beverage mixer

Bread-and-butter plate

Bread or muffin tray

THE JEWELERS' MANUAL

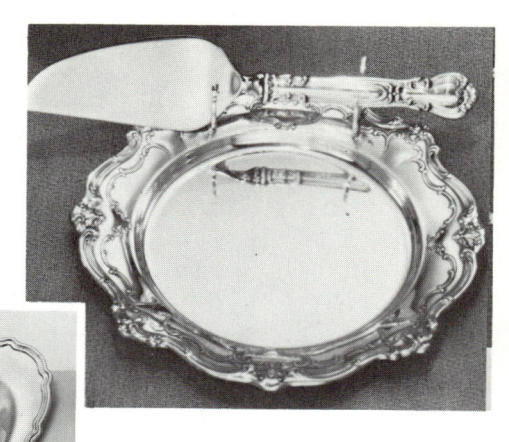

Butter plate and serving knife

Celery or roll tray

Cheese-and-cracker server

Butter dish

Sterling Holloware

Candlistick

Centerpiece

Candelabra

THE JEWELERS' MANUAL

Compotier

Cocktail shaker

Cigarette box

Coasters and match covers

Sterling Holloware

Low compotier

Coffee service

THE JEWELERS' MANUAL

Fruit dish

Double vegetable dish

Sterling Holloware

Goblet

Hurricane lamp

Gravy bowl and tray

Gravy boat and tray

THE JEWELERS' MANUAL

Match covers

Jam jar and tray

Ice bucket

Jigger

Sterling Holloware

Mustard jar

Mayonnaise bowl and ladle

Marmalade set

167

THE JEWELERS' MANUAL

Pipkin and tray

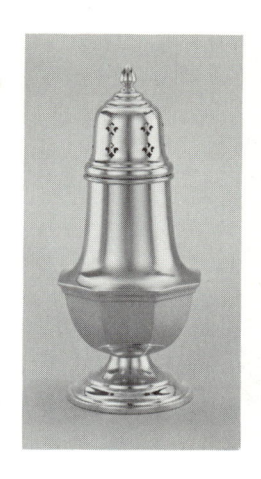

Muffineer, or sugar sifter

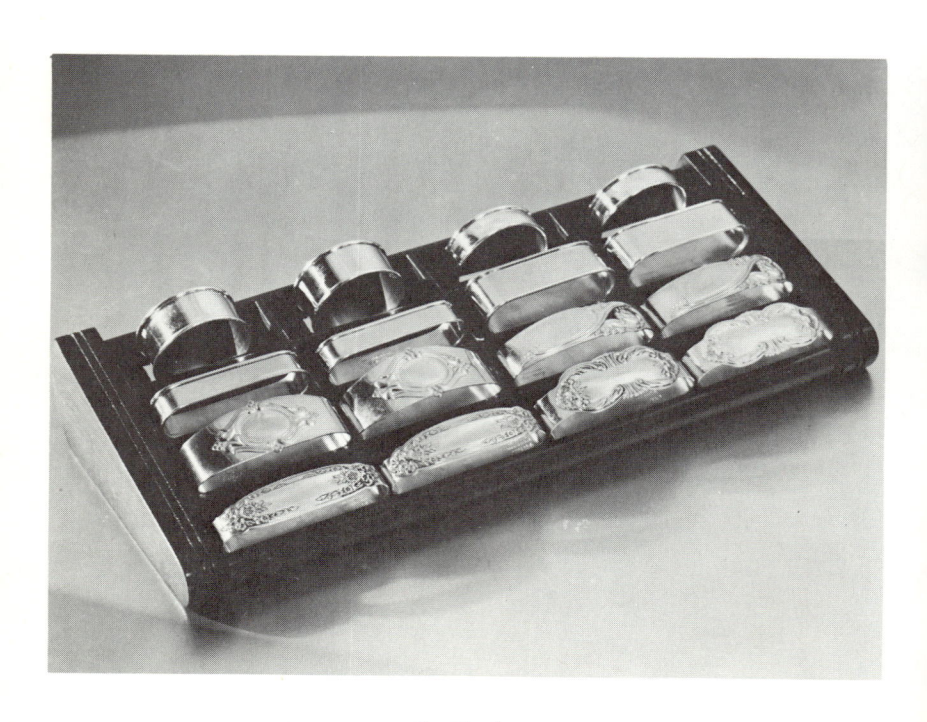

Napkin rings

Sterling Holloware

Porringer or cream-soup dish

Pitcher

169

THE JEWELERS' MANUAL

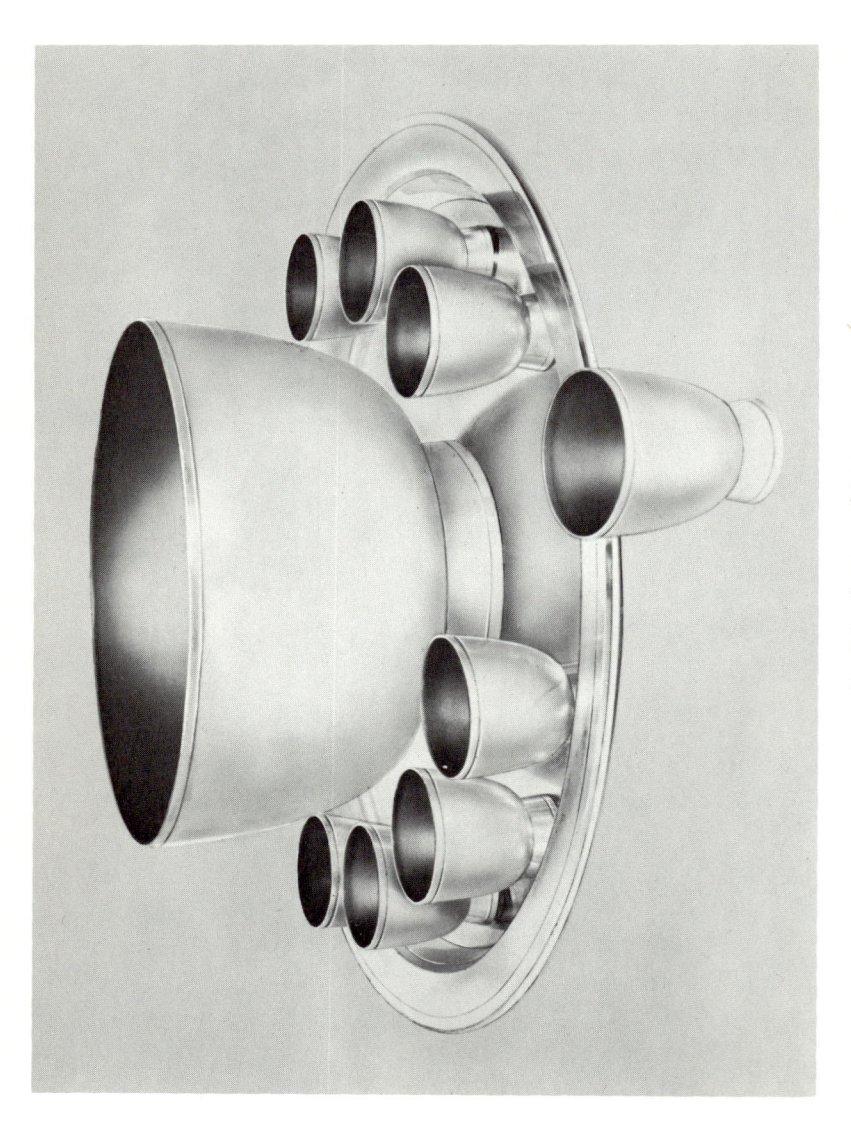

Punch bowl, cups and tray

Sterling Holloware

Sugar, cream and tray

THE JEWELERS' MANUAL

Syrup jug and tray

Sandwich plate

Sterling Holloware

Tea service

THE JEWELERS' MANUAL

Salt and pepper shakers

Vase-candlestick

Tea strainer

Sterling Holloware

Utility bowl and tray

Vegetable bowl

THE JEWELERS' MANUAL

Waiter

Well-and-tree platter

Examples of Styles for Jewelry & Silver Engraving

Examples of Styles for Jewelry & Silver Engraving

Plate 1

Block Roman and old English (60)
Cipher-script monogram (83)
Drop-cipher monogram (82)
Flourished script with acanthus leaf (80)
Modern-script adaptation (75)

Modified combination Roman script (65)
Plain old English (74)
Ribbon, shaded or threaded script (55, 67, 69)
Script inscriptions (56, 57, 63, 64, 82, 83)
Shaded old English (54, 73, 77)

Copyright by V. C. Bergling 1917, 1919, 1944, 1946, 1950. By permission of copyright owner.

THE JEWELERS' MANUAL

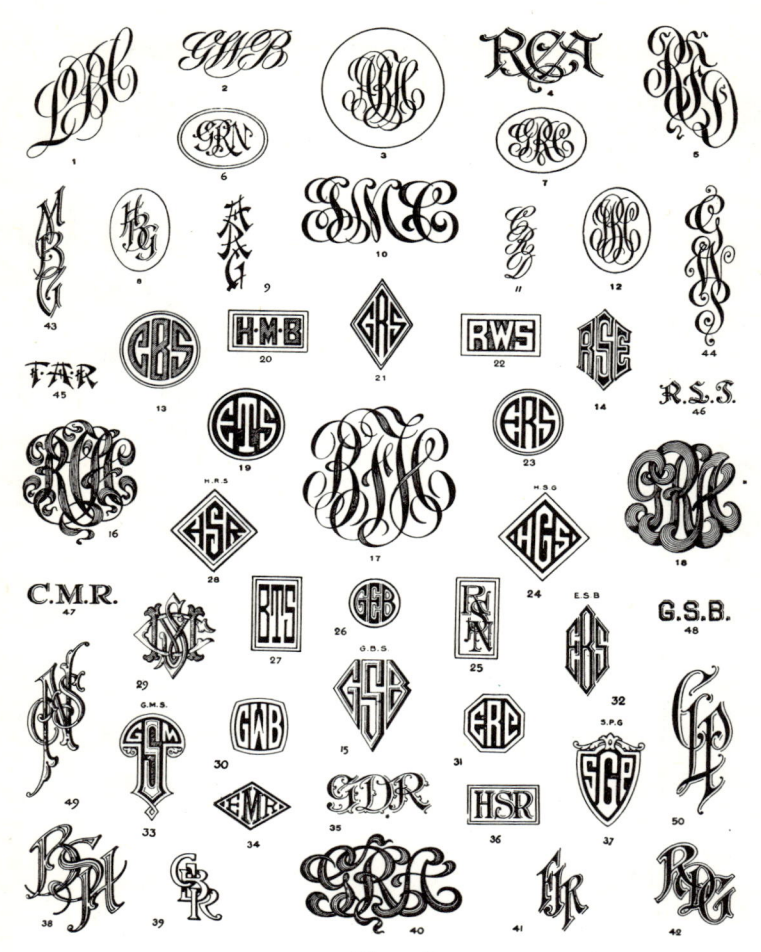

Plate II

Block—plain, fancy, modied (13, 15, 19, 20, 21, 22, 23, 24, 27, 30, 31, 32, 33, 34, 37, 48)
Ciphers—script (1, 2, 3, 5, 7, 10, 12, 16, 17, 18, 40)
Combination of styles, designed by engraver (6, 35, 42, 46, 50)
Dropped-letter monograms (9, 11, 43, 44)
Fancy capitals, sometimes called illuminated capitals when background is engraved (19, 22, 24, 29, 31, 33, 37)
Oriental—Chinese style (9, 45)
Ribbon monograms, entwined ribbon or shaded ciphers (16, 17, 18, 40)
Roman—plain, fancy, modified (4, 8, 14, 25, 26, 28, 36, 38, 39, 41, 43, 47, 49, 50)
Script—plain and flourished (1, 2, 3, 5, 7, 10, 11, 12, 16, 17, 18, 40, 44)
Shaded (10, 13, 14, 16, 17, 18, 20, 40)
Slanted drop-letter monograms, up or down (1, 5, 8, 25, 38, 39, 41, 42, 49, 50)

Ornaments & Designs

Ornaments & Designs

Acanthus	Composite	Corinthian

Cartouche	Cockleshell	Anthemion	Baluster

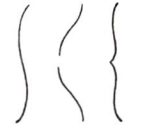

Cyma curves	Egg & tongue	Egg & dart	Doric

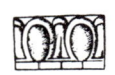

Engine turning	Feather edge	Fiddle pattern	Filigree

THE JEWELERS' MANUAL

Fluting

Francis I influence

Gadroon border

Key

Ionic

Gothic arch

Lotus

Medallion & rosette

Palm

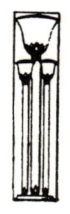

Papyrus

Rococo

Shell

Strap work

Swag

Tuscan

180

Watches and Clocks

How a Watch Works

A watch movement can be divided roughly into five sections: (1) the *mainspring*, which is the powerplant; (2) the *train wheels*, which deliver power to the escapement; (3) the *escapement*, which permits the slow, uniform dissipation of that power, permitting it to move the hands; (4) the *balance assembly*, which is the governor of the watch, since it governs, or controls, the timekeeping; (5) the *mechanism under the dial*, which carries the hands.

The mainspring is a long, thin ribbon of steel or steel alloy; it is coiled inside a container called the *mainspring barrel*. In the conventional watch, the outer end of the mainspring is hooked to the inside wall of the barrel and the inner end is hooked to the mainspring arbor. As the mainspring is wound, it is coiled tightly around the arbor. The spring is constantly trying to return to its original stretched-out position, and this stored energy furnishes the power to run the watch. Since the outer end of the spring is hooked to the mainspring barrel, it will turn the barrel, if it is permitted to do so. The outer rim of the barrel has teeth that engage with the pinion of the center wheel; this passes the power of the mainspring to the center wheel.

The center wheel and the three other wheels make up the train of the conventional watch; they pass the power from one to the other. Each wheel is driven by the preceding one. There is a definite gear ratio between each pair of wheels; this ratio reduces the powerful pull of the mainspring to a more controllable level, which is delivered to the escapement. When the watch is running, these wheels turn at a definite rate. In the conventional watch, the center wheel turns once each hour, and its lengthened arbor protrudes through the center of the dial and carries the minute hand. The fourth wheel turns once each minute and its arbor carries the seconds hand. In the unconventional watches or those having a center sweep-seconds hand, the gear ratio of the wheels must be changed, and often their arrangement in the movement must be changed to permit the wheels that carry the hands to turn at a given rate.

The first member of the escapement is the *escape wheel*, which is also the last wheel of the train. The other member of the escapement is the *fork*, which, when the watch is running, swings from side to side and permits one tooth of the escape wheel to "escape" at a time. The "ticktock" sound that is heard is produced by the escape-wheel striking the *pallet stones* of the fork. The pallet stones are two small rectangular blocks of synthetic ruby or sapphire, so placed in the arms of the fork that they lock the teeth of the escape wheel and permit only one tooth to pass at a time. The faces of the pallet stones and the faces of the escape-wheel teeth are cut at such an angle that as the tooth passes over the face of the pallet stone it delivers an impulse of power, or thrust, to the fork. This impulse is transmitted to the balance by the other end of the fork and swings the balance wheel.

The balance assembly consists of the *balance wheel*, the *hairspring* and the *roller*, which carries the *roller jewel*. The layman may look at a balance wheel in motion and believe that it is going around and around; actually, however, it is only swinging part of the way around, stopping, and then swinging back the other way. This action takes place so rapidly that the wheel appears to be in constant motion. When the balance wheel is at rest, as when the mainspring is run down and no power is being applied to the train wheels, the roller jewel is in a direct line between the arbor of the balance wheel and the fork arbor and is in the slot in the end of the fork.

When the watch is in motion, the fork is held to one side and the pallet stone is holding the escape wheel to keep it from turning. As the balance wheel swings, the roller jewel comes back to the center position, enters the fork slot, and moves the fork to the other side. When this happens, one of the teeth of the escape wheel "escapes," permitting the entire train of wheels to move; at the same time, that tooth gives an impulse of power to the pallet stone. That impulse is passed down the fork and delivered to the roller jewel and balance assembly, sending it on another swing through its arc of motion. It swings until its inertia is overcome by the increasing tension of the hairspring; then it stops and swings back the other way, propelled by the hairspring.

In the conventional watch, this happens eighteen thousand times an hour (three hundred times each minute, five times each second), and the watch is spoken of as an 18,000-*beat watch*. The number of beats an hour is arrived at by setting up a ratio of hairspring strength in relation to the weight of the balance wheel. This ratio must be such that it brings the roller jewel back to the line of centers in the exact fraction of a second necessary to permit the watch to beat exactly five times a second. If it beats faster than that and has a *gaining rate*, it will be necessary to either increase the length of the hairspring or to add weight to the rim of the balance wheel.

Just the reverse is true if the watch has a *losing rate*. If the difference in time is only a few minutes a day, the rate can be changed by moving the regulator. The regulator has a pair of closely spaced, parallel pins that straddle the hairspring; moving them toward or away from the outer end of the hairspring lengthens or shortens its effective length, thus slowing or speeding the timekeeping of the watch.

The *dial train,* or series of wheels and pinions under the dial, provides the parts that carry the minute and hour hands. The minute hand is carried by the arbor of the center wheel of the watch. In order to provide the twelve-to-one gear ratio that is necessary for one hand to make one turn around the dial while the other goes around twelve times, a series of flat wheels and pinions is provided. The wheel that carries the hour hand fits loosely over the pinion that carries the minute hand, so that one can turn freely inside the other. One protrudes a bit farther from the dial than the other, so that the hands can be sandwiched over one another and not touch the dial, the crystal, or one another as they pass.

Factors Contributing to Quality

The quality of a movement can vary from the cheaply made, poorly finished one with seven jewels (or no jewels at all) to the beautifully finished, fully jeweled one found in better watches. To generalize, the quality of finish tends to vary in proportion to the price of a watch. In all but the cheapest, the parts are well finished and plated. There are no rough edges where the recesses have been milled out on the plates. There are no burrs left from the milling process or from drilling or tapping the holes in the plates. The *steady pins,* which hold the plates in proper alignment, fit into the proper holes without having to be forced and permit disassembly without unnecessary prying. The plates are often *damaskeened* (a circular decoration produced by grinding the surface with abrasive end-laps, rotated in a hand tool or in automatic machines). The jewels are properly aligned and correctly set, so that the arbors that fit between them have the correct endshake and freedom of movement. The winding and setting parts are well finished and function smoothly. Accomplishing these things involves considerable handwork in the manufacturing process; naturally, the more of it that is done, the higher is the cost of the movement.

The quality of cases varies from the thin, poorly assembled stamped-out ones to the heavier ones of gold-filled material, karat gold or platinum. Here, again, the amount of labor involved in manufacture, plus the cost of the material, determines the cost of the end product. Some poorly made cases are so thin that they can be twisted and warped by the hand,

and will sometimes do so if they are strapped too tightly to the wearer's wrist. The two sections do not fit tightly and let dust into the movement. Although these are gradations, in general, the heavier, well-made cases are assembled with such precision that the line where the two parts fit together is hardly noticeable. Design plays an important part, too; a good-quality case has artistic merit.

The bracelet or other attachment should not only hold the watch safely on the wrist but should add to its appearance. The quality and design should match that of the watch. If it has a clasp or catch or other moving parts, they should function properly and smoothly.

Wearing a Watch to Bed

This should not be done, if it is a conventional watch and does not have a sealed case that keeps out the small particles of lint; otherwise, it will have to be cleaned more often.

The Meaning of Jewels

Most of the jewels in a watch are bearings for *pivots*. There are three jewels that are not bearings but are placed at certain contact points to reduce friction: the *roller jewel,* which is in the balance assembly, and the two *pallet stones* in the fork. The jewels are made of synthetic ruby or sapphire, because their hardness permits a high polish. By polishing the pivots that run in the jewels, friction is reduced to a minimum; naturally, the less the friction, the smoother the watch runs.

The 17-jewel watch is considered a fully jeweled watch. The pivots of all the train wheels, as well as the pivots of the escapement and balance wheel, run in jeweled bearings. A 21-jewel watch has additional jewels, usually *cap jewels*, which limit the endshake of certain wheels; these permit assembling the watch to closer tolerances and, by reducing friction, permit better timekeeping. Most of the 23- and 25-jewel watches now on the market are self-winding. The additional jewels are placed in the self-winding unit to reduce wear and lengthen the life of the unit.

Winding a Watch

A watch should be wound fully, as far as possible, once each twenty-four hours. There is no danger of overwinding a watch. Modern watches have a ratchet that permits the ratchet wheel to turn back a fraction after the winding pressure is released from the crown. It is commonly known as a *recoiling click*, and releases a bit of the pressure applied to the end of the mainspring when it is fully wound.

The mainspring of a modern watch will keep it running for at least thirty hours after being wound. There is always a reserve of several hours, to take care of the person who forgets to wind his watch at the same time each day. It is best to wind a watch in the morning or at the beginning of the work day. The timekeeping is less affected by the shocks received while being worn when it is fully wound than when it is almost run down. If the watch stops when it is fully wound, it is because something else stopped it, not because of the winding.

Self-Winding Watches

A self-winding watch is wound by a weight that is pivoted at the center of the movement; it swings from side to side as the watch is moved. A series of wheels, reversers, pinions and ratchets changes this swinging motion to a rotary motion. The last pinion of this series engages with the mainspring ratchet wheel and the watch is wound each time the weight moves. It takes several hours of wear to wind the watch fully; when it is wound completely, it has the same reserve of running time as the ordinary watch. It should run for twenty-four hours without being worn, and it can be laid aside at night and still be running in the morning, just as a regular watch.

To keep pressure from being applied to the mainspring after it is wound fully, it is equipped with a safety device. The outer end of the mainspring is not attached to the inner wall of the mainspring barrel, as in the regular watch, but is attached to a bridle that slips and releases a bit of the tension of the mainspring, if it is wound past the desirable maximum.

Some self-winding watches have a rotor that swings through an arc of about 270 degrees; its motion is stopped at each end of its swing by a small bumper spring. Other designs have no bumper springs; the rotor swings around completely in either direction, winding constantly, regardless of the direction in which the rotor swings. These are spoken of as 360-*degree rotors*, or the watch is called a *360-degree-winding watch*.

Most self-winding watches have the conventional winding mechanism, in addition to the self-winding unit, and can be wound with the crown. This takes care of those times when the watch has run down as a result of not being worn for a period of time.

"Shockproof" Watches

The term "shockproof" was outlawed by a May, 1947, FTC order, but the terms *shock resistant* and *shock absorbing* are permitted under certain circumstances.

The balance jewels of a shock-resistant movement are usually held in place by springs that permit a slight movement when the watch is dropped or suffers a blow; this prevents damage to the jewels or pivots. Another type of shock-absorbing device is a balance wheel with flexible, spiral arms (spokes).

Naturally, there is a limit to the amount of shock a watch can absorb. These shock-absorbing devices, however, take care of most shocks received in normal wear; occasionally, they have been known to survive extreme blows or falls.

Antimagnetic Watches

Most modern watches, especially those of better quality, have a hairspring and balance made of an alloy that will not retain magnetism; they are spoken of as being *antimagnetic*. In the early days of watches, the hairsprings were made of steel, which could become magnetized. This would upset the timekeeping of the watch, because the coils of the hairspring would stick together.

Waterproof Watches

Under the terms of a Federal Trade Commission directive, a watch, in order to be called *waterproof*, must pass certain immersion tests. It also must be stated that removal of the back of the case or crystal may again render the watch nonwaterproof.

The sections of a waterproof watchcase are sealed with a gasket that keeps the moisture out. The crown also has an inner gasket that fits tightly against the pendant tube of the case and seals the opening. As long as these seals, or gaskets, function properly, the case will remain waterproof. If the gasket in the crown becomes worn from the wear it receives when the watch is wound every day, it may permit dust and moisture to leak past into the movement. If the gasket that seals the back of the case is broken or distorted when the case is opened, or if it ages and loses its pliability, moisture may reach the movement. The crystals of waterproof cases are usually made of a plastic material and set into the bezel with a press, so that they constantly exert pressure against the bezel. If the crystal shrinks with age, moisture may be permitted to pass; this is also true if the crystal is damaged. The crown, the crystal and the back gasket should be replaced whenever the presence of moisture is suspected.

There is always some air inside the case, and since that air expands when heated and contracts when chilled, there is a movement of air into and out of the case. That movement of air is small; if it occurs, however, it may eventually move some moisture into the case. Sometimes, that small amount of moisture becomes visible on the inside of the crystal when the watch is exposed to a cool temperature, as on a chilly morning. It then condenses on the inner surface of the crystal but disappears, or vaporizes, when the watch becomes warmer. It is inside the case, though, and may produce rust.

Round Versus Square Watches

Round and square watches have the same number of parts and the same general arrangement of parts. The working parts of a fancy-shaped movement are merely arranged differently and the bridges are shaped differently, so that the movement fits into a fancy-shaped case. Sometimes, too, a round movement will be put into a square or rectangular case; this is often done with a self-winding movement, since the rotor swings in a circle and this kind of a movement is usually round in shape.

Chronographs

This is a watch with a center-seconds hand that may be started at zero, stopped to record the time of an event, then returned to zero by operating a button on the outside of the watchcase. It also has the ordinary hour and minute hands, and usually the ordinary seconds hand.

Chronometers

A chronometer is a highly accurate timepiece used for navigation or other purposes requiring extremely precise timekeeping.

Swiss Versus American Watches

Both Swiss and American manufacturers make watches of various qualities. A Swiss watch has no advantage over an American watch, if the two are in the same quality bracket. The two would probably retail for about the same price, too. Swiss manufacturers, however, make many unusual kinds of timepieces, such as chronographs and other special-purpose watches that are not made in America.

The usual Swiss watch is styled just about the same as the American watch, and neither is more difficult to repair than the other. Repair parts can be obtained for Swiss timepieces from any watch-material supply house. Swiss manufacturers make certain that the countries that buy their products are also well supplied with parts.

The Meaning of "Adjusting to Position"

This means adjusting a watch to obtain the nearest possible uniformity of timekeeping in the various positions it may assume in use. A railroad-grade pocketwatch is adjusted to the pendant-up, pendant-left, pendant-right and dial-down positions (and sometimes to the pendant-down position also). The conventional wristwatch is adjusted to the dial-up, dial-down and pendant-down positions.

THE JEWELERS' MANUAL

Cleaning

Most manufacturers recommend a yearly cleaning. If a watch is worn in a very dusty environment or in high temperatures, it should be cleaned more often. Very small watches require more frequent cleaning than larger ones.

The average-size man's wristwatch has a balance wheel that is approximately three-eighths of an inch in diameter. In the widely used standard "train," the balance wheel makes 18,000 oscillations an hour, or 157,680,000 oscillations a year! In one year, the rim of the balance wheel, if it were in contact with the ground and had maintained an even speed, would have traveled 2931 linear miles, or a distance about equal to that from New York to San Francisco! And this great distance would have been covered without any additional lubrication to the balance-wheel pivots, which are the axes of the balance wheel. If this wheel were as large as that of a locomotive, the distance traveled in a year under the conditions listed above would be equal to twenty-eight times around the earth.

Watches are currently being manufactured with fast trains that beat as high as 600 beats per minute or 36,000 beats per hour. Fast train watches are capable of greater timekeeping accuracy than watches of the conventional 18,000 beat.

In any piece of machinery with moving parts, friction develops and with all of man's inventive genius, no method of eliminating friction entirely has yet been devised. Oils of various kinds that produce a microscopic film between two moving parts have been found to reduce friction materially; however, in due time, the volatile components of the oil evaporate and the residue becomes dirty and gummy.

In a watch, the finely polished pivots and bearing jewels are designed to reduce friction, and the cap jewels, in a sense, serve as small oil reservoirs. Yet, despite all precautions, the oil in a watch gradually becomes dry, even when it is not running. In an automobile, several quarts of oil are required, whereas several watches can be lubricated with an amount of oil the size of a pinhead!

It has been found necessary to equip a watch with a motive power (the mainspring) that is capable of driving the entire train, or a series of wheels, for twenty-four hours or more. As a result, the mainspring continues to make the watch run, even against the friction that develops, long after the minute quantity of oil has become dry or lost effectiveness. This causes wear on the moving parts, with resultant damage. If this condition is allowed to exist over a period of time, the movement is eventually ruined.

Watches & Clocks

The Electric Watch

The electric watch is actually a miniature electric motor that can be carefully adjusted to run at a predetermined speed. It makes possible the elimination of the mainspring; therefore, it requires no winding. Its power source is a tiny energy cell, or battery, about the size of a man's shirt button. The cell is rated at 1.5 volts, and has an average life of more than one year. Since the power from this cell is almost constant, the watch is capable of exceptional accuracy.

The balance assembly carries a coil that is impulsed electrically and works in conjunction with two permanent magnets. A combination contact wheel and index wheel and a half-gold/half-jewel pin perform the double duty of making the electrical contact and advancing the train. This wheel is a four-piece assembly: an index pinion, an index hub, a contact wheel, and index wheel. The index pinion is insulated from the hub. Current flows from the energy cell, through the cell lead, the end piece, the lower pivot of the index wheel, to the contact wheel.

As the balance assembly turns counterclockwise, the gold side of the half-gold/half-jewel pin contacts the contact wheel, closing the circuit. Current then flows through the gold half of the pin and the wire "pigtail" to the coil. The current passes through the coil, energizing it, then returns through the coil attachment, the balance, the hairspring, the balance bridge and pillar plate to the positive side of the energy cell.

In addition to closing the circuit while the balance is turning counterclockwise, the gold side of the half-gold/half-jewel pin advances the index wheel; it is a steel wheel fastened to the lower side of the platinum contact wheel. The indexing action is completed and the wheels are held in their proper rest position by two small permanent magnets beneath the index wheel. The index wheel is advanced one tooth for each counterclockwise swing of the balance. The train and hands are caused to rotate by means of this indexing action.

On the clockwise swing, the balance is merely returning. The jewel side of the half-gold/half-jewel pin trips past a tooth of the contact wheel without changing teeth of the index wheel over the index magnets and no electrical contact is made, since the jewel side of the pin is a nonconductor of electricity.

The parts of this contact system are made so that adjustments are unnecessary; in fact, adjustments cannot be made.

The Electronic Watch

The electronic watch is a timekeeper that depends on a mathematically

THE JEWELERS' MANUAL

precise instrument known as a *tuning fork,* such as those used as basic frequency standards for various kinds of precision measurements. In this watch, the balance wheel and escapement mechanism are eliminated.

The source of energy in the watch is a *power cell,* which provides power to an electronic circuit and converts the energy of the cell from direct current to pulses of current; these pulses drive the tuning fork. One tine of the fork is linked, by a ratchet-and-pawl indexing mechanism, to a conventional gear train, which drives the hands.

The Parts of a Watch Mechanism

Illustrations courtesy Elgin National Watch Co., Elgin, Ill.

1. Sweep-seconds hand
2. Minute hand
3. Hour hand
4. Dial
5. Dial-foot screw
6. Hour wheel
7. Cannon pinion
8. Sweep-seconds cock
9. Sweep-seconds cock screw
10. Sweep-seconds pinion
11. Sweep-seconds spring
12. Sweep-seconds wheel
13. Main wheel
14. Main screw
15. Main-wheel washer
16. Ratchet wheel
17. Ratchet-wheel screw
18. Click
19. Click screw
20. Click spring
21. Regulator
22. Balance cock
23. Balance-cock screw
24. Hairspring (complete)
25. Hairspring-stud screw
26. One-piece double roller (complete)
27. Balance wheel
28. Balance staff
29. Upper-balance-jewel dome
30. Jewel-assembly retainer
31. Endstone, or cap jewel
32. Holding spring
33. Balance hole jewel
34. Pallet bridge
35. Pallet-bridge screw
36. Pallet hole jewel
37. Pallet fork and arbor
38. Barrel bridge
39. Barrel-bridge screw
40. Barrel cover
41. Barrel arbor
42. Mainspring
43. Barrel
44. Center wheel (complete)
45. Third wheel (complete)
46. Train bridge
47. Train-bridge screw
48. Fourth wheel (complete)
49. Escape wheel (complete)
50. Winding arbor, or stem (with crown)
51. Bevel, or winding, pinion
52. Winding and setting clutch
53. Minute-wheel clamp
54. Minute-wheel clamp screw
55. Clutch lever
56. Clutch-lever spring
57. Minute wheel
58. Setting wheel
59. Setting-lever screw
60. Setting lever
61. Lower-balance-jewel clamp
62. Lower-balance clamp screw
63. Holding spring
64. Endstone, or cap jewel
65. Balance hole jewel (set)
66. Lower, or pillar, plate

Watches & Clocks

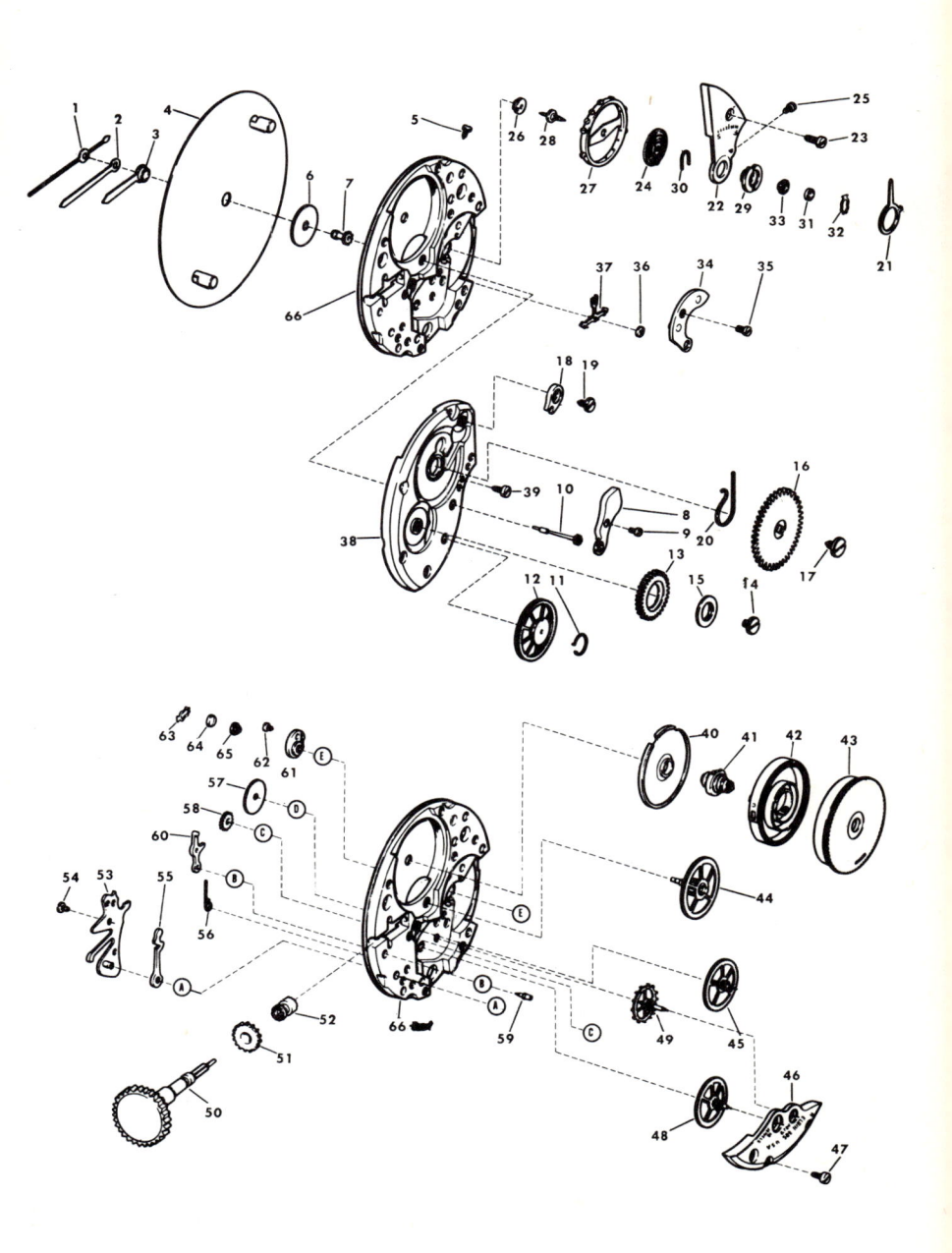

191

THE JEWELERS' MANUAL

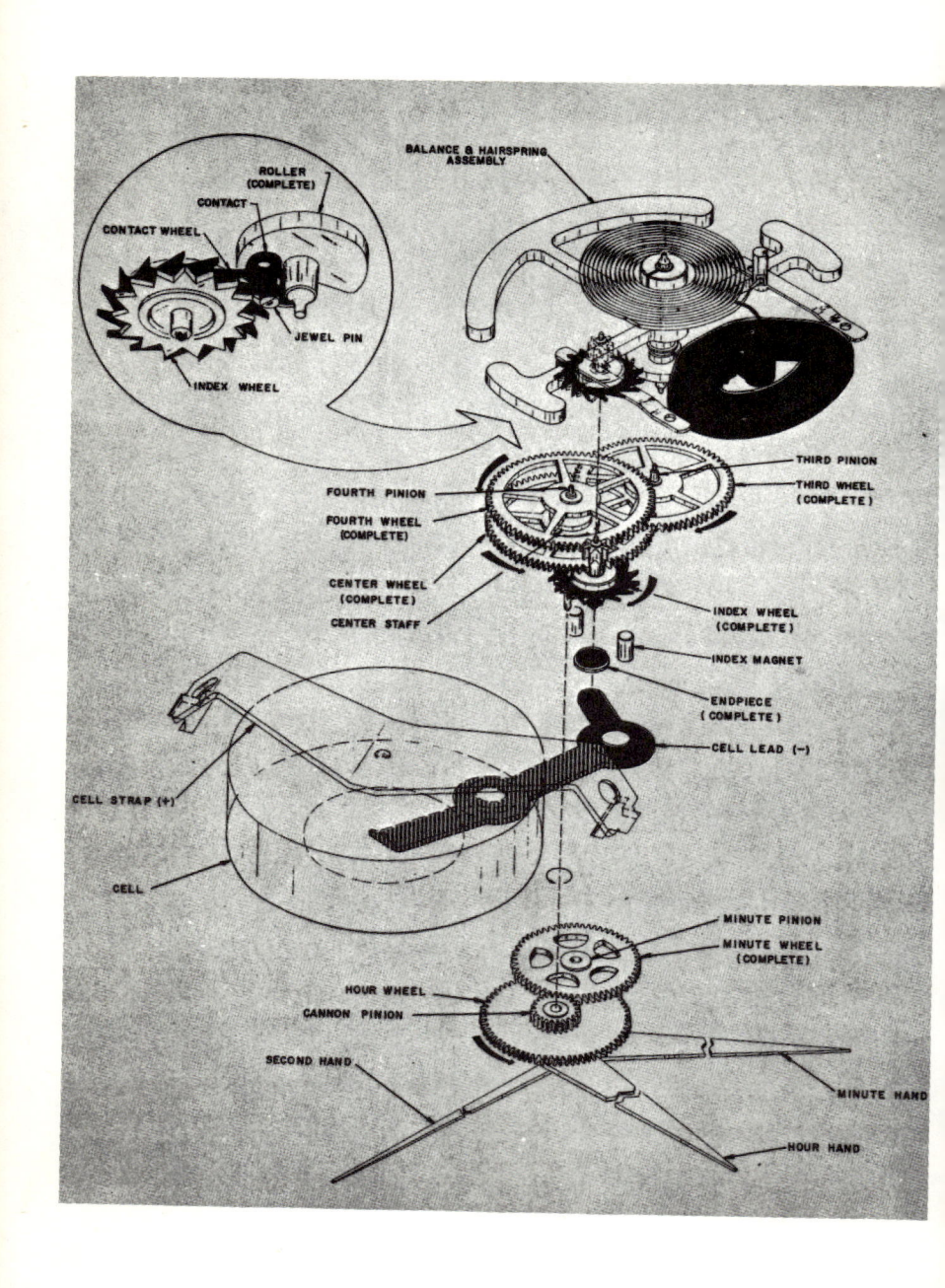

Modern Watch Hands & Their Names

Illustrations courtesy B. Jadow, Inc., New York City

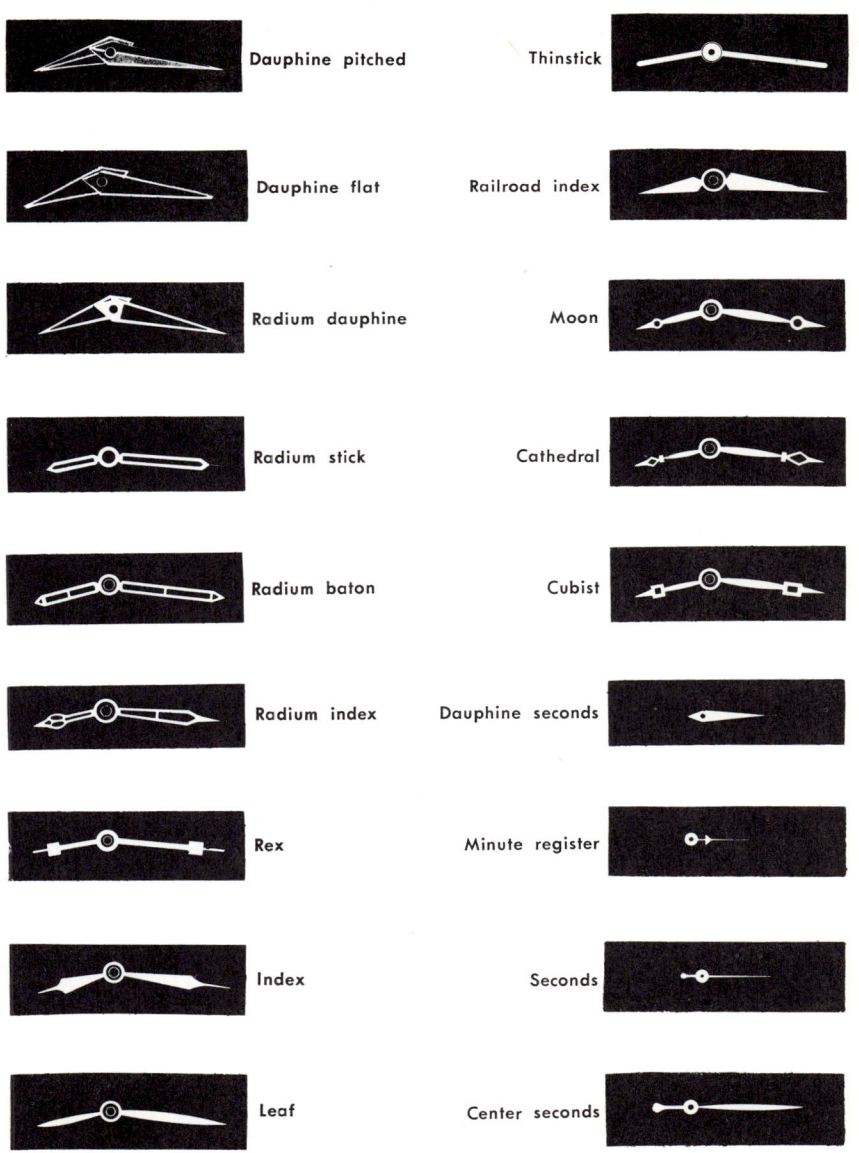

	Dauphine pitched	Thinstick	
	Dauphine flat	Railroad index	
	Radium dauphine	Moon	
	Radium stick	Cathedral	
	Radium baton	Cubist	
	Radium index	Dauphine seconds	
	Rex	Minute register	
	Index	Seconds	
	Leaf	Center seconds	

THE JEWELERS' MANUAL

Watch Sizes

The *Lancashire gauge* for determining watch sizes is of English origin and is the standard commonly used by American watch manufacturers. By this system, 1 5/30 inches was taken as a base figure and was called *naught* (0) size. Every 1/30 of an inch added *increased* the size by one number; every substraction of 1/30 of an inch *decreased* the size by one number. The size of a watch is determined by its width through the center at the narrowest part of the dial side of the lower plate. The following table shows Lancashire-gauge watch sizes in terms of fractions of inches, decimal inches, lignes and millimeters:

Watch Size	Fractions of Inches	Decimal Inches	Lignes	Millimeters
18	1 23/30	1.767	19.89	44.87
17	1 22/30	1.733	19.52	44.03
16	1 21/30	1.700	19.14	43.18
15	1 20/30	1.667	18.77	42.33
14	1 19/30	1.633	18.39	41.49
13	1 18/30	1.600	18.01	40.64
12	1 17/30	1.567	17.64	39.79
11	1 16/30	1.533	17.26	38.95
10	1 15/30	1.500	16.89	38.09
9	1 14/30	1.467	16.51	37.25
8	1 13/30	1.433	16.14	36.41
7	1 12/30	1.400	15.76	35.56
6	1 11/30	1.367	15.39	34.71
5	1 10/30	1.333	15.01	33.87
4	1 9/30	1.300	14.64	33.02
3	1 8/30	1.267	14.26	32.17
2	1 7/30	1.233	13.88	31.33
1	1 6/30	1.200	13.51	30.48
0	1 5/30	1.167	13.14	29.63
2/0	1 4/30	1.133	12.67	28.79
3/0	1 3/30	1.100	12.38	27.94
4/0	1 2/30	1.067	12.01	27.09
5/0	1 1/30	1.033	11.63	26.25
6/0	1	1.000	11.26	25.40
7/0	29/30	.967	10.88	24.55
8/0	28/30	.933	10.51	23.71
9/0	27/30	.900	10.13	22.86
10/0	26/30	.867	9.76	22.01
11/0	25/30	.833	9.38	21.17
12/0	24/30	.800	9.00	20.32
13/0	23/30	.767	8.63	19.47

Watches & Clocks

Watch Size	Fractions of Inches	Decimal Inches	Lignes	Millimeters
14/0	22/30	.733	8.26	18.63
15/0	21/30	.700	7.88	17.78
16/0	20/30	.667	7.51	16.93
17/0	19/30	.633	7.13	16.09
18/0	18/30	.600	6.76	15.24
19/0	17/30	.567	6.38	14.39
20/0	16/30	.533	6.00	13.55
21/0	15/30	.500	5.63	12.70
22/0	14/30	.467	5.25	11.85
23/0	13/30	.433	4.88	11.01
24/0	12/30	.400	4.50	10.16
25/0	11/30	.367	4.13	9.31
26/0	10/30	.333	3.75	8.47

Comparative values of measurement standards: 1 inch = 25.4 millimeters; 1 millimeter = .03937 inch; 1 ligne = 2.25 millimeters.

THE JEWELERS' MANUAL

Basic Shapes & Kinds of Clocks

Photos courtesy Cuckoo Clock Mfg. Co., Inc., New York City; Chelsea Clock Co., Chelsea, Mass.; Henry Coehler Co., Inc., New York City; Hanson Clock Mfg. Co., Rockford, Ill.; Sessions Clock Co., Forestville, Conn.

Antique wall grandfather clock

Banjo clock

Basic Shapes & Kinds of Clocks

Cuckoo clock

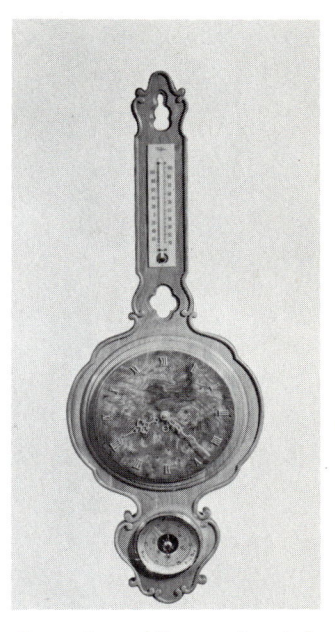

Barometer-and-thermometer clock

400-day clock

THE JEWELERS' MANUAL

Grandfather clock

Grandmother clock

Basic Shapes & Kinds of Clocks

Travel alarm clock

Electric alarm clock

Mantle clock

Tambourine clock

199

Trade Associations

Allied Silversmiths' Association, Inc., 53 W. 56th St., New York City 19.
American Fine-China Guild, Box 229, Nyack, N. Y.
American Gem Society, 3142 Wilshire Blvd., Los Angeles 5, Calif.
American Stone Importers' Association, Inc., 48 W. 48th St., New York, N.Y.
American Watch Association, Inc., 39 Broadway, New York City 6.
American Watchmakers' Institute, Inc., 608½ E. Green St., Champaign, Ill.
Appraisers' Association of America, 22 W. 48th St., New York City.
Canadian Jewellers' Association, 800 Bay St., Toronto 5, Ont., Canada.
China, Glass & Giftware Board of Trade, Inc., 71 W. 23rd St., New York City 10.
China, Glass & Pottery Association of America, Inc., 71 W. 23rd St., New York City 10.
Cigarette Lighter Manufacturers' Association, 303 Fifth Ave., New York City 16.
Clock Assemblers' & Importers' Association, Inc., 1261 Broadway, New York City 1.
Costume-Jewelry Board of Trade of New York, 303 Fifth Ave., New York City 1.
Cultured-Pearl Association of America, Inc., 22 W. 48th St., New York, N.Y.
Diamond Manufacturers' & Importers' Association of America, Inc., 342 Madison Ave., New York City 17.
Eastern Manufacturers' & Importers' Exhibit, Inc., 220 Fifth Ave., New York City 1.
Educational Jewelry Manufacturers' Association, 41 E. 42nd St., New York City 17.
Fountain-Pen & Mechanical-Pencil Manufacturers' Association, Inc., 1426 G St., NW, Washington 5, D. C.
Gemological Institute of America, 11940 San Vicente Blvd., Los Angeles 49, Calif.

Trade Associations

Gem Trade Laboratory of GIA, 580 Fifth Ave., New York City 36.

Gold-Filled Manufacturers' Association, 220 Bates Bldg., Attleboro, Mass.

Industrial-Diamond Association of America, Inc., 24 W. 43rd St., New York, N.Y. 10036.

Jewelers' Board of Trade, Inc., 24 Baker St., Providence, R.I. 02905. York, N.L.

Jewelers' Security Alliance of the United States, 535 Fifth Ave., New York City 17.

Jewelers' Vigilance Committee, Inc., 41 E. 42nd St., New York, N.Y. 10017.

Jewelry Industry Council, 608 Fifth Ave., New York City 20.

Jewelry-Industry Tax Committee, 8575 Georgia Ave., Silver Springs, Md.

Jewelry Manufacturers' Association, Inc., 535 Fifth Ave., New York, N.Y. 10017.

Machine-Chain Manufacturers' Association, 735 Allens Ave., Providence, R. I.

Manufacturing Jewelers & Silversmiths of America, Inc., S75, Sheraton-Biltmore Hotel, Providence, R.I.

Manufacturing Jewelers' Sales Association, Inc., 50 Chestnut St., Providence, R. I.

Metal-Findings Manufacturers' Association, 91 Hartford St., Providence, R. I.

National Association of Costume Jewelers, 303 Fifth Ave., New York City 16.

National Association of Watch & Clock Collectors, Box 33, Columbia, Pa.

National Gift & Art Association, 220 Fifth Ave., New York City 1.

National Wholesale Jewelers' Association, 1900 Arch St., Philadelphia 3, Pa.

Platinumsmiths' Association of New York, Inc., 580 Fifth Ave., New York City 36.

Retail Jewelers of America, Inc., 1025 Vermont Ave., N.W., Washington, D.C. 20005.

Silver-Users' Association, 1725 K St., NW, Washington 6, D. C.

Sterling Silversmiths' Guild of America, 551 Fifth Ave., New York City 17.

THE JEWELERS' MANUAL

United Jewelry Show, Room 1856, Sheraton-Biltmore Hotel, Providence, R. I.

United States Potters' Association; Taylor, Smith & Taylor; E. Liverpool, Ohio.

Watch-Material Distributors' Association of America, Inc., 2135 Wisconsin Ave., N.W., Washington, D.C. 20007.

Watchmakers of Switzerland Information Center, Inc., 730 Fifth Ave. New York City 19.

American Gem Society

The AGS is a professional society of fine jewelers, numbering 900 firms and 1800 individuals in the United States and Canada. Its purpose is to promote high standards of business ethics and encourage gemological education among its members for the protection of the public, while furthering the growth of the fine-jewelry business. Members must adhere to the rulings of the Better Business Bureau, the Federal Trade Commission, and the Society's own code of conduct.

To implement the understanding between retail jeweler and the public, the American Gem Society prepares and distributes informative pamphlets, educational displays, and other aids on the subjects of diamonds and colored stones of every kind. Special advertising aids include a national magazine campaign and retail ad mats, designed for the exclusive use of members. The Society awards the titles of *Registered Jeweler* and *Certified Gemologist* to qualified members and firms. Established 1934.

Headquarters: 3142 Wilshire Blvd., Los Angeles 5, Calif.

American Stone Importers' Association, Inc.

The Precious-Stone Dealers' Association, Inc., was founded in April of 1930 and was known under that name until August of 1946, when the name was changed to its present one. It was felt that the new title was more descriptive of its members.

The principal function of the ASIA is to correct and improve conditions in the industry. Its purposes are to see that tariff laws are equitable; that nomenclature of stones is correct, both from an academic and a commercial standpoint; that smuggling is eliminated; that any deceptive practices of merchants are exposed; that the industry knows there are three classes of stones: genuine, synthetic and imitation; that the industry, both here and abroad, be kept aware of the organization's existence through advertising activities; and that any matter pertaining to stones be referred to the Association.

Trade Associations

The ASIA is strictly a trade group and does not indulge in any business enterprises. It cooperates with the United States Government and other governments whenever requested.

Membership includes firms that import approximately 90% of the synthetic and genuine stones to the United States.

Headquarters: 10 W. 47th St., New York City 36.

American Watch Association, Inc.

The American Watch Association, Inc., is a trade association for firms engaged in the importation of watches and watch movements.

The primary purpose of the AWA is to promote the general welfare of all importers, assemblers and processors of imported watches, cases, movements and parts, as well as to assist wholesalers and jobbers of these products. Its objective is to stimulate the growth of the industry, by obtaining a wider market for its products, and to attempt to correct abuses and unfair trade practices.

The Association disseminates information and statistics concerning the industry, to enable its members to conduct their business more intelligently. It works toward standardization of customs and usages within the trade and aims at maintaining a high consistent standard of product, in order to render better service to the buying public.

Through a continuing information program, the organization attempts to obtain improved public understanding concerning the role played by the industry and the position of its membership regarding pending problems and issues.

A fundamental activity of the Association is to cooperate with the government in efforts to prevent watch smuggling and to apprehend those engaged in such activities.

Headquarters: 39 Broadway, New York City 6.

American Watchmakers' Institute

The AWI is a national organization owned and controlled by and for the watchmaker and watchmaker-jeweler. Its members represent all segments of the watch and jewelry industry—repairmen, jewelers, watch engineers and scientists; however, most members work at the bench, and it is for them primarily that the AWI operates. Memberships composed of individuals and entire guild and state organizations are represented in the fifty states and in many foreign countries.

The AWI attempts to raise the individual and collective standards of the watchmaking profession. It represents an opportunity for bringing about greater public recognition and respect for watchmakers, and in the long run a better economic status for those employed in the industry. It works and speaks for the watchmakers. It aims basically at bringing together men and women in the same field of endeavor for their mutual benefit through varied activities, programs and services.

The Institute conducts educational programs, to help watchmakers increase their skills; provides members with current information on the industry, to help them meet technical and economic problems; establishes recognition and awards programs; and develops public-relations programs, to give the buying public a better understanding of the watchmaker and the retail jewelry industry.

Although a watchmaker does not need to qualify for membership through examinations or certification, members are encouraged to become *Certified Master Watchmakers*, and after qualifying are given recognition as such.

Headquarters: Urbana, Ill.

Canadian Jewellers' Association

The Canadian Jewellers' Association, which includes retailers, wholesalers and manufacturers, was organized in 1918. Its primary function is that of intervention with the government at any level on behalf of the industry. A monthly bulletin keeps members informed of matters related in any way to the trade. A group health- and life-insurance plan is offered. The CJA conducts the National Jewelry-Week program and various meetings across the country among jewelers, including an annual convention.

The Canadian Jewellers' Institute, a subsidiary of the Association, conducts the Retail Jewellers' Training Course, the course in Introductory Gemmology, a library service, and an examination for qualified watchmakers that leads to a certificate.

Headquarters: 800 Bay St., Toronto 5, Ont., Canada

Cultured-Pearl Association of America

The Cultured-Pearl Association of America is an organization of cultured-pearl importers and dealers who are dedicated to maintaining quality standards for the industry; it was founded in 1956.

The purposes of the Association are as follows: to stimulate customer interest in the desirability of cultured-pearl jewelry through a program of national advertising and publicity; to establish ethical business standards for cultured-pearl importers and dealers, to which all members of the Association are committed to adhere; to educate the customer in the many aspects that determine the true value of cultured pearls, and to direct him

Trade Associations

to the recognized professional jeweler for guidance in their purchase; to remain cognizant of both the immediate and long-range interests and requirements of the retail jeweler, and work toward stabilizing the wholesale cultured-pearl market; to spotlight unfair trade practices in the advertising and sales promotion of simulated pearl-type beads, as they relate to cultured pearls, and to work to correct such practices.

Headquarters: 550 Fifth Ave., New York City 36.

Diamond Manufacturers' & Importers' Association of America, Inc.

The DMIAA is a trade organization consisting of importers, cutters and wholesalers of gem diamonds who are banded together for the betterment of the industry.

Its aims and purposes are (1) to maintain and constantly seek new methods to instill confidence of the public in diamonds, so that the United States will continue to be the largest consumer of gem diamonds in the world; (2) to maintain constant vigilance to protect the industry against discriminatory and inequitable legislation and, when possible, to sponsor favorable legislation; (3) to provide information on city, national and international levels, through frequent publications, on matters of importance affecting the everyday transactions of members; and (4) to encourage pleasant and profitable interexchange of business among members.

The various activities of the Association are carried out by committees specializing in disability and life insurance, inter-relations with other trade associations, meetings and entertainment, memorandum transactions, misleading advertising, government regulations, importers' affairs, crime prevention, public relations, labor relations, appraising, tariffs and taxes.

The Association, founded in 1932, is recognized by the U. S. Department of State, the U. S. Department of Commerce, The Chamber of Commerce and the Diamond Trading Co., Ltd., as the official organization of gem-diamond merchants in the United States.

Headquarters: 342 Madison Ave., New York City 17.

Gold-Filled Manufacturers' Association, Inc.

The Gold-Filled Manufacturers' Association, Inc., sponsors a public-relations and advertising program aimed to create an awareness of the quality of gold-filled materials and of the products made from these materials. The Association consists of contributors and members who manufacture gold-filled sheet, wire and tubing and offer it for sale to end-product manufacturers.

THE JEWELERS' MANUAL

No manufacturer of finished products, as such, may contribute to this program; this enables the association to discuss the quality image without obligation to specific items or products.

Principal among the Association's activities is creating an awareness at the manufacturing, retail and consumer levels. The first is done through personal contact and advertising. The second is accomplished through a series of correspondence courses and promotions at retail level, which fortifies sales and buying personnel with information about gold-filled products. The correspondence course is available to all appropriate personnel at no cost to themselves or their retail outlet. Third, the consumer is approached through films and publicity, which is generated principally through radio and TV media.

Headquarters: 203 Bates Bldg., Attleboro, Mass.

Industrial-Diamond Association of America, Inc.

The Industrial-Diamond Association of America, Inc., is the organization of the industrial-diamond dealers of the United States. It was organized in 1945 to promote the general welfare of the industrial-diamond industry and to distribute information among members of the Association and the users of their product. An important added function is to encourage reasearch in the industrial uses of diamonds and to distribute the results of that reasearch. The IDA encourages ethical procedures and seeks to prevent false advertising and misleading articles. It attempts to bring about standardization, by using the same standards promulgated in allied industries.

Headquarters: 587A Turnpike, Pompton Plains, N. J.

Jewelers' Board of Trade

The JBT is a mutual, nonprofit membership corporation. It was organized and is maintained to promote the interests of the jewelry industry, and particularly to provide its members with information and assistance in matters relating to credit.

The association, as it is today, is the result of the amalgamation of several large credit organizations in the jewelry field, with combined experience and activity dating back to 1874. These consolidations have brought increased efficiency, together with broadening and deepening of service to members.

The membership of the Board includes manufacturers, wholesalers and importers of jewelry and kindred lines. Its purpose is to give a highly specialized credit service to its members—a service that is broad, thorough, accurate and constant. Because it is a mutual cooperative

Trade Associations

association, it renders credit service at the lowest possible cost. It also, through certain services not confined to members only, endeavors to promote the general welfare of the jewelry industry.

The Jewelers' Board of Trade is national in its scope. Through its offices in New York City, Chicago, Providence and San Francisco, it maintains a most intimate relation with the jewelry industry in all parts of the country.

Headquarters: 413 Turks Head Bldg., Providence 3, R. I.

Jewelers' Security Alliance of the United States

The Jewelers' Security Alliance was organized on July 13, 1883. It is a mutual, nonprofit, voluntary association of jewelers. The members of the Executive Committee and the Advisory Board serve without compensation.

Applicants for membership are not elected. Every applicant is thoroughly screened before the Membership Committee gives its approval.

Insurance companies that write jewelers' block policies give a credit for membership of $2\frac{1}{2}\%$ of the premium up to $65, which the jeweler pays to insure his stock under a block policy.

Members are eligible to participate in the Alliance Group Insurance Fund, the least expensive form of life insurance available.

When membership is approved, the jeweler receives a warning sign, a reward sign and a certificate of membership to display on windows or doors, indicating that Pinkerton's National Detective Agency, Inc., is the official investigating organization.

The Alliance pays a standard reward of $100 for the arrest and conviction of a thief that commits a crime against a member; the Executive committee may pay a reward up to $5000. The JSA was instrumental in getting the FBI to investigate all jewelry crimes and not wait to be shown that the amount involved was over $5000 or that the crime involved interstate commerce.

The Alliance cooperates with all law-enforcement agencies; prevents the commission of crimes by advocating various burglar alarms and protective devices; supplies guards to traveling salesmen when suspicious circumstances arise; issues an encyclopedia to each member, explaining how to prevent the various kinds of crimes committed by jewelry thieves; sends its bimonthly house organ, the *Detector*, to each member, which contains many subjects of benefit to jewelers; and issues "flash bulletins," which, in the past, have brought about the arrest of many thieves.

When a criminal is caught, the JSA assists the prosecutor to obtain a conviction by furnishing evidence. When necessary, counsel for the

Alliance, a former assistant district attorney, appears for the member at the trial.

A representative of the JSA provides the probation officer and the sentencing judge with information concerning the record of the convicted criminal and insists that adequate punishment be imposed for the crime committed. The Alliance furnishes information to parole officers and, in many instances, opposes the release of a hardened criminal.

Annual dues range from $20 to $65, according to the inventory of the jewelers.

Headquarters: 535 Fifth Ave., New York City 17.

Jewelers' Vigilance Committee

The JVC was organized in 1913 and incorporated under the laws of New York State in 1917. It is composed of representatives of every branch of the jewelry industry. For corporate purposes, it is a membership corporation limited to sixty. Its Board of Directors comprises thirty-six men, many of whom represent the national trade associations, covering every segment of the industry.

The principal objectives of the Committee are summarized as follows: to be prepared to meet promptly any situation that imperils any broad interest of the trade; to protect the trade's prestige and endeavor to maintain public confidence in the jewelry industry, particularly the retailers; to fight any discrimination against the trade through government action; to help maintain fair competition within the industry; to develop and help maintain trade standards on the highest possible level; to assist in the prosecution of violators of the various laws, rulings and regulations pertaining to advertising, correct nomenclature and quality markings; to assist the government to combat smuggling and protect the industry from it; and to keep the trade informed of laws and regulations affecting its business.

Headquarters: 15 W. 44th St., New York City 36.

Jewelry Industry Council

The JIC is the nationwide publicity and promotional organization of the entire industry, with a membership composed of sales-minded jewelry retailers and suppliers. Its basic objective is to keep retail jewelry sales at the highest possible level. This is accomplished by the following activities:

It prepares and releases for newspapers, magazines, radio, television and other communications media a steady stream of publicity stories about the desirability of jewelry-store merchandise. These stories stress the appeal of jewelry for all gift occasions and for self-purchase.

It serves as a public-relations organization for the industry and makes available to those who request it (e.g., writers, students, government agencies, universities) facts about jewelry, jewelry products and the industry itself.

It creates and furnishes sales-promotional material for retailers, including booklets for public distribution, advertising and display ideas for newspapers, direct-mail service, radio commercials, window displays, Christmas portfolios, display cards for gift occasions, speech manuscripts, and fashion reports.

It serves as the statistical and market-research organization for the industry. Through analysis and interpretation of information in government reports, trade publications, surveys and other sources, data is collected and interpreted to help the industry grow and plan for the future.

Headquarters: 608 Fifth Ave., New York City 20.

Jewelry Manufacturers' Association, Inc.

The Jewelry Crafts Association, Inc., was merged with Associate Jewelers, Inc., on July 1, 1961, under the name of Jewelry Manufacturers' Association, Inc. The Jewelry Crafts Association, Inc., was organized in August, 1919, and Associate Jewelers, Inc., in September, 1919. The members of the Jewelry Manufacturers' Association, Inc., manufacture gold rings, mountings, findings, watchcases and platinum jewelry.

The Association is governed by a president, first vice president, second vice president, secretary, executive secretary and a board of governors.

The JMA fosters and promotes high ethical standards and integrity among its members. Its purposes are as follows: (1) to promote the interests of those persons, firms and corporations who are engaged in the business of manufacturing jewelry; (2) to regulate and adjust any problems with the members of this Association and others; (3) to prevent illegal exactions from being perpetrated against the members; (4) to bring about uniformity in relation to employment, wages and hours and sanitary conditons of labor; (5) to interchange information and establish business methods in relation to credit, financial standing of debtors and the sale, interchange and return of merchandise; (6) to act in concert in the event of failing or fraudulent debtors; and (7) to cooperate for the improvement of all conditions relating to said business and to foster, enlarge and encourage a friendly intercourse among its members and their employees and those persons with whom they have dealings.

Headquarters: 400 Madison Ave., New York City 17.

THE JEWELERS' MANUAL

Manufacturing Jewelers & Silversmiths of America, Inc.

The MJSA is the national representative of the American jewelry- and silverware-manufacturing industry. It is a nonprofit trade association, with more than five hundred coast-to-coast members. Its office is manned by a staff of three executives and two clerical assistants.

The activities of the MJSA are numerous. It has been the Washington representative of the industry for the past half century, and has been instrumental in promoting fair and effective government action on numerous issues. It coordinates a freight-transportation service, administers group-insurance programs and pension plans, sponsors a convention and industrial exposition every two years, cosponsors a jewelry show for wholesale buyers twice a year, offers training courses, publishes a monthly national magazine and a buyers' guide in four languages every two years, and conducts a foreign-trade program, which won the President's "E Award" and acts as liaison between manufacturers and other segments of the industry.

Headquarters: 207-11 Sheraton-Biltmore Hotel, Providence 2, R. I.

National Wholesale Jewelers' Association

The NWJA is a trade organization composed of firms that (1) buy and maintain stocks of jewelry and related goods, jewelers' supplies or watch material; (2) sell primarily to the retailer for the resale to the consumer; and (3) render a general distribution service to the retail jewelry trade. Its objectives are to foster and promote a feeling of fellowship and good will among its members, and on broad and equitable lines to advance the welfare of the jewelry trade in the United States; and to establish harmonious relations between manufacturer, wholesaler and retailer.

The activities of the Association are numerous. It makes frequent studies of such important subjects as salesmen's compensation, automobile expenses, memorandum- and prepaid-shipment policies, returned goods, bad-debt reserves, delinquent accounts, repairs, minimum value of orders, etc. Monthly surveys cover percentage changes in sales, inventories and cash collections. An annual study shows a dollar-gross-margin comparison and figures on operating expenses, net profit and turnover. Panel discussions at conventions feature the exchange of new ideas and business methods.

Distribution of periodic news bulletins covering current items of interest in the industry, individual-member activities, and up-to-date news of rulings, regulations and laws of the Federal Trade Commission, Department of Commerce, the Congress and other government agencies are among the other services rendered. Special attention is given to what can and cannot be done under the federal antitrust laws.

Annual dues for active members, based on an average of sales for the preceding three-year period, range from $60 to $125. There is an additional fee of $25 a year for each branch office that is listed in the membership directory and that receives all mailings sent to members.

Headquarters: 1900 Arch St., Philadelphia, 3. Pa.

Retail Jewelers of America, Inc.

The RJA is a national trade association that was formed in 1957 upon the merger of the American National Retail Jewelers' Association and the National Jewelers' Association. The purpose of the organization is to promote the general welfare, standing and prosperity of the retail jewelry industry. Forty-two state jewelers' associations are affiliated with the RJA; membership in a state association automatically establishes membership in the RJA, and vice versa, thus creating a national team for retail jewelers. The organization sponsors and manages an annual National Jewelry Trade Show in New York City.

Headquarters: 711 14th St., NW, Washington 5, D.C.

Sterling Silversmiths' Guild of America, Inc.

The Sterling Silversmiths' Guild of America was founded in 1919 as an organization uniting manufacturers of sterling silver in a common effort to maintain the traditions and standards of the ancient and honorable craft of silversmithing, and to encourage public appreciation and demand for sterling silver.

In performing this function, the Guild conducts a broad public-relations program, with emphasis on the schools. Also, it offers a wide range of dealer aids, to assist sterling retailers in the development of their business.

Headquarters: 551 Fifth Ave., New York City 17.

The Watchmakers of Switzerland Information Center, Inc.

The Watchmakers of Switzerland Information Center, Inc., established in New York in 1947, is an association whose primary function is the promotion of quality Swiss watches in the United States and Canada. In addition, it is dedicated to the service of recognized retail watch outlets and of professional watchmakers. Its members represent approximately six hundred Swiss producers of jeweled-lever watches and watch parts.

THE JEWELERS' MANUAL

Educating consumers on the quality aspects of watches and on fashion and styling, special features and technical innovations of modern Swiss timepieces is done through a continuous national publicity program.

The Watchmakers of Switzerland's trade program features various special store promotions for retailers, aimed at increasing individual storewide or communitywide sales of quality watches.

Numerous merchandising services, including a program of sales training for store personnel, are provided through a staff of regional merchandising directors.

Technical information is furnished to watchmaker-jewelers, to help maintain proficient watch service and repair facilities and to keep them fully apprised of newest developments in the industry. Technical bulletins, parts catalogs and supplements are distributed periodically. Also, special booklets and technical aids are furnished to watchmakers for use in promoting watch service to customers. The organization also functions as a consulting office on repair problems and hard-to-find parts for the trade.

Other material for promotional and merchandising use by jewelers is made available regularly; this includes displays, booklets, ad mats, films and slide kits. Supplementing such aids are consumer lecture material and a nationwide timetelling and watch-educational program for grade schools and high schools.

Another phase of the Information Center's effort consists of a continuous program of market research that is conducted regularly on various aspects of the watch business. This is part of its overall activities aimed toward the advancement of watch and jewelry retailing, which is coordinated with such industry organizations as the Retail Jewelers of America, Inc., Jewelry Industry Council, American Watchmakers' Institute, and the Watch-Material Distributors' Association of America.

Headquarters: 730 Fifth Ave., New York City 19.

Watch-Material Distributors' Association of America

The Watch-Material Distributors' Association of America is an organization of watch-material, -tool and -supply distributors, devoted to the progressive and ethical development of its industry and the preservation of fair and high standards of business conduct between its members and the entire jewelry industry.

Founded in 1946 as a nonprofit, incorporated trade association, the WMDAA has steadily endeavored to improve the standards of service and ethical trade practices between the buyers and sellers of the industry.

Trade Associations

The membership of approximately one hundred twenty-five is composed of two groups: Active Members (wholesalers) and Associate Members (who sell to the wholesalers). The associate Members are the principal manufacturers, importers and agencies for the parts and materials that are sold through the wholesalers (Active Members) to the retail jewelers and watchmakers of the United States. The Active Members serve as the key distribution houses in all the important marketing areas of the country.

An Executive Director, who is appointed by a Board of Directors, administers the headquarters office, supervises the activities of the Association under the direction of the President and Board, and assists the officers and committees in the performance of their duties. He keeps members informed on general matters of interest, including Association activities, trade practices, legislative matters and related government affairs.

The Association holds an annual convention, to discuss problems of mutual interest and exchange views and become acquainted with new developments, techniques and services.

The WMDAA's twenty-eight-minute film, *What Makes it Tick*, gained widespread publicity and enhanced the reputation of the industry with more than one hundred TV showings.

As a means of relaying important Association news, the WMDAA publishes a monthly news letter, *Quotes to Watch*, which keeps members informed on committee work, developments in government regulatory changes and coming events.

Headquarters: 1411 K St., NW, Washington 5, D.C.

Glossary

(Many of the definitions in this glossary are based on those in the Dictionary of Gems & Gemology, by Robert M. Shipley and others.)

A

A. The abbreviation for *avance* on the regulator of Swiss or French timepieces, corresponding to F (faster) on American timepieces.

AA. Plated silverware on which the thickness of the plating is equivalent to that obtained by depositing three ounces of silver on a gross of teaspoons.

abalone pearl. A colored pearl from the abalone, a mollusc found on the seacoast of California and Mexico. It is usually a *blister pearl* and (1) gray with green and pink iridescence, or (2) iridescent dark or pale green. It is rarely seen in the jewelry industry.

aberration (ab'-er-a"shun). The failure of a lens or mirror to bring light rays to the same focus. When caused by the shape of the lens or mirror, it is called *spherical aberration;* when caused by the different refractivity of light of different colors, it is called *chromatic aberration.*

abrasion. (1) A bruise or scratch on a fashioned diamond. (2) The act or process of wearing away by grinding contact; the erosion of both stream bed and transported pebbles and rocks as they are tumbled along by the force of the stream. Abrasion creates waterworn pebbles, in which form many gems are found.

abrasive. A substance used to wear away another substance by friction. Emery, synthetic-corundum powder, diamond powder and other abrasives are used to fashion gemstones.

acanthus. A popular jewelry and silverware ornamentation resembling the serrated leaf of the acanthus tree. See section on ornaments and designs.

achromatic color (ak'-roe-mat"-ik). White, black or any tone of neutral gray; i.e., gray containing no tinge of any hue.

achromatic lens. A lens that is free from *chromatic aberration.*

acid finish. A finish obtained by removing a part of the base metal from the surface of an alloy, leaving it nearer in color to the more precious metal of the alloy.

acid test. (1) Testing precious metals by the *touchstone* method, using *aqua regia.* (2) Detecting a *carbonate* mineral, such as onyx marble or malachite, by the use of *hydrochloric acid.* (3) Eliminating color coatings from diamonds by boiling them in concentrated *sulphuric acid.* (4) The ratio of net-quick-cash assets to current liabilities in a business.

adamantine (ad'-ah-man"-teen). The bright luster associated with diamond. The word also has a connotation of unyielding hardness.

Glossary

adularescence (ad'-you-lar-es"-cence). The name given to *feldspar* (usually *orthoclase moonstone*, or *adularia*) that exhibits a floating, billowy, blue to white light in certain directions as the stone is turned. It is caused by diffused reflection of light from parallel intergrowths of another feldspar of slightly different R.I. from the main mass of orthoclase. It is often called "schiller."

Afganistan lapis. Fine blue, best-quality lapis-lazuli from the Badakshan district of Afganistan or from just over the border in Russia. It is better known in the trade as *Russian lapis*.

African emerald. Emerald from the Transvaal. It is usually yellowish green, flawed, and lacks the rich chrome-green of fine Colombian stones. The calibre-size Sandawana emeralds, although from Rhodesia, are not usually called African emerald.

"African jade." A misnomer for *grossularite garnet*.

African tourmaline. (1) Tourmaline from Africa. (2) Sometimes used in the sense of a color grade, applies to all yellowish-green to bluish-green tourmaline, whether or not from Africa. It is the same as *Transvaal tourmaline*. (3) Fine, almost emerald-green tourmaline from South-West Africa.

agate (agg"-it). One of the many varieties of chalcedony (*cryptocrystalline quartz*). Known best in its curved, banded form, it also occurs in straight, parallel bands (*onyx*) and in a translucent form with dendritic inclusions (*moss agate*). It is found in virtually all colors, usually of low intensity, and translucent to semitransparent. Most gray-banded agate is dyed to improve its color.

"Agni Mani" (or "Fire Pearl"). Glass, supposedly of meteoric origin, has been promoted under this name as being possessed of magical powers. It has little eye appeal and little, if any, value as a gemstone.

AGS. Abbreviation for **American Gem Society.**

a jour (ah-zure"). Any setting that permits a view of the pavilion (back) of the stone.

albite (al"-bite). A species of the *plagioclase feldspar* group of minerals.

alexandrite (al'-eg-zan"-drite). A transparent variety of the mineral *chrysoberyl* that is green by daylight and red (preferably) to almost violet in incandescent artificial light. The finest comes from Ceylon, good from Russia, and inferior from Madagascar. Quality is a function of the extent of color change from daylight to incandescent light and the beauty of the two colors. It is one of the birthstones for June.

alloy. A compound metal resulting from melting two or more metals together. Sterling silver, for example, is composed of $92\frac{1}{2}\%$ *silver* and $7\frac{1}{2}\%$ *copper*.

alluvial stone. A stone that has been transported by water and deposited in seas, lakes or stream beds.

almandite, or almandine (al″-man-dite; al″-man-deen). A transparent, dark, slightly brownish-red to purplish-red species of the *garnet* group. The finest quality is found in Ceylon and India.

Alumag. A trademarked name for *colorless synthetic spinel*.

amalgam. An alloy of mercury and another metal, usually silver.

amazonite (am″-ah-zon-ite). A green, opaque to semitranslucent gem variety of *microcline feldspar*. Sources: Russia, Colorado, Virginia and elsewhere.

amber. A transparent to translucent *fossil resin*, sometimes containing insects or plants. It is usually yellowish or brownish. Other colors are usually artificial, although red and black are known. Sources: principally from the mines in east Prussia and waters of the Baltic Sea; also Sicily and Burma.

American cut (also called ideal cut). A label that has come to refer to fashioned diamonds with the proportions and facet angles that were worked out by trial and error by master American cutters to yield the maximum in brilliancy consistent with a high degree of fire and confirmed mathematically by Marcel Tolkowsky.

American Gem Society. See section on trade associations.

American jade. (1) *Nephrite* from Wyoming or other western states. (2) A deceiving name for greenish *idocrase*.

American pearl. The *fresh-water* pearl of North America.

American Stone Importers' Association, Inc. See section on trade associations.

American Watch Association, Inc. See section on trade associations.

American Watchmakers' Institute. See section on trade associations.

amethyst (am″-eh-thist). A transparent to translucent, pale-violet to deep-purple variety of *crystalline quartz*. Sources: Siberia, Brazil, Uruguay and elsewhere. It is the February birthstone.

amethystine (am′-eh-thiss″-teen). A color designation meaning *violet* to *purplish*, as in *amethystine glass*, *amethystine sapphire* and others.

amorphous (ah-mor″-fuss). A word meaning *without form*. It is applied to gem materials that have no definite, orderly arrangement of atoms, or crystal structure, and hence no external crystal form. The term is sometimes applied incorrectly to crystalline minerals that lack external crystal form.

amulet. An ornament or gem worn as a charm or preservative against evil or mischief, often in-

Glossary

scribed with a spell, magic incantation or symbol.

andalusite (an′dah-loo″-site). A mineral species that is finding increasing use as a gemstone. In gem quality, it is usually prized for its very strong and attractive *pleochroism*: brownish green in one direction and brownish red at 90°. Sources: Ceylon, Brazil and elsewhere.

andradite (and″-rah-dite). A species of the *garnet* group. Because of its high dispersion and transparent green to yellowish-green color, *demantoid* is the most notable variety. From Russia and Germany.

anisotropic (an-ice′-oh-trope″-ik). Crystalline substances in which the velocity of light travel varies with the direction of propagation are said to be *anisotropic*, or *double refractive*.

anklet. An ornament similar to a bracelet but worn just above the ankle.

anneal. To reduce brittleness and increase toughness by heating to a high temperature and then cooling slowly. Usually refers to metals and glass.

anniversary stones. See list of wedding-anniversary gifts.

anomalous, or strain, double refraction (ah-nom″-ah-lus). A doubly-refractive effect in a normally singly-refractive gemstone, a condition resulting from *internal strain*, which, in turn, is caused by inclusions or structural irregularities within the stone. It is seen as irregular, or patchy, extinction when the stone is rotated in the dark position of the *polariscope*. Anomalous double refraction may be encountered in any of the *amorphous* or *cubic* (*isometric*) materials; examples are garnet, diamond, synthetic spinel and glass. In diamond, it often indicates a state of sufficient strain to serve as a warning that the stone should be given special care during cutting, setting and repair work.

anthemion (an-the″-me-on). A jewelry and silverware ornamentation consisting of floral or foliated forms arranged in a radiating cluster. See section on ornaments and designs.

antique. An object that is very old, such as an article of jewelry, silverware, etc. The U.S. Customs admits duty free as an antique any article made before 1830.

apatite (ap″-ah-tite). A transparent green, blue, violet, purple, pink, yellow or colorless gem species; most varieties are light in tone. Sources: Ceylon, Burma, Bohemia, Mexico, Maine and elsewhere. Apatite is more a collector's item than a jeweler's gemstone.

appliqué (ap-plik-kay″). Ornamental work made separately and then applied to an article of silverware or jewelry.

aplanachromatic lens (ah-plan′-ah-kro-mat″-ik). A lens

free from both *chromatic* and *spherical aberration.*

aplanatic lens (ap′-lah-nat″-ik). A lens free from *spherical aberration.*

applied border. An ornamented strip of metal soldered onto an article such as a teapot or vegetable dish.

aquamarine (aq′-wah-mah-reen″). The transparent, very light to medium-dark blue to greenish-blue to bluish-green variety of *beryl*. It is found principally in Brazil; also Madagascar, Russia, Ceylon, California and Colorado. It is one of the birthstones for March.

aqua regia (ak″-wa re″-je-ah). A mixture of nitric and hydrochloric acids (usually 3 to 1), used in the *touchstone* test for karat gold.

arbor. A part of a watch mechanism that rotates or that turns in pivot bearings while holding something that turns, as a pallet arbor, barrel arbor, stem (winding) arbor, etc.

argentan (ar″-jen-tan). A French term for nickel silver, German silver and other nonprecious silver imitations.

"Arizona ruby." A misnomer for *pyrope garnet.*

Arkansas diamond. Any diamond found in Arkansas could be so called, but the term is most frequently used as a misnomer for *rock-crystal quartz.*

Arkansas pearl. *Fresh-water* pearl from rivers in Arkansas, once a larger producer of pearls than any other state.

artificial stone. Either an *imitation* or *synthetic* stone.

assay. The analysis of an ore or alloy to determine constituents and their proportions

assembled stone. Any stone constructed of two or more parts of gem materials, or one of gem and one of glass.

asteria. Any gemstone that, when cut cabochon in the correct crystallographic direction, displays a rayed figure (a star) by either reflected or transmitted light.

asteriated. Like a star, with rays diverging from a center.

asterism. The optical phenomenon of a rayed figure possessed by an asteria.

attachments. A designation used in the watch industry for watchbands, straps, etc.

attach ring. See section on jewelry findings.

Australian opal. Any opal from Australia. However, in the jewelry trade it usually refers to black opal from Australia and often to any black opal, regardless of its source. That from Australia is the finest of all opals.

Australian pearl. (1) A trade grade including silvery-white fine pearl from both the *Pinctada Margaritifera*, which is found in the waters north of Australia, and the *Pinctada Maxima*, of the northwest coast of Australia. (2) As a geographical classification, any pearl from Australian waters.

Australian sapphire. Sapphire from Australia; usually very dark tones of blue, green, bluish green or gray.

aventurescence (ah-ven'-chures"-cence). A display of bright or strongly colored reflections from a translucent mineral. It is seen in *aventurine quartz* and *sunstone* (feldspar).

aventurine (ah-ven"-chureen). (1) Translucent grayish, greenish, brownish or yellowish *quartz*, thickly spangled with greenish or silvery inclusions. Sources: India, China, Russia and Brazil. (2) Less correctly, a variety of *feldspar*, better known as *aventurine feldspar* or *sunstone*. It is characterized by golden reflections.

azurite (az"-u-rite). A blue to violetish-blue, opaque, ornamental stone from Russia, Arizona and many other sources. It is an ore of copper.

B

baguette (bah-get″). A French word meaning *rod*. A style of *step cutting* for small, rectangularly shaped gemstones, principally diamonds. See section on shapes and styles of cutting.

bail. The metal wire or bar, soldered to a wristwatch case, to which the arm strap or bracelet is attached.

Bakelite. A trademarked name for a *plastic* that is made of *phenol* (carbolic acid) and *formaldehyde*. It is used as a substitute for amber and other gem materials; it can be made in various colors.

balance. (1) A scale used for weighing gems or metal, such as a *diamond balance*. (2) A scale made or adapted to obtain the *specific gravity* of a gemstone, known as a *specific-gravity balance*. (3) Includes both the balance (symmetry, etc.) of the design and the physical balance of a piece of silverware when held in the hand. (4) The oscillating wheel that operates in conjunction with the hairspring to govern the timekeeping of a watch.

balance assembly. A group of parts in a timepiece, comprising balance, staff, hairspring and roller.

balance spring. Same as *hairspring*.

balance staff. The staff, or "axle," that supports the balance in a watch.

"Balas ruby." A misnomer for *pink spinel*.

baluster. A style of candlestick or cup having swelled bosses, or protuberances, in the shaft. See section on ornaments and designs.

band bracelet. A bracelet consisting of a continuous band of metal; i.e., not flexible. It may be pierced, solid or stone set.

bangle. (1) A very narrow, nonflexible bracelet. Usually, several are worn together. (2) A small ornament worn suspended from a bracelet or other piece of jewelry.

banjo clock. A clock, the case of which is shaped somewhat like a banjo. See section on basic shapes of clocks.

bar chain. See section on basic styles of jewelry chains.

barleycorn chain. See section on basic styles of jewelry chains.

Baroda Gem. A trademarked name for a *glass foilback* that simulates the appearance of diamond.

baroque (bah-roke″). In the jewelry field, baroque means *irregular in shape*; e.g., baroque pearls, tumble-polished gem materials.

barrel. The hollow, short, cylindrical box in which the mainspring of a watch is housed. The teeth on the outside of the barrel turn the center pinion.

Glossary

barrette (bah-ret"). An ornament with pin and clasp for holding hair in place. See section on jewelry findings.

base. That portion of a faceted stone below the girdle; same as *pavilion*. See section on shapes and styles of cutting.

base metal. Any nonprecious metal.

basket mounting. A style on which the sides of the setting and part of the shank are of openwork design. See section on mountings and settings.

bas-relief (bah-re-leef"). Same as *low relief*; i.e., figures (designs) that extend but slightly from the background. Most figures in cameos, for example, are in bas-relief.

basse-taille (bahs-tah"-ye). In enameling, decoration in which the design is carved at the bottom of a depression and shows through the transparent coat of enamel.

beading. The small round protuberances formed by an engraving tool to secure a stone in a setting. The word is sometimes used to describe a milgrained effect on the edges of metal for ornamentation.

bead setting. A setting in which the prongs that hold the stone are made by a beading tool. See section on mountings and settings.

bearded (or fuzzy) girdle. If a diamond is rounded up too quickly in the fashioning process, the surface of the girdle will lack the smoothness and waxy luster of a finely turned girdle. Consequently, numerous minute, hair-like fractures extend a short distance into the stone. A girdle with this appearance is referred to as being *bearded*, or *fuzzy*.

bearings. Holes or bushings in the framework of a timepiece movement in which pivots run. The bearings of pivots that run at greatest speeds, in good watches, are jeweled to reduce friction and wear.

beat. (1) *Out of beat* is a condition in which a balance or pendulum of a timepiece has uneven extent of motion on the two sides of its line of centers, which is indicated by the uneven sound of its beats. When this is corrected, the balance or pendulum is said to be *in beat*. (2) Beats per hour, or the *train* of a watch, is the number of impulses given to the balance per hour by the escapement, such as 21,600, 19,800, 18,000, 16,200, etc. This number is fixed between center wheel and escape wheel, inclusive, and must be matched by the beat number of the balance assembly.

Behr loupe. A loupe in a hinged mounting for attaching to a spectacle frame.

belcher chain. See section on basic styles of jewelry chains.

belcher mounting. A kind of ring mounting with the setting claws, or prongs, formed in the shank of the ring. See section on mountings and settings.

bellcap. See section on jewelry findings.

bell metal. A type of *bronze.*

belt chain. See section on basic styles of jewelry chains.

bench pin. A wedge-shaped block of wood fixed to a bench to support work during filing, sawing, stone setting, etc.

benitoite (beh-nee″-toe-ite). A transparent pale- to deep-blue gem species, found only in San Benito Co., California. It resembles Ceylon sapphire in color.

beryl (bare″-il). A mineral species that includes the gem varieties *emerald, aquamarine, morganite* and others.

beryl triplet. A triplet, made from two portions of greenish or colorless beryl, with a green cement layer between them. Often incorrectly called "emerald triplet."

bevel-filed chain. See section on basic styles of jewelry chains.

bezel. (1) That portion of a brilliant-cut gemstone above the girdle; same as *crown.* (2) More specifically, the sloping surface between the girdle and the table. (3) Still more specifically, only a small part of that sloping surface just above the girdle; the so-called *setting edge.* See section on shapes and styles of cutting. (4) The groove made in a setting to receive the girdle and the immediately adjacent section of a gemstone. (5) The projecting flange, or lip, inside a lid or cover, fitting the latter to the body of the vessel proper. (6) The grooved ring that forms part of a watchcase, around the dial, into which the watch crystal is fitted. (7) A term more rarely applied to that upper part of a ring setting that holds the stone. See section on jewelry findings.

bezel (or top-main) facets. The eight large, four-sided facets on the crown of a round, *brilliant-cut* gem, the upper points of which join the table and the lower points, the girdle. Some diamond cutters further distinguish four of these as *quoin* or *top-corner* facets. See section on shapes and styles of cutting.

biaxial stone. A doubly-refractive material having two directions of single refraction.

"bicycle tire." A girdle on a round, brilliant-cut diamond that is so thick as to be obvious to the unaided eye.

binding wire. Annealed wire used for soldering purposes.

birefringence (by-re-fring″-enz). The strength, or measure, of *double refraction.* See table of birefringence.

birthstone. A stone that has been chosen as appropriate to a person's time of birth. See section on birthstones.

black center. When the pavilion angle of a diamond brilliant is

Glossary

appreciably too deep, the center of the stone appears black when viewed from above.

black chalcedony. The correct designation for most so-called *black onyx*.

black diamond. (1) When a diamond is dark gray, a very dark green or truly black, it is referred to in the trade as a *black diamond*. Such a stone may be opaque to nearly semitransparent. (2) *Carbonado*, a particularly tough *industrial* variety of diamond. (3) A misnomer for *hematite* or *anthracite coal*.

black onyx (ahn″-iks). The popular name for black, single-colored *chalcedony*, usually artificially colored. Although the word *onyx* is not quite accurate, except for banded material, it has come to be accepted as the usual term for solid color.

black opal. An opal with black or dark-gray body color, exhibiting play of color.

black pearl. In the narrowest usage, a black or almost black pearl, or sometimes a gray pearl. In the broadest sense, a green, blue, blue-green or dark-brown pearl with a pronounced metallic sheen.

Black Prince Ruby. A famous red spinel in the British Imperial State Crown, once thought to be a ruby. It is still uncut. It is almost two inches in length, but its weight is unrecorded.

blemish. Any *surface imperfection* on a fashioned diamond; e.g., a nick, knot, scratch, abrasion, minor crack or cavity, or poor polish. Also a natural on the girdle or an extra facet is usually considered a blemish.

blister pearl. A pearly concretion attached to the shell and therefore not a true pearl. It is flattened, irregular and sometimes contains clay, water, etc., and occasionally a true pearl.

block, plate or square setting. Stones set in a square or a many-sided block. The metal must be clearly cut in a bevel from the outside edge of the setting to the stone, with one or more beads in every corner. See section on mountings and settings.

bloodstone. Dark-green, opaque *chalcedony* with spots of red jasper. Rarely, it is called *heliotrope*. Found in Siberia, India and elsewhere, it is one of the birthstones for March.

blowpipe. A small mouth tube for directing with the breath a jet of flame for soldering jewelry.

blue diamond. A diamond with a distinctly blue body color, even though very light in tone, is a *fancy* diamond. Diamonds that are blue in both daylight and incandescent light are rare, although fluorescent stones that show a blue color in daylight are comparatively common. A blue color may also be induced artificially.

blueground. A miner's name for

kimberlite, the rock that contains diamonds in the South African pipe mines.

"blue Jager" (Yah″-ger) Jager is the color grade for a diamond that has a faint blue body color in daylight. On the apparent assumption that this is not universally known to jewelers, or that competitors call stones "Jager" when they show no blue in daylight, some importers refer to such stones redundantly as "blue Jagers."

"blue river." A confusing and misleading term, since the diamond color grade known as *river* refers only to an extraordinarily transparent, colorless stone. If a diamond has a blue body color, it is incorrect to call it a "river."

"blue Wesselton." A confusing and misleading term for *top Wesselton*, since this grade falls just below the finest classification on the river-to-light-yellow diamond color-grading system; hence, stones in this classification do not have a blue tint.

"blue-white." A term that has been used for many years to refer to a diamond without body color. However, it is applied frequently, but incorrectly, to stones that have a distinct yellow tint. Federal Trade Commission rulings state that it is an unfair trade practice to apply the term to any stone having a body color other than blue or bluish. An American Gem Society ruling prohibits the use of the term by its members. Flagrant misuse has made the term meaningless.

"blue-white Wesselton." A confusing and misleading term for *top Wesselton*, since this grade falls just below the finest classification on the river-to-light-yellow diamond color-grading system; hence, stones in this classification do not have a blue tint.

bob. The weight that, together with a rod, comprises the pendulum of a clock.

body color. The color of a diamond as observed when examined under a diffused light against a hueless background free from surrounding reflections. The diffused light eliminates glaring reflections and dispersion, which would otherwise confuse the color determination.

Bohemian garnet. A term that is used loosely for any intense, dark-red *garnet* or more specifically but less often, for this quality of *pyrope* garnet found in Bohemia. At the turn of the century, small Bohemian garnets were used lavishly to make large quantities of low-karat-gold jewelry.

bolo or lariat tip. See section on jewelry findings.

"borax." (1) Inferior jewelry merchandise. (2) The stores that sell such merchandise at unfairly high prices or by unethical methods. (3) The methods used by such stores.

bort, or boart. The lowest qual-

Glossary

ity of diamond, so badly flawed and imperfectly crystallized that it is suitable only for crushing into abrasive powders for a multitude of industrial purposes. Kasai Province, in the Congo Republic, is by far the world's greatest producer of this material.

Boston link. See section on basic styles of jewelry chains.

boule (bool). French, meaning *ball*. A pear- or carrot-shaped mass that forms during the production of synthetic gem material by the *Verneuil* process.

bourse. French, meaning an exchange or meeting place where merchants transact business. The word is often used for a diamond-dealers' club or similar jewelry-trade association.

bow. See section on jewelry findings.

bowenite. A fine-grained, rich-green variety of *serpentine*, often used as a substitute for nephrite jade. It is sometimes sold incorrectly as "Korean jade." Sources: China, New Zealand and India.

box chain. See section on basic styles of jewelry chains.

box setting. A setting in which the top edges (or bezel) are burnished over the girdle edge entirely around the stone. See section on mountings and settings.

bracelet chain. See section on basic styles of jewelry chains.

bracelet watch. A small watch worn on a bracelet or band on the arm, particularly a wristwatch for ladies' wear.

Braganza Diamond. An unauthenticated Brazilian diamond. It is said to be owned by the Portuguese Government and to weigh 1680 carats, but most authorities believe it to be a topaz. Another name is the *King of Portugal Diamond*.

brass. An alloy of about two-thirds *copper* and one-third *zinc*.

"Brazilian diamond." A misnomer for *rock crystal*.

Brazilian emerald. (1) Light yellowish-green emerald, usually too light in color to be distinguished readily from aquamarine. (2) A deceiving name for *green tourmaline*.

brazilianite. A mineral from Bahia, Brazil, first described in 1945. It is translucent to transparent yellow-green to greenish yellow and resembles chrysoberyl and beryl.

"Brazilian moonstone." A misnomer for *scapolite*.

"Brazilian ruby." A misnomer for *pink topaz* or *tourmaline*.

"Brazilian sapphire." A misnomer for *tourmaline* or *light-blue topaz*.

"Brazilian tourmaline." A misnomer for *andalusite*.

brazing. Same as *hard soldering*.

bridge. A part of the framework of a watch movement, fastened to its base by a screw at each end of the bridge and containing one or more pivot bearings.

bridge ring. Same as *cocktail ring*.

bright cut. Comparatively deep, sharply-cut engraving in metal.

bright finish. A highly polished, mirrorlike finish on gold or silver articles.

brilliancy. The total amount of light reaching the eye, often being reflected from both the interior and exterior surfaces of a gemstone. Given equal transparency and perfection of cutting, the gem species with the highest index of refraction will be the most brilliant. However, in different stones in any given species, brilliancy depends on comparative transparency, facet angles, proportions and polish.

brilliant cut (round). The most common style of cutting for most stones. The standard round brilliant consists of a total of 58 facets: 1 table, 8 bezel facets, 8 star facets and 16 upper-girdle facets and usually a culet on the pavilion, or base. Modifications of the brilliant style of cutting include such *fancy* shapes as the *marquise, half moon, pear shape* and many others. See section on shapes and styles of cutting.

brillianteering. The placing and polishing of the 40 remaining facets on a brilliant-cut diamond after the main bezel and pavilion facets have been placed and polished.

"Bril-Lite." A trademarked name for *colorless synthetic corundum*.

britannia metal. An alloy closely resembling pewter, the usual composition of which is 92 parts *tin*, 6 parts *antimony* and 2 parts *copper*. It is used as a base for less expensive silverplated holloware.

broach. A tool for shaping, enlarging or finishing holes.

bronze. (1) An alloy of *copper* and *tin* and usually *zinc*. (2) A statue or other artistic figure of bronze.

brooch. A clasplike piece of jewelry with pin and catch for fastening to a ladies' garment, especially at the throat.

brooch mounting. See section on jewelry findings.

brown diamond. Although not so frequent in occurrence as yellow body color, brown tints in diamonds are commonly encountered.

brownie. Used loosely, any diamond with a brown tint. However, the name is seldom applied to those more desirable stones of a pronounced color; i.e., *fancy browns*.

brush finish. The soft, dull finish on a metal, produced by a scratch brush.

bubble. Any transparent inclusion in a diamond; e.g., a tiny diamond crystal or a grain of a different mineral.

buckle chain. See section on basic styles of jewelry chains.

Glossary

buckle prong. See section on jewelry findings.

buff. (1) A piece of cloth, leather or felt used with an abrasive to polish metals or gems. (2) To polish with a buff.

buff top. A low cabochon-type top and a faceted back.

bulletin watch. A watch that has won a competitive prize and that has an accompanying certificate from an observatory.

Bultfontein Mine (Bult'-fontane"). The third diamond pipe mine discovered in South Africa (early in 1871), situated just one-half mile from the Dutoitspan Mine. It produces the best colors of the "Big Five" pipe mines, although the comparative perfection of its white stones is below average. Annual production is usually between 300,000 and 400,000 carats.

bunch rings. Mass-produced rings, containing very small center diamonds, made to sell at low prices. They sometimes contain minute uncut diamonds, known in trade as roughs. The name originated when it was common practice to sell such rings tied together in bunches.

Bunsen burner. An apparatus that mixes gas and air, producing a flame. It is used extensively in watch- and jewelry-repair work.

burin. An engraver's tool, prismatic in form, with one end attached to a wooden handle and the other end ground off obliquely to a sharp point.

Burma, or Burmese, jade. The finest known jadeite, from the mines in Mogaung, subdivision of Myitkyina district, Upper Burma. The term is commonly used in the Orient to distinguish it from any and all varieties of nephrite jade.

Burma, or Burmese, ruby. A term used in the jewelry industry for rubies of the finest color (intense, medium to medium-dark purplish red), whether or not from Burma, where most of them are mined.

Burma, or Burmese, sapphire. A term used in the jewelry industry for fine, slightly violetish-blue sapphire, whether or not from Burma. Same as oriental sapphire.

"burner." In a "borax" jewelry-store window, a flashy piece of diamond jewelry, often displayed at or below cost. It is used to attract customers, who are then switched to an inferior item carrying a long markup.

burnisher. A tool of highly polished hardened steel, agate, etc., used to finish the surface of metal by rubbing. Also, to form metal by pressure and movement.

burnishing. (1) To produce a polished surface on metal by rubbing it with a hard, smooth, highly polished burnishing tool. (2) To press or swage a metal corner over the edge of a stone; i.e., to hold it in a setting.

burnt amethyst. Yellow to yellow-brown transparent quartz, produced by heating natural amethyst.

burnt stone. Same as *heated stone*.

butler finish. A finish that duplicates closely the dull, light-gray finish that resulted from the long use of silver and its constant cleaning and polishing by butlers. Today, it is produced by polishing the article to a bright finish and then dulling it with a wire-brush wheel and fine pumice.

button back. See section on jewelry findings.

button pearl. A domelike pearl with a flat or near-flat base.

button shank. See section on jewelry findings.

bye (or byewater). A color-grading term used at the mines for diamond rough having a tinge of undesirable color. Stones in this classification usually fall between the cape and yellow grades when cut.

Glossary

C

cable chain. See section on basic styles of jewelry chains.

cabochon (cab″-oh-shawn). An unfaceted cut stone of domed, or convex, form, or the style of cutting itself. The top is unfaceted and smoothly polished; the back, or base, is usually flat or slightly convex and often is unpolished. The height of the domed top is varied to accomplish various desired effects. With convex top and flat base it is called a simple, or single, cabochon; with convex top and base, a double cabochon. All asterias, cat's-eyes, girasols, most moonstones, opals and turquois are cut cabochon, as well as many translucent or semitransparent jades and other gem minerals. Less desirable specimens of various minerals are also sometimes cut cabochon. The girdle outline may be oval, round, square or any other shape. The backs of almost all transparent or semitransparent cabochons are polished. See section on shapes and styles of cutting.

cairngorm (karn″-gorm). Same as *smoky quartz*.

calcite (kal″-site). A mineral species, some varieties of which are dyed to imitate gemstones. It is the principal component of coral.

calendargraph. A watch that tells the day and the month, as well as the time. It has two dials; one that tells the day and one the month. In addition to the time hands, it usually has a seconds hand. One type tells the phases of the moon. The calendar-and-chronograph combination shows the day and month and has split-second timing.

caliber, or calibre, cut (kal″-eh-ber, or kal″-eh-bray). Stones of square, rectangular, keystone or other shapes that are cut for setting in ring shanks, band rings, bracelets, etc. They are usually very small and set *pavé* in lines or masses, to improve the design or enhance the beauty of a jewel.

"California jade." A misnomer for *idocrase*.

"California lapis." A misnomer for *dumortierite quartz*.

"California moonstone." A misnomer for *chalcedony*.

californite. A green variety of of *idocrase (vesuvianite)*, sometimes substituted for jade. Source: California.

caliper. A device with movable jaws that hold or contact an object to be measured.

cameo. A carved gem that is actually a miniature bas-relief sculpture. Unlike the intaglio, it will not yield an impression in relief. Cameos are commonly carved from materials of differently colored layers, especially onyx, the upper layer being used for the figure and the lower layer serving as the background. They may also be fashioned from shell, coral, synthetics and other substances. See section on shapes and styles of cutting.

Canadian Jewellers' Association. See section on trade associations.

canary diamond. An intensely colored *yellow* diamond. The yellow may be very slightly greenish or slightly orangey, but it must be deep enough to be a distinct asset. Such a diamond is called a *fancy*.

candelabrum (can'-de-lah"-brum); plural, candelabra. A candlestick with several branches; it may be made of sterling, silverplate, glass or other material.

cannon pinion. A hollow cylinder with pinion leaves at its lower end, fitted friction-tight to the centerpost extension of the center pinion of a watch or clock, and forming the first member of of the dial train, with its leaves engaging the teeth of the minute wheel. The minute hand is usually fitted to the top shoulder of the cannon pinion.

cape. (1) A broad range of diamond color grades for stones that show a distinct yellow tint face up (except for small stones in the top part of the range). The term originally referred to the Cape of Good Hope, the popular name for the area that later became the Union of South Africa. Since the average color produced by the South African mines was distinctly more yellow than the Brazilian average, the term *cape* became accepted for strongly yellow-tinted stones. The best grade in the group is variously called *top silver cape, top cape, light cape, fine cape* or *silver cape,* depending on the system used by the grader. (2) Perhaps most commonly, *cape* is used as the color grade below *top cape* in the *river-to-light-yellow* system.

"Cape ruby." A misnomer for *pyrope garnet.*

capillarity. An effect of molecular adhesion and liquid surface tension, whereby a liquid tends to press into the narrower part of a space. The pivot bearings and jewels of a watch are formed to take advantage of capillarity, by which oil is fed to the point where friction requires lubrication.

cap jewel. Also called endstone. In a watch, a flat, unpierced hard bearing (usually synthetic corundum), placed over a hole jewel to make contact with the end of a pivot. The cap jewels over both pivots of an arbor limit its endshake and minimize end friction, compared with the greater friction of shoulder pivots without cap jewels.

carat. A unit of weight for diamonds and other gems. The carat formerly varied somewhat in different countries, but the metric carat of .200 grams, or 200 milligrams, was adopted in the United States in 1913 and is now standardized in the principal countries of the world. It is sometimes incorrectly spelled *karat*, but in the USA karat refers only to the fineness of pure gold and gold alloys.

carbon. (1) An inclusion in a diamond that appears black to the unaided eye. (2) *Carbonado*, a kind of *industrial* diamond.

carbonado (kar-boe-nah"-doe). Black *industrial* diamond. A massive, impure, slightly cellular aggregate of minute diamond crystals, forming a mass with a granular to compact structure. It may be black, brown or dark gray. Bahia, Brazil, is the principal source. It is the toughest form of diamond.

carbon spots. Any black-appearing inclusion or imperfection in a diamond. Actually, black inclusions are rare, although some may occasionally be graphite or small particles of another mineral. Although many diamonds contain inclusions that *appear* black under ordinary lighting, dark-field illumination, plus magnification, shows most to be caused by reflection from cleavages or included transparent crystals.

carbuncle. A cabochon-cut *red garnet*.

carillon (kar"-ih-lon, or kah-ril"-yun). The French word for *chimes*, as in *carillon watch*.

carmen bracelet. The popular name for an extension bracelet with pivoted links, each enclosing a spring concealed between the front and the back, allowing the bracelet to stretch to the required size.

carnelian (kar-neel"-yan). The orange-red, brownish-red or brownish-orange translucent to semitranslucent variety of *chalcedony*; sometimes yellow or brownish yellow. It grades into darker, more brownish colors of these hues, which are called *sard*.

cartouche (kar-toosh"). A symmetrical, ornamental metal tablet, usually oblong or oval, on which can be engraved a design, monogram, maker's mark, etc. See section on ornaments and designs.

carving. Ornamentation of metals accomplished by cutting metal away from the surface. Depth of design is achieved by actually cutting the metal away to form a *bas-relief*, or a true representation of the depth of the design.

case. The protective box covering the mechanism of a watch or clock.

case screw. A screw, with full or three-quarters head, to fasten a watch movement in the case.

Cashmere sapphire (also Kashmir or Kashmere). (1) Any sapphire from Kashmir, a territory claimed by India and Pakistan but now largely in Indian hands. (2) A trade grade for *blue* sapphire, applied to stones of the velvety cornflower color (violet-blue to violetish blue).

casting. Forming an object by pouring molten metal into a mold (usually of sand or similar material) the shape of the desired object. It is often used for duplicating objects. Jewelry of cast metal is less desirable than of rolled or struck metal, because it is softer.

catch. A part into which the pin of a brooch or barpin or the wire of an earring fits to prevent loss. It is also called a *safety catch* or *clasp*, if it has a locking device.

cathedral watch hand. See section on watches.

cat's-eye. (1) When used alone, this term is properly applied only to *chrysoberyl* cat's-eye. (2) Any gemstone that, when cut cabochon, exhibits under a single, strong point source of light a well-defined chatoyant band or streak across the summit of the stone that moves as the stone is turned about. This phenomenon, which resembles the slit pupil of the eye of a cat, is caused by reflection of light from included fibrous crystals or long, parallel cavities or tubes. To describe well-defined eyes correctly in other gem minerals, the name of the mineral should precede the word cat's-eye; e.g., *tourmaline cat's-eye, quartz cat's-eye.* Many other gemstones exhibit a broader or less well-defined band of light, but these are more properly called a cat's-eye effect or a chatoyant effect. (3) A name used incorrectly for so-called *shell cat's-eye.*

celtic cross. A cross with a disc or circle at the juncture of the two arms.

cement filled. Silver holloware that has been loaded with cement or other heavy substance to prevent denting and to add weight to the piece.

center-seconds hand. See section on watches.

Certified Gemologist. A title awarded by the American Gem Society to qualified jeweler-members. To qualify, a person must study colored stones and their identification and diamond grading and appraising. Also, he must prove his proficiency with several written examinations, a diamond-grading examination, and pass a 20-stone identification examination without error. This is the AGS's most advanced title.

Ceylon sapphire. (1) Any sapphire from Ceylon. (2) A trade grade for any light-blue sapphire.

chains, styles of. See section on basic styles of jewelry chains.

chalcedony (kal-sed″-o-nee). (1) The *cryptocrystalline* subspecies of *quartz*, as distinguished from crystalline quartz. Massive, semitransparent to translucent white, gray, black and various tones and intensities of all hues, many of which are known by variety names; such names are in general use in the trade, except for the blue variety. (2) More specifically, the light-blue-gray variety of chalcedony.

champagne diamond. A green-

Glossary

ish-yellow to yellow-green diamond of a sufficiently pronounced color to be an asset. Such a stone is called a *fancy*.

champlevé (shomp-leh-vay"). An enameling process in which the metal ground is removed by engraving or etching with acid, leaving a design in the form of raised ridges or divisions to hold the enamel.

channel setting. Stones set between two ridges of metal with their edges almost touching, usually in a straight line. The sides of the mounting grip the outer edges of the stones. See section on mountings and settings.

charcoal block. A block of charcoal made by charring wood, preferably willow wood, in a closed chamber. It is used by jewelers and watchmakers to hold metal for soldering, annealing and melting.

Charles II Pearl. A pearl found in 1691, presumably in the Americas, and presented to Charles II. It is almost equal in weight to La Peregrina. The two were worn in earrings by the Queen of Spain.

charm. (1) A miniature metal replica of any object for attaching to a charm bracelet. (2) A metal ornament, such as a fob or a key, worn on a watch chain.

chasing. The act or art of ornamenting metals by means of chasing tools; that is, by means of variously shaped tools struck with a hammer. Flat chasing is effected by working the metal from the front by depressing the surface with small punches, leaving the design raised above the background. *Repoussé* chasing is hammered and raised from the back and modeled on the surface with chasing tools.

chasing tool. A steel rod, square or round, usually about four inches in length, one end of which is fashioned into any one of numerous shapes, contours and outlines. They are hardened and annealed and used for hammering (chasing) either raised motifs or indented designs on metal surfaces.

chatelaine watch (shat"-e-lane). A small watch for women's wear, suspended from a hook on an ornamental pin or brooch.

chaton (sha-ton"). (1) The bezel of a ring. (2) Same as *chaton foil*.

chaton foil. (1) An *imitation foilback* or *imitation lacquerback*. (2) More specifically, a *colored* imitation foilback.

chatoyancy (sha-toy"-an-se). A broad term covering any sort of movable, linear light reflection on a cabochon-cut gemstone, whether distinct and well defined (as the narrow, light-colored streak in a fine chrysoberyl cat's-eye) or less distinct (as in the usual tourmaline or beryl cat's-eye).

chevee (sheh-vey"). A flat gem with a smooth, concave depression. If a raised figure is in the depression, it is called a *cuvette*, although the two terms are often used interchangeably in the trade. See section on shapes and styles of cutting.

chime clock. A clock that usually chimes the quarter hours.

chip. (1) A small *rose-cut diamond* or a *single-cut melee*. (2) A cleavage piece of diamond that weighs less than one carat. (3) A small, irregularly shaped diamond. (4) A curved break on a diamond that extends from a surface edge.

chlorastrolite (klor-ast"-rho-lite). A translucent, dark-green curio stone. It has a radial fibrous structure that imparts a silky luster.

choker. A necklace, usually of beads, that fits snugly around the throat.

chronograph. A watch with a center seconds hand that may be started at zero, stopped to record the time of an event, then returned to zero by operating a button on the outside of watchcase, in addition to the ordinary hour and minute hands.

chronometer. Broadly speaking, an instrument for measuring time, but customarily used as meaning a highly accurate timepiece for navigation or other purposes where such accuracy is required.

chrysoberyl (kris"-o-bare-il). A very hard and important gem species, of which *cat's-eye*, *alexandrite*, and green, brown and yellow chrysoberyl are varieties. Sources: Ceylon, Urals, Brazil and China.

chrysolite (kris"-o-lite). (1) A mineral species that is more generally known as *olivine* by mineralogists and *peridot* by gemologists. (2) In gemology, the pale yellow to yellowish-green variety of that mineral species.

chrysoprase (kris"-o-praze). (1) A pale yellow-green variety of *chalcedony*. (2) A misleading name for so-called green onyx (actually, *green-dyed chalcedony*), which is a much darker green.

citrine (sit"-reen). The transparent yellowish to red-orange to red-brown variety of *crystalline quartz*; it is also known as *topaz-quartz*. Sources: Brazil, Madagascar, Spain and elsewhere. It is one of the birthstones for November.

clasp. A device to hold together the ends of a bracelet, necklace, neck chain, etc. See section on jewelry findings.

claw setting. A prong setting in which each of the prongs is curved. If there is a backward tapering of the claw so that a front view shows only the points by which the stones are held, it is called an *invisible-claw setting*. In the *open-claw style*, in which a small stone is set, both the points and hollows of the claw are fully exposed to view.

"clean." A term used by some jewelers to mean absence of internal imperfections only, and by

Glossary

others to describe diamonds with slight imperfections. It is prohibited by the American Gem Society for use by its members. It is also prohibited by the Federal Trade Commission, unless the stone meets the Commission's definition of the term *perfect*.

cleaning (a watch). Removing thickened oil, dirt or rust from watch and clock mechanisms, to be followed by fresh oiling. Cleaning is made necessary more by evaporation and thickening of oil than by foreign matter, a fact that is well to emphasize to watchmakers' customers, who are apt to question even a reasonably frequent need for cleaning.

cleavage. (1) The tendency of a crystalline mineral to break in certain definite directions, leaving a more or less smooth surface. (2) The act or process of producing such a break. (3) One of the portions of such a mineral resulting from such a break. (4) A term sometimes used for a diamond crystal that requires cleavage before being fashioned. (5) A misshapen diamond crystal, particularly one that is flat and rather elongated. The term is used by diamond cutters to refer to such a crystal, whether or not its form results from cleaving. (6) A grading term used at the mines for broken diamond crystals above one carat, of reasonable thickness, and not twinned. (7) A break within a diamond.

cleavage crack. A break parallel to a cleavage plane. It is characterized by a two-dimensional nature; intersections with facets are usually straight lines. It is generally the most damaging kind of imperfection in a diamond, since it affects durability as well as beauty.

cleavage (in diamond). Well-developed cleavage can occur in any of four planes, each parallel to a pair of opposite faces of the octahedron. A less easily developed cleavage parallel to faces of the dodecahedron may also occur. Cleavage planes are known in the trade as the *grain* of a diamond.

cleavage mass. A term used by diamond cutters to refer to any comparatively large portion of a diamond produced by the cleaving operation.

cleaver. The workman who prepares and cleaves diamonds. Also, he is often responsible for planning the entire fashioning from the rough.

cleaver's knife (or blade). A wedge-shaped steel knife for cleaving diamonds.

cleaver's mallet. A rounded wooden mallet that is used to strike the cleaver's knife to cleave a diamond.

cleaver's stick. The holder either for the diamond being cleaved or for the *sharp* being used to dig the groove.

cleaving. A process occasionally used in fashioning diamonds and, but rarely, other stones; the splitting of a stone along a cleavage plane, or grain, into two or more portions, to produce pieces of a size or shape that will produce fashioned stones more economically or of better quality.

click. An adjunct of a toothed ratchet wheel, with a point that enters between teeth and prevents backward movement of the wheel; used in the winding and self-winding mechanisms of timepieces.

click spring. In a watch, a spring pressing on a click, to keep it in place in the teeth of a ratchet wheel.

clip. A jeweled form similar to a brooch but fastened to a garment with a spring, instead of a pin.

clocks, shapes of. See section on basic shapes of clocks.

clock watch. A watch that strikes hours.

cloison. A wire fillet used in *cloisonné* enameling.

cloisonné (kloy-zoe-nay"). A type of enameling in which various colors of enamel are separated by thin wire fillets (*cloisons*) that are first soldered on the base to form a design.

closed culet. A culet on a diamond that is too small to be resolved with the unaided eye and that can be seen only with difficulty under 10x. The term is rarely used to refer to a pavilion point or ridge with *no* culet.

closed table. A term used by some diamond men to designate a small table diameter. However, its interpretation and use varies. It may refer to a diameter less than the American cut 53% (of the girdle diameter) or, more frequently, to a table smaller than about 60%, because so many of the stones cut today have tables well over that figure.

close goods. A grading term used at the mines for diamond crystals of good color and symmetry and free from imperfections.

closing. In a watch, designates contracting diameters of worn pivot holes with a punch — a quick, inexpensive expedient that is inferior in mechanical effectiveness to bushing.

cloud (or cloudy texture). A group of tiny white inclusions in a diamond that together give a cottony or clouded appearance in the otherwise highly transparent stone. A cloud may be so minute that it is difficult to see under 10x, or it may be large enough to deprive the entire stone of brilliancy.

"cloverleaf" or "umbrella," effect. The appearance seen around the culet of a brilliant-cut diamond, the pavilion of which has been subjected to the beam of deuterons or alpha particles in a cyclotron to impart a green color to the stone. Since the penetration of such particles is not great, and the color is concentrated at the maximum depth of penetration, the zone of color forms a scalloped "halo" around the culet that has been likened to the shape of a

Glossary

cloverleaf. It is also sometimes referred to as an "umbrella" effect.

cluster setting. Stones set in a group and held by beaded prongs. Sometimes, they are arranged to impart the illusion of a single larger stone. See section on mountings and settings.

clutch. (1) A device in a stemwind watch that shifts power from the stem to either the winding or setting gearing. (2) The metal clamp that prevents a tiepin or tietack from coming out.

coal-oil blue. A yellow diamond that has an oily-bluish body appearance in daylight; such a stone is better known as a *Premier*. The effect is caused by strong *fluorescence*.

coated diamond. A diamond that has been coated on the pavilion or girdle, or entirely, with a substance that imparts a bluish color and masks a yellowish body color. Although such treatment improves color, it is a deceptive practice. Also called *painted diamond*.

coat-of-arms. The ensigns of heraldry worn in early days; usually embroidered on the garments that partially covered the armor.

cockleshell. See section on ornaments and designs.

cocktail ring. A ladies' finger ring of fancy design, usually employing both small diamonds and small colored stones.

coil pin. See section on jewelry findings.

coin gold or coin silver. In the USA, consists of 10% *copper* and 90% *gold* or *silver*.

coin mounting. See section on jewelry findings.

collection color. A term used at the source for the finest color grade of diamond. It is also misused by some importers and retailers for stones tinted with yellow.

collet. (1) The portion of a finger ring in which a stone is set. (2) Same as *culet*. (3) A split ring of brass that holds the inner terminal of a watch's hairspring, which is pinned to it and fitted to the balance staff.

collet setting. A thin wire (bearing) is soldered to a thin strip of thin, flat gold. The bezel to fit the stone is made of gold with pliers and the ends soldered together. A suitable number of points are formed by filing and the points pressed over the stone. This style of setting is sometimes used for topaz, garnet, amethyst, aquamarine, chrysolite and similar stones.

"Colorado jade." A misnomer for *amazonite*.

colored stone. A gemstone of any species other than diamond. This usage illogically classifies all varieties of such species as colored stones, including colorless varieties, but it does not include colored diamonds. However, it has proved a practicable and satisfactory classification.

Colored-Stone Certificate. A

certificate awarded to those who complete successfully the *Colored-Stone* and *Gem Identification Courses* of the Gemological Institute of America.

color grade. The relative position of a diamond's body color on a colorless-to-yellow scale.

colorimeter. An instrument for measuring color. The first crude diamond colorimeter was developed in the Laboratories of the Gemological Institute of America by Robert Shipley, Jr., in 1940-41; it served to assist in the choice of color-comparison stones used by the GIA for the selection of sets of comparison stones for others. About 1955, the American Gem Society developed an electronic colorimeter; it incorporates a selenium cell that measures the relative transmission of yellow and blue light by a diamond brilliant.

colorless. Devoid of any color, as is pure water or a fine diamond; therefore, distinctly different from white, as in milk (or white) jade.

"commercially clean." The common meaning of this term is "reasonably free from inclusions." If a diamond were without flaws or blemishes, logically, it would be called *flawless* or *perfect*. Sometimes, highly flawed stones are represented as "commercially clean." The obvious misleading nature of the term has led the American Gem Society to prohibit its use by Society members. It is also prohibited by the Federal Trade Commission, unless the stone meets the Commission's definition of the term *perfect*.

"commercially perfect." A clarity classification used to imply that a diamond is "almost perfect." It is most commonly used to mislead the unwary into the belief that a slightly imperfect to imperfect stone has a much higher grade than its actual rating. It is prohibited by the American Gem Society for use by its members. It is also prohibited by the Federal Trade Commission, unless the stone meets the Commission's definition of the term *perfect*.

"commercial (or commercially) white." A misleading term that is used to mean *not white*, but *slightly off color*. It is prohibited by the American Gem Society for use by its members. It is also prohibited by the Federal Trade Commission, unless the stone is devoid of body color.

common opal. Opal without play of color. Most varieties are of no gemological interest or importance; others, because of their color or markings, are set in jewelry.

conch pearl. A concretion from the conch that may be one of several colors. Only the pink, which resembles pink coral, is used in jewelry. It is found principally in the waters off Florida and the Bahamas. It is devoid of nacreous luster; hence, not a true pearl.

concussion mark. A bruise on

Glossary

the surface of a fashioned diamond, caused by a blow from a pointed object. Such a mark is often outlined by minute cleavages and is either four or six sided, depending on the crystallographic orientation of the facet.

convertible piece. A jewelry article that can be detached and the individual parts used for two or more different purposes.

coral. A stonelike mass of calcium carbonate secreted by the coral polyp, a small sea animal. Precious coral is red or pink. Other colors are known, including white, cream, brown, blue and black. Source: Persian Gulf, Japan, Australia and the Mediterranean.

Corinthian. In art, refers to decorative painting in Greece in the 7th century B.C.; in architecture, the most ornate of the three Greek orders, characterized by its bell-shaped capital enveloped with acanthus leaves. A general meaning is *ornate*. See section on ornaments and designs.

corundum (ko-run″-dum). A mineral species of which *ruby* and *sapphire* are varieties. It is one of the most durable of all gemstones, having a hardness of 9 on Mohs' scale. Ruby is found in Burma, Thailand, Ceylon and, rarely, North Carolina; sapphire comes from Kashmir, Burma, Ceylon, Australia and Montana.

costume jewelry. A term ordinarily used to describe jewelry composed of imitations of gems and metals. However, it is sometimes applied to jewelry that consists of inexpensive genuine gems (often *baroques*) and plated metals.

crackled stone. A gemstone in which numerous small cracks have been produced by heating and sudden cooling, at which time the stone may be artificially colored by forcing dye into the cracks.

cream pearl. A fine pearl with a cream-colored body but without any particular hue of orient or overtone. Light-, medium- and dark-cream pearls are distinguished; dark cream is the equivalent of light to medium yellow-brown.

cream or rosé pearl. Same as cream pearl but with a *rosé orient*. Light-, medium- and dark-cream rosé pearls are distinguished.

crest. A figure appearing above the shield of a coat-of-arms and used separately on a finger ring, silverware, personal stationary, etc.

critical angle. Theoretically, the angle of refraction in a denser medium when the angle of incidence is 90° to the normal to a surface. As light traveling in a dense medium, such as a gem, strikes the boundary between it and a medium of lesser density, such as air, it is bent *away* from the normal as it leaves. As the angle to the normal increases, bending increases, until the departing beam is nearly parallel to the surface. At any greater angle to the normal, the light is totally reflected back into the denser medium. The angle to the normal between the last light refracted out and the first totally reflected is called the *critical angle*.

crocus (kro″-kus). Coarse grains of iron oxide that are used for grinding metal or glued onto cloth, which is called *crocus cloth*.

crown. (1) That part of any gem *above* the girdle. See section on shapes and styles of cutting. (2) The knurled part of a watch that is grasped and turned to wind the mainspring.

Crown of the Andes. A gold crown set with 453 emeralds, estimated to weigh 1521 carats; the principal stone weighs 45 carats. It is said to have belonged to Atahualpa (1502-1533), last of the Inca rulers. The Crown was made by the people of Popayan, Colombia, in thanksgiving for having been spared from an epidemic. After six years of labor, it was completed and placed in the statue of the Madonna in the cathedral at Popayan. Since the Crown was brought to the United States, in 1936, it has been exhibited in museums, jewelry stores, gem-and-mineral shows, and by many charities for fund-raising purposes. During this time, it was owned by an American syndicate called Crown of the Andes, Inc. In 1963, it was sold at auction to the Dutch diamond cutter and gem dealer, J. Asscher.

cryptocrystalline (krip′-toe-kris″-tal-in). Indistinctly crystalline, in which the crystalline grains are not discernable even under magnification, although an indistinct crystalline structure can be proven by a polarizing microscope.

crystal. (1) A crystalline solid bounded by plane faces. (2) The glass or plastic that covers and protects a watch dial. (3) In the jewelry industry, the term is often used to mean glass tableware, such as goblets and tumblers. It is also carelessly applied to *rock crystal*. (4) An early term still used by some jewelers to designate the diamond color grade between *top crystal* and *top cape* in the *river-to-light-yellow* system. Diamonds in this classification show a slight tinge of yellow.

"crystalline emerald." A deceiving name for an *emerald triplet*.

crystal structure. An orderly arrangement of atoms, identical in all specimens of any mineral species.

ct. An abbreviation for *carat*.

cubic (or isometric) system. See section on crystal systems.

cubist watch hand. See section on watches.

cuckoo clock. An ornately carved wooden clock, from which the figure of a bird appears and imitates the cuckoo as it strikes the hour. See section on basic shapes of clocks.

Glossary

cufflink back. See section on jewelry findings.

cufflink mounting. See section on jewelry findings.

culet (kew"-let). The small facet that is polished parallel to the girdle plane across what would otherwise be the sharp point or ridge that terminates the pavilion of a diamond or other gemstone. Its principal function is to reduce the possibility of damage to the stone. See section on shapes and styles of cutting.

Cullinan Diamond. The largest gem-quality diamond ever found; it weighed 3106 carats, or about 1 1/3 pounds. It was discovered in the Premier Mine, South Africa, in 1905. The cutting produced nine major gems and many smaller ones, one of which was a 530.20-carat pear-shaped stone known as *Cullinan I*, or the *Star of Africa*, the largest fashioned diamond in the world. *Cullinan II*, the second largest cut diamond in existence, is a 317.40-carat square cut. All are a part of the British Crown Jewels or are the personal possession of the Royal Family. See section on famous diamonds.

cultured pearl. A pearl produced by artificially inducing the formation of a pearl sac, usually by the introduction of a large bead and/or a piece of mantle tissue into the body mass of a pearl-bearing mollusc. Spherical cultured pearls are produced, largely in Japanese waters, in the mollusc *Pinctada Martensii*.

Cultured-Pearl Association of America. See section on trade associations.

cushion cut. The older form of the *brilliant cut*, having a girdle outline approaching a square with rounded corners. Essentially an *old-mine-cut*.

custom made. Jewelry made for an individual. It differs greatly from costume jewelry.

cut (of a gem). The style or form in which a gem has been fashioned; e.g., *brilliant cut, emerald cut*.

cutlery. Knives with a cutting edge.

cut stone. A stone that has been fashioned as a gem, as distinguished from an uncut, or rough, stone.

cutter. (1) One who fashions diamonds, but the term is often applied to a lapidary or any other artisan who fashions colored gemstones. (2) A tool for stamping out thin discs of metal on a lead block.

cutting. A term in general use to mean fashioning, and therefore includes the operations not only of sawing (which technically is the only true cutting operation), but of grinding, polishing and faceting.

cuttlebone. A material of which casting molds are made.

cuvette (koo-vet"). An *intaglio*

with a raised cameolike figure in a polished depression. Also called *chevee* (she-vay″) in the trade. See section on shapes and styles of cutting.

cyanide. In the jewelry trade, a term used to mean a solution of *potassium cyanide,* used to dissolve tarnish on silver or watchcases. It is very poisonous.

cyclotron-treated diamond. A diamond whose color has been changed as a result of bombardment with alpha, neutron or deuteron particles in a cyclotron. The color produced is usually green, bluish green, blue-green, yellow-green, brownish green or black. After a relatively low-temperature heat treatment, yellow, brown, orangey-brown, reddish-brown or brownish-pink stones may result. Few are irradiated by this method today.

cylinder (gem). A stone fashioned as a cylinder. It was carved with designs, inscriptions or names for use on seals. In the ancient business and social world, it was drilled lengthwise for insertion of a cord for carrying or wearing. It was often fashioned of gem materials.

cylinder escapement. A form of escapement that is considered inferior in timekeeping to the lever or chronometer escapement.

cyma curves. An ornamention that is a double curve, concave at the top and convex at the bottom. See section on ornaments and designs.

Glossary

D

damascene (dam-ah-seen"). (1) The art of ornamenting metal by inlaying it with other, usually more precious, metals. (2) The ornamental finish applied to the flat, exposed surfaces of watch movements.

Danish silver. A distinctive style of silverware, representative of the Danish arts and crafts. If made to meet Danish standards, it is 830 parts pure; if for export, 925 fine.

dapping. Forming metal by striking it rapidly with a special punch and die.

dapping dies, or blocks. Metal blocks containing convex depressions into which metal can be dapped into rounded contours.

dapping punches. Domed steel tools for dapping.

dark-field illumination. A method of illuminating diamonds and other gemstones with a strong light from the side while the stone is viewed against a black background. It causes inclusions and imperfections to stand out clearly and reduces confusing surface reflections. This principle, together with *light-field illumination*, is incorporated in the **Gemolite,** or **Gemscope** (trademarks, Gemological Institute of America), the **Diamondscope** (trademark, American Gem Society), plus the **GIA Gem Detector** and the **GIA Diamond Grader.**

dauphine-flat watch hand. See section on watches.

dauphine-pitched watch hand. See section on watches.

dauphine seconds hand. See section on watches.

De Beers Consolidated Mines, Ltd. This company is the major factor in the diamond industry, because it holds a controlling interest in a number of diamond-mining companies and in companies having buying contracts with independent producers. It owns or controls all of the important pipe mines in South Africa and Consolidated Diamond Mines of South-West Africa, Ltd. Williamson Diamonds, in Tanganyika, is owned by De Beers and the government of that country on an equal basis.

De Beers Mine. A diamond pipe mine that was discovered in South Africa in 1871 on a farm owned by D.A. and J.N. De Beer. It ceased operation in 1908 but was reopened in 1961 for eventual full-scale operation.

De Beers Mines. (1) The Bultfontein, De Beers, Dutoitspan, Kimberley and Wesselton diamond pipe mines. (2) Sometimes used to refer to all diamond-mining properties owned or controlled by De Beers Consolidated Mines, Ltd.

decorative stone. A stone used for architectural decoration, as in mantles, columns and store fronts. It is sometimes set in silver or gold-filled jewelry, but usually as curio stones.

demagnetize. To remove effective magnetism from magnetized steel parts of a watch, by passing the watch through a hollow coil of wire in which alternating current flows.

demantoid (de-man″-toid). The green, transparent variety of *andradite* garnet. It is often sold incorrectly as "olivine." Source: Russia.

density. Same as *specific gravity*.

depth percentage. The depth of a stone measured from the table to the culet, expressed as a percentage of the stone's diameter at the girdle, is a relationship used in the analysis of the proportions of a fashioned diamond. In cuts with other than a round girdle, the narrowest girdle diameter is used.

detent. A part in a mechanism used to retain another part in a particular position during a phase of action, as the detent in the setting works of some watches.

Devonshire Emerald. A splendidly-formed emerald crystal of excellent color from the Muzo Mine, Colombia, presented in 1831 to the sixth Duke of Devonshire by Dom Pedro (once Emperor of Brazil). It is now in the British Museum of Natural History. It weighs 1383.95 carats and measures about two inches in diameter and length.

dial down. One of the positions in which an adjusted watch has been timed; i.e., with dial horizontal and face downward.

dial foot. One of the soft metal pins on the back of a watch dial to fasten it to the lower plate of the movement.

dial up. One of the positions in which an adjusted watch has been timed; i.e., with dial horizontal and face upward.

dial screw. The screw in the lower plate of a watch to fasten the dial foot.

dial train. The gearing under a watch dial that reduces the rate of turns, usually from one per hour at the center post to one in 12 hours, to provide motion for an hour hand.

dial washer. A pierced, concave washer made of thin, springy sheet metal placed between the hour wheel and dial in a watch, to hold the wheel into the gearing with the minute pinion.

diamantiferous (dye′-ah-man-tif″-er-us). Diamond-bearing ground or rock.

diamond. A mineral composed essentially of carbon that crystallizes in the *cubic,* or *isometric,* crystal system. It is by far the hardest of all known natural substances (10 on Mohs' scale); only manmade *Borazon* is as hard. In its transparent form, it is the most cherished and among the most

Glossary

highly valued gemstones. It occurs in colors ranging from colorless to yellow, brown, orange, green, blue and violet. Reddish stones are known, but no pure red stones have been reported. Its hardness and high refractive index (2.417) permits it to be fashioned as the most brilliant of gems, and its dispersion (.044) produces a high degree of fire. The specific gravity is 3.52. Sources include various sections of south, west, southwest and middle Africa; central, east and northeast South America; Siberia; India; Borneo; and Australia. It is also found in the United States, but not in commercial quantity.

diamond-angle (or bezel-angle) gauge. A gauge that measures the comparative correctness of the angles for the slope of the bezel facets in relation to the table of a fashioned diamond.

diamond anniversary. An anniversary celebrated upon the completion of 60 (or sometimes 75) years following the event commemorated.

diamond balance. A sensitive scale for weighing gemstones. It is also used for obtaining the *specific gravity* of gems by the *hydrostatic weighing method*. See section on diamond-grading and -merchandising instruments.

Diamond Certificate. A certificate awarded to those who complete successfully the *Diamond Course* of the Gemological Institute of America, which requires passing the diamond-grading and diamond-appraising instruction and practice.

Diamond Corporation, Ltd. The market-control organization of the diamond industry. It was organized in 1930, to purchase the output of the Diamond Producers' Association on a quota basis and to arrange contractual purchase agreements with other producers. Industrial Distributors (Sales), Ltd., is confined to the marketing of crushing bort and drilling diamonds; all other diamonds are marketed through the Diamond Trading Co., Ltd. The Corporation is owned about 80% by De Beers Consolidated Mines, Ltd., and about 20% by its subsidiary, Consolidated Diamond Mines, of South-West Africa, Ltd.

diamond cut. A name used in the colored-stone trade for *brilliant cut*. See section on shapes and styles of cutting.

diamond cutter. (1) Any workman engaged in the cutting and polishing of diamonds. (2) One who *rounds up* rough diamonds as a step in the fashioning of brilliants.

diamond doublet. An infrequently encountered *assembled stone*, consisting either of a diamond crown and a pavilion of another colorless material or two pieces of diamond cemented together.

"Diamond-ite." A trademarked

245

name for *colorless synthetic corundum*.

diamond lamp. Any type of illuminator designed specifically for diamond sales and display purposes.

Diamondlite (trademark, Gemological Institute of America). An instrument for *color grading* diamonds by visual comparison with *master diamonds*. It affords a constant source of artificial light that is the equivalent of north daylight, eliminates reflections from surroundings, and reduces fire. The instrument incorporates an ultraviolet tube for detecting fluorescence in diamonds and other gems. Also called the *Diamolite*. See section on diamond-grading and -merchandising instruments.

Diamondlux (trademark, Gemological Institute of America). A special overhead light fixture, introduced in 1959, for jewelry-store illumination. The unit consists of a combination of special fluorescent tubes, the effect of which is to produce a daylight-equivalent illumination to show objects in their true colors. A unique pattern and type of baffles produces individual light sources, yielding a degree of dispersion and scintillation in gems not seen with other present kinds of illumination. The result is the equivalent of a multitude of spots, but each corrected to true color. See section on diamond-grading and -merchandising instruments.

Diamond Manufacturers' & Importers' Association of America, Inc. See section on trade associations.

diamond paper. A sheet of paper folded to form a pocket in which diamonds and other gems are contained. Usually, a durable paper stock is used. One or more sheets of similarly folded paper may be used to line and strengthen the outer paper. Weight, lot number, and coded or uncoded prices usually are marked on the flap of the paper.

diamond-paper weight. A collapsible frame, consisting of four hinged pieces of thin metal, used to hold diamond papers open while examining stones.

diamond powder. Small particles of diamond that are used in loose form in industrial grinding, for fashioning the harder colored stones (e. g., ruby and sapphire), and for faceting and polishing diamonds. It is also forced or molded into the surface of tools used for grinding, drilling, machining, etc. *Diamond grit* and *diamond dust* are synonymous terms.

Diamond Producers' Association. An association whose membership consists of the Government of the Union of South Africa; the Administrator of the Mandated Territory of South-West Africa; De Beers Consolidated Mines, Ltd.; Premier (Transvaal) Diamond Mining Co., Ltd., Consolidated Diamond Mines

Glossary

of South-West Africa, Ltd.; and the Diamond Corporation, Ltd. It sells to the Diamond Purchasing & Trading Co., Ltd., and Industrial Distributors (1946), Ltd., all of the diamonds produced by its members. These companies have contracts with the Diamond Trading Co., Ltd., and Industrial Distributors (Sales), Ltd., for the marketing of all the diamonds acquired by them. Each of its members receives a quota of the world's diamond trade, after providing for the purchase by the Diamond Corporation of the output of the diamond producers who are not members.

Diamond-Proportion Screen. A device for assessing the proportions of fashioned diamonds for determination of excess weight, if any, in comparison to ideal proportions—especially for demonstrations to customers. A simple screen is used with a StereoZoom-type microscope, but a more complicated telescoping arrangement is needed for microscopes with fixed magnifications. See section on diamond-grading and -merchandising instruments.

Diamond Purchasing & Trading Co., Ltd. A company that buys gem diamonds from the Diamond Producers' Association and from other African diamond sources. It sells them to the Diamond Trading Co., Ltd., for marketing to the world diamond trade.

diamond saw. (1) A saw used for dividing, or separating, diamonds. (2) A diamond-charged blade used as a cutting edge in fashioning colored stones or in various applications in industry.

Diamondscope (trademark, American Gem Society). A binocular gemological microscope, incorporating an illuminator with an adjustable baffle that affords examination of gemstones by either dark-field or light-field illumination. It is used for both the identification of colored stones and the grading of diamonds.

diamond shovel. A small metal scoop, with or without a handle, used to facilitate the handling of large quantities of small diamonds.

diamond sieve. A round, perforated metal plate for rapid grading of loose, fashioned diamonds for size. A number of such plates are usually used, each having perforations of different size.

Diamond Syndicate. In the early days of the South African diamond fields, the word *syndicate* was used to refer to various groups of individuals and companies that held controlling interests in diamond production and distribution. In 1893, a syndicate composed of ten firms offered to purchase all of De Beers Company's diamonds. This seems to have been the embryo of the famous diamond syndicate that became so well known to jewelers in the early part of the 20th century as the price-fixing and market-controlling factor of the diamond industry. In various forms, a diamond syndicate composed of different persons or firms functioned in this capacity, until the crisis of 1929 demanded a marketing organization of a more rigid kind with greater capital. Although the term *syndicate* is no longer meaningful, it is often popularly applied to De Beers Consolidated Mines, Ltd., because it holds a controlling interest in a number of diamond-mining companies and in companies that have buying contracts with independent producers, including the Diamond Corporation, Ltd.

Diamond Trading Co., Ltd. The organization that markets to the diamond trade the gem diamonds it buys from the Diamond Purchasing & Trading Co., Ltd.

diamond-washing cup. A perforated, solid-bronze cup, suspended inside of a glass jar with a glass cover, for washing and cleaning diamonds and other gemstones.

"Diamonite." A trademarked name for *synthetic rutile*.

"Diamothyst." A trademarked name for *synthetic rutile*.

diaper. A pattern consisting of the continuous repetition of one or more units of a design.

dichroism (die″-kro-ism). The property of most doubly-refractive colored minerals of the tetragonal and hexagonal crystal systems of transmitting two different colors in the two different directions of vibration into which light is polarized by the material.

die stamping. The process of applying the design and achieving hardness of metal by striking it with heavy blows from a drop hammer, in which the top and bottom dies are fixed to the head and anvil.

die-struck jewelry. Jewelry formed by pressing the softer precious-metal alloys into dies. It is usually mass produced.

diffraction. An optical phenomenon. The breaking up of white light into minute colored spectra. It occurs on the edges of the tiny overlapping plates of nacre on the surface of a pearl, producing *orient*.

dike (or dyke). When a fissure cutting across the bedding planes of earlier rocks is filled by igneous rock, it is called a *dike*. Diamonds are sometimes found in dikes of *kimberlite*.

diopside (di-op″-side). A mineral species, the green varieties of which are sometimes cut as gems. Sources: Italy, Ontario, New York.

Dirilyte. A trademarked name for a gold-colored metal that contains no gold. It is used in the manufacture of flatware.

disk chain. See section on basic styles of jewelry chains.

dispersion. The property of transparent gemstones to separate white light into the spectrum

Glossary

colors. The interval between such colors varies in different gemstones, and is usually expressed by the measure of the difference between the refractive indices of the red ray and the violet ray. Diamond has the highest dispersion (.044) of any natural, colorless gem. See table of dispersion.

"doctored" pearl. A pearl that has had surface cracks filled, has been artificially colored, or that has been made more spherical by removing certain portions, as in *peeling*.

"dog collar." A wide band of cloth or flexible metal that fits snugly around the neck, often set with gemstones.

dop. Any device that is used to hold a gem during any phase of the fashioning process.

dore (doe-ray"). French, meaning *gilt*.

Doric. The oldest and simplest of the Greek orders of designing. See section on ornaments and designs.

double cable. See section on basic styles of jewelry chains.

double curb. See section on basic styles of jewelry chains.

double-link curb. See section on basic styles of jewelry chains.

double, or XX, plate. Plated silverware on which the thickness of the plating is equivalent to that obtained by depositing four ounces of silver on a gross of teaspoons.

double-oval link. See section on basic styles of jewelry chains.

double ring. See section on basic styles of jewelry chains.

double refraction. The refraction and separation of rays of light into two rays as they pass obliquely from air into minerals of any but the isometric system. The two rays then travel at different velocities and vibrate in mutually perpendicular planes. The *polariscope* or *dichroscope* reveal the presence of double refraction.

double-sunk dial. A watch dial in which the hours-and-minutes circle is depressed, and the seconds are still further depressed.

doublet. An assembled stone of two portions, bound together by a colorless cement or by fusing the parts one to the other.

douzieme (due-zee-em"). One-twelfth of a *ligne* (a ligne is a French measurement for the diameter of a watch, equivalent to 2.255883 millimeters, or .08883 inch).

draw color. When several diamonds are placed together in a diamond paper and light passes through one stone after another, each stone tends to intensify the slight color of the other. The group of stones is then said to *draw color*. The term is also used to describe an individual diamond with a visibly yellow body color.

drawplate. A piece of steel, flattened and pierced with holes of graduated size, for use in changing the shape or reducing the size of wire.

Dresden Green Diamond. An apple-green, almond-shaped diamond weighing 41 carats, believed to be of Indian origin. It is displayed in the Green Vaults in Dresden, Germany. See section on famous diamonds.

dressclip. See section on jewelry findings.

dresser set. Mirror, hairbrush and comb. Sometimes includes manicure articles.

drop. (1) Any small part suspended from a jewel. (2) The slightly raised part on back of a piece of flatware between handle and bowl.

drop cut. Any form of cutting suitable for use in pendants, earrings, etc., such as the *briolette* or *pear shape*.

ductility. The capability of being drawn easily into wire or other forms. It varies in different metals.

Duke of Devonshire Sapphire. A famous sapphire weighing 100 carats, last reported in the possession of the present Duke.

dumortierite quartz (du-mor″-te-er-ite). An opaque, deep-blue mixture of quartz and dumortierite. It is also known by the misleading name of "California lapis." Source: California.

Duplex Refractometer (re′-frak-tom″-eh-ter). A refractometer made by the Gemological Institute of America that employs a large high-index hemicylinder, slotted to reduce parallax, and a moving mirror. Using an auxiliary eyepiece for flat-surface readings, it is the first refractometer designed for both spot and facet readings. See section on gem-testing instruments.

"Dutch gold." A deceiving name for an alloy of about 80% *copper* and 20% *zinc*.

Dutch silver. Authentic Dutch silver, as made in Holland, carries quite highly embossed designs. It is copied by American manufacturers in plated ware. It usually assays no more than 800 fine, as compared to 925 for sterling.

Dutoitspan Mine (Du-toits″-pan). The second diamond pipe mine discovered in South Africa (September, 1870), on the farm Dorstfontein, near the present town of Kimberley. Dutoitspan was the name given to the *pan*, or natural land basin, on this farm. This mine is noted for its large yellow diamonds and for its large proportion of big stones. Annual production is usually between 200,000 and 300,000 carats.

dwt. The abbreviation for *pennyweight*.

dyed pearl. A pearl that has been dyed any one of various colors.

Glossary

E

earnut. See section on jewelry findings.

earwire, or earring. An ornament attached to the ear lobe by a small screw or clip or by a wire piercing the ear. See section on jewelry findings.

earwire pin. See section on jewelry findings.

ebauche (e-bosh"). A term used in Swiss watch manufacturing to denote a watch movement with its principal parts assembled but not yet finished; i.e., a movement "in the rough."

edge up. A diamond positioned so that it is being observed parallel to the girdle plane, a position commonly used for detecting faint tints of color.

Edith Haggin de Long Ruby. A star ruby measuring 1½ inches long, one inch across, and weighing 100 carats. It is a Burmese stone. It is in the American Museum of Natural History, New York City.

Edwardes Ruby. A ruby crystal that was presented to the British Museum of Natural History in 1887 by John Ruskin. It is translucent, of good color, and weighs 167 carats (nearly 1¼ ounces).

egg and dart. A classic repeat design used in applied borders for silverware, gallery strips for jewelry, and molding for clocks. See section on ornaments and designs.

egg and tongue. A repeat design combining oval and tongue, usually embossed or *repoussé*. See section on ornaments and designs.

eighth. A common abbreviation for an *eighth carat,* when referring to the weights of diamonds.

electric clock. A term popularly applied to the synchronous clock, although it is more accurately limited to clocks that contain an electric motor or armature that is independent of an electric power system.

electromagnetic spectrum. A term used in science to designate all wave-motion phenomena, including X-rays, ultraviolet light, visible light, infrared light, radio waves, etc.

electron-bombarded diamond. A diamond whose color has been changed to blue by bombardment with fast electrons in a *Van de Graaff generator.* Such a stone can be detected readily by a *conductometer,* since treated blue stones are nonconductors of electricity and natural blue stones are conductors. Gamma-ray radiation has also been used to produce blue colors.

electroplating. Affixing a plate or layer of one metal on another metal by immersing a piece of each in the proper chemical solution and passing an electric current from one to the other. The current deposits particles of the first metal on the second.

electrum. An alloy of 20% *gold* and 80% *silver*.

elinvar (el″-in-var). An alloy of *steel, nickel* and *chromium,* used for watch hairsprings, that yields a timekeeping rate practically without temperature error.

elk's tooth. Part of the emblem of the Benevolent and Protective Order of the Elks. Genuine elk or other teeth are incorporated in the emblematic jewelry of this lodge, but plastic imitations are frequent.

emblem, or emblematic, jewelry. See section on emblems of fraternal orders and civic groups.

embossing. Ornamentation that is raised in *relief* from a surface; to raise the surface up into bosses, or protuberances; particularly to ornament with relief work. Strictly speaking, the term is applicable only to raised impressions produced by engraved dies or plates that are brought forcibly to bear by mechanical means on the material to be embossed. In embossing, the work is done from the front and by driving down the ground, leaving the design in relief. Thus, it differs from *repoussé*, carving, casting, chasing or hammering.

emerald. (1) The medium-light to medium-dark tones of slightly bluish-green or slightly yellowish-green *beryl*. There is no standard dividing line between emerald and either *aquamarine* or the lighter green variety known as *green beryl.* Colored by chromium, a fine emerald is one of the three most valuable gems; its color is possessed by no other gemstone except top-quality jadeite. The finest emeralds come from Colombia; good ones from Russia; and a few others from Brazil, India and Africa. Emerald is the birthstone for May. (2) A color designation meaning the color of an emerald, as in *emerald jade, emerald glass,* etc., although the meaning is often incorrectly extended to mean any color approaching the green of emerald.

emerald cut. A form of *step cutting.* It usually is rectangular but sometimes is square, in which case it is known as *square emerald cut.* It has rows (steps) of elongated facets on the crown and pavilion, parallel to the girdle, with sets on each of four sides and at the corners. The number of rows, or steps, may vary, although the usual number is three on the crown and three on the pavilion. See section on shapes and styles of cutting.

emerald filter A color filter through which emeralds, some other genuine stones, synthetic emeralds, and some imitations appear reddish, whereas most glass imitations and most green stones appear green. It is of little value in gem testing. See section on gem-testing instruments.

emerald glass. (1) Any green glass, such as is used in the manu-

Glossary

facture of imitation gemstones. (2) An emerald-colored glass made by fusing beryl.

emerald-prong setting. A *prong setting* having the four corner posts flattened off instead of at a 90° angle. This actually makes an octagon-shaped outline, commonly referred to as an *emerald shape*. See section on mountings and settings.

emerald triplet. An assembled stone, two parts of which are quartz, pale beryl or synthetic spinel and the third part usually is a layer of green cement, serving as both colorant and adhesive. It is best detected by observation from the side while immersed in a liquid.

emery. An impure variety of corundum, often used as an abrasive.

"Emperor-lite." A trademarked name for *colorless synthetic corundum*.

Empress Eugenie Diamond. A 51-carat, oval-shaped diamond brilliant. Starting about 1787, successive owners have included Catherine II, of Russia; Emperor Napoleon III; and the Gaekwar of Baroda. It is presently thought to be owned by Mrs. N. J. Dady, of Bombay, India. See section on famous diamonds.

enamel. A vitreous glaze. In jewelry, it is usually fused to a base by heat. The base used in jewelry is always of metal, but it may also have a glass or pottery foundation. It is applied to the metal in the form of powdered glass, often preserved in distilled water. It is dried, placed in a furnace, and heated to a pale-orange heat. The particles of glass melt and run together into a smooth coating. This process is repeated until the desired thickness is obtained. The enamel is then stoned down flush with the metal walls and polished with abrasives. The principal types of jewelry enamels are *cloisonné, plique à jour, champlevé, basse-taille, neillo, painted enamels* and *lacquer*.

enamel painting. A process in which opaque, vitrified colors are fixed on an enamel base.

encrusting. A decoration of gold, platinum or other precious metal that is applied in liquid form and then fired.

endoscope. A pearl-testing instrument that utilizes a hollow needle into which is inserted a tiny metal rod, with its ends both polished to flats at 45° to its length and at 90° to one another. A powerful light comes through the needle and strikes the first 45° mirror and is reflected through an opening in the wall of the hollow needle into the pearl being tested. When the two mirrors are equidistant from the center of a natural pearl, a flash of light is seen reflected from the top metal mirror, having traveled through the pearl's concentric layers.

endshake. The play of an arbor that is permitted between its shoulders and their bearings in a watch or clock plate, or between endstones and the tops of conical pivots.

"Endura emerald." A misnomer for *green glass*.

engagement ring. A ring given in token of betrothal, especially a *diamond solitaire* so given by a man to his fiancé.

engine turning. The process of decorating metal by a hand-controlled cutting machine, which is made to follow the design of a master pattern, or stencil. Engine turning is generally confined to toiletware and novelties. See section on ornaments and designs.

English Dresden Diamond. A 119.50-carat diamond, found in Brazil in 1857. E. H. Dresden, a London merchant and the first owner, had it cut to a 76.50-carat drop shape and sold it to an East Indian for $200,000. Later, it was sold to the Gaekwar of Baroda but is presently owned by Cursetjee Fardoonji, of India. Another name is the *Star of Dresden Diamond*. See section on famous diamonds.

English finish. An electrolytic plating of pure gold that has been highly polished.

engrailed border. The reverse of a scalloped border, composed of semicircular indentations.

engraver. (1) An artisan skilled in the ornamentation of metals by engraving. (2) One who engraves plates of copper and other metals used in the printing of high-grade stationery, coats-of-arms, monograms, etc.

engraver's block. A heavy, usually globular, metal turntable with clamps that hold articles being engraved.

engraving. (1) The ornamentation of metals by means of small hand-pushed (or hammer-driven, especially on steel) chisels, called *gravers*. Engraving differs from carving in that depth is suggested by shaded lines; thus, engraving is akin to a pen-and-ink drawing. (2) An engraved piece. (3) A print made from an inked, engraved plate.

en resille (ahn-ray-see"). A rare form of decoration, requiring great skill and craftsmanship. It is a process in which a base of glass or rock crystal has incised on it fine hairlike lines to form a design. The pattern is lined with gold; the tiny cells thus formed are filled with soft, low-fire opaque or translucent enamels. The resulting effect, after firing and polishing, is not unlike that of a delicately woven net.

EPBM. A stamp used on silverware to mean *electroplate on britannia metal*.

APC. A stamp used on silverware to mean *electroplate on copper*.

epidote (ep"-ih-dote). A yellowish, pistachio-green to dark-green transparent gem mineral. It is rarely seen in the jewelry

Glossary

trade. Sources: Italy, Norway and France.

EPNS. A stamp used on plated ware to mean *electroplate on nickel silver*.

EPWM. A stamp used on silverware to mean *electroplate on white metal*.

escapement. The mechanism that transfers power in a timepiece from the train to the balance or pendulum.

escutcheon (es-kuch"-un). The shield or other space provided for the engraving of a monogram, crest, shield, etc.

essence d'orient. A suspension of guanine crystals in collodion, used for adding a highly lustrous coating to beads to make imitation pearls.

etanche (aye-tawnch"). On Swiss watch cases, means *waterproof*.

etching. A kind of decoration that is produced by what might be called "chemical engraving." The metal is covered with a protective coating through which the desired design is cut and the design eaten into the metal by acid.

euclase (u"-klace). A very rare gem species. It is transparent and light blue, light bluish green or colorless. The blue variety is highly esteemed by gem collectors but is rarely seen in the gem trade. Sources: Russia and Brazil.

European cut. Obsolete. A diamond brilliant whose proportions were worked out mathematically for light falling perpendicularly on the crown. It was never adopted as a common form of cutting. The angle of the pavilion facets to the girdle is 38° 40'; of the bezel facets, 41° 6'. The table is 56% of the girdle diameter; crown depth, 19%; and pavilion depth, 40%. It is not to be confused with the *old European cut*. See section on shapes and styles of cutting.

"evening emerald." A misnomer for *peridot*.

Excelsior Diamond. A 995.20-carat, blue-white diamond, found in South Africa in 1893. It was cut by Asscher's Diamond Co., in Amsterdam, into 21 marquise, brilliant, and pear-shaped stones, ranging from one to 70 carats, and having a total weight of 373.75 carats; each was sold separately. The combined value of these stones at the time of cutting (1903) was approximately $1,000,000. One of the gems, an 18-carat marquise, was displayed by De Beers Consolidated Mines at the New York World's Fair in 1939.

explorer's watch. A term used in England for a *waterproof* watch.

extra facets. Facets in excess of those needed to achieve the planned symmetry of a given style of cutting. They usually result from polishing away nicks, chips, naturals, etc., on or near the surface. Although extra facets are considered blemishes, some disregard small ones that are not visible from above.

extra-fancy gem blue. A term applied by some diamond men to diamonds of fine color; however, it is often misused for lower grades.

"eye clean." A term that implies that no internal flaws are visible to the unaided eye of a qualified diamond-clarity grader. It is prohibited by the American Gem Society for use by its members. It is also prohibited by the Federal Trade Commission, unless the stone meets the Commission's definition of the term *perfect*.

eyelet. See section on jewelry findings.

eye loupe. Any type of magnifier that can be held in the eye socket.

"eye perfect." A term that implies that no internal flaws or surface blemishes are visible to the unaided eye of a qualified diamond-clarity grader. In practice, it seems to be used mostly to describe stones with imperfections that can be seen only with difficulty by the unaided eye. It is prohibited by the American Gem Society for use by its members. It is also prohibited by the Federal Trade Commission, unless the stone meets the Commission's definition of the term *perfect*.

Glossary

F

"Fabulite." A trademarked name for *strontium titanate*.

face. (1) A term used in brillianteering for the entire group of facets that can be placed on a diamond without repositioning it in the dop; viz., two star facets and four upper-break facets or four lower-break facets. (2) In crystallography, a natural, plane surface on a crystal.

facet. (fas″-et). A plane, polished surface on a gemstone.

facet (or faceted) cut. A type of cut gem bounded by plane faces, as distinguished from *cabochon* or other unfaceted styles.

faceting. The operation of placing facets on a diamond or other gem.

face up. A faceted stone positioned with the table toward the viewer, the usual position in which a mounted stone is observed.

face up well. Many diamonds in the intermediate color grades that show color readily in the edge-up position appear to be without noticeable color when viewed table up. Such stones are said to *face up well*. The bright, mirrorlike reflections of the light source in this position mask slight tints of color. For example, some well-cut stones that grade in the *top-cape* grade, and most of those that fall in the *crystal* and *top-crystal* categories, seem colorless or nearly so under a strong, white-light source when observed face up.

"false lapis." A misnomer for *lazulite*.

fancy cut. Any style of diamond cutting other than the round brilliant or single cut. Fancy cuts include the *marquise, emerald cut, heart shape, pear shape, keystone, half moon, kite, triangle* and many others. Also sometimes called *fancy-shaped diamond* or *moderne cut*.

fancy diamond Any diamond with a natural body color strong enough to be attractive, rather than off color. Red, blue and green are very rare; orange and violet, rare; strong yellow, yellowish-green, brown and black stones are more common.

fancy pearl. A pearl with a body color of white or cream and a *rose'* orient, superimposed on an overtone of some hue such as blue-green, violet, purple, blue or green.

fancy sapphire. (1) A sapphire of any hue other than blue or colorless, although colorless is included by some. (2) Also, assorted lots of sapphire, and sometimes entirely different mineral species of every conceivable color, are incorrectly sold under this term.

fashioning. A term that includes sawing, cleaving, rounding up, facet grinding and polishing, and other operations employed in preparing rough gem material for use in jewelry.

fault. A little-used term that is essentially synonymous with *flaw* and *imperfection*.

faultless. A less-commonly used term than *flawless*, but having essentially the same meaning. As a word approximately synonymous with *flawless*, it is subject to the same restrictions under Federal Trade Commission Trade Practice Rules.

feather. When the plane of cleavage or fracture in a diamond is viewed at right angles to it, the appearance is often reminiscent of a feather. Thus, cleavage and fracture cracks in diamonds are often called *feathers*.

feather edge. A decoration suggesting a series of feathers, used as a border on silverware. See section on ornaments and designs.

Federal Trade Commission. A United States Government body that oversees interstate commerce and cooperates with representatives of various industries, including the gemstone and jewelry trades, to establish trade-practice rules that govern the representation to the public of the products of those industries.

feldspar. A group of closely related mineral species, the only gemologically important of which are *orthoclase* (*moonstone*), *microcline* (*amazonite*), *labradorite*, *albite* and *oligoclase*.

fiddle pattern. A 19th-century design for spoons and forks. Its characteristic features were round ends, straight sides, and sharp corners where the handle rounded away into the stem. See section on ornaments and designs.

fifth. A common abbreviation for a *fifth carat*, when referring to the weights of diamonds.

fifty-nine-twenty line. A sharp absorption line seen in the spectrum of most yellow and brown diamonds in which the color has been improved artificially by neutron bombardment and subsequent heat treatment. The application of this line to the detection of such diamonds was first described by Robert Crowningshield in *Gems & Gemology*, Vol. IX, No. 4; Winter, 1957-1958.

figaro chain. See section on basic styles of jewelry chains.

file test. A test that is used principally to separate glass imitations from diamonds, since a jeweler's file (hardness, about $6\frac{1}{2}$) will scratch glass but not diamond. However, many natural and artificial stones that might be confused with diamond are harder than a file and thus cannot be separated from diamond by such a test. In addition, the thin edges of a diamond or other valuable stones harder than the file may be damaged, giving the impression of a lower hardness.

filigree. (1) Ornamental work of very fine wire, often with toothed

Glossary

or notched edges that give the effect of fine beading. It is bent into designs and soldered together, sometimes to a metal background. (2) Because such work is called filigree when the background is omitted, all types of openwork (sawed, pierced, etc.) are sometimes less correctly referred to by this name. See section on ornaments and designs.

filter. Any colored glass or plastic used to filter out certain colors of the spectrum.

findings. Parts of jewelry produced in quantity for use in manufacturing or repairing jewelry; e.g., *catches, spring rings, gallery strips, pintongues.* See section on jewelry findings.

fine gold. Gold of 24-karat quality. The term *solid gold* should be applied only to fine gold.

fine rust. A name for the greenish or bronze *patina* of bronze.

fine silver. Pure silver; 1000 fine.

finial (fin″-e-al). The pointed ornament (usually turned) sitting at the very top of a clock, tea kettle, coffee pot, lamp, etc.

finish. (1) The cutting quality of a diamond is judged not only by its proportions and facet angles but by the excellence of its polish, the smoothness of its girdle surface, the exactness of its symmetry, and the size of its culet. These details of cutting comprise a fashioned diamond's *finish.* (2) The polish, texture and color of metal surfaces. Kinds of finish are *plain polished; acid finish; Roman finish; rose finish; English finish; India (green or smut) finish; matt, satin, brush, pumice* and *sand finishes;* and *patina.*

finishing. In a watch factory, the operations involving handwork, finishing of parts and regulating, as distinguished from the production of parts.

fire. Flashes of the different spectrum colors seen in diamonds and other gemstones as the result of *dispersion.*

fired zircon. Any zircon whose natural color has been changed or entirely eliminated by heating. The colors thus induced often revert partially.

fire opal. Transparent to translucent orangey-yellow, red, brownish-orange or brownish-red opal. It may or may not have a play of color. Principally from Mexico.

fisheye. A diamond whose pavilion is exceedingly shallow, producing a glassy appearance and a noticeable dearth of brilliancy.

fishtail setting. In setting a row of diamonds, the fishtail is formed by curving the holding prongs toward each other. The prongs are formed by splitting a single center post to hold adjacent diamonds. The curving of the metal to the side leaves a notch in the center, giving the appearance of a fish's tail; hence, the name. See section on mountings and settings.

fissure. An elongated cavity in a diamond's surface. It may or may not have occurred along the line where a cleavage reached the surface.

Fl. The abbreviation for *flawless*, the top imperfection, or clarity, grade of diamond.

flange. A reinforcing rib, or rim, set inside the bezel, forming a bearing for the setting.

flash plating. A thin coating of metal, little more than to permit necessary polishing.

flat. A flat diamond crystal or a portion thereof; it may or may not be a portion of a *macle*.

flat chasing. Shallow, indented chasing done with a blunt-edged tool. Unlike engraving, it does not cut away any silver, but merely displaces and depresses it along the lines of the pattern.

flat curb. See section on basic styles of jewelry chains.

flat-filed chain. See section on basic styles of jewelry chains.

flatware. Sterling or silverplated knives, forks, spoons, etc., as distinguished from bowls, platters, trays, plates and similar pieces. See section on flatware and holloware items.

flaw. Any *internal* or *external imperfection* on a fashioned diamond; e. g., a feather, fissure, carbon spot, knot, etc. Some diamond men limit its use to internal faults only, using the term *blemish* for surface faults. The terms *flaw* and *imperfection* are usually used interchangeably.

flexible bracelet. Any bracelet consisting of links or units joined together by links or rods, permitting flexibility.

flexible extension bracelet. A type of bracelet used for watches or jewelry, with links actuated by springs that allow for extension.

floating opal. Small pieces of gem opal, placed in glycerine in transparent drop-shaped or spherical glass containers, for use principally as a drop on a neck ornament.

floor clock. Same as *grandfather*, or *hall*, clock, usually of colonial design. See section on basic shapes of clocks.

floral setting. The style in which pearls and other gems are set in the form of flowers, leaves, etc., the stems being formed by the cuts made by the graver.

Florentine Diamond. A light-greenish-yellow, 137.27-carat Indian diamond, fashioned in the form of an irregular, 9-sided, 126-facet double rose cut. Legends link this famous gem with such well-known persons of history as Charles the Bold, Pope Julius II, the Grand Duke of Tuscany and Empress Maria Theresa, who placed it in the Hapsburg Crown. Later, it was displayed in the Hofburg, Vienna, where it was valued at $750,000. Its present whereabouts is unknown. Also known as the *Tuscan*, the *Grand Duke of Tuscany*, the *Austrian Diamond*, and the *Austrian Yellow*

Glossary

Diamond. See section on famous diamonds.

flower agate. (1) Any *moss agate*. (2) Translucent *chalcedony* containing inclusions of other minerals, sometimes red, brown, yellow or green, arranged in flowerlike forms, often of both red and green colors. (3) A term often applied to any *moss agate* or *mocha stone* with flowerlike markings.

fluorescence (floo'-oh-res"-cence). The property of changing the wavelength of radiation to one in the visible range; for example, the visible wavelengths emited by a material when excited by invisible radiation (such as X-rays, ultraviolet rays or cathode rays), as well as by certain visible wavelengths. It is exhibited by ruby, kunzite, yellow-green synthetic spinel, some diamonds and opals, and many other substances.

fluorite (floo"-oh-rite). A transparent to translucent green, blue, violet, yellow, orange, red, brown or colorless ornamental stone. It is seen in the jewelry trade as carved lamp bases, figurines and other carvings, and occasionally as imitations of other gems. Sources: England, Switzerland, Norway, Illinois and elsewhere.

fluting. A style of surface ornamentation having parallel channels, or grooves, usually running up and down like the fluted upright of a candlestick, the body of a bowl, or the base of a teapot. See section on ornaments and designs.

fob. An ornament attached by means of a short ribbon, chain, etc., to a watch to remove it from one's pocket.

foilback. An inexpensive gemstone or a piece of faceted glass that has been backed with a thin leaf of metallic foil, either silver or other color, to simulate the brilliancy of a diamond or to impart or improve the color of a colored stone.

foliation. Ornamental tracery in the form of leaves, vines, etc.

fork. In a lever-escapement watch, the acting end of the lever arm that is a part of the pallet, and through which power is applied to the roller jewel at each impulse to the balance.

Four C's. A phrase coined for advertising purposes that sums up the numerous factors affecting diamond value into four categories: *color, clarity, cutting* and *carat weight*.

four-hundred-day clock. A mantle clock with torsion pendulum, driven by a mainspring and running for a year or more without rewinding. See section on basic shapes of clocks.

four-point diamond. (1) A diamond that weighs four one-hundredths of a carat. (2) A diamond whose table has been cut parallel to a possible face of the cube.

foxtail chain. A chain, tightly braided of fine wire, on which beads are strung.

fracture. The chipping or breaking of a stone along a direction other than a cleavage plane. Types of fracture include *conchoidal* (kahn-koy"-dal), or *shell-like; splintery; granular; even* and *uneven.*

Francis I influence. See section on ornaments and designs.

French-gray finish. A gray finish that is distinctly darker in tone than any other silver finish.

French rope. See section on basic styles of jewelry chains.

fresh-water pearl. A concretion with orient and pearly luster, found in a fresh-water mollusc. The *Unio* genus of fresh-water clams is the host in North American waters.

friction jeweling. Jeweled bearings for pivots in watches, in which the synthetic jewels are pressed friction-tight into the framework of the movement, instead of being set by burnishing metal over the edge of the jewel.

friction staff. A type of balance staff for watches, in which the staff is fastened to the balance by a friction fit in a hole in a hub in the balance, instead of being riveted into a hole in the balance arm.

frosting. Various finishes on metals that look like frost. It is produced by sandblasting, steel bristles, chemical action, etc.

full-cut brilliant. A *brilliant-cut* diamond or colored stone with the usual total of 58 facets, consisting of 32 facets and a table above the girdle and 24 facets and a culet below. On colored stones, the girdle is usually polished, but seldom on diamonds. See section on shapes and styles of cutting.

Glossary

G

gadroon border. An ornamental border consisting of fluting or reeding, usually short in proportion to its width and often approaching the oval or almond shape. With a shell at the corners it is called a *shell-and-gadroon border*. See section on ornaments and designs.

gaining rate. In adjusting or regulating timepieces, the term is applied to timepieces that run faster than the standard rate of time; the opposite of a losing rate.

galalith. A plastic used to imitate ivory, tortoise shell, amber, etc.

gallery wire. Strips of ornmental metal used in making bezels or settings for mountings. See section on jewelry findings.

garnet. (1) A name that encompasses a number of closely related mineral species. Several chemically similar elements replace one another freely in the garnet group; as a result, the properties and appearance of the different garnet minerals differ appreciably. The garnet group is comprised of the following species and varieties: *pyrope, almandite, rhodolite, andradite* (*dematoid*), *grossularite* (*hessonite*), *spessartite* and *uvarovite*. (2) As an adjective, a color designation meaning *dark red*, as in the term *garnet glass*.

garnet doublet. The most common doublet: that with a very thin top of red garnet and a glass base. It is made in every color in which glass is made.

gas bubbles. Spherical bubbles seen in glass and synthetics, a characteristic that helps separate these materials from most genuine gems, in which the inclusions are usually angular.

gem. (1) A cut-and-polished stone that possesses the necessary beauty and durability for use in jewelry; also, a fine pearl. (2) An especially fine specimen; e. g., a *gem diamond*. In this use, the meaning depends on the ethics and the range of qualities handled by the seller. (3) As an adjective, a prefix; e. g., *gem quality*, *gem crystal*, etc. (4) As a verb, to decorate with gems.

gem color. Approximately synonymous with *perfection color*. However, it is often used in lieu of a definite grade to imply that a diamond of average to good color is actually exceptional in color.

Gem Detector. An inexpensive binocular microscope mounted on a dark-field illuminator base and equipped with a mechanical stoneholder. See section on diamond-grading and -merchandising instruments.

gem gravels. Gem-bearing gravels of present or former rivers or lake beds.

gem material. Any rough material, either natural or artificial, that can be fashioned into a jewel.

gem mineral. Any mineral species that yields varieties that have sufficient durability and beauty to be classed as gemstones.

Gemolite (trademark, Gemological Institute of America). An illuminator-magnifier combination for diamonds and other gems. It utilizes wide-field binocular magnifications with the Stereo-Zoom method of magnification change and a base designed for the examination of gems by either dark- or light-field illumination. The base contains a diffuser; an adjustable baffle; a diaphragm, to adjust to various lighting needs; and a turntable, to permit the instrument to be turned around to the customer. Accessories enable demonstration of proportions and color to be made to customers. See section on diamond-grading and -merchandising instruments.

Gemological Institute of America. See description of GIA elsewhere in book.

gemologist. One who has successfully completed recognized courses of study in gem identification, grading and pricing, as well as diamond grading and appraising; e.g., A *Gemologist* or *Graduate Gemologist* of the Gemological Institute of America or a *Certified Gemologist* of the American Gem Society.

gemology. The study of gemstones; their identification, grading and appraisal.

Gem Refractometer. An inexpensive refractometer, introduced to the trade in 1949 by the Gemological Institute of America. It employs a fixed hemicylinder and a simplified optical system that can be used for obtaining the refractive index of cabochon-cut stones as well as flat, polished surfaces.

Gems & Gemology. The quarterly journal of the Gemological Institute of America.

gem species. A mineral species with varieties suitable for use as gemstones.

gemstone. Any mineral or other natural material that has the necessary beauty and durability for use as personal adornment.

Gem-Trade Laboratories, Gemological Institute of America. See description under GIA, elsewhere in the book.

geode (jee″-ode). Cavities in clay or other formations that have been lined with a layer of quartz or other mineral. Weathering and erosion have subsequently carried away the host rock, leaving a hollow ball, the interior walls of which are usually studded with crystals.

German silver. Same as nickel silver.

GIA (Gemological Institute of America) Color-Grading System. A color-grading system for colorless to yellow diamonds

Glossary

that utilizes the letters D through X for a colorless-to-yellow scale. These grades are set in relation to a series of *master diamonds* that are maintained in the GIA's Los Angeles Laboratory. This range of the alphabet was purposely chosen to avoid confusion with other trade systems employing letters starting at the beginning of the alphabet.

GIA Color Grader. An accessory manufactured by the Gemological Institute of America to facilitate the color grading of diamonds under binocular magnification and to demonstrate it readily to the layman. See section on diamond grading and -merchandising instruments.

GIA Diamond Grader. A binocular microscope mounted on an illuminator base. It is equipped with a mechanical stoneholder, iris-diaphragm light control, light- and dark-field illumination, tilt back, and a turntable. Accessories for proportion and color grading extend its range. See section on diamond-grading and -merchandising instruments.

GIA Dichroscope (die"-kroscope). An instrument designed to detect the different colors that emerge from *pleochroic* (i.e., *dichroic* or *trichroic*) gems. It contains a rhomb of Iceland spar (calcite) and a lens in a short tube. The calcite is long enough so that its high birefringence separates the two images of the aperture enough to appear side by side. When examining a pleochroic stone, the two images show different colors. See section on gem-testing instruments.

GIA Gemologist Diploma. A diploma awarded to those who complete successfully the correspondence courses in gemology that are prepared and conducted by the Gemological Institute of America.

GIA Thermal Reaction Tester. An instrument made by the Gemological Institute of America that provides a rheostat-controlled, electrically-heated metal point to detect oiling, paraffin treatment, plastic imitations, etc. See section on gem-testing instruments.

GIA Spectroscope Unit. An instrument designed and manufactured by the Gemological Institute of America to provide the precise lighting necessary to maximize the usefulness of the spectroscope. The variable-intensity transmitted beam is passed through a prism to reduce heating in the specimen, an iris diaphragm controls and directs beam size, and a folding arm permits light to be reflected from above. The scale is lighted and three motions are possible on the spectroscope. See section on gem-testing instruments.

gilding. The process of electroplating a thin layer of pure gold on another metal. Bowls of spoons, tines of forks, the inside of mayonnaise and other bowls (holloware), etc., are often gilded to either reduce the possibility of tarnish from sulphur-containing foods or for ornmentation.

gilding metal. Brass with a low content of zinc, sometimes used as a base metal for gold-plated jewelry.

gilt. (1) Base metal dipped in a gold solution, which is also said to be *gold dipped*. (2) Base metal with a thin *electroplate* of fine gold.

girdle. The outer edge, or periphery, of a fashioned stone; the portion that is usually grasped by the setting or mounting; the dividing line between the crown and pavilion. See section on shapes and styles of cutting.

girdle (or break) facets. The 32 triangular facets that adjoin the girdle of a round brilliant-cut stone, 16 above and 16 below. Also called *upper-* and *lower-break facets*, *upper-* and *lower-girdle facets*, *top-* and *bottom-half facets*, *skew facets*, *skill facets* or *cross facets*. Facets are sometimes placed directly on the girdle, in which case the stone is usually said to have a *faceted girdle*. See section on shapes and styles of cutting.

girdle reflection. When a diamond has a pavilion that is too shallow or flat, the girdle is seen reflected in the table.

girdle thickness. The width of the outer edge, or periphery, of a fashioned diamond or other gemstone.

girdling (also called rounding up, bruting or cutting). The step in the fashioning process of a diamond in which the stone is given a circular shape. The stone is held in a *lathe,* or *cutting machine,* and another diamond, called a *sharp,* which is affixed to the end of a long dop that is supported by the hands and under an armpit, is brought to bear against the stone being shaped. An older method consisted merely of rubbing two diamonds together until the desired shape was obtained.

glass. (1) An amorphous solid, made usually by fusing a mixture of silica and one or more other metallic oxides. It is more a physical state than a definite material, being most easily visualized as a congealed liquid. (2) A term used synonymously with *crystal* for any transparent material covering the dial of a watch.

glassie. (1) Used at the diamond mines as a grade for well-shaped, transparent crystals of good color and without visible inclusions. (2) Also sometimes used to refer to a fashioned diamond that lacks brilliancy.

glyptography (glip-tog"-ra-fe). The art or process of engraving gems.

Gnaga Boh Ruby (Dragon Lord Ruby). A fine Burmese ruby that weighed 44 carats in the rough and 20 carats after cutting.

Goldconda. (1) A city in India

Glossary

that was the center of the diamond trade in the 17th century. (2) The ancient alluvial-diamond deposits to the south and east of the city of Golconda, along the Pennar, Kistna and Karnul Rivers; also called the *Kistna Group*. (3) Rarely used to denote a very fine color grade of diamond.

gold. A yellow-colored metallic element and precious metal, used for coins and jewelry since prehistoric times. Its hardness is 2 to 2.5, which is too soft for jewelry, unless alloyed, and the specific gravity is 19.3. It is unaffected by heat, air or most corrosive agents, but is dissolved by aqua regia. Gold is the most ductile and malleable of all metals: theoretically, a grain may be drawn into a wire 1 1/4 mile long and worked into a gold leaf .0000033 inch thick that would cover an area of six square feet.

gold beating. The method of producing *gold leaf* by beating with a hammer.

gold electroplate. The more accurate term for *gold plate*.

golden beryl. Golden-yellow beryl.

golden sapphire. Yellow to greenish-yellow or orangey-yellow sapphire.

gold filled. A layer (or layers) of karat gold, joined to the base-metal alloy and then rolled or drawn to the desired thickness, as distinguished from *gold dipped*,

gold plated, gilt, etc., but similar to *rolled-gold plate.*

gold jewelry. Jewelry made wholly or in part of *karat gold*. It is less accurately applied to gold-filled or gold-plated jewelry.

gold leaf. An extremely thin layer of gold. 23-karat gold is commonly used for sign painting; 14 to 18 karat for stamping leather.

gold plate. A base metal, usually gilding metal or other gold-colored metal, upon which a thin plate of fine gold has been deposited by *electrolysis*. Hence, it is *gold electroplate*, as distinguished from *rolled-gold plate.*

gold quartz. Milky quartz containing inclusions of gold. It is sometimes cut as a curio stone.

goldsmith. A person or firm that specializes in the manufacture of gold jewelry or other articles made of gold and its alloys.

goldstone. A translucent brown glass containing numerous inclusions of copper. A poor but popular imitation of *sunstone*. It is now also made with a blue background color, as well as brown.

goods. Mining companies, marketers of rough, cutters, importers and wholesalers often refer to categories of their diamond merchandise as *goods*.

Gothic arch. See section on ornaments and designs.

graded goods. Diamonds that have been graded by the cutter, importer or wholesaler before offering to the retailer, in contrast to *melange* offerings.

Graduate Gemologist. One who holds the *Graduate in Gemology Diploma*, awarded by the Gemological Institute of America, after successful completion of both its correspondence and residence courses in gemology.

grain. (1) Cleavage, sawing or polishing directions in diamond. When used alone, the word usually refers to *cleavage direction*. (2) One-quarter of a metric carat (.0500 grams), a unit of weight commonly used for pearls and sometimes other gems.

grainer. Diamonds with weights near multiples of one-quarter carat, or one grain, are referred to as *grainers*, qualified by the appropriate numerical designation; e.g., *four-grainer* for a *one-carat* stone.

grandfather clock. A *floor clock*, usually of colonial design. See section on basic shapes of clocks.

grandmother clock. A *floor clock*, smaller in height and general proportions than the grandfather clock. See section on basic shapes of clocks.

granulation. A granular ornament made by soldering large numbers of rounded metal grains onto a gold or silver background in such a way as to express a pattern.

graver. (1) A hand-cutting tool used by an engraver. (2) Also, a turning tool of a different style used on a lathe.

gray finish. A duller or whiter finish for silver than a butler finish. A gray finish is sometimes produced by the use of a slow-moving cotton buffing wheel and fine pumice.

gray gold. An alloy of *gold* and *iron* and sometimes *silver*.

grease table. A device for separating diamonds from other heavy minerals after concentration of heavy minerals from the crushed blueground. Since water does not adhere to the surface of a clean diamond, diamonds adhere to the grease. Other minerals are wetted and are washed over the slanted, rocking tables.

Great Mogul Diamond. Found in India in the mid-17th century, this legendary stone is said to have weighed 787.50 carats. Tavernier, the French jeweler and traveler, saw the diamond in 1665 and described it as a 280-carat rose cut, resembling an egg cut through the middle; at that time, it was owned by Shah Jehan, builder of the Taj Mahal. It is thought to have been stolen by the Persians when they looted Delhi in 1739. Some authorities believe that the *Orloff* and the *Great Mogul* are one and the same, and that the latter was broken up to escape detection. See section on famous diamonds.

Greek finish. Another name for *rose finish*.

Glossary

Greek key pattern. A border consisting of narrow fillets, or lines, at right angles to one another; also known as *Greek fret pattern*.

green chalcedony. Chalcedony that has been artificially colored green. If naturally colored, it is called *chrysoprase*.

green diamond. A naturally green, yellowish-green, apple-green or olive-green diamond of a sufficiently pronounced color to be an asset. Such a stone is called a *fancy*.

green finish. Same as *India finish*.

green garnet. Usually *demantoid garnet*, but may refer to *grossularite garnet*.

green gold. *Gold* alloyed with *silver* and, in 14 kt. and 10 kt., with smaller amounts of *zinc* and *copper*. 18 kt. is 75% gold and 25% silver.

green onyx (ahn″-iks). The usual trade designation for *green-dyed chalcedony*.

grinding. In the fashioning process, the preliminary shaping of a colored stone.

grisaille (gre-zay″; greh-zale″). A type of enamel in which white enamels are applied progressively on a dark background, producing a gray monochrome effect. Where the enamel is either left thin or omitted altogether, shadows are produced. A thick application (several coatings with successive firings) of enamel is used to produce the whitest tones. Some areas may be tinted lightly with a final layer in color.

grizzly. A screen used for sorting blueground at the diamond mines. 1¼-, 2- and 5-inch screens are used.

grossularite (gros″-u-ler-ite). A species of the *garnet group*. Translucent to semitranslucent white, yellow, pink and green varieties are sometimes sold incorrectly as "jade." The transparent yellow-brown to orangey-brown variety is known as *hessonite*. It is found in Ceylon, Italy, California and elsewhere. Nontransparent green grossularite is found in Oregon and the Transvaal.

guard chain. See section on jewelry findings.

guard ring. A narrow finger ring, plain or set with gems. Originally, such a ring was worn to prevent the loss of a more valuable ring; hence, the name.

gun-metal finish. A deep blue-black finish.

gypsum (jip″-sum). A soft mineral that yields a few curio stones. The *alabaster* variety is often carved into lamp bases, figurines and similar articles.

gypsy mounting. A ring that holds a gemstone so that its girdle is completely covered, as in bezel set, but in this case there is no bezel. Instead, a seat is cut in the

269

metal shank and the edges burnished over the stone. After polishing, the entire top surface of the ring is smooth and flush with the girdle of the stone. See section on mountings and settings.

Glossary

H

hairclip. See section on jewelry findings.

hairspring. A metal spring of spiral, helical or combined form attached to the balance of a watch to govern its motions. The balance and the spring together constitute the balance assembly, which is the true timekeeping element.

hairstone. Any variety of transparent to translucent *quartz* containing hairlike inclusions of other minerals.

half-quarter repeater. A watch that strikes every 7½ minutes.

hall clock. A standing clock six feet or more in height. See section on basic shapes of clocks.

hallmark. See section on silverware.

hammered finish. That produced by imparting a multitude of tiny dents in a metal's surface. The random pattern of a hand-hammered surface is regarded as particularly desirable by connoisseurs.

handless watch. A watch with a dial on which time is shown by numerals appearing in openings in the dialplate; the numerals are on rotating discs under the dial.

hand remover. A tool for taking hands off watches. It may be of various forms, but all work on the principle of a pair of wedges to exert force without damaging dial or hands.

hands. The pointers that turn around the dials of timepieces, indicating hours, minutes and seconds. Early clocks and watches had only an hour hand; the concentric minute hand was introduced shortly after 1650 and the seconds hand about 1700. See section on watches.

hand wrought. Made from a flat piece of silver or other metal entirely by hand tools.

hard mass (or masse). A trade term used originally for a special glass of an unusual hardness of 6 or more. It is now misused to mean any glass, especially green glass artificially flawed to imitate emerald, and sometimes to mean synthetic sapphire or spinel.

hardness. The resistance a substance offers to being *scratched*, a property that is sometimes useful in the identification of gemstones and their substitutes. See table of relative hardness of gem materials.

hardness points. Small, pointed pieces of minerals of different hardness, affixed to small metal handles. They are held in the hand and used for testing the hardness of another mineral, by ascertaining which point will scratch it. Minerals of hardness 6 to 10 are usually used as the points. Damage to a stone is such a great danger that gemologists avoid this method of testing, except under unusual circumstances. See section on gem-testing instruments.

hatpin. A pin sufficiently long to pass through a woman's hair and hat. The head of the pin is ornamental.

Hatton Garden. The center of the wholesale gem and jewelry district in London, England.

hawk's-eye. Transparent, colorless *quartz* that contains parallel, closely-packed, bluish needlelike crystals of another mineral. When cut cabochon, it resembles the eye of a hawk.

"healed" pearls. Those in which surface or subsurface cracks have been repaired by experts.

heated stone. A stone that has been heated to change its color, such as blue zircon, or to improve its color, such as many aquamarines.

hematite (hem″-ah-tite). An opaque mineral, yielding pigments when red and earthy, and fashioned as intaglios and other carved gems when dark gray to black with metallic luster. Incorrect names are "bloodstone" (its ancient name) and "black diamond." Sometimes, it is used to imitate black pearls. Sources: England, Scandinavia, USA (Lake Superior region).

Hemetine. A trademarked name for an imitation of *hematite*. It has since been outlawed as misleading.

"Herkimer diamond." A misnomer for *rock crystal*.

hessonite (hes″-o-nite). The yellow-brown to orangey-brown, transparent variety of *grossularite garnet*. It is also known as *hyacinth garnet* or *cinnamon stone*.

hexagonal system (hex-ag″-oh-nal). See section on crystal systems.

hiddenite (hid″-den-ite). A pale but intense yellow-green variety of *spodumene*. Sources: Madagascar and North Carolina.

holloware. A term that refers to various sterling and silverplated dishes used for containing and serving food (e.g., bowls, pitchers, service plates, butter plates), as distinguished from silver flatware. See section on flatware and holloware items.

hollow pearl. Same as *wax-filled pearl*.

hololith ring. A finger ring cut from one piece of gem material.

hook chain. See section on basic styles of jewelry chains.

hoop earring. See section on jewelry findings.

Hope Cat's-eye. A large, nearly hemispherical chrysoberyl cat's-eye, about 1½ inches in diameter. It was once in the Hope collection.

Hope Chrysoberyl. A 45-carat flawless, yellowish-green, oval, brilliant-cut chrysoberyl now in the British Museum of Natural History. It is called by the Museum "a matchless specimen." It was once in the Hope collection.

Hope Diamond. A 44.50-carat

dark-sapphire-blue Indian diamond. Although its early history is controversial, this famous stone appeared on the market in 1830 and was purchased by Henry Thomas Hope. In 1908, it was purchased by Abdul Hamid II, Sultan of Turkey; and in 1911 by Edward B. McLean, of Washington, D.C. It became the property of Harry Winston, New York City gem dealer, in 1947, and in 1958 he presented it to the Smithsonian Institution, where it is on display. See section on famous diamonds.

Hope Pearl. An 1800-grain pearl, somewhat cylindrical but swelling at one end; white, but brown tinted at one end. It was once in the Hope collection, but now is in the British Museum of Natural History. It is thought to be the largest known precious pearl. Length, 2½ inches; circumference, 3½ to 4½ inches.

horology. The science of time measurement, including the art of designing and constructing timepieces.

horse-timer. Another name for a *stop watch*.

hub. A female die.

hubcutter. Same as diecutter.

hue. The principal attribute by which a color is distinguished from black, white or neutral gray; the attribute by which colors, when they are arranged in their orderly spectrum sequence, are perceived as differing from one another. Thus, technically, each wavelength in the visible spectrum propagates a different hue. Red, yellow and green, as well as greenish yellow, yellow-green and yellowish green, are different hues; whereas pink (light red), maroon (dark red) and brownish red are colors that have the same hue but that differ in other attributes.

"Hungarian cat's-eye." A misnomer for *quartz cat's-eye*.

hunting case. A watchcase on which the dial is covered by a lid that may be thrown open by pressing a button on the pendant. It differs from an openface case, in which the dial is covered only by a glass or crystal.

hyacinth. (1) A variety of *zircon*. The term is applied by some authorities only to the red and orange varieties, many of which have been heat treated. Others use it interchangeably with *jacinth* to mean yellow-orange, red or brown zircon. It is sometimes used loosely to mean any zircon. (2) The word is also used as a color designation meaning *orange-red* to *orange*, as in *hyacinth garnet* and *hyacinth sapphire*.

hydrostatic weighing method. The determination of the *specific gravity* of a gemstone or other substance by weighing it immersed in water and also in air. The S.G. is then stated as the ratio between the weight in air and the loss of weight in water.

I

Idar-Oberstein. A famous center for colored-stone cutting in West Germany. Some diamond cutting is done in the vicinity, also.

ideal cut (also called American cut). Those proportions and facet angles that were calculated mathematically by Marcel Tolkowsky to produce maximum brilliancy consistent with a high degree of fire in a round diamond brilliant are considered by many diamond men to constitute the *ideal cut*. These figures, computed as a percentage of the girdle diameter, are as follows: total depth, 59.3%, plus girdle thickness; crown depth, 16.2%; pavilion depth, 43.1%. The bezel angle is 34° 30′ and the pavilion angle is 40° 45′.

identification (of a gemstone). The testing of the physical and optical properties of a stone, to determine whether or not it is genuine, and, if genuine, its species.

idocrase (i″-doe-krase). Same as *vesuviante*. A mineral species, the green *californite* variety of which is sometimes mistaken for jade. Sources: California, Siberia, Italy, Canada.

Illuminator Polariscope (polare″-ih-scope). An optical instrument that consists basically of two polarizing filters. The filter through which light enters is called the *polarizer*; that through which observations are made is called the *analyzer*. The instrument is used to ascertain whether a gemstone possesses *single* or *double refraction* and, to a lesser extent, to detect *anomalous double refraction*, which indicates *internal strain*. See section on gem-testing instruments.

Industrial Diamond Association of America, Inc. See section on trade associations.

illusion setting. A *prong setting* in which a wide ring of metal surrounding the girdle of a stone is highly polished to act as a mirror. It creates the illusion that the stone is larger than its actual size. See section on mountings and settings.

imitation. In its broadest sense, anything that simulates a genuine, natural gem. Gemologically, the term is applied only to glass, plastics and other *amorphous* materials, as distinguished from synthetics and assembled stones.

imitation pearls. Beads made of glass, wax or other substances and coated or lined with *essence d'orient*, as distinguished from natural or cultivated pearls.

immersion cell. Any cell used to immerse a gemstone in a liquid as a means of overcoming reflection and refraction from its surface, thus providing more efficient observation of its interior. Immersion cells usually have glass bot-

Glossary

toms, to facilitate their use with microscopes, polariscopes, etc. See section on gem-testing instruments.

imperfect. The diamond imperfection grade at the low end of the *flawless-to-imperfect* (or *perfect-to-imperfect*) scale. An imperfect diamond contains imperfections that are visible face up to the unaided eye or that have a serious effect on the stone's durability. The Gemological Institute of America recognizes three grades in the broad imperfect range.

imperfection. A general term used to refer to any *external* or *internal* flaw or blemish on a fashioned diamond; e.g., a feather, carbon spot, fissure, knot, scratch, natural, etc. The terms *flaw* and *imperfection* are usually used interchangeably.

imperfection (or clarity) grade. The relative position of a diamond on a *flawless-to-imperfect* scale. A number of imperfection-grading systems are used by various importers and retailers, perhaps the most common of which begins with either *flawless* or *perfect*, followed by *very, very slightly imperfect, very slightly imperfect, slightly imperfect* and *imperfect*. In some systems, *piqué* is substituted for one or more of the grades mentioned; perhaps most frequently it is inserted in place of *imperfect* or between *slightly imperfect* and *imperfect*. Often, several grades, such as *first piqué, second piqué*, etc., are employed. Some grading systems utilize letters or numerals for the respective grades. In others, internal and external grades are given separately.

imperial jade. The finest, evenly colored, emerald-green translucent to semitransparent *jadeite*.

inactive patterns. Silverware patterns that have been discontinued by the manufacturer, but the dies of which have been retained at the factory. Replacements, or even full services, can usually be obtained for such patterns.

incised. Cut or carved areas; a design in which the decoration is below the surface, as in an *intaglio*.

inclusion. Any internal foreign object, or any crystal or grain of the same material as the host, or any break in a diamond or other gemstone can be called an inclusion. Breaks such as fractures and cleavages, however, are not always considered inclusions.

incrustation. An overlay of gemstones, gold, silver or other ornamental material on the surface of another substance, usually in a design.

"indestructible pearl." A misnomer for an imitation pearl containing a *glass center*, as distinguished from a *wax-filled* glass sphere.

index watch hand. See section on watches.

India (green or smut) finish. An olive-green smudge in the background, the raised surfaces being relieved to produce a pleasing contrast with the background. It is used on green-gold alloys.

Indian cut. A clumsy form of the *single cut,* adopted by East Indian cutters for the purpose of retaining maximum weight in the cut stone.

"Indian jade." A misnomer for *aventurine quartz.*

industrial diamond. As a general term, it refers to nongem-quality diamonds that are suitable only for industrial tools, abrasives, drills, etc. Gem-quality crystals, however, are also used for tools and particularly for dies, where lack of both internal strain and flaws is required. In this capacity, such a stone would also be called an industrial diamond.

infrared. That part of the electromagnetic spectrum beyond the red end of the visible spectrum, containing the so-called heat rays, which produce *luminescence* in certain gems and other substances. Infrared extends from wavelengths of about .7 micron to 100+.

inherent vice. If an insured gemstone is said to have suffered damage, the insurance adjustor must determine whether damage has occurred and, if so, whether it is attributable to some characteristic weakness in the stone (e.g., a preexisting cleavage); such weakness is called *inherent vice.* If damage has occurred, it is fully recoverable from the insurance company only if inherent vice is not involved.

inlay. In some silverplated ware, an additional coating or piece of silver embedded (before the electroplating process) in the base metal of certain parts of an article that receive the greatest amount of wear, such as the heel of a spoon.

in situ. A mineral found in place in a primary rock (e. g., diamond in kimberlite), rather than in a position to which it has been transported by such agencies as water, wind, glacial action or gravity, is said to have been found *in situ.*

insulators. Heat-resistant substances inserted between the handle and the body of such articles as kettles, teapots, etc.

intaglio (in-tal″-yo). A carved gem that may be used as a seal, in which the design has been engraved *into* the stone. Intaglios differ from cameos, in that the figure is incised in the intaglio and raised in the cameo. See section on shapes and styles of cutting.

intensity (of a color). The comparative brightness (vividness) or dullness of a color; therefore, the variation of a hue on a *vivid-to-dull* scale.

interference. When light waves originating at different sources or that have traveled different path distances then travel the same path simultaneously, reinforcement or cancellation takes place. Thus, two red rays may interfere to produce

Glossary

more intense red, as in many opals, or to cancel one another.

internal strain. A stress set up in a gemstone as a result of structural irregularities or distortion, usually brought about by inclusions in the stone.

invar. An alloy of 36% *nickel* and 64% *iron*, which has a very low coefficient of expansion. It is used in horology for precision-clock pendulum rods and integral watch balances.

iolite (i"-oh-lite). A mineral that, when transparent and blue to blue-violet, is sometimes cut as a gem for collectors. It is also known as *dichroite* or *cordierite*. Its pleochroism is very strong. A frequently used misnomer is "water sapphire."

Ionic. One of the three orders of Greek architecture. See section on ornaments and designs.

iridescence (ear-ih-des"-cence). The exhibition of prismatic colors in the interior or on the surface of a mineral, caused by interference of light from thin films or layers of different refractive index.

iridio-platinum. An alloy that usually contains 90% or more of platinum. The remaining percentage is of iridium, which is necessary to produce an alloy sufficiently hard for use in mountings. If it is 10% iridium, it is known as *hard platinum;* if 5%, *medium-hard platinum.*

iridium (i-rid"-e-um). A metal of the *platinum* group. It is used for hardening platinum and for the tips of penpoints. Its specific gravity is 22.4 and its hardness, 6½.

iris agate. Banded agate that, in thin sections, displays *iridescence.*

iron pyrites. A popular name for *pyrite.*

irradiated diamond. A diamond that has been subjected to bombardment by fast electrons, neutrons, deuterons, or other subatomic particles. The purpose of irradiation is to make the stone more attractive and desirable by introducing a pronounced color.

isochronism (i-sock"-ro-nizm). In the action of a watch balance or any other governor of a timepiece, the conditions in which all vibrations are made in equal periods of time.

isometric system (ice-oh-met"-rik). See section on crystal systems.

isotropic (ice'-oh-trope"-ik). Meaning *singly refractive.* The inability of a gem to polarize light passing through it, thus permitting light to pass through as a singly-refracted beam. Diamond, spinel, garnet and other minerals of the *cubic,* or *isometric,* crystal system, as well as glass and other amorphous materials, are isotropic.

ivory. The hard, creamy-white, opaque, fine-grained substance, consisting of a peculiar form of dentine that comprises the tusks of elephants; also, the dentine of the tusks of other large mammals. In a broader sense, the dentine of any tooth.

J

jade. A gemological group of two minerals, *jadeite* and *nephrite*, of different chemical composition but rather closely related in appearance and in physical properties, especially their unusual toughness and in uses that include jewelry, carved objects, and various ornamental objects. Jade occurs in large compact masses, and its color is often unevenly distributed.

jadeite. A semitranslucent to almost semitransparent mineral, which, in its finer qualities, is a more valuable jade than nephrite. White, green and mixtures of these two colors are the most common; also gray, mauve, lavender, pink, reddish and orangy to brown. The structure of the tougher qualities consists of closely matted fibrous crystals. *Chloromelanite* is a dark-green to almost black variety. Upper Burma is the principal source.

Jager (Yah"-ger). A diamond that displays a faint tint of blue in daylight or under other light sources that are rich in ultraviolet.

Jagersfontein Mine (Yah"-gers-fon-tane"). The first diamond-pipe mine in South Africa, discovered in 1870 on the Jagersfontein farm near Fauersmith, Orange Free State. Although the mine produces a large proportion of cleavage fragments and heavily spotted goods, it has a high yield of fine colors, including stones that are faintly blue in daylight. Annual production is usually between 100,000 and 150,000 carats.

japanning. A sort of lacquering or pseudoenameling, usually black. It is used on cheap jewelry and for the numerals on watch dials.

jasper. An opaque red, yellow, brown, dark-green, grayish-blue or lavender, fine-grained, impure *chalcedony (cryptocrystalline quartz)*. Widely distributed.

"Java Gem." A trademarked name for *synthetic rutile*.

jet. A black variety of *lignite* (brown coal); a fossilized coniferous coal. Source: England and Spain.

jewel. (1) A fashioned gemstone or a pearl. (2) Any ornament made of gold or platinum of more than 10-kt. fineness, whether or not set with a genuine or synthetic gemstone or with a genuine or cultured pearl. (3) A badge or ceremonial ornament containing genuine or artificial gems, enamel or the like. (4) A bearing for a pivot in a watch or other precision instrument, usually made of synthetic corundum.

jeweled watch. A watch that contains jewels used as bearings in the movement; usually 7, 15, 17 or 21.

jeweler. One who makes jewelry. The term is also used more loosely for any jewelry repairer or merchant.

Jewelers' Board of Trade. See section on trade associations.

Jewelers' Camera. A camera designed to meet the photographic needs of jewelers; from less than actual size to many-time enlargements of set and unset diamonds and colored stones, large or small jewelry articles for advertising artwork, appraisals, stock records, reference files of attractive merchandise and many other uses. Background contrast and highlighting are provided by a new development in lighting that consists of three independent, adjustable sources located at the base, at the sides and near the lens. For each of the jeweler's major uses, lighting combinations and settings have been worked out to speed and simplify operation. Polaroid film, as well as conventional color and black-and-white roll film, may be used. This instrument is manufactured by the Gemological Institute of America. See section on diamond-grading and -merchandising instruments.

"jewelers' olivine." A misnomer for *demantoid garnet*.

Jewelers' Security Alliance of the United States. See section on trade associations.

"jewelers' topaz." A misnomer for *citrine*.

Jewelers' Vigilance Committee. See section on trade associations.

jeweling. In timepieces and other instruments, the use of polished synthetic-stone bearings for pivots and other parts acting with friction. Jeweling gives mechanical advantages by lessening friction, power consumption and wear of parts. In timepieces, the pivot bearings are jeweled with hole and cap jewels; in the escapement, jewels are used in the form of pallet stones and roller jewels.

jewelry. Any personal ornament wrought from precious metals or any ornament that can be worn as a substitute for it, such as shell jewelry, plastic jewelry, etc. In industry usage, the term includes (1) any article worn or carried wholly for personal adornment, or (2) any article worn or carried for utilitarian needs that is made of precious metals, set with precious gems, or made in imitation of any utilitarian article made of precious metals and set with gems. It differs in meaning from jewel.

Jewelry Industry Council. See section on trade associations.

Jewelry Manufacturers' Association, Inc. See section on trade associations.

jobber. A wholesaler, as distinguished from an importer or manufacturer, either of whom may sell to jobbers or retailers or both.

jobbing-stones. An assortment of stones, mostly glass or synthetics, kept for use in replacing lost or broken stones in customers' jewelry.

job envelope. The coin envelope in which a retail jeweler keeps an

Glossary

item or items during repair and remodeling.

job shop. Same as *trade shop*.

"Johannes Gem." A trademarked name for *synthetic rutile*.

joint. See section on jewelry findings.

Jonker Diamond (Yon"-ker). A fine-quality, 726-carat diamond, found in South Africa in 1934. It was purchased by the Diamond Producers' Association for $315,000 and later sold to Harry Winston, New York City gem dealer, for a reported $700,000. After cutting by Lazare Kaplan, of New York, a marquise and eleven emerald cuts resulted. The largest stone, the *Jonker*, was a 66-facet emerald cut that weighed 142.90 carats; later, it was recut to 125.65 carats and 58 facets. After being owned briefly by King Farouk, of Egypt (when its estimated value was $1,000,000), it became the property of Queen Ratna, of Nepal. See section on famous diamonds.

Jubilee Diamond. A 650.80-carat African diamond, found in 1895. It was named in honor of Queen Victoria's Diamond Jubilee, in 1897. It was cut into a 245.35-carat cushion-shaped brilliant of excellent quality and exhibited in Paris in 1900. Thereafter, it was owned by an Indian industrialist and a London firm. Since 1937, the gem has been the property of Paul-Louis Weiller, of Paris, who loaned it to the Smithsonian Institution in 1961 for display. Its present value is estimated to be $1,500,000. See section on famous diamonds.

jump ring. A wire ring, so made that its two ends can be temporarily separated, thus permitting the connection of another ring. It is used for attaching charms to be worn on chains, etc. It is also called a *split ring*. See section on jewelry findings.

junk box. A jeweler's container of damaged or otherwise comparatively valueless jewelry, salvaged mostly from outmoded or worn-out pieces.

K

"Kandy spinel." A misnomer for *almandite garnet*.

karat. A unit of weight to express the proportion of gold in an alloy or the quality of a gold alloy. Pure gold is 24 karats. One karat is 1/24 part by weight of gold in any article. Any alloy of gold is known by its proportion in weight of fine gold; e.g., 18 karat is 18/24 fine gold, or 75% of the weight of the entire article; 10 karat is 10/24, or 41.67% fine gold. The balance may be an alloy of other metals, commonly a combination of silver and copper and occasionally zinc. Nickel is used in white gold, and palladium has been used at times. The meaning of the term is entirely different from *carat*.

karat gold. Alloys of gold with other metals, as distinguished from *fine gold*, and provided that the alloy contains ten parts or more of gold; i.e., 10-karat gold.

karat needles. A set of needles, each one of which is tipped with a different gold alloy. They are used for comparison to the unknown being tested in the *acid test* for precious metals.

karat tolerance. The word *tolerance* refers to the specified allowance for error in weighing, measuring, etc., or for variations from a standard. The permissible variation for karat gold is one-half karat, or 20.8 parts per thousand on gold not containing solder and one karat on an entire piece containing solder. Laws do not provide for minimum karat. The method of determining whether a gold alloy legally conforms to a karat-and-fineness mark stamped on it is to make an assay. The assay determines the fineness; e.g., 10 karat must contain 416.7 parts of fine gold per 1000; 18 karat, 750 parts per 1000; or within the tolerance provided for in the United States Stamping Law.

"Kenya Gem." A trademarked name for *synthetic rutile*.

kerf (kurf). An Anglo-Saxon word referring to the groove that is cut in a diamond preparatory to the *cleaving* operation.

key, or Greek key. See section on ornaments and designs.

key release. See section on jewelry findings.

keystone. When a retail price is followed by *keystone*, it means that cost to the retailer is 50% of that figure.

key winder. An old-fashioned watch wound by a key, instead of a stem.

Kimberley Mine. July, 1871, is the usually accepted date for the discovery of diamonds at Colesburg Kopje, on the farm Vooruitzigt, Cape Province, South Africa. The pipe was originally known as De Beers New Rush and later shortened to New Rush; finally, it

Glossary

was named Kimberley. The mine was closed in 1914, after being worked to a depth of 3610 feet. The huge crater, in the city of Kimberley, is called the "Big Hole."

kimberlite. The name applied to the type of basic igneous rock (a serpentinized biotite-peridotite) that is the host rock of diamonds in all primary diamond deposits discovered to date.

"Kimberlite Gem." A trademarked name for *synthetic rutile*.

"king topaz." A deceiving name for *citrine,* or *topaz-quartz*.

kite facets. An alternate term for the *main bezel facets,* the outlines of which resemble a kite. See section on shapes and styles of cutting.

knife-edge girdle. A girdle of a diamond that is so thin that it can be likened to the edge of a sharp knife. Since such a girdle is easily chipped, an ideal girdle has an appreciable thickness.

knot. (1) An included diamond crystal that is encountered at the surface of a stone during the polishing operation and that stands out as a small, raised surface on the finished stone. (2) An included diamond crystal that is encountered by the saw blade. Since the softest directions available for sawing and polishing are used by the cutter, and since included crystals have a different orientation from the surrounding mass, they almost always have a harder direction than that being exploited. (3) A small section of a twinned stone in which the grain differs from the main mass.

knot lines. A term used by some cutters for the *twinning lines* on or within a diamond.

knuckle. One of the tubular sections that, together with the hinge pin, forms the hinge on a locket or watch case.

knurled. When an ornamentation is cut into steel rolls and then impressed from the rolls into silver (e.g., borders on bowls or dishes) or other metals, the ornamental surface is said to be *knurled*.

Koffyfontein Mine (Kof'-e-fon-tane"). The third largest diamond pipe mine in area in the Union of South Africa and one of the earliest discoveries (1870) in the Orange Free State. De Beers obtained full control of the mine in 1911. Formerly an important producer, it was operated until 1931. It is located between the Kimberley and Jagersfontein Mines.

Kohinoor Diamond (Ko"-uh-nur). One of the world's most renowned diamonds, with a recorded history that began in 1304, when it was an old Indian cut of 186 carats. For hundreds of years thereafter, it was the subject of mystery, violence and intrigue, involving such famous and infamous persons as Sultan Baber, the first Mogul emperor; Shah Jehan, who built the Taj Mahal; and Nadir Shah who conquered Delhi in 1739. In 1849, the stone was acquired by the British East India Co. and presented to Queen Victoria, who had it recut to a 108.93-carat oval brilliant; before recutting, it was valued at $700,000. Since then, it has been one of the prized possessions of British royalty. See section on famous diamonds.

"**Korean jade.**" An incorrect name that is sometimes used with a variety of jade substitutes, including bowenite, steatite and serpentine.

K, or kt. The abbreviation for *karat*.

krinkle chain. See section on basic styles of jewelry chains.

kunzite (koonts"-ite). The transparent pink to light-violet variety of *spodumene*. Sources: Southern California, Madagascar, Brazil.

kyanite (ki-"-ahn-ite). A colorless, green, brown or blue gem mineral that is cut occasionally for collectors. Sources: Brazil, Switzerland, India, Massachusetts, Pennsylvania, North Carolina, Montana and elsewhere.

L

labradorescence (lab′-rah-door-es″-cence). The phenomenon possessed by *labradorite* that displays flashes of a laminated iridescence of a single bright hue that changes gradually as the stone is moved about in reflected light.

labradorite (lab″-rah-door-ite). A feldspar that is best known for a light-interference effect resulting in vivid colors (particularly blue, green or yellow) over large areas. The cause is interference in laminae caused by repeated twinning. Transparent yellow labradorite is a curiosity. Sources: Labrador, Finland, Russia, Colorado.

lace chain. See section on basic styles of jewelry chains.

lacquer. (1) A colorless varnish applied to silverware to prevent the air from reaching its surface and producing a tarnish. (2) An unfused enamel that is often used on cigarette boxes, compacts, etc., on whose large surfaces it is less apt to chip, although it scratches and becomes dull more easily than fusible enamel. It is sometimes called *French flexible enamel*.

landscape agate. Agate with irregularities in banding that remind some imaginative viewers of country scenes.

lap. A horizontally revolving, circular metal disc, usually eight to 18 inches in diameter, against which gems are held to be ground, polished or faceted. Cast iron for diamonds; copper, gun metal, lead, pewter, wood, cloth, leather, etc., for colored stones.

La Pellegrina Pearl. A pearl of 111½ grains, described as one of the world's finest. It was last known in Russia, in 1827.

La Peregrina Pearl. A pearl of 134 grains, found in Panama or Venezuela about 1570 and presented to Phillip II, of Spain. It is thought to have burned in a fire at the palace in 1734. It is also called *Phillip II Pearl*.

lapidary (or lapidist). A cutter, grinder and polisher of colored stones. In the trade, a lapidary is not necessarily an engraver of gems, this being considered a specialized art. A cutter and polisher of diamonds is classed as a *diamond cutter*, as distinguished from a lapidary.

lapis. The popular name for *lapis-lazuli*.

lapis-lazuli (lap″-iss-laz″-u-li). An opaque gemstone that is made up primarily of the mineral *lazurite*; it is noted for the intensity of its violetish-blue color. Gold-colored grains of *pyrite* are usually present. The more patches of white or gray *calcite*, the lower the grade. Sources: Afghanistan, Russia, Chile, Colorado.

lapis matrix. Lapis-lazuli with especially large patches of white or gray.

lapped border. Same as *rolled edge.*

lapper (or blocker). A diamond cutter who specializes in placing the first 18 (main) facets on a brilliant-cut diamond (17, if there is no culet).

lapping. The grinding or polishing of colored stones on a lap, by the use of water and (1) diamond dust rolled or hammered into a soft metal lap, or (2) a mixture of abrasive grit, usually silicon carbide. In diamond cutting, lapping is the process of placing the first 18 (main) facets on a brilliant (17, if there is no culet); it is also known as *blocking.*

La Regente Pearl. An egg-shaped pearl of 337 grains, once a French court jewel. It was sold in 1887.

La Reine des Perles (The Queen of Pearls). A fine, round oriental pearl weighing 27½ carats, stolen with other French crown jewels in 1792. It is thought by some to have been purchased and renamed *La Pellegrina Pearl.*

lariat slide. See section on jewelry findings.

lavalliere (lahv-ah-lear"). An article of jewelry; a *pendant* suspended on a neck chain.

lazulite (laz"-u-lite). A light-to dark-blue, transparent to opaque mineral that resembles lazurite somewhat in color. It is rarely cut, except for collectors.

lazurite (laz"-u-rite). A semi-transparent to opaque, light to intense blue to violet-blue mineral. It is the principal constituent of *lapis-lazuli.*

lead glass. Any glass that contains a large proportion of *lead oxide.* The addition of this oxide raises the refractive index, dispersion and specific gravity above that of ordinary glass. It is the most common glass imitation of diamond, and is also used to imitate many colored stones. It is also known as *flint glass* or *strass.*

leaf watch hand. See section on watches.

lemel (le"-mel). Sweepings from jewelry shops that are collected to be sent to refiners for gold and platinum recovery.

lentille. A watch crystal in which the edges are rounded off.

lever escapement. The type of escapement long considered as best for use in watches. It is a detached-type escapement, with pallet-fork-and-arbor assembly between the escape wheel and the balance.

Leveridge gauge. A millimeter dial micrometer, designed by A. D. Leveridge, for measuring various shapes of mounted and unmounted diamonds and colored stones, as well as spherical pearls. An accompanying set of tables is used for translating measurements into weights. It is the most accurate of the gauges designed specifically for weight estimations. See section on diamond-grading and -merchandising instruments.

Glossary

lever set. A type of handsetting mechanism for watches, in which a lever is pulled out from the side of the dial to shift the mechanism from winding to setting condition. This type of setting is favored by railroad-inspection rules, because with it, it is impossible to leave the watch in a setting position accidently, which could cause an error in timekeeping.

light-field illumination. A kind of illumination in which the light source is directly behind the gemstone being observed. This principle, together with *dark-field illumination*, is incorporated in the *Gemolite*, or *Gemscope* (trademarks, Gemological Institute of America), the *Diamondscope* (trademark, American Gem Society), plus the *GIA Gem Detector* and the *GIA Diamond Grader*.

light yellow. A trade term used by some dealers to cover a wide range of colors in the low end of the diamond color-grading scale. Stones in this broad classification show a very obvious yellow tint to the unaided eye.

ligne (leen″-yuh). An ancient French unit of measurement, still used for designating the diameters of watches, especially those of European origin. A *ligne* is the equivalent of 2.255883 millimeters, or .08883 inch.

limpid. A diamond is said to be *limpid* if it is without body color and very transparent.

Linde Star. A trademarked name for synthetic star ruby and synthetic blue, white and black star sapphire made in the United States by Linde Air Products Co.

liner. A graver that produces, with one cut of the tool, a series of closely spaced, parallel lines.

"lithia emerald." A misnomer for *green spodumene*.

long-and-short chain. See section on basic styles of jewelry chains.

loose goods. Polished but unmounted diamonds.

lot. (1) A group of rough diamonds offered for sale by the Diamond Trading Co. to firms invited to view its *sights*. A lot usually includes a wide variety of material. (2) Also applied by diamond merchants to their regroupings of these diamonds according to color, make, and comparative freedom from imperfections after fashioning.

lotus. An ornamentation patterned after the Egyptian water lily. See section on ornaments and designs.

loupe (loop). Any small magnifying glass mounted for use in the hand as a *hand loupe*, or so that it can be held in the eye socket or attached to spectacles as an *eye loupe*. A loupe may contain a single lens (uncorrected) or a system of lenses (corrected), which in commercial usage range from 2 to 20 power or more. The usual jeweler's or watchmaker's loupe is uncorrected and magnifies from 2 to 3 times; *aplanatic* *loupes* (those that are corrected for spherical aberration) vary from 6 to 20 power. See section on diamond-grading and -merchandising instruments.

"loupe clean." A term that is usually misleading, since it is used to describe diamond qualities to suggest that no flaws are visible under magnification. If this were true under 10x examination by an experienced man using a corrected loupe, the term *perfect* or *flawless* would be used. It is prohibited by the American Gem Society for use by its members. It is also prohibited by the Federal Trade Commission, unless the stone is flawless.

louped. A trade term meaning that a gemstone has been examined and probably graded by using a loupe.

loving cup. A large urn-shaped metal vessel, usually with two or more handles, awarded as a trophy in contests.

low relief. (1) Extending but slightly from the background, as the figures in most cameos. (2) When inclusions in a transparent mineral have a refractivity near that of the host, they are said to have *low relief*.

low-square setting. A replica of the upper half of the *square-prong* setting. It is frequently used for repair or replacement work. See section on mountings and settings.

Lucite. A trademarked name for a transparent *plastic* that is widely used to imitate various colored stones.

lugs. The bails, or loops, on a wristwatch case for attaching the bracelet to the case.

luminescence (loo'-meh-nes" cence). A general term used to describe the emission of visible wavelengths of light by a gemstone or other substance when excited by radiation of different wavelengths, electrical discharge, heat, friction or a similar agency.

lumpy girdle. An unnecessarily thick girdle on a brilliant-cut diamond.

lumpy (or thick) stone. A cut diamond that is unnecessarily deep, resulting in a loss of brilliancy.

luster. The appearance of a mineral's surface in reflected light. It depends principally on the relative smoothness of the surface (polish) and the refractive index, which governs the amount of light reflected. It is described as *adamantine, pearly, metallic, silky, vitreous, resinous* or *waxy*.

Glossary

M

macle (mack″-al). A term used in the diamond trade for a flat, triangular rough diamond, which is a twinned crystal of the spinel type.

Madagascar aquamarine. As a trade grade, any aquamarine that is darker and more violetish blue than the usual light-greenish-blue variety.

magnetization. The condition in a watch caused by too close proximity to heavy electric currents and magnetic fields, in which the steel parts become magnetic and exert forces on each other that ruin the accuracy of timekeeping. This condition may be removed rather easily by demagnetizing.

Maiden Lane. The New York City street that was once the center of the gemstone and jewelry industry in America. Although it is still important, Maiden Lane has been replaced by 47th Street as the key area.

main facets. The large *crown* and *pavilion* facets of a brilliant-cut gemstone; on step-cut stones, the *center* row of facets on the pavilion. See section on shapes and styles of cutting.

mainspring. The spiral coil of steel "ribbon," the unwinding of which furnishes motive power for portable timepieces. It is a spring that runs much longer than a day, so that its weaker phase is not reached by the time it should be rewound, thus obtaining more uniformity of power.

mainspring barrel. A casing of metal, recessed to contain the mainspring of a timepiece, with or without its outer rim cut with gear teeth to form the first wheel in the train.

mainspring hook. A metal hook, either on the periphery of a barrel-arbor hub or inside the rim of the barrel, engaging a hole at either end of the mainspring. Its function is to hold the spring in action during the winding and running of a timepiece.

mainspring winder. A tool for winding a watch's mainspring for replacement in its barrel, instead of twisting the spring into the barrel with the fingers, which may result in malformation of the spring coil.

make. The quality of *proportions* and the *polish* and *symmetry* of a fashioned diamond; e.g., good make, poor make, full make.

malachite (mal″-ah-kite). An opaque, bright-green ornamental and decorative mineral often banded in lighter and darker layers. An ore of copper. From Arizona and numerous overseas localities, including Africa and Russia.

malleable. Capable of being hammered or rolled out without breaking, as are precious metals.

Manufacturing Jewelers & Silversmiths of America, Inc. See section on trade associations.

marcasite (mar‴-kah-site). (1) An opaque bronze to grayish mineral with metallic luster. (2) A trade term for *pyrite*, with which costume jewelry is sometimes paved, which has a more brassy color but is more durable than marcasite.

marine chronometer. A very accurate, portable timepiece that is used for navigation of ships, for carrying the time of a known meridian to use in connection with local time of the ship's position obtained by observation with a sextant.

mark. A term used by a few jewelers in selling diamonds as a substitute for the more conventional imperfection terminology; for example, slightly marked or very slightly marked, in place of slightly imperfect or very slightly imperfect.

marquise (mar-keez″). A style of diamond cutting in which the girdle outline is boat shaped. The shape and placement of the facets is of the *brilliant* style. See section on shapes and styles of cutting.

mass. A term sometimes used for rough diamond during the early phases of the fashioning operation.

master (or key) diamonds. Fashioned diamonds of known color grades that are used as comparison stones when grading diamonds for body color.

Matan Diamond. A 367-carat stone, found in Borneo in 1787, that once belonged to the Rajah of Matan. Since it is rarely shown and never leaves the royal treasury, an accurate description is impossible; however, a replica made from hearsay shows an unfaceted pear shape. Some researchers believe it to be rock crystal. See section on famous diamonds.

"Matara," or "Matura, diamond." A misnomer for *colorless zircon*.

matched pearls. A term often interpreted to mean pearls that are duplicated exactly as to all of the color attributes of hue, tone and intensity. With the number of pearls that are necessary for a necklace, this is practically an impossibility. Pearls may, however, be matched as to luster, body color, and predominant color of orient. Thus, a necklace may consist entirely of light-cream *rosé* pearls but they will vary slightly in one or more color attributes, usually tone and intensity.

matrix. The rock in which a mineral is contained, portions of which contain pieces of the mineral; e.g., *opal matrix, turquois matrix*.

matt finish. A soft finish with a dull sheen. It is produced by glass, brass or steel scratch brush, powdered pumice or by sandblasting.

Glossary

It is used on platinum and all colors and qualities of gold.

mauve diamond. A light-violet, light-purple or light-bluish-violet diamond of a sufficiently pronounced color to be an asset. Such a stone is called a *fancy*.

mean-time screws. Screws with threads fitted friction-tight in a balance rim, to be turned in for regulating a watch to run faster or turned out to run slower.

medallion. A decorative metal disc, usually oval or round, cast like a coin or sometimes inset in a dish. It also refers to a decorative motif for holloware and flatware. See section on ornaments and designs.

medallion and rosette. See section on ornaments and designs.

"Medina emerald." A misnomer for *green glass*.

melange (may-lahnzh"). From the French, meaning a *mixture* or *medley*. It is used in the trade to mean an assortment of diamonds of mixed weights and/or qualities and of sizes larger than *melee*.

melee (anglicized pronunciation: mel"-e). From the French, meaning a *confused mass*. (1) In the trade, the term is used collectively to describe small (up to .20 or .25 carat) brilliant-cut diamonds, whether full cut or not. Usually, all small gemstones used to embellish mountings, settings or larger gems are called *melee*. (2) A grading term used at the mines for unbroken diamond crystals (round, octahedral or slightly distorted octahedra) of less than one carat that do not pass through a .070 sieve.

mesh. A woven fabric of metal, used in bracelets, bags, etc.

metric. Referring to measurements, the units, or subdivisions, of which are expressed in units of ten.

"Mexican diamond." A misnomer for *rock crystal*.

"Mexican onyx." A misnomer for *marble*.

mi-concave crystal. A watch crystal that is slightly curved and appears to be of uniform thickness.

microcline (mi"-kro-kline). A green, pink, pale yellow or white mineral of the *feldspar* group. The only gem or ornamental variety is *amazonite*.

micrometer. A device for measuring small distances, usually reading to .001 inch, or .01 millimeter. It is used to measure gems and thickness of metals. See section on diamond-grading and -merchandising instruments.

microscope. An optical instrument that affords magnification of objects. A *monocular* microscope permits the use of only one eye at a time; a *stereoscopic binocular* microscope is equipped with paired objectives and oculars and provides uninverted three-dimensional viewing. See section on diamond-grading and gem-testing instruments.

milgraining. Applying by means of a tool a line of globular projections of metal around a setting that holds a gem, or in other places on a piece of jewelry when such treatment improves the general appearance.

milky diamond. A diamond that has a milky or hazy appearance. This condition is usually caused by clouds of exceedingly minute inclusions. Excessively flourescent diamonds sometimes have a milky appearance in daylight.

millimeter. .03937 of an inch; hence, there are 25.40 millimeters in an inch.

mineral. A natural, inorganic substance that has a characteristic chemical composition and usually a definite crystal structure; the latter is sometimes expressed in geometric external form or outline.

mineralogy. The science of minerals.

minute-register hand. See section on watches.

minute repeater. A watch that will strike the nearest minute when a slide or button is operated.

minute wheel. In a dial train of a watch, the wheel with teeth engaging the leaves of the cannon pinion, and with a pinion fastened to it that turns the hour wheel.

Miridis. A trademarked name for *synthetic rutile.*

misnomer. An incorrect name. It usually implies that a stone is more valuable than it is; e. g., "Herkimer diamond" for quartz.

mixed cut. A combination of brilliant cut above the girdle, with usually 32 facets and often a larger and higher table, and step cut below, with the same number of facets. It is often used for colored stones, especially fancy sapphires, to improve color and retain brilliancy. A variation of a mixed cut with an emerald-cut crown is sometimes used.

mocha stone (mo″-kah). White, gray or yellowish *cryptocrystalline quartz* with brown to red iron-bearing or black manganese-bearing dendritic inclusions. A form of *moss agate.*

modern, or moderne, cut. Any modification or combination of table cut, step cut and brilliant, used especially in connection with diamond. It includes baguette, triangle, keystone, half moon and others.

Moe gauge. A caliper-type gauge that, together with accompanying tables, is used to estimate the weights of either mounted or unmounted round brilliant-cut diamonds by measurements of width and depth. It is not a precision instrument. See section on diamond-grading and -merchandising instruments.

Moh's scale. The most commonly used scale of relative hardness of minerals: diamond, 10; corundum, 9; topaz, 8; quartz, 7; feldspar, 6; apatite, 5; fluorite, 4; calcite, 3; gypsum, 2; talc, 1. Each mineral of a given hardness scratches

Glossary

all of those with a lower number. The divisions are not equal, having been chosen arbitrarily by the German mineralogist, Mohs. The difference between 9 and 8 is considerably greater than between any of the lower numbers, and between 9 and 10 is greater than between 9 and 1.

moldavite (mol″-dah-vite). A bottle-green to brownish-green *natural glass* thought to be of meteoric origin.

mollusc. A soft-bodied, nonsegmented invertebrate animal that typically possesses a hard shell. The shell may be univalve, as in the snail, or bivalve, as in the oyster, cockle and mussel. Some species produce nacreous pearls. Also spelled *mollusk*.

Monel metal. An alloy composed of about 70% *nickel* and 30% *copper*. It is very resistant to corrosion.

moneyclip. See section on jewelry findings.

monochromatic light (mon′-o-kro-mat″-ik). Light of a single hue, limited to one wavelength or a very limited number of adjacent wavelengths.

monoclinic system. See section on crystal systems.

monogram. Letters combined into a pleasing design by interweaving, etc. See examples of styles for jewelry and silver engraving.

monometallic balance. A watch balance made of one metal throughout. It is used in combination with a hairspring of alloy metal in which there are practically no changes of elastic force under changing conditions of heat and cold. A monometallic balance does not compensate, because, with its hairspring combination, it is not needed.

"Montana jet." A misnomer for *obsidian*.

moonstone. (1) A term applied correctly only to *adularia* (precious moonstone), which is an interlayering of *orthoclase* and *albite*, two semitransparent to translucent *feldspars*. (2) Incorrectly applied, without proper prefix, to milky or girasol varieties of chalcedony, scapolite, corundum, etc.

moon watch hand. See section on watches.

morganite. The transparent, light-purplish-red variety of *beryl*. Sources: Brazil, Madagascar and California.

mosaic (mo-sa″-ik). Pieces of colored stone, porcelain or enamel, inlaid into cement to form a decorative design, the whole polished to a smooth surface.

moss agate. A term used generally for any translucent *chalcedony* that contains inclusions of any color arranged to resemble moss, ferns, leaves or treelike patterns. Little if any distinction is made between it and *mocha stone*.

mother-of-pearl. The iridescent lining of the shell of any pearl-bearing mollusc. It is usually of the same color, composition and general quality as the pearls produced by the particular mollusc.

mounted goods. (1) Diamonds that have been set in rings. (2) Diamonds set in any kind of jewelry.

mounted stone. A stone fixed in a setting, as in jewelry.

mounting. That portion of any piece of finished jewelry without the gemstone or gemstones for which it was designed; e. g., *ring mounting, pendant mounting, brooch mounting.* See section on mountings and settings.

mounts. Small pieces of ornamental metal (wires, casts, stampings, etc.) soldered to a silverware article for decoration.

movement. The mechanism of a watch or clock, as distinguished from the case.

movement-holder. A device for holding watch movements during assembly or other work.

"Mr. Diamond." A trademarked name for *colorless synthetic corundum.*

Multifacet Diamond (trademark). A name used to describe a standard *brilliant cut* upon whose girdle had been polished at least 40 flat facets.

Muzo emerald. Colombian emerald from the ancient Muzo Mine, about 75 miles NNW of Bogotá, which produces the finest known emeralds.

Glossary

N

nachgehen (nahk″-gay-hen). On the movement of a German watch or clock, means *slower*.

nacre (nay″-ker). The iridescent substance, principally *aragonite*, of which *pearl* and *mother-of-pearl* consist.

naif (pronounced knife). Also spelled *naife, naive* or *nyf*. A word of French derivation, meaning the natural, unpolished faces of a diamond crystal; its luster or "skin." Other meanings, less frequently used, are as follows: (1) A well-formed diamond crystal, as distinguished from a distorted one. (2) A thick or pointed diamond crystal, as distiguished from a flat one. (3) A diamond crystal, possessing bright, or splendent, faces.

Nassak Diamond. The origin and size of the rough of this diamond are unknown. It first appeared in India as a triangular stone that weighed more than 90 carats. At that time, it was in a Hindu temple, where it was said to have been an eye of an idol of the god Shiva. Successive owners included the Marquis of Hastings, the first Marquis of Westminster and a Paris jeweler. By this time (1927), it had been recut to 80.59 carats, still triangular in shape. Harry Winston, New York City gem dealer, acquired the stone and refashioned it to a 43.48-carat emerald cut. Since 1944, it has been the property of Mrs. William B. Leeds, New York City. Another name is the *Eye of Shiva Diamond*. See section on famous diamonds.

National Bureau of Standards. A part of the US Bureau of Commerce, which, among numerous other duties, establishes standards for the qualities of precious metals and for the testing of timepieces.

National Wholesale Jewelers' Association, Inc. See section on trade associations.

natural. A trade term for a portion of the original surface of a rough diamond that is sometimes left by the cutter on a fashioned stone, usually on the girdle.

natural glass. Vitreous, amorphous, inorganic substances occurring in nature that have solidified too quickly to crystalize.

natural stone. A stone that occurs in nature, as distinguished from a manmade substitute such as a synthetic or imitation stone.

Naval Observatory. The national astronomical observatory at Washington, D. C., where time determinations are made for broadcasting time signals by radio and wire for Navy and civilian use.

necklace hook. See section on jewelry findings.

negative crystal. An angular cavity within a crystal or fashioned gemstone, the outline of which coincides with a possible crystal form of the mineral in which it occurs.

nephrite (nef″-rite). One of the two species of *jade* and the toughest of all gemstones. The mineral is translucent to opaque and usually spinach green (often called "spinach jade"); it is also gray, brown, reddish, bluish, lavender or, rarely, yellow or black. Sources: China, Siberia, New Zealand, Wyoming, Alaska and California.

nick. A minor chip out of the surface of a fashioned diamond, usually caused by a light blow.

nickel "silver." A misleading term for an alloy containing no silver. When used as a base for silverplated ware, it usually consists of 65% *copper*, 5% to 25% *nickel*, and 10% to 30% *zinc*.

niello (nye-el″-oh). The art of decorating metal by filling engraved designs with a blue-black alloy. The alloy (composed of silver, lead, etc.) is introduced at high temperature. The metal thus decorated resembles a dull, metallic enamel.

Nizam Diamond. An unauthenticated stone, thought to have been found in India and still to be in the treasury of the Nizam of Hyderabad. It is reported to have weighed either 340 or 440 carats in the rough and 277 carats after cutting. Models show a concave-based, elongated, dome-shaped stone, covered with irregular, concave facets. See section on famous diamonds.

nulled. A gadroonlike ornament but convex and rounded, instead or flat or quarter round.

O

obsidian (ahb-sid″-e-an). A natural volcanic *glass;* an ornamental stone, rarely cut as a gem. Many early civilizations fashioned black-obsidian utensils and sculpture. Solidified out of lava, it is a rock. Colors include black, gray, yellowish, reddish and greenish. It occurs in numerous localities throughout the world.

obsolete patterns. Silverware patterns that are no longer available, because the dies have been worn out, destroyed or broken by the manufacturer.

"Occidental cat's-eye." A misnomer for *quartz cat's-eye.*

"Occidental topaz." A misnomer for *citrine.*

odd-beat watches. Watches with balances that beat more or less than 18,000 beats an hour.

odd-shaped crystals. A trade term denoting watch crystals of shapes other than round.

off-center culet. A diamond that has been cut from distorted rough, or one that has been repaired after breakage, often has a culet that is considerably displaced from the normal position centered under the girdle. This is done to save more weight, but at the expense of beauty. Facet angles are steep on one side and flat on the other, thus increasing light leakage.

off-center table. Distorted diamond rough is sometimes cut in a manner that places the table nearer the girdle at one point than elsewhere. It is the result of the opposite crown facets being cut at different angles. An off-center table may be inclined to the girdle plane.

off-color diamond. (1) In the American trade, any diamond that has a tinge of undesirable color, especially yellowish or brownish, that is easily apparent to the unaided but practiced eye without comparison with a stone of known color. (2) A term that has been used at the South African diamond mines for the grade of rough diamonds below the *cape* and *bye* grades.

oilcup. The concave recess formed around the pivot hole on the upper side of a jeweled bearing, or on the metal of a nonjeweled bearing in a watch or clock, for holding a supply of oil.

oilers. Tools for applying oil to parts of timepieces. They are blades made of fine gold or steel wire set into a handle, with a flattened point charged with a small quantity of oil by dipping it into a bench cup.

oilie. (1) In the American diamond industry, a little-used term that is synonymous with *Premier diamond.* (2) In some European countries, the term applies to diamonds having a blue-green tint.

oilsink. A V-shaped cut turned

into the part of an arbor in a watch or clock immediately next to the base of the pivot, to keep oil from overflowing onto the arbor by capillary action.

oils, watch. Liquids used for lubricating the parts of timepieces. The two principal types are classified as to the source of the raw materials, as *animal oils* and *mineral oils*. Most of the animal oil used in American horology is from the blubber of porpoise or blackfish. Today, most horological lubricants are synthesized from mineral sources, primarily petroleum.

old gold. Gold or gold-filled articles bought to be melted and refined.

old-mine cut. (1) An early form of *brilliant cut* with a nearly square girdle outline. (2) Incorrectly applied to a somewhat more modern style of brilliant cut that also has a much higher crown and smaller table than the modern brilliant cut, but whose girdle outline is circular or approximately circular—a style of cutting that is more properly called a *lumpy stone* or an *old-European cut*. See section on shapes and styles of cutting.

old-miner. An abbreviated form of *old-mine-cut diamond*.

old Sheffield. Sheffield plate made before 1840.

oligoclase (ahl″-ih-go-klace). A species of the *feldspar* group, a variety of which is *sunstone*.

olivine (ahl″-ih-veen). (1) The mineralogical name for the gem species *peridot*. (2) A name still sometimes used in the trade to mean "demantoid garnet."

onglette (ohn-let″). A sharply-pointed *graver*.

onyx (ahn″-iks). (1) One of the many varieties of *chalcedony*. The same as banded agate, except that the alternately colored bands of onyx are always *straight* and *parallel*. The most common kinds are black and white or gray, black and red to brownish red, and white and red to brownish red. That banded only with various tones of gray or gray and white is more specifically known as *onyx agate*. Stone cameos are carved principally from onyx. (2) A noun applied incorrectly to dyed, unbanded black or green chalcedony. (3) A qualifying adjective that means *parallel banded*, as in the term *onyx marble*.

opal. An *amorphous* mineral in great demand as a gemstone, when it displays its unique play of color. Caused by light interference set up by slight differences in refractivity in adjacent sections of the mass, opal with a black or dark-gray background and a vivid play of color is valued above similar material but with a white, colorless or orangey body. Common opal (without play of color) is found in a variety of colors.

open culet. A culet that is larger than necessary; usually, one that

Glossary

is visible to the unaided eye. It may be described as *medium large, large* or *very large*.

open-faced watch. A pocket watch with a thin crystal over the dial and without a hinged metal cover, such as a hunting case.

opening a diamond. In the diamond-cutting industry, a trade term used to describe the operation of polishing a "window," or facet, on the surface of a heavily coated or rough-surfaced diamond, so that a clear view of the interior can be had before proceeding with the work. A window must be oriented properly, so as to eliminate distortion caused by refraction of light.

open table. A term that is sometimes used to refer to the table on a *spread*, or *swindled*, diamond. To some, any table diameter of 60% or more of the girdle diameter is open; to others, open means 65% or more.

optical black. An intense black finish for *brass*, produced by immersion in a platinum-chloride solution and used for oxidizing metal name plates, etc.

optic sign. The kind of double refraction possessed by a mineral. In *uniaxial* stones, the sign is *positive* when the constant refractive index is the lower numerically; *negative* when the constant is the greater index. In *biaxial* stones, which have three optical directions, the R.I. of the intermediate, or beta, ray is the criterion: if its R.I. is nearer that of the low, or alpha, ray, it is said to have a *positive* sign; if it is nearer the high, or gamma, ray, it is said to be *negative*.

Optivisor. A simple binocular magnifier that is worn on the head by jewelry repairmen and manufacturers and by diamond and colored-stone graders. Many diamond graders believe that their efficiency in color grading is increased slightly by low magnification. See section on gem-testing instruments.

orange diamond. A diamond of a distinct orange tint, which is properly called a *fancy*.

ordinary ray. That ray of light that has the same refractive index, regardless of the direction in which it travels through a uniaxial material.

O'Reilly Diamond. A 21.25-carat diamond that was the first (1866) to be found in South Africa. In its cut form (a 10.73-carat round brilliant, mounted in a ring), it is owned by Peter Locan, an Englishman, and is known as the *Eureka Diamond*. In 1959, this historically important stone held a place of honor in the *Ageless Diamond* exhibition in London.

orient. The minute play of color on, or just below, the surface of a gem-quality pearl.

"oriental amethyst." A misnomer for *violet sapphire*.

"oriental emerald." A misnomer for *green sapphire*.

oriental moonstone. Genuine moonstone, as distinguished from moonstonelike chalcedony.

oriental pearl. (1) A trade name applied to any naturally-occurring *Pinctada* pearl, and therefore not to cultured, abalone, mussel or fresh-water pearl. (2) More specifically, such a pearl fished in the Orient only. This usage is not general, however, since many pearls fished elsewhere are sold in India and are thereafter indistinguishable from those fished in the Orient proper.

"oriental topaz." A misnomer for *golden sapphire.*

Orloff Diamond. A 199.60-carat diamond, set in the Russian Imperial Scepter and displayed in the Kremlin Museum, Moscow. It is shaped like half of a small egg, rose cut on top, and flat and unfaceted on the bottom. It was named for Count Gregory Orloff, who purchased the stone in Amsterdam and gave it to Empress Catherine, in 1774. Some authorities believe the *Orloff* and the *Great Mogul* are one and the same. See section on famous diamonds.

ormolu (or″-moe-loo). An alloy of *copper, tin* and *zinc,* resembling yellow gold. It is used in mounts for furniture, clocks, etc.

ornamental stone. A term applied to attractive natural materials that are not practical for jewelry purposes but are useful for fashioning into ornamental objects, such as ash trays and lamp bases; e.g., *onyx, alabaster.*

orthoclase (or″-tho-klase). A species of the *feldspar* group. Thin, alternate layers of orthoclase and *albite* give rise to the floating, bluish-light effect called *adularescence* in moonstone.

orthorhombic system (or′-thorom″-bik). See section on crystal systems.

osmium (ahz″-me-um). A white metal of the *platinum* group. Its hardness is 7 (the hardest metal known) and the specific gravity is 22.5. Osmium alloys are used for the tips of penpoints, compass bearings, etc.

out-of-round diamond. Any brilliant or other style of round-cut diamond that does not have a truly circular girdle outline to the eye; a stone with a girdle circumference that is appreciably oval or squared but not constituting a fancy shape.

overbanking. A faulty condition in a lever escapement, in which failure of the guard, or safety action, allows the fork to pass over to the wrong side of the line of centers; then the roller jewel, instead of entering the fork slot, comes to rest against the outside of one of the fork horns, stopping the watch, instead of unlocking the escape wheel for the next impulse.

overblue. A term applied to a diamond that has a bluish cast in

Glossary

daylight; usually a *fluorescent* stone.

overcoil. The portion of the outer coil in a watch hairspring that is bent upward and formed into a terminal curve; for example, a *Breguet hairspring*.

overlay. An additional coating of silver electroplated on certain desired parts of an article, such as the back of teaspoon bowls.

oxidation. A popular name for *oxide finishes* and *tarnish*. Tarnish on silver is a silver *sulphide*, rather than silver oxide; however, the process of tarnish formation is a form of oxidation.

oxide finish. A popular name for a black finish on metals, obtained by immersion in platinum chloride or potassium sulphide. It is usually used as a background for designs made by polishing the raised parts.

oyster pearl. A concretion found in common edible oysters. It is generally black or purple or a mixture of black and white or purple and white. It is devoid of nacreous luster, possessing neither beauty nor value and hence not a true pearl.

P

paillons (pay″-lons). Decoration of enamel through the use of tiny ornaments (paillons), which are stamped out with a sharp-edged punch from very thin sheets of fine gold in the forms of stars, flowers, birds, etc.

palladium (pal-lay″-de-um). A soft, light-weight metal (hardness, 4-4½; specific gravity, 12.0) of the *platinum* group. When alloyed with a small amount of ruthenium and rhodium, it is used in jewelry, largely as a substitute for platinum. It can also be hardened with nickel. It was once used in amounts of about 15% as the coloring agent for white gold. It has been used for plating other metals, although ruthenium is favored; also for watch hairsprings, since it cannot be magnetized.

pallet. Part of an escapement, usually a detainer against which a tooth of the escape wheel rests during the condition known as *lock*. Another function of most pallets is to act as the part through which an escape-wheel tooth imparts power, through a lever, to the balance. Pallet jewels are usually made of synthetic corundum, but in inexpensive watches and most clocks, they are made of steel.

palm. See section on ornaments and designs.

palmette. A conventional ornament of very ancient origin, closely related to the Egyptian lotus and Greek anthemion. It consists of radiating petals springing from a calyxlike base. The outermost, usually green, leaves or petals of a flower are called the calyx.

paper marks. The fine scratches or abraded facet edges on *paperworn* diamonds.

paperworn diamond. A diamond with abraded facet edges or scratches, often on both crown and pavilion, resulting from being carried loose in a paper with other diamonds.

papryrus (pah-pye″-rus). See section on ornaments and designs.

parcel. A group of diamonds offered for sale.

Pasha of Egypt Diamond. A 40-carat Indian diamond, described as an octagonal brilliant of good quality (weight in rough, unknown). The stone was named for Ibrahim, Pasha of Egypt, who purchased it in 1848. It remained in the Egyptian Treasury for many years, but was last reported to have been offered for sale in England. See section on famous diamonds.

paste. A jeweler's term used to mean any kind of *glass* gemstone imitation.

patina (pah-teen″-ah). In its strictest sense, the condition of a metal, stone or painted surface after many years exposure to the atmosphere. Most commonly, it re-

Glossary

fers to the coating on bronzes, brasses and other metals. *Surface oxidation* is often artificially induced to similate the patina of centuries of use.

patina finish. A term applied by some silverware manufacturers to a slight variation of the *butler finish*, which is produced by first applying a highly polished bright finish and then dulling it with a hairlike wire brush and finely powdered pumice.

pavé (pah-vay"). Many stones set flush with the surface and very close together, so as to show the least amount of metal. A piece of jewelry made in this manner is said to be *paved*.

pavilion. That portion of a faceted gemstone below the girdle; same as *base*. See section on shapes and styles of cutting.

pavilion facets. (1) Those facets on any fashioned stone located on the *pavilion*, or *base* (i.e., *below* the girdle), as opposed to the *crown* facets, which are located *above* the girdle. (2) A term sometimes used synonymously with *pavilion - main,* or *bottom - main,* facets to denote, in the case of brilliant-cut stones, the large facets that extend from the girdle to the culet; on *step-cut* stones, the *center* row of facets on the pavilion. Some diamond cutters further distinguish four of the pavilion-main facets as *quoin* or *bottom-corner* facets. See section on shapes and styles of cutting.

pawl. A pivoted catchpiece, or click, with a point to catch and hold the teeth of a ratchet wheel, as in the winding mechanism of timepieces

pearl. A calcareous concretion formed naturally in the body mass of a mollusc and possessing the iridescent effect known as *orient*.

pearl grain. One-fourth metric carat.

pear-shape cut. A variation of the *brilliant cut*, usually with 58 facets, having a pear-shaped girdle outline. See section on shapes and styles of cutting.

peeling. Removing the outer layer or layers of a pearl, in the hope that a lower layer will be of better quality.

peening. Drawing, bending or flattening metal with a hammer.

pendant. (1) An ornament that hangs, usually from a chain. See section on jewelry findings. (2) The part of a watch through which the winding stem passes and that is capped by the crown.

pendant bow. The ring or hoop on the pendant of a watchcase, to which is fastened the swivel of of a watch chain.

pendant mounting. See section on jewelry findings.

pendant up, pendant-right, pendant-left, pendant down. Positions in which a watch may be placed to note its timekeeping in adjusting to positions; these are called the *vertical positions*. The other positions are *dial up* and *dial down*.

pendeloque (pahn″-dah-loke). A modification of the *round brilliant cut*. It has an outline similar to the *pear shape*, but with the narrower end longer and more pointed. See section on shapes and styles of cutting.

pendulum. The weight, or bob, and its supporting rod that swings from side to side in a clock.

"perfect cut." A term used to imply that a diamond or other gemstone has been cut to ideal proportions and is well finished. Ideally proportioned stones are extremely rare. The American Gem Society prohibits the term for use by its members.

peridot (pear″-ih-doe). A mineral species that yields yellowish-green gemstones. If deep in color, it is called *peridot;* if light, *chrysolite*. Sources: St. John's Island (Red Sea), Burma, Ceylon, Arizona and elsewhere. It is one of the birthstones for August.

Perigem. A trade name for light-yellow-green *synthetic spinel*.

period. A design or style that typifies those associated with a given time and place; e.g., the simple lines and motifs of the American Colonial days, or the fluted effects of the time of Queen Anne are easily recognized periods in antique silver.

Persian Gulf pearl. At present, the best quality of oriental pearl, noted for its fine color, shape and orient. It is principally from the vicinity of Bahrein Island, in the Persian Gulf. The term is also deceivingly applied to imitation pearl.

Persian turquois. (1) A trade term for the finest quality of turquois (intense light to medium blue), which in early times came from Persia (now Iran), although some may have been mined in Turkestan or Tibet. (2) The term is also used to refer to poor-quality turquois from various present-day mines in Iran.

petrified wood. Fossilized wood in which the cells have been entirely replaced by crystallized silica and hence converted into quartz or opal or, less often, other substances. It is usually easy to identify since it reveals, more or less, the original structural pattern of the wood.

pewter. Old pewter was a tin-lead alloy. Modern pewter is largely tin with other metals added, such as copper or antimony, so that the resulting alloy will be comparatively hard.

Pforzheim. A city in West Germany that is an important center for the manufacture of costume jewelry, silverware, watches, jewelry chains and similar products. There are also diamond-cutting plants.

phenakite (fen″-ah-kite). A very rare, transparent to translucent mineral of little gem value, except to collectors. It is colorless or light yellow, red or brown. Sources: Russia, Brazil, Tanganyika, Mexico, Maine and Colorado.

phenomenal gem. A gemstone exhibiting an optical phenomenon, such as *chatoyancy*, *play of color*, etc.

phosphorescence (fos'-fo-res"-cence). A variety of *luminescence*. A property possessed by some gemstones of continuing to emit visible light in darkness after exposure to X-rays, cathode rays, ultraviolet light or visible light. It differs from *fluorescence*, which is an emission of visible light *during* exposure. Phosphorescence is a continuance of luminescence *after* removal of the exciting rays, and a phosphorescent stone or other object is said to *phosphoresce*, or glow.

pick, or pick price. Terms used when the buyer is permitted to select (or pick) the most desirable stones in a lot.

pickling. Cleaning a piece of jewelry work, usually after it has been soldered, by boiling in a weak acid pickle.

piercing. Cutting away parts of a flat sheet of metal, thus producing a design.

pigeon's-blood ruby. Ruby of the finest color quality: intense, medium to medium-dark purplish red. It is likened to the arterial blood of a freshly-killed pigeon.

Pigott (or Pigot) Diamond. A fine-quality Indian diamond, variously said to have weighed from 47 to 85.80 carats. It was named for Baron George Pigot, Governor of Madras, who acquired it from an Indian prince in 1775. After changing hands several times, Ali Pasha, ruler of Albania, purchased the stone in 1818. Following a dispute with the Sultan of Turkey, overlord of Albania, the Pasha was fatally wounded and ordered an aid to shatter the diamond. Since then, there has been no trace of the stone, although there is no actual evidence of its distruction. Only a model, made previously in England, remains. See section on famous diamonds.

pile-treated diamond. A diamond whose color has been changed to green or yellowish green (or, if treated too long, to black) by bombardment in a nuclear reactor. Subsequent heat treatment may result in still further color change.

pillar plate. The lower plate of a watch or clock.

pinback. A metal plate on which is a pin, joint and catch. An attachment to make a brooch. See section on jewelry findings.

pinclip. See section on jewelry findings.

pin-cushion design. A piece of jewelry made up of a collection of wires, the ends of which are set with ornaments or stones or have rounded ends. It is sometimes set with stones in between the wires. Pins and brooches are made up in pinwheel fashion or pin-cushion effect. Wires often radiate from center clusters of stones, somewhat like the spokes of a wheel, or they are placed in inclined circles to give depth to the piece.

pinfire opal. Opal exhibiting pinpoint color flashes, smaller and usually less regularly spaced than the patches in harlequin opal.

pinguard. See section on jewelry findings.

pinion. A member of a watch's train of gears; specifically, a gear wheel of a relatively small diameter. It is usually without wheel spokes and is comprised only of teeth, called *leaves*, and the *core*, or *body*, left by cutting the leaves out of a solid piece of material.

pink diamond. A term often used loosely in the trade to describe any light-red, purplish-red or purple stone. Such a diamond is called a *fancy*.

pinked topaz. Pink topaz, the color of which has been induced artificially by heating yellow or brown varieties.

pink gold. Same as red gold, but with a smaller percentage of copper and some silver.

"pink moonstone." A misnomer for *scapolite*.

pink sapphire. Light-red corundum, as distinguished from medium to dark tones of red or slightly purplish red, which is ruby. The dividing line between ruby and sapphire is a matter of opinion.

pin-lever escapement. The escapement usually used in inexpensive alarm clocks and nonjeweled watches. Although not adapted for fine timekeeping, it has advantages of economy in manufacturing costs.

pin mounting. See section on jewelry findings.

pinstem. A stem with one pointed end and one that attaches to a pivot. It is used for pins and brooches. See section on jewelry findings.

pipe. The common name for a vertical, columnar mass of rock that cooled and solidified in the neck of a volcano. When these rock masses consist of *kimberlite*, they often contain diamonds. They occur in Africa, Arkansas, India, Russia and elsewhere.

piqué (pe-kay″). From the French, meaning *pricked*. A term used by some importers as an imperfection grade. The original use of the word was confined to those stones that had tiny, difficult-to-find inclusions. It has been used with increasingly poor stones until 1st, 2nd and 3rd piqué grades now sometimes fit in between *slightly imperfect* and *imperfect*. Some importers still use the terms 1st, 2nd and 3rd piqué for grades just below *flawless* or *perfect*, and others for categories of the *imperfect* grade.

pit. An indentation on the surface of a diamond. It may be caused by a blow, by a *knot* being pulled out from the surface during the

Glossary

polishing operation, or by the surface intersecting a negative crystal. A fairly large indentation is usually called a *cavity*; a minor one, a *nick*.

pivot. The portion at the end of an arbor in a watch, formed to run in a hole or bearing to allow rotary motion of the arbor; or a similar part at the fulcrum of a lever to allow angular motion; or a fixed pin on which a part turns on a hole or pipe in a part.

PK. The abbreviation for *piqué*.

placer. Alluvial or glacial deposits in which minerals are found; usually an accumulation of sand and gravel containing gold, gem material or other valuable minerals.

place setting. The basic utensils necessary for eating a correctly served meal. It usually consists of a salad fork, fork, knife, teaspoon, soup spoon, and butter spreader; a four-piece place setting usually eliminates the latter two.

plain polished. Polished without any ornamentation or other additional treatment of the metal.

plane polarized light. Light that has passed through a polarizing substance (such as the Polaroid in a polariscope), so that its vibration direction has been confined to a single set of parallel planes.

planishing. Hammering to make smooth or plane, as a metallic surface; to condense, toughen or harden by hammering lightly.

plastic. A substance that can be shaped by flow at some stage in its manufacture, but that retains the final condition into which it is formed. Transparent to translucent plastics of all colors are used to simulate natural gems, especially those with a resinous luster, such as amber.

plate. A term formerly applied extensively in England to sterling coin or sterling silver, used only by churches and later by private families. It is still used when referring to sterling silver, especially in England; hence, the occasionally heard term "family plate." It is not to be confused with plated silver.

plate-cut stone. An opaque gemstone with a flat, parallel top and back and beveled, or stepped, sides.

plated ware. Ware of inexpensive metal electroplated with a more expensive metal.

plates. In watches and clocks, the flat metal parts of the framework or movements, comprising the lower, or pillar, plate and upper plate, pierced with drilled or jeweled holes that form bearings for the pivots of the acting parts.

platinum. A soft, heavy (hardness, 4-4½; specific gravity, 21.5), light-gray precious metal. When alloyed with 10% iridium, it is known as *hard platinum*; with 5% iridium, as *medium-hard platinum*. It is used in the most expensive jewelry. It is unsatisfactory as a plating for other metals. Substitutes: palladium and white gold.

platinum metals. Platinum, iridium, palladium, ruthenium, rhodium and osmium.

platinumsmith. A person or firm specializing in the manufacture of platinum articles.

play. Freedom allowed in fitting parts of timepieces to work together.

play of color. An optical phenomenon consisting of flashes of a variety of prismatic colors. It is caused by interference of light in thin films of limited lateral extent within or near the surface of a gem, seen in rapid succession as the gem is moved, as in *opal*. It is one of the causes of the *orient* in pearls, but differs from *change of color, dispersion* and *opalescence*.

pleochroism (ple″-oh-kro′-izm). The property of most doubly-refractive colored minerals of exhibiting two or three different colors when viewed in different directions. It is rarely distinguished by the unaided eye, but becomes apparent when viewed through a *dichroscope*. Characteristic colors and strength of pleochroism may assist in gem identification. See table of pleochroic colors.

plique-à-jour (pleek-ah-zhoor″). Similar to *cloisonné* but without a metal background. Transparent colored enamel is held between metal strips and exposed on both sides of the article.

PM. The abbreviation for "push money," a premium placed on shopworn or slow-moving merchandise to encourage its sale by an employee.

"pocket peddler." Sellers of diamonds and other jewelry who operate without the benefit or cost of maintenance of an office or store.

point. In weighing diamonds, one hundredth part of a carat, each one hundredth being called a *point*; e.g., 32 hundredths (.32) of a carat is called 32 *points*.

poising. The art of equalizing the weight of a watch balance at all points around its circumference. It is very important for securing uniformity of timekeeping rates in different positions.

polarizing microscope. A microscope that is equipped to observe the behavior of a stone under polarized light. It is one of the mineralogist's key tools in identification.

Polar Star Diamond. A 40-carat Indian diamond of fine color and purity. Once owned by Joseph Bonaparte, eldest brother of Napoleon I, it went to Russia in the 1820's and became the possession of Prince Youssoupoff, whose family owned it for more than a century. Later, it was sold to Cartier, of Paris, and is presently owned by Lady Deterding, Russian-born former wife of the late oil magnate, Sir Henry Deterding. See section on famous diamonds.

polished girdle. A girdle that has been lapped to yield either a lustrous, curved surface or a series of flat, polished surfaces (facets). Diamonds with smooth, polished surfaces have been marketed under such trademarked names as *Circle of Light*, *Halo Cut* and *Brilliant Circle*. *Multifacet* is a trademarked name for a 40-facet girdle.

polisher. A term used to describe any workman who places and polishes any of the facets on a diamond.

polishing. (1) The reduction of a rough or irregular surface to a smooth flatness or curvature. (2) Applying the final finish to silverware articles. The process consists of both burnishing and polishing.

polishing mark. A groove or a scratch left by the lap on a facet of a diamond or other gemstone. Parallel grooves left on a diamond's facet during its initial placement should be removed during the final polishing, so that they are not visible under 10x; otherwise, they are considered defects of finish.

precious cat's-eye. The cat's-eye variety of *chrysoberyl*.

precious jade. True *jadeite* or *nephrite*, more often the former.

precious metals. Metals that are more beautiful, rare, easily worked and resistant to corrosion than most other metals, and that also have the desirable durability for use in jewelry, coinage and the arts. Included are *gold*, *silver* and the *platinum metals*.

precious opal. Opal with *play of color*, as distinguished from common opal.

precious stone. As contrasted with so-called semiprecious stones, this classification includes the more important and comparatively more valuable gems. However, fine qualities of other gems are much more valuable than poor qualities of diamond, ruby or emerald; therefore, such a division is meaningless. In the strictest sense, all genuine gem materials are precious.

precious topaz. Genuine topaz, as distinguished from *citrine* (topaz-quartz, or "jeweler's topaz").

Premier diamond. A diamond that appears bluish in daylight and yellowish in artificial (incandescent) light; a yellow stone that fluoresces strongly in a blue color. The term is usually applied to fluorescent stones that seem cloudy or oily in daylight.

Premier Mine. (1) The name that was given originally to the Wesselton Mine; references prior to 1903 are to that mine. (2) After 1903, the name referred to the mine located 25 miles east of Pretoria, South Africa. Industrial diamonds represent about four-fifths of the total production.

The remainder are gemstones, some of which, particularly those of a blue color, are of very fine quality. Now controlled by De Beers Consolidated Mines, Ltd., annual production is usually between 1,000,000 and 1,500,000 carats.

Presidente Vargas Diamond. A 726.60-carat Brazilian diamond, found in 1938, and named in honor of the then president of that country, Getulio Vargas. After changing hands several times, Harry Winston, New York City gem dealer, purchased it and, in 1941, had it cut into 29 stones, the important ones of which were emerald cuts. The largest of these, which weighs 48.26 carats, bears the name *Vargas*, it is reported to be owned by Mrs. Robert W. Windfohr, of Ft. Worth, Texas. See section on famous diamonds.

pressed amber. Fragments of genuine amber that have been heated and softened, homogenized and compacted. It is characterized by an obvious flow structure or by a dull spot left by a drop of ether.

program clock. A master clock that rings bells at desired times, as in schools and factories.

prong. The projection of metal that overlaps the edge of a stone and secures it to the setting. Common prong types are *emerald prong, illusion, fishtail, belcher* and *Tiffany*. See section on mountings and settings.

ProportionScope. The ProportionScope combines lenses and movable mirrors to project the silhouette of a diamond on a screen. Diagrams and scales on the screen, as well as a "zoom" range, enable the instrument to analyze the proportions of round brilliant-cut diamonds, as well as fancy-cut diamonds.

pumice. An extrusive volcanic rock so full of gas vesicles that it floats on water. It is used in powdered form as an abrasive for cleaning and buffing.

pure. A rarely used term that refers to comparative perfection in a diamond; more or less synonymous with *clean*.

pusher. A square steel rod, in a round-shaped handle, used to push bezels or points of crown settings around a stone.

pyrite (pi"-rite). Popularly called "iron pyrites." A pale bronze- or brass-yellow mineral with a bright, metallic luster. It is generally sold in the jewelry trade as "marcasite," which is less durable and no more valuable or attractive. Sources: Saxony, Bohemia, Czechoslovakia, Spain, New Jersey, Colorado, Pennsylvania and elsewhere.

pyrope (pi"-rope). A transparent, dark, very slightly brownish-red to intense pure red species of the *garnet* group; the latter is sometimes substituted for ruby. Sources: South Africa, Arizona, Colorado and elsewhere.

Glossary

Q

quadruple, or XXXX, plate. Plated silverware on which the thickness of the plating is equivalent to that obtained by depositing eight ounces of silver on a gross of teaspoons.

quarter chimes. In clocks, a different combination of notes played each quarter hour.

quarter repeater. A watch that will strike the nearest quarter hour when a slide or button is operated.

quartz. The most common and widely distributed mineral. It includes many varieties of ornamental stones and gemstones of many colors, some crystalline and some cryptocrystalline. Among the varieties are amethyst, citrine, agate, aventurine, bloodstone, tiger's-eye and many others.

quartz cat's-eye. Chatoyant quartz, usually grayish green or greenish yellow, but may ocur in other colors. It never equals the sharp eye of the finest chrysoberyl variety.

"quartz-topaz." A misleading name for *citrine*.

Queen Pearl. The most famous American fresh-water pearl. Found in Notch Brook, near Patterson, New Jersey, in 1857, it was pinkish and weighed 93 grains. It was purchased by Tiffany and Co. and was sold to a French gem dealer, who sold it to Empress Eugenie.

queen's metal. An alloy of antimony, tin, bismuth and lead. It is used somewhat as is britannia metal but less often, except as the base of cast ornaments for silver-plated holloware.

R

R. An abbreviation on the regulator of Swiss or French timepieces corresponding to F (faster) on American.

radiograph. A photograph taken with a broad X-ray beam. A radiograph of a pearl, if properly taken and developed, discloses to an experienced eye the nature of its interior structure.

radium-baton watch hand. See section on watches.

radium-dauphine watch hand. See section on watches.

radium dial. An incorrect name for the dial of a timepiece. The numerals and hands are coated with any substance that is luminous in the dark; radium itself is too expensive.

radium-index watch hand. See section on watches.

radium-stick watch hand. See section on watches.

radium-treated diamond. A diamond whose color has been changed (usually to greenish) as a result of being exposed to the radioactive emanations of radium salts. Because of the prolonged radioactivity of diamonds thus treated and consequent danger of injury to the finger of the wearer, this form of coloration is not practiced commercially.

railroad-index hand. See section on watches.

railroad-time inspection. A system of rules in force on many railroads for assuring accurate timekeeping of watches used by employees. Essentials of the system are: a periodic check and record of the timekeeping of each watch; an inspection of the mechanical condition of each watch at longer intervals, the inspector ordering any cleaning or repairs found needed; a specification of grades and types of watches that employees are required to carry. The inspecting is usually done by retail jewelers appointed in towns served by the railroad. These local inspectors report to a general inspector, an official of the railroad.

railroad watch. A watch of a model and grade specified by the rules of the time-inspection service of a railroad, and required to be used by all employees concerned with the operation of trains. Specifications, in general, require a watch that is fully jeweled; adjusted to five positions, heat and cold, and isochronism; and capable of performance in timekeeping of a minimum error of plus or minus thirty seconds a week.

"Rainbow Diamond." A misleading name for *synthetic rutile*.

"Rainbow Gem." One of the many names under which *synthetic rutile* has been sold.

"Rainbow Magic Diamond."

Glossary

A misleading name for *synthetic rutile*.

raise. To fashion metal by beating or pounding the background.

ratchet. (1) The adjustable part of a link watch bracelet. (2) A wheel with teeth, as in a watch, in which a click, or pawl, engages to prevent backward motion.

rate. A numerical statement of the error of a timekeeper; its gain or loss per day.

raw edge. A term applied to silver holloware pieces whose edges have not been turned over or mounted with a border.

rebanking. In a watch, a fault in the action of a *lever escapement*, usually caused by a too-strong main-spring, in which excess of balance motion carried the roller jewel too far, until it strikes and rebounds from the outside of a forkhorn, instead of stopping and reversing its motion by tension of the hairspring. The rebounds cause erratic speeds of balance motion; hence, erratic timekeeping.

reconstructed ruby and sapphire. Terms often mistakenly used for *synthetic* ruby and sapphire. Prior to the advent of the *Verneuil* process, ruby, but not sapphire, apparently was synthesized by melting fragments of natural ruby; if so, accumulation lines should differ from those of *Verneuil* boules. However, some boule tips show irregular striae; as a result, identifying a true reconstructed ruby is all but impossible.

recorder. (1) A clock with accompanying mechanism that stamps a time record on cards of employees. (2) The dial on some chronograph watches that records elapsed time.

red diamond. The rarest of all fancy-colored diamonds. However, the term is often used to mean red-brown or rose-colored stones. Diamonds of the full red color of ruby are perhaps unknown.

reducing gearing. A train of wheels and pinions in which pinions turn wheels, resulting in each successive mobile running slower than its driver, an example being the dial train of a timepiece.

reed, or reeding. A style of decoration for silverware, consisting of a parallel series of narrow hemispherical embossings, usually used as a border.

refining. The recovery of certain metals from masses of other alloys or combinations, such as old gold.

refraction. The bending of light rays. The deflection from a straight path suffered by a ray of light as it passes obliquely from a medium of one optical density to another medium of different optical density, as from air into water or from air or water into a gemstone. The degree of bending is related to the change in the velocity of light and the angle at which the light impinges.

refractive index. A measure of

the amount a light ray is bent as it enters or leaves a gemstone, expressed by numerals that indicate the comparative bending power of different gems. It is defined as the sine of the angle of incidence divided by the sine of the angle of refraction, or the velocity of light in air divided by its velocity in the substance. Other factors being equal, the higher the R.I., the greater the brilliancy. See refractive-index table.

refractometer (re'-frak-tom"-eh-ter). An optical instrument for measuring the *refractive index* of a gemstone. See section on gem-testing instruments.

Regent Diamond. A fine-quality 410-carat diamond, found in India about 1701. It was first owned by Thomas Pitt, Governor of Madras, who had it cut to 140.50-carat cushion-shaped brilliant. Later names connected with the long and intriguing history of the great gem included the Duke of Orleans, Regent of France, for whom the stone was named; Louis XV, in whose crown it was set; Marie Antoinette; and Napoleon Bonaparte, who had it set in the hilt of his coronation sword. The diamond was stolen in the French jewel robbery of 1792, pledged for funds to help Napoleon in his rise to power, secreted in a French chateau during World War II, and came to its final resting place in the Apollon Gallery of the Louvre Museum. It was featured in the Museum's *Ten Centuries of French Jewelry* exhibition in 1962. See section on famous diamonds.

Registered Jeweler. A title that is awarded by the American Gem Society to qualified retail jewelers. After membership in the Society is attained, the title is secured by successful completion of comprehensive proctored examinations based on prescribed coursework.

register service. A jewelry store's record of a person's patterns in silverware, china and glassware. An up-to-date record is kept, so that gift suggestions can be made to friends and relatives of the registered person.

regulating. Making the mean, or average, timekeeping rate of a watch faster or slower, by moving the regulator or adding weight or substracting it from the balance.

regulator. A device for holding the hairspring curb-pins in a watch, by which they may be moved to various concentric positions on the overcoil of the spring, having the effect of lengthening the spring to make the watch run slower or shortening it to make it run faster.

repeater. A watch or clock that strikes the time, but only when a finger piece on the case is operated.

repoussé (rep-oh-say"). (1) Raised and modeled designs and motifs. (2) The method of ornamenting sheet metal by beating it out from the back and on the top with hammers, punches or other tools. (3) The term is popularly used to mean a combination of *repoussé* and *chasing*.

Retail Jewelers of America. See section on trade associations.

rex watch hand. See section on watches.

rhinestone. (1) Historically, *rock crystal*. (2) In the jewelry industry, the commonest usage is for *foilback imitations of diamond*, but the term is used for other colored foilbacks and occasionally for colorless glass.

rhodium (roe″-de-um). A metal of the *platinum* group, infrequently used to harden platinum alloys; also, with ruthenium, to harden palladium alloys. Hardness, 5; specific gravity, 12.4. It is frequently used to plate silverware to prevent tarnish, or to plate white gold or other metals to imitate platinum.

rhodolite (ro″-doe-lite). A rare, brilliant, transparent, purplish-violet type of *garnet* that represents a combination of *almandite* and *pyrope*. Sources: Ceylon and North Carolina.

rhodonite (roe″-don-ite). A translucent to opaque, pink to red-brown ornamental mineral. The pink variety is used for beads, brooches, buttons, Easter eggs and similar items. Source: New Jersey, Siberia, Germany, Italy, Colorado, Montana and elsewhere.

R.I. The abbreviation for *refractive index*.

riffle file. A bar with a file at either end, the center section being used as a handle.

ring. Jewelry in the form of circlets, usually made of one of the precious metals, commonly worn on the finger or ear. They are often set with a gem or gems, and some are used as seals. Rings are used primarily for personal adornment; often, however, they are combined with such purposes as betrothal, marriage, school matriculation, memberships in fraternal orders or civic groups, to display family crests or birthstones, and as a convenient method of transporting realizable assets.

ring blank. See section on jewelry findings.

ring chain. See section on basic styles of jewelry chains.

ring clamp. A ring holder used in jewelry manufacturing and repairing. It consists of two semi-conical members of wood, held together by a metal band in the center and activated by inserting a wedge between the members at the base end.

ring mandrel. A tapered steel rod upon which rings are sized, and often shaped, by blows from a rawhide mallet.

ring sizes. A series of graduated rings, marked with standard ring sizes, to designate the inside diameter of a finger ring. In the USA, a set numbered from 0 to 13. See table of United States and British ring-size equivalents.

ring stick. A tapering rod of

wood covered with metal, used for determining ring sizes by fitting the ring on the stick and reading the sizes indicated on it.

ringstone. Any stone that is suitable for use in a finger ring.

river. An early trade term still used by some dealers to designate the finest color grade of diamonds; i.e., an extraordinarily transparent, colorless stone.

river-to-light-yellow system. A widely used color-grading system for the most commonly encountered color range of diamonds; i.e., the *colorless-to-yellow* range. The usual grades include *river, top Wesselton, Wesselton, top crystal, crystal, top cape, cape, dark* (or *low*) *cape, very light yellow, light yellow* and *yellow*.

rock crystal. The transparent, colorless variety of *quartz*, which is widely distributed. Its low refractive index results in low brilliancy, so it is usually used for beads, etc., rather than for ringstones.

rococco (ro-ko″-ko). A florid style of the 18th century, characterized by light and fantastically curved lines, imitating rock work, shells, foliage or scrolls. It usually refers to any style that shows extravagant curvature or ornament. See section on ornaments and designs.

Roebling Opal. An opal in the Smithsonian Institution, said to be the largest mass of precious opal known: weight, 2610 carats. It was found in Virgin Valley, Nevada.

rolled edge. On an article of jewelry or silverware, a rounded metal border that has been lapped or rolled over the edge and spun underneath it.

rolled-gold plate. Same as gold filled, but usually of lower quality. Layers of gold are mechanically affixed onto one or both sides of an alloy of base metal.

roller jewel. A pin, usually made of synthetic ruby or sapphire, set perpendicularly in the roller, that works in the slot of the fork of a *lever-escapement watch* during unlocking of the escapement and impulse.

Roman finish. An electrolytic deposit of 24-karat (fine) gold, dulled by a scratch brush made of fine brass or steel wires.

Roman gold. Gold with a Roman finish.

rose cut (rosette). An early style of cutting that is thought to have originated in India and to have been brought to Europe by the Venetians. In its most usual form, it has a flat, unfaceted base and a somewhat dome-shaped top that is covered with a varied number of triangular facets and terminates in a point. The rose cut is now used primarily on small diamonds. See section on shapes and styles of cutting.

rose-finished gold. Yellow gold with a background finished with

Glossary

a pink or orange smudge and the relieved surfaces polished.

rose gold. Another name for *pink gold*.

rosé pearl (roze-ay"). A trade term for a pearl with a pinkish *orient*.

rose quartz. The light-red, translucent variety of *crystalline quartz*. When cut cabochon, it sometimes exhibits a star. It fades rather easily. Sources: Madagascar, Brazil, South Dakota and elsewhere.

Rothenio-Palladium. A trademarked name for palladium hardened with rhodium and ruthenium.

rottenstone. An abrasive powder used in jewelry, watch work, and the final polishing of colored stones. It is essentially silica particles that remain after the calcite has been leached from a siliceous limestone.

rouge. Iron oxide; a buffing compound for polishing.

rough girdle. If a diamond is rounded up too quickly in the fashioning process, the surface of the girdle, instead of having the smoothness and waxy luster of a finely turned girdle, will be rough or granular. This condition may also be accompanied by numerous hairlike fractures extending into the stone.

round-filed chain. See section on basic styles of jewelry chains.

ruby. The red variety of *corundum*. Intense, medium to medium-dark purplish red (so-called pigeon's blood) is best, intense red is fine, and dark red is less desirable. Star ruby is rare. In the jewelry industry, the finest purplish-red stones, principally from Burma, are known as *Burma*, or *oriental, rubies;* less valuable, darker red, principally from Thailand, as *Siam rubies;* and light red, from Ceylon and elsewhere, as *Ceylon ruby* or *pink sapphire*. The birthstone for July.

Rutania. A trademarked name for *synthetic rutile*.

ruthenium (ru-then"-e-um). A metal of the *platinum* group, used to harden platinum or palladium; also, occasionally on penpoint nibs. Hardness, 6½; specific gravity, 12.2.

S

safety catch. A catch that locks the point of a pinstem in place. See section on jewelry findings.

safety pinion. A center pinion that unscrews on the center arbor of a watch, if a mainspring breaks, to protect the train from shock and breakage.

Saint Edward's Sapphire. A fine blue sapphire, reputedly worn by King Edward about 1042. It was refashioned as a rose cut and is now in a diamond-paved cross that surmounts the British Imperial State Crown.

Sancy Diamond. A 55-carat pear-shaped diamond, one of the first with symmetrical facets. It was named for the French ambassador to Turkey, Nicholas Harlai, the Signeur de Sancy, who bought it in Constantinople about 1570 and brought it to France. Thereafter, its history was checkered, involving such famous names as Henry III, Henry IV, Queen Elizabeth I, James II and Louis XIV. In 1792, it was stolen with other famous jewels during the French Revolution, reappeared in 1828 and sold by a French merchant to Russian Prince Demidoff, owned by an East Indian for two years, and displayed at the Paris Exposition of 1867 by the French jeweler, Bapst. Finally, in 1906, the diamond was purchased by William Waldorf Astor as a wedding present when his son married the late Lady Astor. It was featured at the *Ten Centuries of French Jewelry* exhibition at the Louvre Museum in 1962. See section on famous diamonds.

sandblast finish. A frosted finish produced on the surface of metals by exposure to a highly pressurized stream of sand.

sanding. The operation in fashioning gemstones during which deep scratches left by grinding are removed by garnet paper, emery cloth or silicon-carbide paper.

sapphire (saf″-ire). Any gem corundum other than ruby. In the jewelry industry, the word generally means *blue sapphire;* other colors are known as pink sapphire, yellow sapphire, purple sapphire, etc. These, as a group, are distinguished from blue as *fancy sapphires.* Sources: best-quality blue from Cashmere; fine blue from Burma, Thailand and Montana; lighter blue from Ceylon; and other colors principally from Ceylon, Australia and Montana. The birthstone for September.

sard. The translucent brown to reddish-brown variety of *chalcedony.*

sardonyx (sar″-doh-niks). *Chalcedony* with straight, parallel bands or layers of reddish brown to brown alternating with other colors. The name is applied incorrectly to carnelian and, more often, to sard. Cameos and intaglios

Glossary

are frequently cut from sardonyx. One of the birthstones for August.

satin finish. A dull finish, smoother than that produced by sandblasting, exhibiting a soft, pearllike luster.

sautior (so-twar"). A chain or ribbon worn around the neck, sometimes with a short length of chain added in front, from which a watch, lorgnette, jewel or other ornament can be hung.

sawed stone. (1) Any diamond that has been sawed during the fashioning process. (2) A *spread*, or *swindled*, stone is occasionally referred to as a sawed stone by some dealers, since spread stones are usually cut from sawed rough, in contrast to lumpy stones, which represent the greatest weight savings from a whole octahedron.

sawing. In fashioning, this process of grinding a narrow slit through a gemstone is usually accomplished by a metal disc charged with an abrasive. Phosphor bronze charged with diamond dust is used for diamonds and other valuable gemstones, sheet iron and diamond dust for less valuable ones, and the mud saw for inexpensive ones.

scarab. A gemstone or other substance fashioned into a conventionalized representation of a scarabaeus beetle, which was worshipped by the ancient Egyptians as a symbol of fertility and resurrection. It was fashioned by them in minerals, metals or ceramics, especially *faience*, with inscriptions on the base. They were used as talismans and ornaments and were buried with the dead. These and modern scarabs have been mounted in jewelry, especially finger rings and bracelets. Their intaglio-cut bases are also used as seals. All modern seal rings are probably a development of the scarab and cylinder.

scarf pin. A pin worn in a scarf or a necktie, usually set with a gem.

"scientific emerald." A misnomer for a green *doublet* or *triplet*.

scintillation. Scintillation in gemstones can be defined broadly as an alternating display of reflections from the polished facets of a gemstone that is seen by the observer when either the illuminant, the gemstone or the observer is in motion—a flashing or twinkling of light from the facets. Comparative scintillation, or the degree of scintillation, is determined by (1) the number of facets on the stone that will reflect light to the eye as the stone is moved about (i.e., the number of individual reflections); (2) the quality of the polish of the facets, since the more highly polished the facets, the brighter the reflections and hence the stronger the reflections from them; and (3) the brilliancy of the stone and thus the degree to which light is returned to the eye after refraction into the stone and back out through the crown.

"scotch topaz." A misnomer for *citrine*.

scratch brush. A wire-bristled brush, used to produce various dull finishes on metals by scratching their surfaces.

screwcase. A watchcase in which the back and bezel are held to the center by screw threads, cut on the shoulder wall of the center and inside the back and bezel rims.

scroll. An ornament or design resembling a loose roll of paper; often a spiral form.

scroll chain. See section on basic styles of jewelry chains.

seal ring. Any finger ring that can be used to emboss an emblem in sealing wax.

seconds hand. The hand on a timepiece dial that indicates the 60 seconds of a minute; usually, it is a prolongation of the lower pivot of the fourth pinion in a watch. See section on watches.

seed pearls. Small, round, nacreous pearls that weigh less than one-fourth pearl grain.

self-winding clock. A clock in which the weight or spring is wound by an electric motor, which is automatically started and stopped by the clock movement. It is not to be confused with a *synchronous* clock.

self-winding watch. A class of watches in which the mainspring is wound by a pedometer weight that operates a click-and-ratchet attached to the barrel arbor. It is also called an *automatic watch*.

semiprecious. An indeterminate and misleading classification that includes all gemstones other than the so-called precious stones; i.e., diamond, ruby, emerald, sapphire and pearl. It does not recognize the fact that a poor-quality ruby may be far less costly than a fine specimen of jadeite, for example. *Gemstone* is a term that is being used with increasing frequency to include all fashioned gem minerals.

semitranslucent stone. One that transmits some light, as through the edges of an otherwise opaque cabochon.

semitransparent stone. One that transmits light but only hazily; i.e., not water clear.

serpentine (sur″-pen-tine). A mineral species, greenish varieties of which, including *bowenite*, are often used as jade substitutes.

set. A term used by the brillianteerer in a diamond-cutting plant to refer to a group of facets consisting of two star facets and the accompanying four upper-girdle facets.

setter. The skilled craftsman who sets fashioned gemstones in rings and other kinds of jewelry.

setting. (1) That portion of a mounting that actually holds the stone, as distinguished from the rest of the mounting to which the setting is attached, such as the shank of a ring. See section on mountings and settings. (2) To some persons, the word setting refers only to a gemstone, usually for a ring.

S.G. The abbreviation for *specific gravity*.

shackle. A link used to fasten two parts together, so that one may be turned, as a charm on a chain may be turned.

Shah Diamond. An 88.70-carat, partially polished, bar-shaped, engraved diamond, found in India. The first inscription shows it was owned by an Indian prince in 1591; the second, by Shah Jehan (builder of the Taj Mahal) in 1651; and the third, by the Shah of Persia in 1824, which means that it was probably part of the loot carried off by the Persians after the sack of Delhi in 1739. In 1889, the Persian Government sent the diamond to the Czar, in St. Petersburg, in appeasement for the accidental killing of the Russian Ambassador by the Persian mob. During World War I, it was sent to the Kremlin for safekeeping, where it has remained since. See section on famous diamonds.

shallow stone. A diamond on which the pavilion main facets are placed at an angle of less than 39° or 40° to the girdle plane. If the angle is much less than this, the loss in brilliancy gives the diamond the very glassy appearance that diamond men associate with a *fisheye*.

shank. That part of a finger ring that surrounds the finger, exclusive of the setting (if it is a gem-set ring) or the seal (if it is a signet ring).

sharp. A diamond used to groove another diamond in preparation for the cleaving operation, or to abrade and shape a diamond in the *girdling (rounding up, cutting or bruting)* process.

Sheffield plate. True Sheffield plate was made by heat rolling together sheets of copper, brass or other metal and silver in the desired proportions. The process, discovered in 1742, was virtually abandoned about 1840 with the introduction of electroplating.

shellac mounting stick. A holder consisting of a wooden disc with a handle. Shellac is melted on the surface of the disc and pieces of jewelry are embedded in it and thus secured for engraving, setting, etc.

shell cameo. A cameo carved from shell, almost always with a raised figure cut from the white layers and the background cut away to the darker layers.

shell cat's-eye. The "door" (operculum) of a sea snail. It is domed and oval or round with round markings of yellowish to white and reddish to dark brown and green. It does not have either the long narrow pupil of a gemstone cat's-eye or the movable effect of that "eye."

shell-gold jewelry. Jewelry consisting of very thin sheets of karat gold formed into a three-dimensional design, the hollow interior of which contains lead or soft solder.

shell motif. See section on ornaments and designs.

ship's-bell's strike. A striking work for clocks that sounds time signals the same as those struck on a ship's bell for calling labor shifts, or watches, of the crew. At 12:30 PM, one bell is struck; every half hour the striking adds a bell, until eight bells are struck, at 4 PM. The cycle is repeated throughout the day and night, so that eight bells is sounded further at 8 PM and 12 noon. After any two strokes, the next one occurs at a slightly longer interval than between the two preceding strokes, so that they can be counted in pairs, thus: 0, 00, 00-0, 00-00, 00-00-0, 00-00-00, 00-00-00-0, 00-00-00-00.

shirt stud. See section on jewelry findings.

"shockproof watch." Once applied to watches having spring-controlled balance jewels, "shockproof" is outlawed by FTC regulations.

shock-resistant watch. A watch in which the balance jewels are mounted so that they have a light spring-controlled movement under impact of pivots when the watch suffers a blow or fall. It is designed to prevent damage to jewels and pivots. The use of the term "shockproof" has been outlawed by a May, 1947, FTC order (since it is manifestly impossible to manufacture a completely shockproof watch), but both *shock resistant* and *shock absorbent* are permitted under certain circumstances.

shoulder. The upper portion of a ring shank, near the setting.

shoulder pivot. A form of pivot for arbors of watches and clocks, used in bearings without endstones, the endshake being limited at each bearing by contact of the shoulder with the plate or jewel.

SI. The abbreviation for *slightly imperfect.*

sideshake. In a watch, play or freedom of pivots to move sideways in their bearings.

sight. When parcels and lots of rough diamonds are offered periodically by the Diamond Trading Co. to invited buyers, both the event and the lot selected for a company are known as *sights*.

signet ring. A finger ring engraved with an initial, monogram, crest, coat-of-arms or other design, or set with a stone bearing designs of this kind. If the engraving is sufficiently deep, it may be used as a *seal ring.*

silica. Silicon dioxide, found in nature in the forms of quartz, chalcedony, opal, diatomaceous earth and sandstone. It is used in the manufacture of glass, ceramic glazes and high-quality clayware bodies.

silicon carbide. An artificial abrasive that is between corundum and diamond in hardness.

Glossary

Although it is usually green and nearly opaque, patents were taken out on colorless material a number of years ago.

silk. Microscopically small, needle-like inclusions in *ruby* and *sapphire;* subsurface reflections from them produce a whitish sheen resembling the sheen of silk fabric. The inclusions are generally conceded to be tiny crystals of rutile.

silver. A white, metallic element; one of the precious metals. Hardness, 2½-3; specific gravity, 10.5. It is used in the manufacture of jewelry, silverware, coins and in many branches of science and industry. It is harder than gold, softer than copper, more malleable and ductile than any metal except gold, and an excellent conductor of heat and electricity. It can be rolled so thin that it transmits light. It has a strong affinity for sulphur to form tarnish.

silverplate. A base metal coated with silver by an *electroplating* process.

silversmith. An artisan or a firm that specializes in the manufacture of silver jewelry, tableware or other objects.

simulated stone. Any substance fashioned as a gemstone that imitates it in appearance. It is a term that is used widely in advertising.

single cut. A simple form of cutting that has a circular girdle, a table, eight bezel facets, eight pavilion facets, and sometimes a culet. It is used mostly for small diamond *melee*. Same as *mazarin cut.*

single, or standard, plate. Plated silverware on which the thickness of the plating is equivalent to that obtained by depositing two ounces of silver on a gross of teaspoons.

sister hook. See section on jewelry findings.

sixth. A common abbreviation for a *sixth carat,* when referring to the weights of diamonds.

skylight watch. An open-face watch with a wide bezel and a glass of small diameter.

"slave's diamond." A misnomer for *colorless topaz.*

sleeve. In the pendant of the case of a watch having a negative-setting work, a split-steel tubular spring with interior projections engaging a slot in the stem, to hold the stem in position either for winding or setting the watch.

slightly imperfect. A grade of relative imperfection in a diamond. It signifies a more flawed condition than *very slightly imperfect* but less than *imperfect.* In general, stones are called *slightly imperfect* only if the flaws they contain are not visible face up to to the unaided eye of a trained observer.

slightly yellow. A diamond color grade that is used by some dealers for a stone showing an obvious yellow tint to the unaided eye.

slitting. A term used for the sawing of colored stones by a diamond saw or other discs charged with abrasives.

slug. An irregular, distorted freshwater pearl or intergrowth of such pearls.

smithsonite. An ore mineral of *zinc* that occurs in many lovely pastel colors. The greenish varieties sometimes substituted for jade.

smoky quartz. A smoky grayish-brown, smoky yellow to almost black variety of transparent *crystalline quartz*. It is also called *cairngorm*. Sources: Scotland, Ceylon, Spain, Switzerland, Maine, New Hampshire, Colorado and elsewhere.

"smoky topaz." A misnomer for *citrine* or *smoky quartz*.

smut finish. Same as *India finish*.

snake chain. See section on basic styles of jewelry chains.

snap. See section on jewelry findings.

snap ring. Same as *spring ring*.

socket. A ring or tube into which the catch of a clasp or fastener fits.

sodium-vapor lamp. A *monochromatic* light source for use with optical instruments. It is of particular value when used with a *gem refractometer*, because the resultant reading consists of a sharp shadow edge, rather than the broad spectral band produced by a white-light source.

soft-metal silverware. A popular trade term for *silverplated* *holloware*, the base of which is *britannia metal* or *pewter*.

soldered curb. See section on basic styles of jewelry chains.

soldering. Joining metals together by melting between them an alloy that flows at a lower temperature than those being joined. *Hard soldering* is done at a red-hot temperature and makes a stronger union, rarely becoming unjoined. *Soft soldering* is done with solder that flows at lower temperatures, forming a weaker bond.

solders. Alloys used in soldering. *Hard solders* are alloys of gold, silver or brass and melt when red hot. *Soft solders* are alloys of lead and tin, those with the addition of bismuth melting at the lowest temperature.

solid gold. Fine gold, or gold of 24-*karat* quality. For any other use, the term has no legal standing and should not be used because of ambiguity. It may mean 24 karat to some and to others, any karat, as distinguished from gold filled or gold plate. However, the terms *solid 14-karat gold* and *solid 18-karat gold* are not considered objectionable by the Federal Trade Commission.

solitaire. A ring containing a single gem, and often extended to mean a ring containing one important gem, with comparatively unimportant stones set in the shank.

"Soochow jade." A misnomer for *serpentine* or *steatite*.

"soude emerald." A misnomer for a *green triplet*.

spandrel. A scroll- or leaflike design, usually executed in brass, squaring off the face of a hall clock or other large clock.

"Spanish topaz." A misnomer for *citrine* or *smoky quartz*.

species. A mineralogical division indicating a *single mineral*. All the varieties in any one species have the same basic chemical composition, structure and basic properties, such as refractive index, specific gravity and hardness, but may vary widely in color, form and transparency.

specific gravity. The ratio of the density of any substance to that of water at 4° C. The S.G. of gems is usually determined by *hydrostatic weighing* or, for approximate values, by the use of *heavy liquids*. See table of specific gravity.

specific-gravity attachments. The accessories used in conjunction with a *diamond balance* for obtaining the *specific gravity* of gemstones by the *hydrostatic weighing method*. They consist of a beaker stand, beaker, wire stone basket and wire counterbalance. See section on gem-testing instruments.

specific-gravity liquids. High-density liquids that are used to determine the *specific gravity* of gemstones. If a gem's specific gravity is lower than the density of the liquid, it will float; if it is the same as that of the liquid, it will remain suspended; if it is higher than that of the liquid, it will sink. The most commonly used liquids for testing gems are *methylene iodide* (S.G., 3.32), *bromoform* (S.G., 2.89), and bromoform diluted with *xylene* (zy″-lene) to a density of 2.62. A saturated solution of a 50-50 combination of *thallium malonate* and *thallium formate* in water (*Clerici's solution*) has a density of about 4.15 at room temperature. See section on gem-testing instruments.

spectroscope (spek″-tro-scope). An optical gem-testing instrument for forming and examining spectra by the dispersion of light into its component wavelengths. See section on gem-testing instruments.

spectrum. Radiant energy spread so that the component wavelengths are arranged progressively. In visible light, the wavelengths from longest to shortest are as follows: red, orange, yellow, green, blue, violet. Spreading radiant energy with instruments for analysis is accomplished by dispersing the energy through a prism or a diffraction grating.

sphene (sfeen). A mineral species, the transparent yellow to greenish varieties of which have extraordinary brilliancy and fire. It is not frequently used in jewelry. Sources: Switzerland, Ceylon, France, Madagascar, Russia, Mexico and elsewhere. Its mineral name is *titanite*.

spinel (spi-nel″). A mineral species that has transparent red, orange, blue, violet and purple varieties. It is hard and brilliant. Sources: Burma, Ceylon and elsewhere.

"spinel ruby." A misnomer for *red spinel.*

spinning. A method of forming or shaping pieces of silver holloware by revolving a flat disc of silver over a piece of wood or steel that has been made in the shape the silver is to assume. By means of a tool, the silver is spread over the rotating form, finally achieving the desired shape.

split ring. Same as *jump ring.*

split-seconds watch. A *chronograph,* or *timer watch,* with two sweep-seconds hands that can be operated in turn to time two successive happenings, as the finish of the first and second horses in a race.

spodumene (spod″-u-meen). A mineral species that occurs in transparent form in light tones of rose, lilac, violet, green or yellow; also colorless. It is difficult to cut, since it cleaves easily. Sources: Madagascar, Brazil, North Carolina, California and elsewhere.

spread stone. A diamond that has been cut with a large table and a thin crown, to retain greater weight from the two sawn pieces of an octahedron than is possible by using ideal proportions.

spring-drive clock. A class of clocks in which motive power is provided by winding a mainspring; differentiated from *weight-driven* clocks.

spring hinge. See section on jewelry findings.

spring ring. A hollow ring that can be partly opened (and again closed) by means of an enclosed spring. Thus, it can be easily attached to, and removed from, another ring; for example, when a spring ring and a closed ring of metal are used on the ends of a necklace. See section on jewelry findings.

square emerald cut. A form of *step cutting* with a square girdle outline but modified by corner facets. See section on shapes and styles of cutting.

square setting. Same as *block setting*

square-prong setting. A *four-prong* setting with 90° angles at the four corners and a dovetail or similar piercing along the flat sides. See section on mountings and settings.

staff. A pivoted shaft, or arbor; specifically, the arbor on which is mounted the balance of a watch or other timepiece.

stained stone. A stone whose color has been altered by the use of a coloring agent, such as a dye, or by impregnation with a substance such as sugar, followed by either chemical or heat treatment, which usually produces a permanent color. Many materials are stained, but *chalcedony* is particu-

Glossary

larly adaptable to this kind of color alteration.

stainless steel. An alloy composed mainly of steel, nickel and chromium, generally having greater strength than ordinary steel and possessing unusually high resistance to corrosion, tarnish or stain by air, water and acids.

standard time. The time used by agreement for regulating civil affairs in each of practically all countries of the world. It is based on sideral-time determinations made in national astronomical observatories, which are translated into mean solar time of the local meridians of the observatories. In 1884, an international congress was held in Washington, D. C., where what is known as *standard time* was adopted. As far as the USA is concerned, the agreement was made to recognize four zones, east to west, each to have uniform time within its area and to have a difference of exactly one hour between any zone and a zone adjacent to it.

star. A rayed figure, consisting of two or more intersecting bands of light; an optical phenomenon caused by reflected light from inclusions or channels, and brought to sharp lines in gem materials by cabochon cutting. Stars usually have four, six or twelve rays, but three- , five- , seven- and nine-rayed stars occur, or are possible due to the absence of inclusions in a portion of the stone.

star facets. The eight triangular facets that bound the table of a round *brilliant-cut* gem between the main bezel facets. See section on shapes and styles of cutting.

Star of Artaban. A 316-carat blue star sapphire in the Smithsonian Institution.

Star of Este Diamond. A 26.16-carat, fine-quality Indian diamond, said to have belonged to the Este family, an ancient ruling house of Lombardy, Italy. Archduke Ferdinand, of Austria-Este, whose assassination in 1914 precipitated World War I, inherited the diamond. After his death, it presumably reverted to Emperor Charles, of Austria. It disappeared after Charles was deposed, in 1919. However, a large diamond of similar history was reported to have been purchased by Farouk, at that time King of Egypt, in 1950. See section on famous diamonds.

Star of India. A 563.35-carat blue star sapphire, thought to be the largest in the world. It is comparatively free from flaws and has a well-defined star. It is on display at the American Museum of Natural History.

Star of South Africa Diamond. A 47.75-carat oval brilliant, cut from rough of 83.50 carats, that is credited with starting the South African diamond rush, in 1869. It was found near the Orange River by a native, traded to a farmer, and sold to a cutter in Hopetown for $56,000. The cutter then sold the finished gem to the Earl of Dudley for $125,000; the Countess Dudley wore it in a hair ornament, surrounded by 95 smaller diamonds. Its present location is unknown. An alternate name is the *Dudley Diamond*. See section on famous diamonds.

Star of the South (Estrella do Sud) Diamond. A 261.88-carat Brazilian diamond, found by a Negro slave woman in 1853. The rough was sold for about $15,000 and cut in Amsterdam into a 128.50-carat, oval-shaped colorless stone. It was shown at the London Exhibition of 1862 and the Paris Exhibition of 1867. Later, it was sold to the Gaekwar of Baroda for $400,000. More recently, the large gem was reported to be in the possession of Rustomjee Jamsetjee, of Bombay. See section on famous diamonds.

star quartz. *Rose* quartz that exhibits a star. Often it is backed with a blue mirror or other blue substance to imitate star sapphire.

star ruby. A ruby with six rays. Usually, there is a wider color latitude in stones called star rubies than in transparent stones. Pink, purple and even violet star sapphires are often sold as star rubies.

star sapphire. A sapphire that normally has six rays; rarely, twelve. Blue, gray and black are the most frequent, although light purplish gray occurs often and other colors rarely.

star setting. A style of setting a stone in a flat piece of metal. The girdle is seated just below the edge of the metal and is secured by beads that are raised by starting considerably back from the edge of the hole with a pointed graver. The resultant long line is further widened on both sides of the beads to form the tapered points of the star.

star stone. In general, any stone in which a rayed figure can be seen.

Star*Tania. A trademarked name for *synthetic rutile*.

steatite (ste″-ah-tite). A soft, ornamental stone; a variety of *talc*. It is a poor but frequent substitute for jade, especially greenish, gray or almost white carved jade. Another name for steatite is *soapstone*.

stem. A shaft in a stem wind timepiece that operates the winding and setting mechanisms.

stem-wind watch. A class of watches in which the mainspring is wound by turning a crown on the stem, which passes through the pendant of the case.

step cut. One of the two basic classifications of cutting styles; i. e., *step cut* and *brilliant cut*. In step-cut styles, all facets are four sided and in steps, or rows, both above and below the girdle. All facets are parallel to the girdle and therefore, except those on the corners, long and usually narrow. The number of rows, or steps, may vary, although the usual

Glossary

number is three on the crown and three on the pavilion. Different shapes of step cuts are usually described by their outline; for example, *rectangular step cut, square step cut, octagon step cut.* A rectangular step cut with cut corners is called a *cushion step cut* or, more popularly, an *emerald cut.* See section on shapes and styles of cutting.

sterling silver. A metallic alloy consisting of 92½% silver and 7½% copper, the latter for hardening and stiffening purposes. This proportion is a legal requirement. It is also called *silver* or *solid silver.* Sterling silver does not refer to the thickness of an article but to the fineness of the silver. The word sterling is derived from Easterling, the name of a 12th-century group of German traders who paid for merchandise with a silver coin, the content of which they rigidly controlled at a time when debasement of coins was common.

Sterling Silversmiths' Guild of America. See section on trade associations.

Stewart Diamond. A slightly yellowish, 296-carat South African diamond, found in 1872. The two prospectors who made the discovery sold the rough for $30,000 to a merchant named Stewart, who later resold it for $45,000; the name Stewart, however, was retained. For years the largest alluvial diamond in existance, it was eventually cut to a fine-quality, 123-carat brilliant. The present ownership is unknown. See section on famous diamonds.

stone. (1) Any small piece of rock or mineral. (2) In the gem trade, the term usually implies a cut-and-polished natural gemstone. However, an artificial reproduction of, or substitute for, such a mineral is often referred to incorrectly as a stone.

stone gauge. (1) A device for measuring gemstones, such as a *Leveridge gauge.* (2) A series of sizes, each of which is numbered, established as a standard and guide for ordering gemstones. (3) A card or plate with the various stone sizes shown as circular holes or printed circles of appropriate diameter for each size.

strap work. See section on ornaments and designs.

streak. The color of the *powder* of a mineral or gemstone.

stretching a ring. Sizing a ring to a slightly larger diameter, by placing it on a tapering steel rod, or mandrel, and hammering it with a soft hammer.

"Strong-ite." A trademarked name for *colorless synthetic corundum.*

strontium titanate. A manufactured transparent gem material possessing a high degree of brilliance and dispersion and little or no body color. It resembles diamond in appearance. It is singly refractive, has a refractive index of 2.409, a specific gravity of 5.13, a hardness of 5 to 6, and the dispersion is .190. The chemical composition is SrTiO$_3$. First produced by the Titanium Division of the National Lead Co. in 1955, it was distributed initially under the trade name of *Starilian;* the present trade name is *Fabulite*.

Stuart Sapphire. A blue sapphire set in the back of the British Imperial State Crown. It measures 1½ by 1 inch.

substitute. In gemology, any substance represented to be, or used to imitate, a more valuable or better-known gemstone; e.g., plastic, glass, doublet, synthetic ruby or natural spinel all could be substitutes for genuine ruby.

sunstone. A translucent gray to white or colorless *feldspar* that contains tiny yellowish or reddish spangles. In fine quality it is reminiscent of moonstone but with a golden reflection, instead of bluish. Sources: Norway, Madagascar, California, Russia and elsewhere.

surface enamel. A thin layer of enamel fused over a metal surface that is decorated in colors similar to that of porcelain painting. The process, although less complicated than for enclosed enamels, requires greater artistic skill.

swag. An ornamental design in the form of a festoon or wreath. See section on ornaments and designs.

sweater-guard clip. See section on jewelry findings.

sweating. A form of *inlay,* in which a small block of silver is sweated into the heel (base) of some silverplated forks and spoons, thus protecting this part of the article that receives the most wear.

swedged cable. See section on basic styles of jewelry chains.

swedged curb. See section on basic styles of jewelry chains.

sweep-seconds hand. A hand driven from the center of the movement of a watch, of a length equal to the radius of the minute circle on its dial, indicating seconds, making one turn on the dial in one minute.

swindled stone. A term used to denote a saving of weight at the expense of beauty in the brilliant cutting of diamonds; it usually refers to a greatly *spread* stone.

swirl pin. See section on jewelry findings.

"Swiss lapis." A misnomer for *dyed jasper*.

swivel. (1) A swivel joint that can be attached to a brooch, concealed so that it can be worn as a pendant. The chain attaches to the swivel. See section on jewelry findings. (2) A clasp attachment that is usually used on the end of a watch chain or fob that holds the watch. It rotates completely on a shaft.

symmetry. Parts that correspond in size, shape and relative position on opposite sides of a dividing line or median plane or that are distributed about a center or axis. When referring to a fashioned dia-

Glossary

mond, the term means the exactness of placement and shaping of opposed facets and other portions of the stone. Symmetry is judged on the basis of the degree to which these opposed features yield exact mirror images.

synchronous clock. A clock of the type known to most as an *electric clock*. It is propelled by its own AC motor, the speed of which is synchonized to that of an electric generator in an electric power plant. The number of cycles per second of this generator, and of the synchronized clock, is regulated by a master clock.

"synthetic alexandrite." A misnomer for *synthetic alexandrite-like corundum*.

"synthetic amethyst." A misnomer for *synthetic sapphire* or *spinel*.

synthetic corundum (ko-run″-dum). Reproduction of the structure, composition and properties of corundum by man. Commercial synthetic corundum is made by the *Verneuil* method; i.e., by melting alumina in an oxyhydrogen flame. It is produced in boules; long, slender rods; and many other shapes. It is detected most effectively by the nature of its inclusions, which differ from those of genuine corundum.

synthetic diamond. Using equipment capable of achieving extremely high temperatures and pressures, the General Electric Co. succeeded in synthesizing tiny industrial diamonds in 1955. Subsequent refinements in technique and apparatus, using a temperature of 9000° F. and pressures up to 3,000,000 pounds per square inch, have enabled G.E. scientists to produce 1/10-carat sizes on a commercial scale and sizes above one carat on an experimental basis. Typical crystals are more irregular and rough surfaced than natural diamonds of similar size, although many have regular crystal faces. Colors are usually light tones of green, gray-black or yellow; however, in bulk they appear black, because of the presence of black inclusions. The manmade stones are used primarily for resinoid- , vitrified- and metal-bonded grinding applications. Many other firms, both in the United States and abroad, make industrial diamonds, including De Beers Adamant Laboratory in South Africa.

synthetic emerald. A synthetic reproduction of genuine emerald. The properties differ from those of its natural counterpart, but structure and composition are those of emerald. It is made commercially in California by Carroll Chatham, in sizes that yield cut gemstones of not more than a few carats. Linde Air Products Co. coats prefaceted natural beryl with synthetic emerald.

synthetic rutile (roo″-teel). A manufactured transparent gem material that has been produced commercially since 1948 by the Linde Air Products Co. and the National

Lead Co. It is noted for its high degree of dispersion (.330), which is considerably greater than diamond's .044. It is double refractive, has a refractive index of 2.62-2.90, a specific gravity of 4.25, and a hardness of about 6 to 6½. The chemical formula is TiO_2. Colors include pale yellow, brownish red and greenish blue to bluish green. It is sold under many trade names, including *Miridis, Kenya Gem, Titania, Titangem, Tiru Gem, Johannes Gem, Diamothyst* and a host of others.

synthetic spinel (spi-nel"). Made in many colors by the same method as synthetic corundum and in similar forms, except that the boules usually exhibit four lateral faces at right angles to one another. It was produced accidentally, prior to 1909, in search for a method of manufacturing synthetic blue sapphire.

synthetic stone. A reproduction of a stone that has the same physical, optical and chemical properties as the genuine stone it reproduces. Many gem minerals have been made synthetically as a scientific experiment, but only corundum, spinel, emerald, rutile and strontium titanate have been made commercially and cut as stones for the trade.

"synthetic zircon." A misnomer for *synthetic sapphire* or *spinel*.

Glossary

T

table. The large facet that caps the crown of a faceted gemstone. In the standard round brilliant, it is octagonal in shape and is bounded by eight star facets. See section on shapes and styles of cutting.

table reflection. The table of a diamond is usually mirrored in the pavilion as the viewer looks through the table. The size and darkness of the reflection provides an accurate guide to the angle of the pavilion facets.

table size. The size of the table of a fashioned diamond, expressed as a percentage of the stone's narrow-girdle diameter, is a dimension used in proportion analysis.

taille de epergne (tah″-ye de a″-purn). The reverse of *champlevé*, the ornamentation being engraved and filled with enamel, generally blue or black.

talisman. A charm, often a gemstone, that is supposed to produce unusual effects, such as protecting the wearer or bringing him good luck, etc.

tambourine clock. A *mantle clock* with a compound curved top. See section on basic shapes of clocks.

tarnish. A coating on metals or other materials, such as glass, caused usually by oxidation of the constituents. The black tarnish on silver is *silver sulphide*.

teeth. In watch gearings, the cogs on a wheel; differentiated from leaves, which are the cogs on a pinion.

tektite. A natural silicious glass, found as loose, rounded, pitted fragments in various parts of the world. It is thought to be of meteoric origin. A variety sometimes used for gem purposes is *moldavite*.

tetragonal system (teh-trag″-oh-nal). See section on crystal systems.

thick crown. A term that designates a crown thickness that is noticeably deeper than the 16.2% (of the girdle diameter) encountered on an ideally cut diamond. Since most diamonds today are cut with spread tables and resultant thinner crowns, a thick crown is seldom seen, except on stones cut much earlier.

thinstick watch hand. See section on watches.

third. A common abbreviation for a *third carat*, when referring to the weights of diamonds.

threaded barrel. See section on jewelry findings.

threaded pin. See section on jewelry findings.

Thrilliant. A trademarked name for *colorless synthetic corundum*.

tiara (te-air″-ah; te-are″-ah). A head ornament that resembles the front one-quarter of a crown; a *frontlet* or *coronet*.

tiebar. See section on jewelry findings.

tietack. See section on jewelry findings.

Tiffany Diamond. A 128.51-carat, golden-yellow cushion-cut diamond, named for the famous Fifth Avenue jewelers who own it. Found in South Africa in 1878, the rough weighed 287.42 carats. Millions of persons have seen the stone in a number of expositions and in Tiffany's store. Its reported value is approximately $600,000. See section on famous diamonds.

Tiffany setting. A *six-prong* setting, generally round in shape and flaring out slightly from the base to the top, having long, slender prongs that hold the stone. The term is sometimes applied to a *four-prong* setting. See section on mountings and settings.

tiger's-eye. A yellow or yellowish-brown ornamental and gem variety of *quartz*. Pseudomorphous after crocidolite asbestos. It is colored by limonite, which, by heating, probably turns to hematite and produces a red to brownish-red tiger's-eye. Gray is produced by an acid treatment; other colors are made by dyeing and staining. When it is cut with a flat surface parallel to the fibers, a changeable silky sheen is seen as the stone is turned. It is a popular stone for cameos and intaglios. When cut cabochon with the base parallel to the fibers, a cat's-eye effect is produced.

Principal source: Asbestos Mountains, west of Griquatown, South Africa.

timer. A chronograph watch, stopwatch, etc., with a mechanism to stop a running seconds hand.

time recorder. (1) An electrically operated instrument that records on paper tape the beat of a watch or any of the five sounds pertaining to a properly set escapement. In the jewelry trade, the term is more properly used to mean a *constant-time recorder*, which is an instrument that records on paper the timekeeping rates of watches. (2) A term sometimes used for a *watchman's clock*.

timing washer. A pierced disc of thin metal, used to place on balance screws to increase weight and make a watch run slower. The same weight of washers must be placed on opposite screws, to maintain poise.

Timur Ruby. The largest known (361 carats) red spinel, famous for six centuries and thought to be a ruby for most of that time. Known as *Kriraj-i-Alman* (The Tribute of the World), it was seized by Timur in Delhi in 1398. It continued to change hands usually in the same manner, until it was presented to Queen Victoria by the East India Co., in 1851. Now among the British Crown Jewels, it is still uncut, and bears inscriptions in Persian indicating six of its royal owners.

Glossary

tip. See section on jewelry findings.

"Tiru Gem." A trademarked name for *synthetic rutile*.

"Titangem." A trademarked name for *synthetic rutile*.

Titania. A trademarked name for *synthetic rutile*.

Titania Brilliant. A trademarked name for *synthetic rutile*.

"Titania Midnight Stone." A trademarked name for *synthetic rutile*.

Titanium Rutile. A trademarked name for *synthetic rutile*.

"Titanstone." A trademarked name for *synthetic rutile*.

toggle. A short piece of wire or chain that connects two pieces or parts of jewelry. See section on jewelry findings.

toiletware. A general term applied to combs, brushes, mirrors, manicure sets, and other dresser and vanity sets.

tone. The attribute of a color that determines its position on a light-to-dark scale. Thus, light gray is a light tone and dark gray is a dark tone. Pink is a light tone of red and maroon is a dark tone.

topaz. Best known in a transparent yellow-brown color, topaz is also popular in pink, light-blue and reddish-brown colors; colorless stones are well known, too. It is sometimes called *precious topaz*, to distinguish it from *citrine*, or *topaz-quartz*, with which it has long been confused by less well-informed jewelers. Sources: Brazil, Ceylon, the Urals, California, Maine, Colorado and elsewhere. One of the birthstones for November.

topaz-quartz. Same as *citrine*.

top cape. An early trade term still used by some dealers to designate the diamond color grade between *crystal* and *cape* in the *river-to-light-yellow* system. Diamonds in this classification have a yellowish cast that is visible to the unaided eye.

top crystal. An early trade term still used by some dealers to designate the diamond color grade between *Wesselton* and *crystal* in the *river-to-light-yellow* system. Diamonds in this classification show a very slight tinge of yellow.

top Wesselton. An early trade term still used by some dealers to designate the diamond color grade just below the finest, or *river*, classification in the *river-to-light-yellow* system. It was originally defined as a colorless stone, but less transparent than a river; today, it is often applied to an exceedingly faintly tinted stone.

tortoise shell. The mottled brown-and-yellow shell of the hawksbill sea turtle. It is used for combs, jewelry novelties, toiletware, etc. It is imitated by plastic.

touchstone. Black quartz, or sometimes basalt, smoothly ground and used with *aqua regia* to determine the gold content of an article. A needle of known karat fineness is used to make a mark on the touchstone beside a mark made with the material of unknown gold content. The mark of the needle with the same karat content as the unknown should be dissolved at the same rate, when the acid is applied to both marks simultaneously.

touch watch. A watch with raised studs at the dial numerals and a heavy hand, for reading time in the dark by feeling with a finger.

toughness. The resistance that a gemstone offers to *blows* and *breakage*, as distinguished from resistance to scratching, which is hardness.

tourmaline (toor"-mah-leen). A mineral species, gem varieties of which are transparent and of all major hues. Sources: Ceylon, Brazil, Madagascar, California, Maine and elsewhere. One of the birthstones for October.

Trade Practice Rules. The United States Federal Trade Commission, at the request of representatives of an industry, undertakes to promulgate rules setting forth fair-trade practices, as agreed upon by groups speaking for the majority of the members of that trade. The first Trade Practice Rules for the jewelry trade were published in 1938 and revised in 1957.

trade shop. A shop in which repairing and, usually, special-order manufacturing is done, as contrasted to a large jewelry-manufacturing factory or shop.

train. In a watch or clock, the series of wheels and pinions between the power plant (the mainspring or weight) and the escapement. This is what is meant by saying merely *the train*, although sometimes it is called the *time train*. There are gear trains in some horological mechanisms, but they are always referred to, and qualified as to their special purposes, as *dial train, striking train*, etc.

translucent. Passing light imperfectly. A translucent material transmits light, but objects cannot be resolved through it. Translucent gem material is not suitable for brilliant cutting, but only for cabochons, beads, etc.

transparent. Passing light clearly. A transparent material transmits light and objects can be seen clearly, even through a considerable thickness.

traveling clock. The present-day type of portable timepiece for transient use. It is usually in a leather case with hinged covers that can be opened and set up so as to expose the dial to view; folded, the covers protect the dial. See section on basic shapes of clocks.

treated stone. A heated, stained or coated stone, or one that has been treated with X-rays, radium or in a cyclotron to improve or otherwise alter its color. Also, a

Glossary

stone that may have been treated to disguise flaws, as are "doctored" pearls or opals, the cracks of which have been filled with oil or other liquid.

trichroism (tri″-kro-izm). The property of some doubly-refractive colored minerals of the orthorhombic, monoclinic and triclinic crystal systems of transmitting three different colors in the three different planes into which transmitted light is polarized.

triclinic system (tri-klin″-ik). See section on crystal systems.

trigon (tri″-gon). A triangular indentation occurring as a growth mark on diamond octahedron faces. The sides of the trigon are reversed with respect to the face on which it occurs.

triple cable. See section on basic styles of jewelry chains.

triple, or XXX, plate. Silver-plated ware on which the thickness of the plating is equivalent to that obtained by depositing six ounces of silver on a gross of teaspoons.

triplet. An *assembled* stone of two main portions, bound together by a layer of cement that is colored to reproduce the color of the stone being imitated.

tripoli cake. A commercially prepared abrasive; also known as *tripoli*.

troy weight. See table of units of weight at end of glossary.

truing. On watch balances or other wheels, the operation of correcting any irregularity of form that would make the part run untrue in circular motion. Truing a watch balance is a necessary preliminary to poising it, which, in turn, is necessary to produce good timekeeping in varying positions of the watch while in use.

tube bracelet. A bracelet formed from a round or oval-shaped tube of metal. It may be modified to take stones, watches, etc.

turning. The method of executing round, rodlike ornaments or shafts, either with a wood or metal lathe and a cutting tool.

turquois (tur″-koiz; tur″-kwoiz). The most important opaque gem mineral. The best quality is an intense blue, between light and medium in tone; light blue-green and yellowish green are less desirable. The finest quality came from Iran (Persia), called *Persian turquois* in the trade. Other sources: Arizona, New Mexico, Colorado, Nevada. One of the birthstones for December.

turquois matrix. When a veining of other mineral matter is present with turquois, the combination is known as *turquois matrix*.

Tuscan. See section on ornaments and designs.

tweezers. A tool for quick and efficient handling in watch and jewelry work. It consists of a pair of spring-metal arms that are fastened together at one end. The spring metal keeps the jaws opened, except when closed by the fingers. See section on gem-testing instruments.

twelve-hour dial. A watch or clock dial that shows the day divided into two periods of 12 hours each, instead of into hours from one to 24, which is a 24-*hour dial*.

twenty-four hour dial. A watch or clock dial that shows the day divided into hours from one to 24, instead of into two periods of 12 hours each, which is a 12-*hour dial*.

twin crystal. Any physical unit comprising two or more crystal individuals of a single species that differ from one another in orientation. The difference in orientation is systematic, in the sense that one individual represents a reflection across some plane with respect to the adjacent individual, or reflects rotation about some axis with respect to the adjacent. The contact between any two twin units may or may not be planar.

twinning lines. Visible lines on or within a fashioned diamond, caused by *twinning* in the crystal. Since the orientation on one side of a twin plane differs from that on the other, the best polishing direction for one is a poorer one for the other; as a result, a line remains at the surface. Also called *knot lines*.

Glossary

U

ultraviolet lamp. A source of ultraviolet radiation used for exciting *fluorescence* in gemstones and other materials. The commonly used long-wave lamp has a peak wavelength emission at approximately 3660 Angstrom units (one Angstrom unit=one ten-millionth of a millimeter). The short-wave lamp has its principal emission peaks at 2537, 2553, 2650 and 2645 A.U., but, depending on the filter, may also emit long wavelengths. The filter on the short-wave lamp is subject to deterioration and has an average effective life of approximately one year. The filter on the long-wave unit, on the other hand, is stable. See section on gem-testing instruments.

uniaxial stone. A doubly-refractive stone that has one direction of single refraction.

upper jewel. The one of a pair of these parts that is nearest the observer, as looked at with a watchcase open; the one that is in the balance bridge, or balance cock; train hole jewels in the top plate.

"Uralian emerald." A term that could be used correctly for Russian emerald, but more often it is a misnomer for *demantoid garnet*.

V

variation. The amount of difference in the rate of a timepiece under different conditions; e.g., when compared running at a higher and lower temperature.

variety. In gemology, a *division of a species*, based on color, kind of optical phenomena, or other distinguishing characteristics of appearance. For example, *emerald* and *aquamarine* are each a variety of *beryl*, and *cat's-eye* and *alexandrite* are varieties of *chrysoberyl*.

"Vega Gem." A trademarked name for *colorless synthetic corundum*.

vermeil (vur″-mil). (1) Gilded silver; also, gilded bronze or copper. (2) A red varnish applied to a gilded surface to give it luster.

vermicelli (vur′-mih-cel″-e). Designs consisting of small curves, scrolls, etc., used in engraving silverware.

Verneuil process (Ver-nay″). The method announced in 1902 by Verneuil, a French chemist, for manufacturing *synthetic corundum*. In addition, the process is used today to produce *synthetic spinel*, *synthetic rutile* and *strontium titanate*.

vernier (vur″-ne-ur). A small, movable auxiliary scale for obtaining fractional parts of a fixed scale.

very slightly imperfect. A diamond-imperfection grade between *very, very slightly imperfect* and *slightly imperfect*. As used ethically, this grade includes stones that are lightly flawed, with flaws easily located but not obvious under 10x.

very, very slightly imperfect. The imperfection grade that is immediately below *flawless* or *perfect*. Ethically employed, this term is applied to stones with minute surface or internal blemishes that are difficult to locate under 10x by a trained eye.

"Vespa Gem." A trademarked name for *colorless synthetic corundum*.

Victoria Diamond. A 469-carat South African diamond, discovered in 1884. The largest stone cut from it weighed 184.50 carats, and is said to have been sold to the Nizam of Hyderabad for $100,000. It is also called the *Great White* or *Imperial Diamond*. See section on famous diamonds.

VSI. The abbreviation for *very slightly imperfect*.

VVSI.. The abbreviation for *very, very slightly imperfect*.

Glossary

W

"Walderite." A trademarked name for *colorless synthetic corundum*.

watch. A portable timepiece. Today, it is a timepiece that is carried in the pocket or worn on the lapel, on the wrist, etc. It is differentiated from semiportable timepieces (e.g., marine chronometers, navigators' deck watches and traveling clocks), which are carried about but not on the person.

watch-cleaning machine. A set of jars for holding cleaning and rinsing solutions, with electric-motor-driven receptacles that move watch parts immersed in the solutions and effect cleaning and rinsing. Usually, there is a heater for drying the parts after rinsing.

watch hands. See section on watches.

watchmaker. In present-day usage, one who repairs watches and who is presumably able to make certain parts for any watch for replacement in repairing it.

Watchmakers of Switzerland Information Center, Inc. See section on trade associations.

watchman's clock. A clock that records the time a watchman reaches certain stations on his rounds.

Watch Material Distributors' Association of America. See section on trade associations.

watch-rate recorder. An instrument for obtaining instantly a record of the deviation of the timekeeping rate of a watch from a standard rate.

water. A term occasionally used as a comparative quality designation for the color and transparency of diamonds, rubies and other gemstones; e.g., *diamonds of the first water, rubies of the second water*.

Waterbury watch. The first watch made in America (1880), designed specifically to sell at a very low price. It was named for Waterbury, Conn., where it was made.

waterproof. A term used in describing certain varieties of watches. Under the terms of a Federal Trade Commission directive issued in April, 1947, the term may be used only when a watch is, in fact, waterproof, as a result of having been immersed for five minutes in water under an atmospheric pressure of 15 pounds per square inch and, also, immersed completely for five minutes in water under an atmospheric pressure of 35 pounds per square inch. If, after these tests, no water has penetrated the case, the watch may be termed waterproof. However, it must be stated that removal of the back of the case, etc., may render the watch nonwaterproof.

"water sapphire." A misnomer for *iolite*.

wax-filled pearl. An imitation pearl consisting of a glass bead filled with wax.

wedding ring. A round band of precious metal that is given to the bride, and sometimes to the groom, as part of the wedding ceremony. It may or may not be set with gems.

weight clock. A clock with weights pulling on cords or chains, wound on drums attached to the main wheel, as motive power for time and striking trains. It is differentiated from *spring clocks*, which use mainsprings for motive power.

well. The dark, nonbrilliant center that is seen through the table of a diamond cut with too deep a pavilion. This condition is caused by excessive light leakage from the overly thick pavilion. *Black center* is used more often to describe this condition.

Wesselton. An early trade term still used by some dealers to designate the diamond color grade between *top Wesselton* and *top crystal* in the *river-to-light-yellow system*. Only the faintest tint of color is visible under ideal grading conditions.

Wesselton Mine. An important diamond pipe mine in South Africa, discovered in 1890. The name was taken from the Wessel's Estate, which owned the farm upon which the discovery was made. It was first known as the Premier Mine, but the name Wesselton soon became accepted through popular usage. The overall quality of the production is fairly low, many are small, and some are coated; however, many fine white diamonds and fancy yellows are produced. Annual production is usually between 300,000 and 400,000 carats.

white diamond. A stone that faces up colorless to the unaided eye. White is below *blue-white* in the *blue - white - to - yellow* color-grading system. Many obviously tinted stones are misrepresented as of "white" grade.

white gold. Karat gold alloyed with 10% to 20% nickel and sometimes smaller amounts of zinc or copper and traces of tin, manganese, etc. It was first used as a substitute for platinum, to which it is inferior in almost every way. It is harder and tougher than yellow gold. Occasionally, a softer alloy, or about 15%, is used in jewelry.

white metal. A term applied to *pewter* or *britannia metal* in the silverplate industry.

white opal. Opal with a body color of any light color, as distinguished from black opal.

white stone. A trade term for *rhinestone* or any other *colorless imitation* of diamond.

Willard clock. Clocks made more than one hundred years ago by the Willard family. The name is

Glossary

now used to mean a *banjo clock*, which the Willards created. See section on basic shapes of clocks.

wire bracelet. A bracelet formed by a series of wires, soldered together to form a semirigid piece. It may involve considerable filigree work, or merely two wires that are separated at the center of the bracelet to permit mounting a bezel for stone setting.

wooden clocks. Clocks with movement plates, wheels and pinions made of wood instead of metal. The two principal examples of the type are early Black Forest (German) clocks, made between 1650 and 1750, and Connecticut wooden clocks, made there in great numbers between 1810 and 1840.

wristwatch. A small watch on a bracelet or strap to be worn on the wrist. Some tradesmen distinguish such watches intended for men's wear as *wristwatches*, and smaller watches worn by women as *bracelet watches*.

X

X-ray diffraction pattern. A pattern produced on photographic film when an X-ray beam strikes a crystal and secondary X-ray beams are generated by reflection from planes of atoms within the crystal. The nature of such a pattern is directly dependent on the manner in which the atoms within the crystal are arranged in space.

Y

yellow diamond. A diamond with a yellow body color. The tone of the color may be exceedingly light or very pronounced.

yellow gold. Karat gold alloyed with copper and silver in approximately equal quantities.

yellow ground. Weathered *blue-ground*, the rock that contains diamonds in the South African pipe mines.

Z

"Zenithite." A trademarked name for *strontium titanate*.

zircon (zur″-kon). A mineral species that yields exceptionally brilliant, transparent gemstones. The most popular color is blue, but colorless is common and red, orange, yellow and green varieties are sometimes seen. Colorless and blue stones are produced by heating light-brown rough. Sources: Viet Nam, Thailand, Ceylon and elsewhere.

Weights & Measurements

Weights and Measurements

The following table lists the units of weights and measurements most commonly employed in the jewelry trade, together with certain other units possessing interest value only. Each unit named is followed by its correct abbreviation (in parentheses) and its equivalent in one or more units of the same quantity.

1 Carat (c. or ct.) = ... 0.00705478 oz. av. = 100 points = 1/5 g. = 200 mg. = 3.08647 gr. = 4 pearl grains.

1 Pennyweight (dwt.) = ... 0.003428571 lb. av. = 0.0041667 lb. t. = .05 oz. t. = 0.0548571 oz. av. = 24 gr. = 1.5517 g. = 1.555.17 mg.

1 Pearl grain = ... 1/4 ct.

1 Kilogram (kg.) = ... 2.20462 lb. av. = 2.6792285 lb. t. = 32.15076 oz. t. = 35.273957 oz. av. = 643.01 dwt. = 15,432.35639 gr. = 1,000 g.

1 Gram (g.) = ... 0.03527 oz. av. = 0.03215 oz. t. = 0.5430 dwt. = 15.4324 gr. = 0.001 kg. = 5 ct. = 1,000 mg.

1 Milligram (mg.) = ... 0.015432 gr. = 0.001 g. = 0.005 ct.

1 Millimeter (mm.) = ... 0.0393700 inch.

1 Grain (gr.) = ... 0.0020833 oz. t. = 0.0022857 oz. av. = 0.041667 dwt. = 0.0648 g. = 0.3240 ct. = 64.798919 mg.
(Note: the grain troy equals the grain avoirdupois.)

1 Pound troy (lb. t.) = ... 0.8822857 lb. av. = 12 oz. t. = 13.1657 oz. av. = 240 dwt. = 5,760 gr. = 0.3732418 kg. = 373.24177 g. = 1,866.12 cts.

1 Ounce troy (oz. t.) = ... 1.09714 oz. av. = 20 dwt. = 480 gr. = 31.103481 g. = 155.51 ct.

1 Pound avoirdupois (lb. av.) = ... 1.21528 lb. t. = 14.5833 oz. t. = 16 oz. av. = 291.667 dwt. = 7,000 gr. = 0.4535942 kg. = 453.5924 g. = 2267.962 cts.

1 Ounce avoirdupois (oz. av.) = ... 0.9114883 oz. t. = 18.22917 dwt. = 437.5 gr. = 28.3495 g. = 141.75 ct.

Bibliography

Gemology

The Agate Book, by H. C. Dake. Mineralogist Publishing Co., Portland, Ore., 1951. 64 pp., ill. $2.

The Book of Agates & Other Quartz Gems, by Lelande Quick. Chilton Books, Philadelphia, 1963. 232 pp., ill. $9.95.

Diamond Technology, by Paul Grodzinski. NAG Press, Ltd., London, 1953. 784 pp., ill. $10.

Gem Materials Data Book, by Charles J. Parsons & Edward J. Soukup. Gemac Corp., Mentone, Calif., 1957. 36 pp., ill. $2.

Gemmologia, by Speranza Cavenago-Bignami. Ulrico Hoepli, Milan, Italy, 1959. 1110 pp., ill. $26.34.

Gemmologists' Compendium, by Robert Webster. NAG Press, Ltd., London, 1947. 241 pp., ill. $4.35.

Gems & Gem Materials, by Edward H. Kraus & Chester B. Slawson (5th ed.). McGraw-Hill Book Co., New York, 1947. 325 pp., ill. $7.25.

Gems: Their Sources, Descriptions & Identification, by Robert Webster (two volumes). Butterworth & Co., Ltd., London, 1962. 804 pp., ill. $32.50.

Gemstones, by G. F. Herbert Smith (13th ed.). Pitman Publishing Corp., New York, 1958. 560 pp., ill. $12.50.

Gem Testing, by B. W. Anderson (2nd ed.). Emerson Books, Inc., New York, 1959. 324 pp., ill. $11.50.

Handbook of Gem Identification, by Richard T. Liddicoat, Jr. (6th ed.). Gemological Institute of America, Los Angeles, 1962. 396 pp., ill. $8.75.

Handbook of Gems & Gemology, by Charles J. Parsons & Edward Soukup. Gemac Corp., Mentone, Calif., 1961. 160 pp., ill. $3.

Inclusions as a Means of Gemstone Identification, by Edward J. Gubelin. Gemological Institute of America, Los Angeles, 1953. 220 pp., ill. $6.75.

A Key to Precious Stones, by L. J. Spencer (2nd ed.). Emerson Books, Inc., New York, 1947. 237 pp., ill. $3.95.

Physical Gemmology, by Sir James Walton. Pitman Publishing Corp., New York, 1952. 304 pp., ill. About $5.

Bibliography

Popular Gemology, by Richard M. Pearl. John Wiley & Sons, Inc., New York, 1948. 316 pp., ill. $4.

Practical Gemmology, by Robert Webster. NAG Press, Ltd., London. 180 pp., ill. $4.95.

Properties of Gem Varieties of Minerals, by Edward Wigglesworth. Gemological Institute of America, Los Angeles, 1948. 65 pp., $4.75.

The Story of Diamonds, by Austin, Mercer & Shipley (3rd ed.). Gemological Institute of America, Los Angeles, 1946. 92 pp., ill. $2.25.

The Story of the Gems, by Herbert P. Whitlock. Emerson Books, Inc., New York, 1940. 354 pp., ill. $6.50.

Wonders of Gems, by Richard M. Pearl. Dodd, Mead & Co., New York, 1963. 63 pp., ill. $3.

The World of Jewel Stones, by Michael Weinstein. Sheridan House, New York, 1958. 430 pp., ill. $15.

History, Lore & Romance of Gems & Jewelry

Adventures in Jade, by James L. Kraft. Henry Holt & Co., New York, 1947. 81 pp., $3.

Antique Jewelry, by Ada Darling. Century House, Watkins Glen, N.Y., 1953. 200 pp., ill. $6.

Antique Jewelry, by Erich Steingraber. Frederick A. Praeger, New York, 1957. 191 pp., ill. $12.50.

Antique Jewelry, by Etienne Coche de la Ferté. Hallwag, Ltd., Berne, Switzerland, 1962. 24 pp., ill. $2.

Chinese Jade Carving, by S. Howard Hansford. Lund Humpheries & Co., Ltd., London, 1950. 145 pp., ill. $6.

Chinese Jade Throughout the Ages, by Stanley C. Nott. Charles E. Tuttle Co., Rutland, Vt., and Tokyo, Japan, 1962. 193 pp., ill. $15.

Chinese & Japanese Cloisonné Enamels, by Harry M. Garner. Charles E. Tuttle Co., Rutland, Vt., and Tokyo, Japan, 1962. 120 pp., ill. $12.50.

Chinese Snuff Bottles, by Lilla S. Perry. Charles E. Tuttle Co., Rutland, Vt. and Tokyo, Japan, 1960. 160 pp., ill. $12.50.

Collecting Antique Jewelry, by Mona Curran. Emerson Books, Inc., New York, 1962. Ill. $4.50.

The Cultured Pearl—Jewel of Japan, by Norine C. Reece. Charles E. Tuttle Co., Rutland, Vt., and Tokyo, Japan, 1958. 107 pp., ill. $2.95.

Diamond, by Emily Hahn. Doubleday & Co., Garden City, N. Y., 1956. 314 pp., $3.95.

THE JEWELERS' MANUAL

Famous Diamonds of the World, by Robert M. Shipley (6th ed.). Gemological Institute of America, Los Angeles, 1955. 61 pp., ill. $1.75.

5000 Years of Gems & Jewelry, by Frances Rogers & Alice Beard. J. B. Lippincott Co., Philadelphia, 1947. 309 pp., ill. $6.

Greek and Roman Jewellery, by R. A. Higgins. Methuen & Co., Ltd., London, 1961. 268 pp., ill. About $10.

A History of Jewellery, 1100-1870, by Joan Evans. Pitman Publishing Corp., New York, 1953. 240 pp., ill. $17.50.

A History of the Crown Jewels of Europe, by Lord Twining. B. T. Batsford, Ltd., London, 1960. 707 pp., ill. About $60.

Italian Jewled Arts, by Filippo Rossi. Harry N. Abrams, Inc., New York, 1954. 233 pp., ill. About $25.

Jade—Stone of Heaven, by Richard Gump. Doubleday & Co., Inc., Garden City, N.Y., 1962. 256 pp., ill. $7.95.

Jade—A Study in Chinese Art & Religion, by Berthold Laufer. P. D. Perkins, Pasadena, Calif., 1946. 370 pp., ill. $12.50.

Jewelry & Amber of Italy, by Rodolfo Siviero. McGraw-Hill Book Co., New York, 1960. 426 pp., ill. $25.

Jewels & Gems, by Lucile McDonald. Thomas Y. Crowell Co., New York, 1940. 288 pp., ill. $2.

Jewels & the Woman, by Marianne Ostier. Horizon Press, New York, 1958. 324 pp., ill. $7.50.

Mexican Jewelry, by Mary L. Davis & Greta Pack. University of Texas Press, Austin, Texas, 1963. 262 pp., ill. $6.50.

Modern Jewelry, by Graham Hughes. Crown Publishers, Inc., New York, 1963. 256 pp., ill. $15.

The Opal Book, by Frank Leechman. Ure Smith, Ltd., Sydney, Australia, 1961. 255 pp., ill. $7.95.

The Pearl Hunter, by Leonard Rosenthal. Vantage Press, New York, 1952. 214 pp., ill. $3.

The Pearl & I, by Leonard Rosenthal. Vantage Press, New York, 1955. 223 pp. $3.

The Pearl King, by Robert Eunson. Charles E. Tuttle Co., Rutland, Vt., and Tokyo, Japan, 1955. 243 pp., ill. $1.50.

Precious Stones, by Edward Gubelin. Hallwag, Ltd., Berne, Switzerland, 1963. 48 pp., ill. $2.

The Queen's Necklace, by Frances Mossiker. Simon & Schuster, New York, 1961. 620 pp., ill. $7.50.

Bibliography

Rings Through the Ages, by James R. McCarthy. Harper & Bros., New York, 1945. 202 pp., ill. $2.50.

A Roman Book on Precious Stones, by Sydney H. Ball. Gemological Institute of America, Los Angeles, 1950. 338 pp., $6.75.

The Story of Jade, by Herbert L. Whitlock and Martin L. Ehrmann. Sheridan House, New York, 1949. 222 pp., ill. $15.

The Story of Jewelry, by Marcus Baerwald and Tom Mahoney. Abelhard-Schuman, New York, 1960. 220 pp., ill. $6.50.

A Treasury of Jewels & Gems, by Mona Curran. Emerson Books, Inc., New York, 1961. 152 pp., ill. $4.50.

The True Book About Diamonds, by Eric Bruton. Frederick Mueller, Ltd., London, 1961. 144 pp., ill. About $1.25.

The Valley of Rubies, by Joseph Kessel. David McKay Co., Inc., New York, 1960. 199 pp. $3.95.

Victorian Jewellery, by Margaret Flower. Duell, Sloan & Pearce, New York, 1951. 271 pp., ill. $10.

Mineralogy, Mineral Collecting & Localities

California Gem Trails, by Darold J. Henry (3rd ed.). Lowell R. Gordon, Long Beach, Calif., 1957. 101 pp., ill. $2.50.

Colorado Gem Trails & Mineral Guide, by Richard M. Pearl (2nd ed.). Sage Books, Denver Colo., 1958. 176 pp., ill. $2.95.

Dana's Manual of Mineralogy, by C. S. Hurlbut, Jr., (17th ed.). John Wiley & Sons, Inc., New York, 1959. 609 pp., ill. $11.50.

Field Book of Common Rocks and Minerals, by Frederic Brewster Loomis. G. P. Putman's Sons, New York and London, 1923. 352 pp., ill. $3.50.

A Field Guide to Rocks & Minerals, by Frederick H. Pough (3rd ed.). Houghton, Miffin Co., Boston, 1954. 330 pp., ill. $4.95.

Gem Hunter's Guide, by Russell P. McFall (2nd ed.). Science & Mechanics Publishing Co., Chicago, 1958. 188 pp., ill. $3.95.

Gemstones & Minerals—How and Where to Find Them, by John Sinkankas. D. Van Nostrand Co., Princeton, N. J., 1961. 387 pp., ill. $8.95.

Gemstones of North America, by John Sinkankas. D. Van Nostrand Co., Princeton, N. J., 1959. 675 pp., ill. $15.

Gem Trails of Texas, by Bessie W. Simpson (2nd ed.). Gem Trails Publishing Co., Granbury, Tex., 1962. Ill. $2.50.

Getting Acquainted With Minerals, by George L. English & D. E. Jensen (2nd ed.). McGraw-Hill Book Co., New York, 1958. 336 pp., ill. $7.50.

THE JEWELERS' MANUAL

How to Know the Rocks & Minerals, by Richard M. Pearl. McGraw-Hill Book Co., New York, 1955. 192 pp., ill. $3.50.

Midwest Gem Trails, by June Culp Zietner (2nd ed.). Mineralogist Publishing Co., Portland, Ore., 1960. 80 pp., ill. $2.

Mineralogy, by Edward H. Kraus, Walter F. Hunt & Lewis S. Ramsdell. McGraw-Hill Book Co., Inc., New York, 1959. 664 pp., ill. $9.

Minerals & How to Study Them, by Edward S. Dana, revised by C. S. Hurlbut (3rd ed.). John Wiley & Sons, Inc., New York, 1949. 323 pp., ill. $6.50.

New Mexico Gem Trails, by Bessie W. Simpson (2nd ed.). Gem Trails Publishing Co., Granbury, Tex., 1961. Ill. $2.50.

Northwest Gem Trails, by H. C. Dake (2nd ed.). Mineralogist Publishing Co., Portland, Ore., 1956. 80 pp., ill. $2.

The Rock Book, by Carol Lane Fenton & Mildred Adams Fenton. Doubleday & Company, Inc., Garden City, New York, 1948. 348 pp., ill. $6.

Rocks & Minerals, by Herbert S. Zim & Paul R. Shaffer. Golden Press, New York, 1957. 160 pp., ill. $1.

Gem Cutting

The Art of Gem Cutting, by H. C. Dake (6th ed.). Mineralogist Publishing Co., Portland, Ore., 1956. 128 pp., ill. $2.

The Art of the Lapidary, by Francis J. Sperisen (revised ed.). Bruce Publishing Co., Milwaukee, Wis., 1961. 390 pp., ill. $8.

The Book of Gem Cuts, MDR Manufacturing Co., Los Angeles. Vol. I: 22 pp., ill., $2.50 (1949); Vol. II: 26 pp., ill., $2.50 (1962).

A Check List of Cabochon Gem Materials & Their Lapidary Features, by J. Lester Cunningham. Gemac Corp., Mentone, Calif., 1963. 40 pp., ill. $1.50.

Facet-Cutters' Handbook, by Edward J. Soukup (2nd ed.). Gemac Corp., Mentone, Calif., 1962. 64 pp., ill. $2.

Gemcraft—How to Cut & Polish Gemstones, by Lelande Quick & Hugh Leiper. Chilton Co., Philadelphia, 1959. 198 pp., ill. $7.50.

Gem Cutting—A Lapidary's Manual, by John Sinkankas (2nd ed.). D. Van Nostrand Co., Princeton, N. J., 1962. 297 pp., ill. $11.75.

Gem Cutting, by J. Daniel Willems (2nd ed.). Charles A. Bennett Co., Peoria, Ill., 1952. 224 pp., ill. $4.50.

Gem Tumbling & Baroque-Jewelry Making, by Arthur Earl & Lila Mae Victor (11th ed.). Victor Agate Shop, Spokane, Wash., 1962. 58 pp., ill. $2.

Bibliography

How to Cut Gems, by Dan O'Brien. Dan & Marie O'Brien, Hollywood, Calif., 1953. 50 pp., ill. $1.

Jewelry, Gem Cutting & Metalcraft, by William T. Baxter (3rd ed.). McGraw-Hill Book Co., New York, 1950. 360 pp., ill. $7.50.

Revised Lapidary Handbook, by J. Harry Howard (2nd ed.). J. Harry Howard, Greenville, S. C., 1946. 220 pp., ill. $3.

Jewelry Making & Repairing, Silversmithing & Enameling.

The Book of Old Silver, by Seymore B. Wyler. Crown Publishers, Inc., New York, 1960. 401 pp., ill. $5.

Cabochon Jewelry Making, by Arthur and Lucille Sanger. Charles A. Bennett Co., Inc., Peoria, Ill., 1951. 128 pp., ill. $3.50.

Coppercraft & Silver Made at Home, by Karl Robert and Nora Kramer. Chilton Publishing Co., Philadelphia, 1961. 175 pp., ill. $7.50.

The Design & Creation of Jewelry, by Robert von Neuman. Chilton Publishing Co., Philadelphia, 1961. 256 pp., ill. $7.50.

Enamel Art on Metal, by Edward Winter. Watson-Guptill Publications, New York, 1958. 159 pp., ill. $9.75.

Enameling on Fine Metal, by Louis-Elie Millenet. D. Van Nostrand Co., Princeton, N.J., 1947. 112 pp., ill. $2.50.

Enameling—Principles & Practice, by Kenneth F. Bates. World Publishing Co., Cleveland, Ohio, 1951. 208 pp., ill. $3.95.

Handmade Jewelry, by Louis Weiner (2nd ed.). D. Van Nostrand Co., Princeton, N. J., 1960. 224 pp., ill. $4.95.

Handwrought Jewelry, by Lois E. Franke. McKnight & McKnight Publishing Co., Bloomington, Ill., 1962. 222 pp., ill. $7.95.

How to Make Modern Jewelry, by Charles J. Martin and Victor D'Amico. The Museum of Modern Art, New York, 1949. 96 pp., ill. $2.50.

Indian Silversmithing, by W. Ben Hunt. Bruce Publishing Co., Milwaukee, Wis., 1952. 160 pp., ill. $4.75.

Jewelers' Workshop Practices, by Leslie L. Linick. Paulson Press, Chicago, 1948. 516 pp., ill. $4.95.

Jewelry & Enameling, by Greta Pack. D. Van Nostrand Co., Princeton, N. J., 1961. 337 pp., ill. $6.50.

Jewelry, Gem Cutting & Metalcraft, by William T. Baxter. McGraw-Hill Book Co., New York, 1950. 256 pp., ill. $6.75.

Jewelry Making & Design, by Augustus F. Rose and Antonio Cirino. The Davis Press, Inc., Worcester, Mass., 1949. 300 pp., ill. $8.95

THE JEWELERS' MANUAL

Jewelry Making as an Art Expression, by D. Kenneth Winebrenner. International Textbook Co., Scranton, Pa. Ill. $6.50.

Jewelry Making for Schools, Tradesmen & Craftsmen, by Murray Bovin. Published by Murray Bovin, Long Island, N. Y., 1959. 159 pp., ill. $4.25.

Jewelry Making for the Beginning Craftsman, by Greta Pack. D. Van Nostrand Co., Princeton, N. J., 1957. 78 pp., ill. $3.75.

The Jewelry-Repair Manual, by R. Allen Hardy and John J. Bowman. D. Van Nostrand Co., Princeton, N.J., 1956. 166 pp., ill. $4.85.

Metalsmithing for the Artist-Craftsman, by Richard Thomas. Chilton Publishing Co., Philadelphia, 1960. 173 pp., ill. $7.50.

Metalwork & Enamelling, by Herbert Maryon (4th ed.). Dover Publications, Inc., New York, 1959. 335 pp., $8.

Refining Precious-Metal Wastes, by C. M. Hoke. Metallurgical Publishing Co., New York, 1940. 362 pp., ill. $7.50.

A Silversmith's Manual, by Bernard Cuzner (2nd ed.). NAG Press, London, 1949. 192 pp., ill. $4.

Silverwork & Jewelry, by H. Wilson. Pitman Publishing Corp., New York, 1948. 496 pp., ill. $5.75.

Workshop Methods for Gold- and Silversmiths, by Christian Schwann. Chemical Publishing Co., New York, 1960. 144 pp., ill. $4.

Your Jewelry, by Leslie Auld. Charles A. Bennett Co., Inc., Peoria, Ill., 1951. 131 pp., ill. $2.75.

Engraving

Art Alphabets & Lettering, by J. M. Bergling (8th ed.). V. C. Bergling, Publisher, P.O. Box 523, Coral Gables, Florida. $11.00.

Art Monograms & Lettering, by J. M. Bergling (20th ed.). V. C. Bergling, Publisher, P.O. Box 523, Coral Gables, Florida. $11.00.

Engraving on Precious Metals, by A. Brittain, S. Wolpert and F. Morton. NAG Press, Ltd., London. 228 pp., ill. $7.80.

Heraldic Designs & Engravings, by J. M. Bergling, Mnl. V. C. Bergling, Publisher, P.O. Box 523, Coral Gables, Florida. $13.50.

The Jewelry Engravers' Manual, by R. Allen Hardy and John J. Bowman. D. Van Nostrand Co., Princeton, N.J., 1954. $4.25.

Ornamental Designs and Illustrations, by J. M. Bergling (4th Ed.), V. C. Bergling, Publisher, P.O. Box 523, Coral Gables, Florida 33134. $11.00.

A Practical Course in Jewelry Engraving, by A. Winters. Modern Technical Supply Co., New York. Ill. $3.50.

Bibliography

Horology

American Clocks & Clockmakers, by C. W. Dreppard. Charles T. Branford. Co., Newton Center, Mass., 1947. 312 pp., ill. $5.95.

Bench Practices for Watch Repairers, by Henry B. Fried. Roberts Publishing Co., Denver, Colo., 1954. 270 pp., ill. $4.95.

The Book of American Clocks, by Brooks Palmer. MacMillan Co., New York, 1950. 318 pp., ill. $9.75.

Britten's Watch- and Clockmakers' Handbook, Dictionary & Guide, by J. W. Player (15th ed.). D. Van Nostrand Co., Princeton, N. J., 1955. 600 pp., ill. $15.

Britten's Old Clocks & Watches & Their Makers, by G. H. Baille, Clutton and C. A. Ibert (7th ed.). E. P. Dutton & Co., Inc., New York, 1956. 518 pp., ill. $25.

The Chronograph, by B. Humbert. Journal Suisse d' Horologerie et de Bijouterie, Lausanne, Switzerland. 154 pp., ill. $7.

Complicated Watches, by Emanual Seibel and Orville R. Hagens. Roberts Publishing Co., Denver, Colo., 1945. 132 pp., ill. $2.50.

Complicated Watches & Their Repair, by Donald DeCarle. NAG Press, Ltd., London, 1956. 174 pp., ill. $7.80.

Electrical Timekeeping, by F. Hope-Jones (2nd ed.). NAG Press, Ltd., London, 1949. 275 pp., ill. $6.

The Horolover 400-Day Clock-Repair Guide, by Charles Terwilliger (4th ed.). Horolover Co., New York, 1959. $3.95.

The Mechanism of a Watch, by J. Swinburne. NAG Press, Ltd., London, 1950. 88 pp., ill. $2.50.

The Modern Clock, by Ward L. Goodrich. North American Watch, Tool & Supply Co., Chicago. 502 pp., ill. $4.95.

Modern Clocks—Their Repair & Maintenance, by T. R. Robinson. NAG Press, Ltd., London, 1955. 289 pp., ill. $7.50.

Practical Clock Repairing, by Donald DeCarle. NAG Press, Ltd., London, 1952. 240 pp., ill. $7.50.

A Practical Course in Horology, by Harold C. Kelly. Charles A. Bennett Co., Inc., Peoria, Ill., 1944. 192 pp., ill. $3.25.

Practical Watch Repairing, by Donald DeCarle. NAG Press, Ltd., London, 1946. 299 pp., ill. $6.

Precision Time Measures, by Charles T. Higgenbotham. North American Watch, Tool & Supply Co., Chicago. 345 pp., ill. $4.50.

The Science of Clocks & Watches, by Arthur L. Rawlings (2nd ed.). Pitman Publishing Co., New York, 1948. $6.95.

THE JEWELERS' MANUAL

Scientific Timing, by Charles Purdom. Roberts Publishing Co., Denver, Colo., 1947. 142 pp., ill. $4.50.

Some Outstanding Clocks Over 700 *Years*—1250-1950, by H. Allen Lloyd. Leonard Hill Books, Ltd., London, 1958. 160 pp., ill. $15.

The Story of Watches, by Camerer Cuss. Philosophical Library, New York, 1952. 176 pp., ill. $7.50.

Swiss Self-Winding Watches, by B. Humbert. Journal Suisse d'Horologerie et de Bijouterie, Lausanne, Switzerland, 1951. 217 pp., ill. $7.

The Swiss Watch-Repairer's Manual, by H. Jendritzski. Journal Suisse d'Horologerie et de Bijouterie, Lausanne, Switzerland, 1953. 182 pp., ill. $7.

Time & Timekeepers, by Willie I. Milham. MacMillan Co., New York, 1923. 609 pp., ill. $3.95.

Timing Manipulations, by James L. Hamilton. Roberts Publishing Co., Denver, Colo., 1954. 64 pp., ill. $3.

Watch & Clock Escapements, by W. J. Gazeley. Heywood & Co., Ltd., London, 1956. 294 pp., ill. $7.

Watch & Clock Encyclopedia, by Donald DeCarle. NAG Press, Ltd., London, 1959. 307 pp., ill. $10.

The Watch Escapement, by Henry B. Fried. B. Jadow Co., New York, 1960. 174 pp., ill. $4.95.

Watchmakers & Clockmakers of the World, by G. H. Baille (3rd ed.). NAG Press, Ltd., London, 1951. 388 pp., ill. $8.

The Watchmaker's Lathe & How to Use It, by Donald DeCarle. NAG Press, Ltd., London, 1952. 154 pp., ill. $7.50.

Watch Repair, by Harold C. Kelly. Charles A. Bennett Co., Inc., Peoria, Ill., 1957. 284 pp., ill. $4.95.

The Watch Repairer's Manual, by Henry B. Fried (2nd ed.). D. Van Nostrand Co., Princeton, N. J., 1961. 310 pp., ill. $6.95.

China & Glassware

The Book of Pottery & Porcelain, by Warren E. Cox. Crown Publishers, Inc., New York, 1944. 1158 pp., ill. $10.95.

The Complete Book of Pottery Making, by John B. Kenny. Greenberg Publishing Co., New York, 1949. 242 pp., ill. $7.50.

5000 *Years of Glass*, by Frances Rogers and Alice Beard (revised ed.). J. B. Lippincott, Philadelphia, 1948. 314 pp., ill. $6.

The Making of Fine Glass, by Sidney Waugh. Dodd, Mead & Co., New York, 1947. 95 pp., ill. $3.

Bibliography

The Practical Book of Chinaware, by Harold D. Eberlein and Roger W. Ramsdell (revised ed.). J. B. Lippincott, Philadelphia, 1948. 320 pp., ill. $5.

Dictionaries & Reference Works

Britten's Watch- & Clockmakers' Handbook, Dictionary & Guide, by J. W. Player (15th ed.). D. Van Nostrand Co., Princeton, N. J., 1955. 600 pp., ill. $15.

The Diamond Dictionary, by GIA Staff. Gemological Institute of America, Los Angeles, 1960. 317 pp., ill. $8.75.

Dictionary of Gems & Gemology, by Robert M. Shipley (5th ed.). Gemological Institute of America, Los Angeles, 1951. 261 pp., $5.50.

Dictionary of Marks—Pottery & Porcelain, by Ralph M. and Terry H. Kovel. Crown Publishers, Inc., New York, 1953. 278 pp., ill. $3.

A Directory of American Silver, Pewter & Silverplate, by Ralph M. and Terry H. Kovel. Crown Publishers, Inc., New York, 1961. 352 pp., ill. $5.95.

Fundamentals for the Retail Jeweler, by Raymond P. Brown. Canadian Jewellers' Institute, Toronto, Canada. 387 pp., ill. $6.

Hallmarks & Date Letters, by Arthur Tremayne. NAG Press, Ltd., London, 1944. 38 pp., ill. $1.

Handbook of American Silver & Pewter Marks, by C. Jordan Thorn. Tudor Publishing Co., New York, 1949. 289 pp., ill. $3.50.

Illustrated Professional Dictionary of Horology, by G. A. Berner. Watchmakers of Switzerland Information Center, Inc., New York, 1962. 1007 pp., ill. $10.

The Jewelers' Dictionary (2nd ed.). Jewelers' Circular-Keystone, Philadelphia, 1950. 265 pp,. ill.$6.

The Retail Jeweler's Handbook, by A. Selwyn. Chemical Publishing Co., New York, 1955. ill. $10.

The Sterling Flatware Pattern Index. Jewelers' Circular-Keystone, Philadelphia (issued annually). With binder, $27.50; without binder, $17.50.

Trademarks of the Jewelry & Kindred Trades (6th ed.). Jewelers' Circular-Keystone, Philadelphia, 1950. 388 pp., ill. $7.50.

Periodicals

American Horologist & Jeweler, 2400 Curtis St., Denver 5, Colo.

le Bijoutier, 1448 Rue Beaudry, Montreal 24, Canada.

China, Glass & Tablewares, 23 E. 26th St., New York City 10.

THE JEWELERS' MANUAL

Deutche Goldschmiede Zeitung; Ruhle-Diebener—Verlag KG; Wolfschlugener Strabe 5a, Postfach 250; Stuttgart-Degerloch, Germany.

Diamant, Editorial & Administration Offices, Consciencestraat 18, Antwerp, Belgium.

The Diamond News & South African Jeweler, 8 Cheapside, Kimberley, South Africa.

Earth Science, 406 Grover St., Joliet Ill.

Gemologia, Alameda Glete 463, Caixa Postal 8.105, Sao Paulo, Brazil.

Gems & Gemology, 11940 San Vicente Blvd., Los Angeles 49, Calif.

Gems & Minerals, 1797 Capri Ave., Mentone, Calif.

Gold, Silber, Uhren & Schmuk; Konradin-Verlag Robert Kohlhammer GmbH; Danneckerstrasse 52, Postfach 625; Stuttgart, Germany.

Guilds, 3142 Wilshire Blvd., Los Angeles 5, Calif.

Horological Journal, NAG Press, Ltd., Finwell House, 26 Finsbury Square, London E. C. 2, England.

Jewelers' Circular-Keystone, Chestnut & 56th Sts., Philadelphia 39, Penna.

Jewelers' Digest, 109 Lindberg Dr., NE, Atlanta 5, Ga.

Jewelers' Outlook, Temple Court Bldg., 5 Beekman St., New York City 38.

The Journal of Gemmology, Saint Dunstan's House, Carey Lane, London E. C. 2, England.

Lapidary Journal, 3564 Kettner Blvd., San Diego, Calif.

Metal Fabricator, 104 Shaw Ave., Edgewood, R. I.

Modern Jeweler, 1211 Walnut St., Kansas City 6, Mo.

National Jeweler, 6 W. 57th St., New York City 19.

Northwestern Jeweler, 225 Washington Ave., Albert Lea, Minn.

l'Orafo Valenzana, Piazza don Minzoni 1, Valenza Po (Alessandria), Italy.

Pacific Goldsmith, 657 Mission St., San Francisco 5, Calif.

Southern Jeweler, 75 Third St., NW, Atlanta 8, Ga.

Technica, 52 Rue d'Artois, Brussels 1, Belgium.

Watchmaker, Jeweler & Silversmith, Heywood & Co., Ltd., Drury House, Russell St., London W. C. 2, England.

West Central Retail Jeweler, P.O. Box 2636, Wichita, Kans.

Zietschrift der Deutschen Gesellschaft für Edelsteinkunde, Gewerbehalle, Idar-Oberstein 2, Germany.

What is Gemology?

Gemology is the study of the identification, grading and appraising of those minerals and other substances that possess sufficient beauty and durability to be worn as ornamental objects.

In pursuing this study, the student acquires a knowledge of many fascinating subjects. He becomes proficient in grading diamonds and other gems for color, perfection and quality of cutting. He studies the structure of the gem market and learns to appraise accurately. He learns how gems are formed, where they are found, how they are mined, in what colors and qualities they are available and at what price. He becomes thoroughly familiar with the identifying features and characteristics of gem materials and their substitutes. He is taught the use of gem-testing instruments and identfication techniques. In short, the gemologist is trained to be a diamond-and-gem expert.

How do Gemologists Serve?

The nature of the gemologist's training is such that he can be a key factor in almost any branch of the jewelry industry. His services are essential in determining the manner in which rough gem material can be fashioned to produce maximum beauty and weight retention. He is competent to grade and price the finished work of the lapidary. He is qualified to test and identify cut gemstones and to distinguish between genuine gems and their substitutes.

In the retail store, the trained gemologist is well equipped to buy diamonds and other gemstones. He is helpful in deciding how and where the finished gems can be used in attractive and saleable jewelry. Gemological training cultivates his esthetic senses and develops a genuine enthusiasm for the beauty of the finished product, thus making it possible to select merchandise that will most effectively fulfill the needs and desires of his customers. In short, his sales effectiveness is maximized.

Buying, selling, appraising, testing, lecturing, planning displays, advising customers on the care and handling of gems and jewelry —these and many more functions constitute the services of today's gemologist.

Training Required

The educational preparation of a gemologist is covered by the successful completion of courses in *Diamonds, Colored Stones* and *Gem*

THE JEWELERS' MANUAL

Identification and final examinations, offered by the Gemological Institute of America. The Institute is a nonprofit organization whose function it is to serve the jewelry industry; its services and correspondence courses are offered througout the world. Supplemental resident courses are offered regularly in New York City and Los Angeles and occasionally in major cities throughout the country. Although there are short courses of a popular nature given at several universities, complete professional training is offered only at the Gemological Institute.

The scheduled courses usually require from two to three years to complete; however, students have completed them in less than a year. Others have taken several years to complete their training.

Stones and all other study materials are provided with the courses. However, if the primary interest of the student is in identification, gem-testing instruments are most helpful. Although they are not furnished, the essential instruments are inexpensive.

Opportunities

Gemologists are employed in a wide variety of positions in the jewelry industry. Among the positions available are buyers, sorters and graders of rough gem material; appraisers; diamond graders; retail buyers; retail and wholesale salesmen; and many others. By far the largest number of gemologists are in the retail field, where they either own their own establishments or are employed by the retailer. The retail field is not noted for top salaries, so those who prepare by special training for the jewelry industry usually contemplate either ultimate ownership of a store or anticipate employment in a managerial capacity. Incomes in either of these situations are likely to be much more satisfactory. Gemological studies may be pursued while the person is gaining experience in the branch of the trade he finds most attractive.

Since no two gemstones are exactly alike, there is unending pleasure for one who enjoys working with them. The pleasure of opening the eyes of a customer to the inherent loveliness of a gemstone is one the gemologist never ceases to enjoy. Interest in, and appreciation for, diamonds is at an all-time high; however, the colored-stone field is largely underdeveloped in this country. Thus, the entire field of gemology represents a promising and rewarding career for those persons whose interests lie in this direction.

The added knowledge and obvious increase in effectiveness in selling and other facets of the gemologist's work should assure advancement.

The Gemological Institute of America

The Gemological Institute of America, known to most jewelers as GIA, or "the Institute", is the educational, research and testing center of the jewelry industry. A major purpose of this endowed, non-profit institution is to provide professional training and other services for both jewelers and the public.

When Robert Shipley founded the Institute in 1931, its sole function was to train jewelers primarily in the fundamentals of gemology. Today's organization has evolved from that beginning, both in the training offered and in its activities. A number of technical services have been added to its functions, including publishing, laboratory services and the development of diamond-grading, gem-testing, and merchandising instruments for the jewelry profession.

Educational Activities

Since it often is difficult for a jeweler to leave his business for an extended period of time, much of the Institute's training is provided on a home-study, or correspondence, basis. For the student who desires resident training, however, full-time programs are conducted in Santa Monica and New York City. Combined resident and home-study programs also can be arranged. One-week classes in Diamond Grading and Appraising, Gem Identification, Jewelry Design, and two-week classes in *Diamond Setting, Jewelry Repair, Wax Carving* and *Modeling,* and *Faceting* are conducted in major cities throughout the country and abroad, or wherever a group of at least fifteen jewelers request a class. Enrollment is limited. A seven-week class in *Engraving* also is taught at the Santa Monica Headquarters.

The correspondence courses offered by GIA include *Diamonds, Colored Stones, Gem Identification, Jewelry Retailing, Jewelry Design, Pearls* and *Creative Display.* Upon successful completion of the *Diamond Course,* the GIA Diamond Certificate is awarded. Successful completion of the *Colored Stone* and *Gem Identification* Courses is required for the Colored Stone Certificate. Upon successful completion of all three courses. the coveted *GIA Gemologist Diploma* is awarded. The scope of training reflected in this diploma is comprehensive — the gemologist is the professional man of the jewelry industry. Successful completion of the two short classes in *Diamond Grading and Appraising* and *Gem Identification* makes the gemologist eligible for the *Graduate Gemologist Diploma.*

THE JEWELERS' MANUAL

GIA maintains five Laboratories, all of which are engaged to a degree in research. The basic purposes for the Laboratories are to develop new methods for the detection of new synthetics and alterations to enhance apparent value and to provide the public, the jewelry industry and regulatory agencies with unbiased testing and grading facilities. Four of the five Laboratories also are known as Gem Trade Laboratories; two in New York City, one in Los Angeles and one in Santa Monica.

The original Gem Trade Laboratory in New York City is by far the largest and most important gem testing and diamond grading Laboratory in the world. It has been under the Direction of Robert Crowningshield since 1950. The second New York Laboratory opened in 1978. It is under the direction of Bert Krashes. Both Crowningshield and Krashes are Vice-presidents of GIA. The Santa Monica Gem Trade Laboratory is the only one in which diamonds are color graded for master color comparison sets. It is under the direction of Charles Fryer. The rapidly growing Los Angeles Laboratory is managed by Peter Yantzer.

The fifth Laboratory located in Santa Monica is devoted entirely to research and is the responsibility of Vincent Manson, Ph.D. It is equipped with very sophisticated instrumentation, permitting, for example, the determination on an almost instantaneous basis of the composition of gem materials, as well as spectrophotometric determinations. Many other facilities are included in the Laboratory's arsenal.

Special Instruments

A wholly-owned subsidiary of the Institute, Gem Instruments Corporation, designs and manufactures professional gem-testing, diamond-grading, and gem-merchandising instruments. Included among the instruments familiar to most jewelers are the *Gemolite*, the *Illuminator Polariscope*, the *Duplex II Refractometer*, the *DiamondLite*, the *DiamondLux*, the *GEM Diamond Grader*, the *GEM Color Grader, Mini-Lab*, and many others. Gem Instruments Corporation has the services of the talented designers Kenneth M. Moore and Gale M. Johnson, both of whom are Vice-presidents of the corporation.

The Gemological Institute of America

Publishing

Another important service to the jewelry industry is publication of authoritative reference works and professional journals in the field of gems and related subjects. The quarterly journal Gems & Gemology commenced publication in 1934. A number of books and pamphlets also have been published. In addition to *The Jewelers' Manual*, some of the books include *The Diamond Dictionary, Diamonds... Famous, Notable & Unique, Handbook of Gem Identification*, and the *Dictionary of Gems & Gemology*.

Staff

The technical and teaching staff of the Institute consists of specialists who are trained and experienced in the gem and jewelry field. Intimate association with jeweler's problems over a long period of time ensures that the training and other services offered by GIA are keyed to the needs of jewelers in every branch of the industry.

The Gemological Institute of America

The President is Richard T. Liddicoat, Jr., who directs the four branches of the organization from its Santa Monica Headquarters. Among the widely known Graduate Gemologists on the Santa Monica staff are Robert A. Earnest, Charles Fryer and Michael D. Waitzman. Dennis Foltz, personnel administrator for the West Coast staff of technical personnel, also heads home-study instruction, where he is assisted by Betsy Schuster, Jan Arnold, Sharon Thompson, and many other Graduate Gemologists. Resident course instructors include Ray Page, Jim Lucey, Archie Curtis, Bill Boyajian and many more. Those teaching both residence and correspondence courses include Jill Fisher and Burt Streeter. J. Michael Allbritton is in charge of the one-week classes in Diamond Grading and Appraising and Gem Identification and is assisted by Janice Mack, Doug Hucker and Mark Ebert. A. Richard Shalberg is in charge of the Jewelry Crafts Classes. Among the other long-term key administrative employees are T.J. Barrows and Margaret Orozco; Raymond Ouderkirk is comptroller. The Headquarters staff numbers over 150.

The staff of the Eastern Division includes Robert Crowningshield, Director of the New York Gem Trade Laboratory; Bert Krashes, Director of the new Gem Trade Laboratory; Eunice Miles, staff gemologist, and instructors John Cubitto, David Fowler, Paul Holt, Ingrid Nolte, Thomas Yonelunas and many others, plus many administrative aides. The staff now numbers well over 60.

The Los Angeles Gem Trade Laboratory is directed by G.P. Yantzer, Jr. He is assisted by Sally Ehmke, Sheryl Stewart, Paul Bianchi and a staff of 25.

Locations

The Institute has four locations. Its modern 50,000 square-foot Headquarters building is located at 1660 Stewart Street, Santa Monica, California 90404. The Eastern Division maintains two separate Gem Trade Laboratories in addition to offices and classrooms at 580 Fifth Avenue, New York, New York 10036. The greatly enlarged Los Angeles Laboratory is located at 606 South Olive Street, Los Angeles, California 90014. The home-study courses are conducted from the Santa Monica Headquarters and instructors from both facilities conduct diamond, colored-stone and other classes throughout the nation.